27/10/11 | 2 - FEB 2019 | NC

"GET IN THERE!"

*To the Lawton twins, Anthony and Zoë, in the hope that it
may bring to life the grandfather they never got to know*

"GET IN THERE!"

Tommy LAWTON
My friend, my father

By Barrie Williams and Tom Lawton Junior

VSP

Published by Vision Sports Publishing in 2010

Vision Sports Publishing
19–23 High Street
Kingston upon Thames
Surrey
KT1 1LL

www.visionsp.co.uk

ISBN 13: 978-1907637-00-1

© Barrie Williams and Tom Lawton Junior

Editor: Jim Drewett
Design: Doug Cheeseman
Copy editing: Ian Turner
Back cover pic: PA

Typeset by Palimpsest Book Production Limited, Falkirk, Stirlingshire

Printed and bound in the UK by CPI Mackays, Chatham, ME5 8TD

CONTENTS

OUR THANKS

Our thanks are due to people who have helped us in compiling this tribute to Tommy Lawton: Thanks to Mick Holland on the sports desk at the *Nottingham Post* and to the Post's Picture Editor, Steve Mitchell; to David McVay and Andy Smith, authors of *The Complete Centre Forward*; to John Mounteney, former vice chairman of Notts County; to all those, far too numerous to mention, who recorded the fine detail of Tommy's scoring exploits in books, magazines and newspapers between 1935 and 1956; to Patrick Collins and Jack Culver of the *Mail On Sunday;* to Jim Drewett and Toby Trotman of Vision Sports Publishing, who shared our enthusiasm for this extraordinary story from the outset and thanks, above all, to the man who told Tommy Lawton stories better than anybody else . . . Tommy Lawton.

Foreword by
SIR TOM FINNEY

A fter the Second World War Tommy Lawton and I were regular members of the England team.

   In fact Tommy was around the England squad for a decade and you have to wonder how many caps he would have won had the war not intervened.

   The memory of Tommy heading goals with such awesome power after a pinpoint cross from Stanley Matthews still makes my spine tingle to this day.

   If I were to select an England team of all time greats, from any generation, then Tommy Lawton would be my centre forward.

   Tommy Lawton was a wonderful friend and a footballer who will forever remain in a class of his own.

Sir Tom Finney, August 2010

"Certain footballers straddle their eras like titans, their pre-eminence so palpable that any attempt to place them in a pecking order is meaningless. So it was with Tommy Lawton, the princeliest, the most complete, simply the best centre forward in Britain as the 20th century approached its halfway mark.

Lawton carried with him the unmistakable aura of stardom, radiating charisma and, even in quiet moments on the field, emitting a wholly distinctive brand of cool menace. Though a powerfully built six-footer, he combined the physical strength expected of a big man with the nimbleness of a ballet dancer. His movement over the ground was graceful, seemingly languid at times, but that was an illusion. In fact, he was quick, often blindingly so, and he had a habit of pouncing with sudden venom to score goals seemingly out of nothing.

His control of the ball was commendable and the power of his shot was ferocious, but it was in the air that Tommy Lawton attained his full and glorious majesty. Indeed, shrewd contemporary judges assert that no more brilliant header of the ball ever lived. His muscular legs and abdomen enabled him to spring to prodigious heights and he was blessed with a sense of timing that verged on the uncanny.

Indeed, such was his expertise that at times he appeared to defy gravity, creating the optical illusion of hovering while the ball homed in on that wide forehead, the sleek, dark hair and prominent beak of a nose intensifying the impression of some ravenous raptor closing on its prey."

Ivan Ponting, *The Independent*

INTRODUCTION

More than 50 years after he last kicked a ball in earnest , there are many football experts who still say that Tommy Lawton was the greatest centre forward ever to play for England. In an age in which the word legend is applied far too carelessly to sports personalities who don't even come close to the fame and adulation he enjoyed, the name of Tommy Lawton still shines. One of the few true stars of the beautiful game, Tommy Lawton is the only footballer whose ashes are on display at the National Football Museum. Such is his status to this day.

A teenage sensation as a prolific goal scorer with Burnley and Everton in the 1930s, Tommy played his first game for his country at the age of 19 and his record as the youngest debutant to score for England stands to this day. The Second World War deprived him of many full England international caps (wartime international matches having been deemed semi-official by the FA, which chose not to award caps to those selected) but even so, between 1938 and 1948, Tommy achieved a phenomenal scoring rate of 22 goals in 23 peace time appearances for his country and 24 goals in 23 wartime internationals. After the war, he played for Chelsea, Notts County, Brentford and Arsenal and when his playing career ended in 1956, he had scored 635 goals in 731 games. A truly incredible record.

Tall, strong and handsome, Tommy Lawton was a national cult figure in the days of Brylcreem and wide partings – a household name who was as much a heart throb to the girls who adored his film star good looks and easy charm as he was a hero to the men who idolised his athletic prowess and soccer skills, particularly his ability to head a football as hard, fast and accurately as other professional players could kick it. He was also a rebel; a defiant working class Lancashire lad who despised snobbery, pretension and 'lah-de-dah' folk; renowned for his outspoken disagreements with the boardroom bosses and uncompromising rows with the 'stuffed shirts' of the soccer establishment.

Tommy Lawton was a fantastic talent who became a hostage to his own fame, often a fool with his money, a soft touch for the hangers-on. Unable to cope with a cruel fall from stardom, his middle years were dogged by poverty, scandal and shame.

The great Tommy Lawton ended up, disgraced and desolate, in a police cell. In the last decade of his life, he regained his rightful status and respect in the football world after a local daily newspaper brought his fate to national attention and gave him a job as a football writer.

Written by Barrie Williams, a newspaper editor who was Tommy's close friend and confidante in those later years, with his son Tom Lawton Junior, who grew up during some of his dad's darkest days, this is an exclusively personal version of the enthralling story of a real soccer legend.

We hope that *"Get In There!"* will come to be regarded as the definitive account of the life and times, the triumphs and torment of England's greatest goal scorer – a title which, on goals per game, we are still entitled to claim for him. We hope that it will be the ultimate and lasting tribute to Tommy Lawton's fantastic achievements on the field of play, but we have also tried to ensure that nothing from his often troubled personal life is 'swept under the carpet.' Tommy would have approved of that. He always said that there were lessons for all young soccer stars to be learned from the mistakes he made in his life and those lessons are as relevant today as they ever were. This is as much the story of the man as it is of the footballer. It is also, through association with Tommy's life, a story of football spanning more than 70 years.

We believe that readers will find much food for thought in the stark comparisons between the way in which star footballers were treated and paid in Tommy's days compared with the power and wealth of today's multi-millionaires. The exploitation of lads like Tommy in the 'slave trade' that was professional football in England from the 1920s right up to the 1960s was an absolute disgrace. Tommy had been a resolute and outspoken campaigner against the iniquitous maximum wage, so he never begrudged the modern day stars their status and riches. But, if he was alive today, would he think that the pendulum has now swung far too much in the other direction?

Football has always been all about opinions and we'll be delighted if *"Get In There!"* succeeds in providing fuel for debate. Tommy would have loved to have sat down to discuss it all with you, preferably over a pint, and he'd have been thrilled to know that his story had been capable of provoking a response so many years later.

Barrie Williams and Tom Lawton Junior

"Only Tommy bloody Lawton!"

Chapter One

AND WHO THE BLOODY HELL ARE YOU?

It was a mid-September day in Nottingham in 1984.

A weakening sun shone from a pale blue sky and there was a hint of autumn chill to the air, the harbinger of what Nottingham folk call 'Goose Fair weather', a reference to the centuries old October funfair which is a massive local attraction but requires an extra layer of clothes in deference to summer's end.

On an inner-city playing field two teams of schoolboys were engaged in battle on the football pitch, their shrill, excited shouts piercing the silence of the quiet afternoon.

From the distance, an elderly man approached the pitch.

His shoulders were stooped and his head was bowed. He wore a dirty beige raincoat, the collar of which was heavily stained with grease from the lank jet-black hair which clung to it.

The shabby old outer garment and its wearer's defeated demeanour gave him a tramp-like appearance but underneath, a sparkling white shirt and spotless bright red tie suggested a different story, as did the brilliant shine on his well-worn black shoes.

He carried a Co-op plastic bag, containing a few slices of boiled ham, thinly cut to keep the cost down, a small tin of garden peas and four potatoes: supper for him and his wife, who had issued a strict reminder as to the thickness of the ham.

As he got close to the football pitch, the man lifted his drooping head and stopped to watch the game.

The tracksuited schoolteacher in charge of the kids' match was sprinting up and down the touchline like a demented greyhound. "RUN, RUN, RUN," he was bellowing at his young charges. "MOVE, MOVE, MOVE."

A pained expression shot across the face of the watching man. He walked up to the overanimated schoolteacher and in a subdued voice with a polite tone he told him, "Now then, son. Never mind all this 'Run, run, run' stuff. Get them to *play* the ball, *dwell* on the ball, *love* the ball. Teach them to take their time – and to *think* about what they're doing."

"Oh, yeah," the teacher replied rudely . . . "and who the bloody hell are *you*?"

"Nobody, son," said the man sadly. "Nobody at all."

As he trudged away from the scene of this encounter, the man's whispered second answer to the teacher's discourteous question was a very different one . . . "Only Tommy Lawton, you prat! Only Tommy bloody Lawton!" Then he sighed, a seriously depressed sigh. "But who cares?"

This was Tommy Lawton, 'England's greatest ever centre forward'. He was 64 years old now. Soon it would be his 65th birthday.

"Next month, Tommy Lawton will be an old-age pensioner and nobody gives a damn about him," he told himself. He recalled a line from one of the countless articles written about him: "His name is mispronounced in awe in every country in the world."

"Mispronounced?! Chance would be a fine thing these days. Now they don't even know me. Not even in Nottingham. Nobody knows Tommy Lawton any more."

This walk home from the shops was one that Tommy took often.

It wasn't a shortcut – on the contrary, it took him considerably out of his way. But it killed some of the time that passed so agonisingly slowly in a life of gut-wrenching inconsequence and boredom that had once known superstardom, glamour and global fame.

He took this walk mainly because it allowed him to feel cut grass under his feet; fabulously fast feet, they had been, gracing the glorious green stages of the massive soccer stadia at the top clubs he played for – Arsenal, Chelsea, and Everton, of rival clubs like Manchester United and Tottenham Hotspur, of international pitches all over the world. Now, when the grass of those inner-city Nottingham playing fields had been freshly cut he was able to savour the same evocative aroma which once carried the tingling excitement and avid anticipation of the arrival of every new football season. Tommy loved that smell.

But that was where the familiarity ended these days – and where once there had been international hero worship for the awesome Tommy Lawton, today there was just a thoughtless insult from an arrogant young man who was teaching hopeful kids bad football habits.

"Christ," Tommy muttered to himself as he sat down on a bench. "How are the mighty fallen! And as for that bloody teacher," he pondered as he drifted into deep, distant memories of his own childhood. "What would Bunny Lee have made of him . . .?"

Dreaming of fame

Chapter Two

THE LAD IS BETTER THAN GOOD

"Lawton, I'm not happy with your left foot," Bunny Lee told seven-year-old Tommy Lawton ". . . and I know how to deal with that."

Mr Lee was the sports master at Tonge Moor Council School in Bolton, Lancashire. The lads at the school, all from poor working-class homes, were responsible for his nickname because they reckoned his prominent front teeth made him look like a rabbit. The gentle mocking was entirely affectionate, though. They all loved Bunny, mainly because they could sense in him a shared childlike fervour for the game of football, around which their young lives revolved. And better still, Bunny was not just keen. He had a sound knowledge of the game which earned him great respect, not only from the kids but from their fathers, too.

Young Lawton, tall for his tender years and strong beyond them, had just got into the school team and was immensely proud to have done so. But, promising though the lad looked, Bunny was not entirely happy with him.

He told Tommy: "If you're going to be any good you need to be two-footed and your shot with your left foot is much too weak. Report to me after school at four o'clock and we'll sort it out."

After school, Tommy reported to the dirt pitch on which the school

4

team trained to find Mr Lee holding a strong leather football boot in one hand and a flimsy, light plimsoll in the other.

" Now then, Tommy – the plimsoll goes on your right foot; the boot goes on your left. Now, go and stand near that wall."

Bunny then picked up a full-sized, laced leather football. This was very heavy for a seven-year-old. Dry, it weighed 15 ounces. Wet, it weighed a good deal more. The strong rubber inner tube was covered with 18 thick tanned leather sections in six panels of three strips each stitched together by hand with five-ply hemp. A considerable missile!

Suddenly, Bunny threw it hard at the boy with the instruction "Hit it back to me with your left foot . . . only with your left foot." When Tommy obliged, the ball was returned to him in a flash. "Again," shouted the master, ". . . and again . . . and again . . . and again." The ball was flying back to Tommy as fast as he could kick it and when, frequently, he instinctively hit it with his unprotected right foot it hurt. "Left foot," bellowed Bunny, time and time again. "Left foot, left foot!"

The boy got the message.

After half an hour, Bunny told him, "That's enough for today. Now then, lad, be here tomorrow afternoon at four o'clock and every afternoon at four o'clock until we get it right."

Tommy was there, every afternoon, week after week after week. And they did get it right. Bunny told the youngster, "That'll do for me now, lad. We'll cut it down to once a week now."

Tommy sprinted all the way home: "Dad, Dad – Bunny says my left foot's as good as my right! Now, I'm a two-footed player!"

The boy's immense pride was shared by the recipient of his news but he was not going to show it: "That's good; well done, son," he said. "But you've still got a long, long way to go."

That was a belief shared by Bunny Lee, a perfectionist who was to keep young Tommy's left foot sessions going for another year – not just shooting but passing, placing and side footing the heavy ball, all with the 'left peg' which had been useless when they started.

Bunny's interest in the lad and the special training to which he gave so much of his own time so selflessly was appreciated with great gratitude by 'Dad' – who, in truth, was not Tommy's father.

The boy had been born into a home which was much better off than the one from which he now made his daily journey, frequently interrupted by impromptu games of football along the way, to and from that school, which thanks to dedicated schoolmasters like Bunny Lee shone as a bright beacon of hope and happiness amid the unrelenting, grinding poverty and hardship which was working-class Lancashire life in the 1920s.

His mother Elizabeth and father Thomas Lawton lived at 43, MacDonald Street in Farnworth, a suburb of Bolton, when their big, bouncing baby arrived on 6th October 1919.

Thomas, an Irishman from County Cork, was a signalman on the Lancashire and Yorkshire Railway. Lizzie, a Lancashire lass and right proud of it, was a weaver at the Harrowby Mill.

The combined earnings of this handsome young couple meant that they lived considerably more comfortably than most of their neighbours and their baby Tommy was strong and healthy, while the newborns of many working-class parents were weak and sickly, quite often not making it beyond the crib.

Lizzie gave up her coveted mill job to look after her baby and Tommy was much loved and well cared for. But when he was 18 months old, Thomas left Lizzie and her baby.

Lizzie went back to live with her mum and dad, taking baby Tommy with her. Her father, James Hugh Riley, became 'Dad' to Tommy and the boy became devoted to his grandfather, who brought him up as his own. Tommy never called him anything but Dad and that was just the way Jim Riley wanted it to be.

The Rileys' small terraced house, off the Folds Road near the centre of Bolton, was badly over-crowded. In just two rooms and a tiny scullery downstairs and two bedrooms and a box room upstairs lived grandfather and grandmother Riley, their four sons Jack, Fred, Harold and Jim, daughter Lizzie and her child.

Like so many working-class families in the 1920s, they were poor. But it was a truly happy home, in which love and laughter could drive away the gloom. This big family packed like sardines into their poky little house looked out for each other, as did their equally poverty-stricken neighbours who all shared far more than their communal outside lavatories. These were real communities. If you stuck together you survived together and the spirit induced by collective hardship was indomitable.

Twenty-two identical houses stood in a row on a cobbled street which, now and again, would resound to the clip-clop of horses' hooves as carts delivered coal, milk and greengroceries. When the carts clattered to a halt it was the signal for 22 front doors to open, facilitating the emergence over diligently polished red-tiled doorsteps of the women. They would gather around the carts in their pinafores and headscarves, exchanging good-natured double entendres with the vendors and gossiping.

The stories would be of how hard it was to cope, but they always did. They were miracle workers, these women in their hairnets who smelled of carbolic soap. With just a paltry few shillings they would feed their families

seven days a week, holding their lives together in the face of seemingly insu-
perable odds, striving to keep them clothed, clean and contented, often going
without themselves.

Young Tommy's nan was the matriarch, minder and mentor of the Riley
household. A tall, formidable woman with a fierce pride reflected in the
ramrod-straight demeanour with which she always carried herself. She was
a towering figure in that household, commanding enormous respect from
all the Rileys but it was love, not fear, which cemented their esteem for
her. They never questioned her, always obeyed her, appreciated her and
adored her. She was their rock of comfort.

When there was no money in the house to buy food, a frequent occurrence, Tommy's nan would tell him, "Go round to the grocer's, there's a
good lad, give 'em this list and tell 'em I'll pay as soon as we can afford
to."

The tick was rarely refused. Broke they might have been. But these were
proud, scrupulously honest folk and the local traders knew they would get
their money eventually. Besides, if they didn't buy the food they sold, who
would?

Skinny scrag ends of neck of mutton would be augmented by ten times
as many potatoes, plus onions and carrots, in pots of 'scouse', which were
stewed and reheated for days (but never boiled, for 'a stew boiled is a
stew spoiled') on black-leaded cooking ranges fuelled by frugally fed coal
fires.

Scouse, cheap but nourishing staple food, was a simple, un-thickened
stew, a dish which had spread through working-class Northern communities from Liverpool which, in turn, had been introduced to it by sailors
from Norway, where it was called lob's course. In Liverpool, it became
lobscouse and got shortened to scouse.

One pot of scouse would feed a large family for a whole week, more
potatoes, carrots, onions and water being added as the days passed and
evidence of the meat diminished. If the housewife's pathetic purse would
not even run to the few scrag ends of meat at the start of the week, it
became a potato stew they called blind scouse. Not only did Scouse
become the name by which people from Liverpool would for ever be
known, it drove hunger from the homes of countless poor families.

Hot water was a luxury saved for weekends and Monday washdays.

Young Tommy Lawton loved Mondays. He would be greeted home
from school by the clean, fresh smell of washing airing on the clothes
maiden in front of the fire, competing for stimulation of the nasal senses
with the mouth-watering aroma of delicious, newly baked homemade
bread. Flourishing her huge, bone-handled bread knife with extravagant

flair, Nan would bear down on one of her perfect loaves, cut the boy a thin slice of warm bread, then sprinkle sugar over it: "Come and get a sugar buttie, Tommy."

The invitation was unnecessary!

Poor as they were, these children never even contemplated hunger, for shielding them from its real possibility was as much a part of the selfless duty of the women as striving to keep it from their door. Only later, in adulthood, would they appreciate just how closely hunger had called. Then it confirmed and deepened their love and admiration for their brave, strong mums and grandmas.

Too often for their own pride and the women's patience, the men would be around in the daytime, too. Work was desperately hard to find. The Rileys were a family of coalminers. The men – Dad, Jack, Fred, Harold and young Jim – all dug coal for a living but the Lancashire coalfield was a despondent place to be in the 1920s. The intense problems of working seams that were becoming uneconomic as well as mercilessly tough to mine were compounded by a slump in 1921 and the General Strike of 1926. Pits were closing; thousands of miners were being laid off.

The Riley men could only get work sporadically – rarely more than just one day a week – and this meant that Lizzie's job in the comparatively sound cotton industry was providing the only full-time and reliable wage coming into that house of seven adults and a child. Lizzie had to make sure that her weekly pay packet contained as much as she could possibly earn and the cotton mill gaffers made sure that their workers earned every single penny. Lizzie was working from 6:30 am to 6:30 pm in the exhausting heat and noise of the weaving sheds, so young Tommy saw little of his mother.

In these circumstances, the boy knew instinctively that he had to try to be 'a man' but when he couldn't measure up to that demand, Nan was always there for him, to wipe away the tears, to bathe the scraped knees, to listen to the tales of imagined wrongs and injustices perpetrated against him in his boy's world.

Most of his time when he was not in school was spent with his uncles. Jack, Fred, Harold and Jim all doted on 'Our Lizzie's lad' as much as their dad did and Tommy looked up to the uncles. He was never exposed to the shame these proud coalminers endured, having to rely so much on their sister's wage, because the whole family were diligent about protecting the boy as much as they could from the unpleasant realities of living through such grim times.

All the Riley men were football mad. Before the Great War of 1914–18, Granddad Jim had been a good amateur player with Turton Rovers, a top

Lancashire team. His sons had all inherited their father's devout love of the game.

Football provided both a way of passing the time that hung heavily for so many fit, able-bodied yet jobless Lancashire men in the 1920s and a means of restoring some of their natural masculine pride.

It was the dominant topic of conversation around the table at every family meal at the Rileys' and young Tommy sat spell bound, his attentive gaze shifting from Dad to Jim; Jim to Harold; Harold to Fred and back to Dad as the men discussed the fine points of the game and the feats of its stars – particularly those of their local heroes, Bolton Wanderers, who won the FA Cup in 1923 and 1926.

The talk was of Teddy Vizard, the Welsh 'wizard' winger; Billy Butler, a local lad and a miner who played on the wing for England, too; of goal-keeper Dick Pym, a Devonian fisherman now an adopted son of Lancashire; of defenders Harry Nuttall, Jimmy Seddon and Fred Kean, all capped by England; of inside forward Joe Smith; and above all, of centre forward David Jack. There were stories to be told about all of them.

Tommy heard those stories so often he could recite them. But he could never hear them too often. Every story sounded fresh and new each time to a boy who imagined himself to be there on the football pitch with his uncles' heroes. Every story put a picture in his head: every picture was vivid and real and every time there was something different in that picture.

He loved all the stories. And each of his uncles had their well-rehearsed favourites. The one Jack liked telling most was about goalkeeper Dick 'Pincher' Pym.

"Before 'e played for Wanderers, Pincher were the goalie for Exeter City, down in Devon," Jack narrated with relish. "In 1914, Exeter went on tour to South America, where Pincher bought a parrot in Brazil. Well, back 'ome in Exeter, Pincher's parrot became Exeter City's mascot. Everybody loved that parrot. But the poor bird didn't take well to the English climate and it died. They were all so upset at Exeter City that they buried the parrot, with full ceremony, under one of the goals.

"The next 'ome game after the parrot's funeral, Exeter lost. Then they lost the next . . . and the next . . . and the next. They 'ad the worst run of 'ome defeats the club 'ad ever known. They just couldn't understand why they kept losing at 'ome.

"Then one day, the captain of the team said 'e reckoned this run of bad luck must be because they'd buried Pincher's parrot in the goal. 'That must be it,' they all agreed. So they dug 'im up. And they started winning again.

"Now, their mascot's a seagull!"

At the end of the story, Tommy always asked the same question, even though he knew the answer off by heart: "What did they call Pincher's parrot, Jack?" And that was the signal for the whole family to shout in unison with Jack's reply: "A bloody jinx!"

None of the Riley men had been able to watch Bolton Wanderers' FA Cup final triumphs in 1923 and 1926 but from what they'd heard, read and had passed down from mates with mates who knew somebody who had a mate who'd actually been there, they could each recount every minute of both those matches with as much attention to detail as if they'd stood in the front row of spectators.

On 28th April 1923 Bolton's Cup final opponents had been West Ham United. It was the first match to be played at the new Wembley Stadium, in the presence of King George V.

Bolton had got to the final by winning 1-0 in every round from the third round on and their great hero David Jack had scored the single goal every time. West Ham, by contrast, had put five goals past Derby County in the semi-final.

When the story of this match was told, frequently, around the Rileys' table Uncle Jack was the unchallenged narrator and match commentator. Tall and slim, with the same jet black hair and sparkling brown eyes as all the Rileys, Jack had earned the respect of the whole family as Jim's second-in-command at its head. Thus, his commentary was received with undivided attention by all, save for Nan who was darning socks. When they were all sitting comfortably, Jack began.

"When our great Wembley Stadium opened it were a year ahead of schedule and it were reckoned to be the best venue in the whole world. It could hold 125,000 spectators. Nobody'd ever seen anything like that.

"Those numbskulls at the FA were worried that the Cup final wouldn't fill the stadium so they'd been pushing it like mad, advertised it everywhere to get as many people there on the big day as they could.

"Well, come the day of the match, the newspapers reckoned that because West 'Am were playing and because of the novelty for all of seeing the grand new national stadium there'd be around 115,000 London folk there and around 5,000 travelling down from Bolton. If they'd been right, the stadium would 'ave been 5,000 people short of full. But the FA, the papers, everybody, got it wrong . . . and 300,000 turned up at Wembley!

"Gates were opened at half past eleven in the morning for kick-off at three o'clock and at first there were an orderly flow into the ground – but by one o'clock it were obvious that far too many people were coming in and at a quarter to two it were decided they'd 'ave to close the gates.

"Well, by now Wembley Way were a seething mass of humanity and them in charge were really panicking. They got messages to all the railway stations to try to stop this great flood of folk but nobody took any notice. They just kept coming in their tens of thousands. More and more and more of 'em. All the roads were blocked by people and the Bolton players 'ad to abandon their bus a mile from the stadium and walk to Wembley!

"Every copper in London were sent to the stadium to try to disperse this huge horde of people but by then it were far too late and at quarter past two that great crowd stormed the gates. The blokes on the turnstiles 'ad just locked 'em and buggered off so people just climbed over the turnstiles to get in. There were no trouble. No fighting. No pushing or shoving. It were all good natured, with folk 'elping each other over the turnstiles. But inside, it were getting terrifying. All them already in the lower tiers began to fear for their lives: they could be crushed to death and they would 'ave been, so they did the only thing they could . . . they climbed over the fences and swarmed onto the pitch.

"So there it were. Chaos. Only a quarter of an hour to go before kick-off for the FA Cup final, the first at England's swanky new national stadium, the King of England in attendance . . . and there were thousands of people all over the pitch, singing *God Save the King* and expecting to see a game of football while all the lah-de-dah officials were saying they'd have to call off the flippin' match!

"Then something magical happened. Mounted policemen 'ad been summoned to try to clear the pitch but they were getting nowhere . . . until one copper on a huge white 'orse took charge. Billy the 'orse were called. And he were a beauty. A big, proud beast who stood out from all the rest because of 'is size and 'is brilliant, shiny white coat. This 'orse were really special.

"Billy's rider were PC George Scorey and 'e said that when he first got there and rode that lovely big white 'orse onto the field, picking 'is way through the dense crowds, he thought it were impossible to do anything. But he saw an opening near one of the goals and rode towards it. Then Billy the 'orse started to ease people back, gently pushing 'em with 'is nose and swishing 'em with 'is tail, and gradually a goal line could be seen. Then, PC George told people at the front to join 'ands and 'eave backwards until they could see the touchlines – then to sit down where they were. At this point, Billy the 'orse took over. No kidding, that lovely big 'orse understood what were expected of 'im and he went on gently moving people back until all the touchlines were clear and everybody were sitting down behind the lines. At a quarter to four, 45 minutes late, the FA Cup final kicked off. And that would never 'ave been possible without that wonderful 'orse. That's why they called it 'the White 'Orse Final'. And that's what they'll call it for years to come.

"So, they kicked off. Can you imagine the excitement? Folk were sitting on the outside of the pitch, close enough to touch the players. After just two minutes, Jack Treadern of West 'Am, who were supposed to be policing David Jack, took a throw in, got tangled up with the crowd and couldn't get back on the pitch! Well, our David needed no invitation to go straight for goal and shoot so flippin' 'ard that the ball not only beat the goalkeeper but knocked out a spectator who were stood pressed up against the net!

"A few minutes later, the crowd got so excited they forgot to stay behind the lines and 'undreds of 'em surged back onto the pitch. The ref 'ad to stop play and mounted police 'ad to come back again to clear 'em off. This time, quite a few of 'em got 'urt and 'ad to be treated by the Red Cross while all the players could do was stand and watch.

"After that, Wanderers never let up. They were too strong for West 'Am who 'ad been relying on the speed of their wingers Richards and Ruffell. Wanderers' plan were to rush 'em every time they got the ball and it worked a treat. We dominated the game. Jack Smith scored a second goal in the second 'alf. West 'Am disputed the goal but there were nowt wrong with it and it were all over bar the shouting.

"And that's 'ow Bolton Wanderers won the FA Cup final of 1923."

Tommy loved all this football talk with his grown-up uncles but better still were their games of football, which he was allowed to join in every Sunday.

On weekdays, Tommy and his school pals would play spontaneous matches, their coats and jackets placed on the cobbled streets for goal posts, a tin can substituting for the flat, patched-up old leather ball when it finally became so worn out it was useless – a can would have to do until Christmas when one of them might be lucky enough to get another ball as a present.

As many as 20 lads would join in these games. With their 'short' trousers almost down to their ankles, well-darned, home-knitted woollen jumpers over faded grey shirts, falling over each other in hot pursuit of the soft ball or the tin can, they might not have looked much like top footballers, but in their own minds there was absolutely no doubt that they were and each lad had his own hero whose identity he borrowed for the duration of the match.

Most of them idolised David Jack, the hugely popular Bolton Wanderers centre forward. But Tommy had a different hero: Dixie Dean of Everton. As his pals squabbled over who was going to be David Jack, Tommy told them, "You be who you like. I'm Dixie Dean."

Those games were great fun, but Tommy's biggest football thrill came from the men's games with his uncles on Sundays.

The Riley family routine on Sundays was church in the morning and church in the evening and for young Tommy this heavy helping of religion was topped up by even more at Sunday School in the afternoon, but he was always out of Sunday School in time to play in the regular matches at the pit-top ground. These were serious games played by big, hard miners for side stakes of sixpence a man. The 'tanner a man' was the key to the fierce intensity of these games, for it paid for a night out with a pint of beer and a packet of cigarettes.

No place for a child, you'd have thought, but Tommy's uncles knew a good thing when they saw it and they had no qualms about picking their nephew for their team. He was very much a boy among men but he could *play* – and he was quick. They put him out on the wing to protect him from at least some of the rough and tumble that went on in the middle of these needle matches but he still got clattered. Young 'un or not, there was a tanner at stake!

So, Tommy learned how to be clever enough to dodge the flying tackles and keep hold of the ball. Cries of "Ooh, ya young bugger!" frequently rang out from the pit top as the kid on the wing left a burly miner on his backside and made a beeline for goal.

Those pit-top matches meant Tommy had no fear of anybody on a football pitch – and he was still barely nine years old.

But the football-mad youngster was worried when he was told he was being moved to a new school, Castle Hill, which had been built nearer to the Rileys' home. There was much fascination in the locality about the brand new modern building. It was single storey, an innovation of much interest and wonder, as were the folding glass doors opening out onto the playground. But all the excitement was wasted on Tommy. Only one thing mattered to him: football.

"Bunny won't be there, will he, Dad?" Tommy complained to his grandfather. "And what if they don't like football much? What if I can't play the same there?"

Fred Milner was very proud to have been appointed headmaster of the new Castle Hill School. It was the culmination of a teaching career to which he had been dedicated for more than 20 years. He stood at the window of his study and surveyed the schoolyard and the generous playing field beyond. His new school looked modern, felt modern, smelled modern. It gave him a real sense of achievement. "This'll do, Fred lad," he told himself with a smile of satisfaction. Young Tommy Lawton would have been relieved and delighted if he could have seen the headmaster walk out of the building, across the playground and onto the lush new turf of the playing field where he stopped and buried his heels into the grass. "This'll be grand," he thought. "We'll have the best school football team anybody's ever known."

Tommy need not have feared. Fred Milner's dedication to teaching was matched by his fanaticism for football and it took Tommy no time at all to show Mr Milner what he could do with a ball at his feet. He was immediately picked for the school team, playing with and against boys of 12 and 13, three or four years older but certainly not three or four years stronger. Those tanner-a-man matches at the pit top had seen to that. When you'd mixed it with fully grown miners, older kids were of no significance whatsoever and he was so big for his age, anyway, that he was as comfortable as he looked in their company.

In fact, for the watching officials of Bolton schools football, this lad Lawton looked far more than comfortable. He excelled. And later they selected him to represent Bolton Town Schools.

The pride and joy with which that news was greeted by the men of the Riley household was matched by that of his mother when they learned that Tommy – so happy in Fred Milner's school – had wasted no time in his lessons, either. He had won a scholarship to an even better school, Folds Road Central.

It was 1930. Eleven-year-old Tommy was the family's hero.

Mam and Nan decided they should have a family party to celebrate the lad's success. "Now, don't go overdoing it, we don't want 'im getting a big 'ead," Jim Riley cautioned. But the women ignored that.

It was a frugal affair, with fish-paste butties and a celebration cake made with more love than fancy ingredients, but to young Tommy it was a banquet. A banquet in *his* honour. His young heart was bursting with happiness and his devoted family shared his happiness. One by one they entertained the boy with a 'turn' – a song here, a monologue there.

His mam had a lovely voice. "Our Lizzie sings like a nightingale," her brothers boasted. Lizzie and all the women mill workers sang all day. It was their way of breaking the mind-numbing monotony of their jobs. Raven-haired Lizzie was a big, strong girl, strikingly attractive and self-confident, qualities which were equally evident in the singing voice with which she was capable of overcoming the clattering cacophony of the mill.

Her party piece for young Tommy's big day was *On the Sunny Side of the Street*. This was a song of the Great Depression, written a year after the Wall Street Crash and intended to lift the spirits of the masses by getting them to believe that the gloom and doom would not last for ever.

That song had as much resonance and relevance in a Bolton back street as it did in the Bronx: the resolute men, women and children of both were fighting an endless battle against desperately hard times. Its sentiments made them feel better. And Lizzie sang it beautifully.

Walked with no one and talked with no one
And I had nothing but shadows.
Then one morning you passed
And I brightened at last.
Now I greet the day and complete the day
With the sun in my heart.
All my worry blew away
When you taught me how to say:

Grab your coat and get your hat
Leave your worries on the doorstep
Life can be so sweet
On the sunny side of the street
Can't you hear the pitter-pat?
And that happy tune is your step
Life can be complete
On the sunny side of the street.

I used to walk in the shade,
With those blues on parade
But I'm not afraid,
Because this rover crossed over.

That last line was the signal for the rest of the family to join in. Dad, Nan, Jack, Fred, Harold, Jim and Tommy all knew what came next and the roof of the tiny terraced house was raised as they all chorused:

And if I never had a cent
I'd be rich as Rockefeller
With gold dust at my feet
On the sunny side of the street.

Jim Riley's contribution to Tommy's family concert was a favourite Stanley Holloway monologue. *Sam, Sam, Pick up Tha Musket* it was called and it celebrated the stubbornness of the proud working classes who, despite their poverty, demanded the right to be treated with respect by their so-called 'betters'.

15

Jim also demanded respect when he performed it – and absolute silence, in which the rest of the family sat dutifully as he cleared his throat and began:

It occurred on the evening before Waterloo
And troops were lined up on parade.
And Sergeant inspecting 'em, he were a terror
Of 'oom every man were afraid.

All except one man who were in t' front rank,
A man by the name of Sam Small.
And 'im and the Sergeant were both daggers drawn.
They thought nowt of each other at all.

As Sergeant walked past 'e were swinging 'is arm
And 'e 'appened to brush against Sam
And knocking 'is musket clean out of 'is 'and
It fell on the ground with a slam.

"Pick it oop," said Sergeant, abrupt like but cool
But Sam with a shake of 'is 'ead said,
"Seeing as tha knocked it out of me 'and
P'raps tha'll pick the thing oop instead."

"Sam, Sam, pick oop tha musket,"
The Sergeant exclaimed with a roar,
Sam said, "Tha knocked it down, reet!
Then tha'll pick it oop, or it stays where it is ont' floor."

The sound of high words
Very soon reached the ears of an officer, Lieutenant Bird,
'Oo says to the Sergeant "Now what's all this 'ere?"
And the Sergeant told what 'ad occurred.

"Sam, Sam, pick oop tha musket,"
Lieutenant exclaimed with some 'eat.
Sam said, "'E knocked it down, reet! Then 'e'll pick it oop
Or it stays where it is, at me feet."

It caused quite a stir when the Captain arrived
To find out the cause of the trouble.

And every man there, all excepting Old Sam
Were full of excitement and bubble.

"Sam, Sam pick oop tha musket,"
Said Captain for strictness renowned.
Sam said, "'E knocked it down, reet! Then 'e'll pick it oop
Or it stays where it is, ont' ground."

The same thing occurred when the Major and Colonel
Both tried to get Sam to see sense.
When old Duke o' Wellington came into view
Well, the excitement were tense.

Up rode the Duke on a lovely white 'orse
To find out the cause of the bother.
'E looks at the musket and then at Old Sam
And 'e talks to Old Sam like a brother.

"Sam, Sam pick oop tha musket,"
The Duke said as quiet as can be.
"Sam, Sam, pick oop tha musket
Coom on, lad, just to please me."

"All right Duke," said Old Sam, "just for thee I'll oblige
And to show thee I meant no offence."
So Sam picked it oop; "Gradeley, lad," said the Duke.
"Right-o, boys, let battle commence!"

That last line of *Old Sam* was always delivered with a theatrical flourish by Jim Riley. When he slammed his enamel tea mug down on the table to accentuate the happy conclusion to this tale of one small man's decency and defiance triumphing over the big bad bosses' bullying and bluster, the rest of the family stood as one, cheered and clapped with great gusto – and in that amusing monologue there was a message of deep meaning for young Tommy Lawton, one he was to carry with him through the rest of his life: "Always stand up for yourself and never let them lah-de-dah buggers do you down!"

One by one, the rest of the Rileys completed the family concert. Only Nan was not expected to perform a solo. That wouldn't be right, so while they all clapped and cheered everyone's 'turn' Nan simply smiled and nodded her head in unspoken endorsement of the acclaim.

For young Tommy, this was a day that should never end . . . every one of the family who loved him and cared for him gathered in recognition of his achievements in the classroom and, more importantly for him, on the football field.

But the family joy was short-lived.

One day soon after the party, Tommy burst through the door of the little terraced house as he always did after school, expecting the usual cheery greeting. But this time there was just an eerie silence. The curtains were drawn and the room was in semi-darkness. His 'dad' sat on a wooden chair with his head in his hands. Sobbing.

His mam took her boy's hands into hers. "It's your nan, Tommy. She's passed away."

It had been sudden. Nan hadn't suffered. Years of selfless sacrifice and unrelenting toil dedicated to her life's mission of making a happy home out of hardship and poverty had finally taken their toll. She was worn out. And she'd just gone.

Tommy cried himself to sleep.

With Lizzie working just about every waking hour in the mill, Nan had always been there for young Tommy. Lizzie loved her son and he her but the family couldn't survive without her weekly wage packet so she couldn't be there on the countless occasions that a child needs comforting, consoling and correcting. Nan, despite all her onerous family duties, had always provided that, always filled the gap his mother was forced to leave. "Now," grief-stricken Jim Riley told himself, "you'll 'ave to look out for the lad."

Tommy was now a pupil at Folds Road Central. Again, he had feared that his football might suffer at a new school. Again, he was wrong.

Much later, in adult life, he was to observe, "My fears were daft, really, because every man in Bolton was either football mad or raced whippets!" So it was to be at Folds Road Central: the elderly headmaster Mr F P 'Pop' Lever didn't race whippets.

One of the first questions he put to young Lawton was, "Do you play football?" The question was asked in ignorance of the fact that the boy had just been picked to represent Bolton Town Schools. "I'm quite a good player," the new pupil told the headmaster. He was given a trial for the school team, was picked immediately and became its star performer, scoring goal after goal after goal.

The medal with which Tommy was presented for representing the town's schools became his pride and joy. Its inscription was economical but to the boy it told an epic story of the two goals he had scored, clinching a 2-1 victory for his side. He read it over and over again:

T Lawton, Bolton Town Schools Football, 1930.

Now, that medal sat proudly on the mantelpiece at home, polished lovingly by his mam while the rest of the Rileys, except for Jim, made an exaggerated point of admiring it frequently: "Just the first of many, our Tommy," Jack told him. The lad's chest all but burst with pride, for this was praise indeed, but his grandfather warned," Now then, now then. 'E's got a long, long way to go yet."

Pop Lever soon became the latest convert to the growing belief in Lancashire schools football that "this lad Lawton looks very special" and though he wouldn't tell the lad himself, no one's faith in that belief was stronger than Jim Riley's.

With Nan gone, Jim devoted himself to Tommy's progress in life and in football: caring for him; nursing him; advising him; protecting him; comforting, coaxing, cajoling and coaching him. Jim became the stone on which his young charge's future was founded. Nothing was too much trouble for him, no problem too small to be dealt with, no difficulty too minor to be resolved. Everywhere the boy went, his grandfather went with him. Every game of football the lad played was watched by Jim. There was no money for tram or bus fares so this odd couple walked to every game, often a distance of many miles. Jim, a tall, straight, well-built man, marched on with an air of purposeful self-importance while the boy – several paces behind his grandfather, football boots, hung around his neck by the laces, bouncing on and off his chest, synchronised with his jaunty young step – tried to emulate the lengthy grown-up stride of his leader.

Jim carried the rest of the boy's football kit, which he'd lovingly washed and ironed, in a brown paper bag – determined that his Tommy would not be just the best player on the pitch, but the smartest, too. And he always was, despite his old, second-hand red-and-black quartered shirt having long ago faded to pink and grey. It would have to do. They couldn't afford a new one. But if it was freshly laundered every time, Jim reasoned, it would still look crisp and good on the lad. There was no money for luxuries like new studs for the boy's football boots, either. When they wore out, as they frequently did, Jim would make new ones out of bits of spare wood. The wooden studs were nailed into the boots which were old hand-me-downs made of thick brown leather stretching high above the ankles, with long white laces and solid toe caps. They were Tommy's pride and joy and he kept them immaculately clean.

It wasn't just on the football pitch that Jim's passion for smart appearance, no matter how impoverished he was, held sway. The same applied to everyday life. And it rubbed off on the boy. He never went to school without making sure that his faded and well-worn but always spotlessly clean clothes looked as smart as could be. And this applied particularly to his shoes.

"It doesn't matter 'ow old yer shoes are," Jim lectured the lad frequently. "A bit of spit an' elbow grease and they'll always look good. And always make sure that you shine the *heels as well*. Remember, lots of folks look at yer from the back." Polish the heels as well . . . It was a mantra that was to stay with young Tommy Lawton for the rest of his life.

The football-mad pupils of Folds Road chalked a set of goalposts on the school wall and – watched from his study window by the equally addicted headmaster – they spent every break from lessons practising shooting and heading with a tennis ball. Whenever Pop Lever saw a boy performing at something below his exacting standards, he opened his study window and shouted, "You boy – come here!" After explaining and correcting the pupil's perceived indiscretion he sent him back into the fray with an impatient wave of his hand. But for all the headmaster's impromptu coaching, shots would go astray, often into the Church Army hall next door, whereupon the lads would just jump over the school wall to retrieve their ball. But one day, they encountered a big problem. The premises were now guarded by a huge mongrel dog with social shortcomings to match its dubious provenance.

The guard dog had gleefully arrested the stray tennis ball and having dropped it between its feet, was snarling an invitation to the boys to go and get it. There were no takers and the delay thus induced in the football irritated the watching Pop Lever. "Boys, boys, why have you stopped?" demanded the headmaster. "Please, sir, yon big dog's got our ball!" With a confident flourish, Pop left his study, strode across the yard, clambered over the wall and confronted the animal. "You, dog. Drop that ball at once!"

The demand went unheeded, despite repeated and heated exhortations from the headmaster, whose exalted status was clearly a matter of some indifference to the triumphant mongrel. Deciding to employ discretion as the better part of valour, while trying to retain the dignity of his position in front of his watching pupils, Pop turned and was walking slowly back towards the wall, head held high, when the dog suddenly flew at him from behind. "Sir, sir," the boys shouted, "Run, run!" The headmaster had to abandon all decorum, flee the ferocious dog and scramble, red-faced, panting, scholarly gown a dishevelled rag around his neck, over the wall to safety, helped by his young charges whose genuine concern for their much-loved mentor became involuntarily subservient to the raucous laughter which, as hard as they tried, they were unable to suppress.

Such indignity would have been enough for many a headmaster who would have taken the easy way out and stopped the schoolyard sessions. Not Pop Lever. The next time the lads went out to play, he had paid for a high wire fence to be erected all along the top of the school wall. When the first misdirected volley sent their tennis ball crashing against the new fence and back into the playground, the face at the study window wore a broad smile of satisfaction.

The school had no playing field of its own and games lessons, mostly football training taken by games master Nobby Foster, were on the nearest public recreation ground. It was two miles from the school. Nobby and the kids were so keen to get there and start playing that they ran all the way.

Tommy always led that chase, so eager and so fast that not even Nobby, a very fit man, could keep up with him. Recognising the boy's promise and hearing Pop Lever, a good judge of a footballer, rave about his potential, Nobby gave young Lawton frequent one-to-one extra training. At the end of every one of these sessions, the lad's reaction was always the same: "When can we do that again, sir?"

"Tommy, do you never tire of football?" an exhausted Nobby panted after one particularly long session – then immediately answered his own question: "That were a daft thing to ask, were it not, lad?!" Tommy, as fresh as when the training had started, laughed and told him, "Yeah. Daft, sir. 'Cause *I'm* going to play for England!" Nobby nodded and, with a smile of admiration, replied, "Do you know, lad. I think you probably will."

As well as all the extra training he was getting at school, Tommy's Friday nights were reserved for training with his grandfather. And these were very special nights. Jim would take the boy up to 'Scotchman's Stump', on the moors between Bolton and Chorley. Tommy and his grandfather loved it up at Scotchman's Stump, where the air was so fresh and clean. Jim Riley always filled his lungs with exaggerated inhalation and his appreciative observation was always the same: "Tommy, lad, the air oop 'ere is like fine wine."

"Aye, it is, Dad," Tommy always agreed, as if he knew the slightest thing about wine, fine or otherwise.

Jim stood, taking in that air, while timing Tommy as he sprinted 100 yards then counting as he did his exercise routine. First ten press-ups, then touching his toes, first left foot, then right foot, ten times, then stretching out his arms to kick his hands, first left hand, then right hand ten times. Then immediately another 100-yard sprint.

With Jim shouting encouragement, this process was repeated for as many times as it took for Tommy to shout back, "Enough!" Then, after a short rest, it would start all over again. Jim knew that if it was left to the lad, he would carry on until he dropped and unlike Tommy, he also knew, instinctively, when "enough" really was enough.

"Time to go now, Tommy." "Right you are, Dad." And off home the pair would go, Jim with a protective arm around the boy's shoulder, talking football as they walked.

There, the old tin bathtub was taken down from the nail by which it hung in the tiny backyard, brought inside in front of the fire and filled with saucepans of hot water for Tommy to soak away the sweat and strain of his exhausting endeavours. There was, the boy thought, nothing to match that feeling. Then there would be pobbies, lumps of bread soaked in warm milk, for supper and a welcoming bed in which contented dreams were of scoring the winning goal at Wembley.

There was much sadness among the Folds Road pupils when dear old Pop Lever retired. They loved the man. Most headmasters ruled by fear, enforced by the cane. Pop was unusual. He spared the rod. Not that that meant he didn't command respect. One disapproving look from him was as much to be avoided as six of the best. And he had an in-built lie detector so efficient that attempting to fool it was futile. None of the kids was sadder to see Pop leave than Tommy Lawton. The old headmaster had taken an interest in the lad's football potential which went way beyond the call of duty.

Yet again, young Tommy found himself fearing what would happen to his football with Pop gone from the school. Yet again, he had no need to worry. Mr Bill Horrocks, successor to Pop, didn't race whippets either! He took just as keen an interest in the school football team and in its exciting centre forward as did his predecessor. And in any event, retirement did not mean the end of Pop's interest in young Lawton nor in his determination to see the boy's remarkable potential realised.

With Jim Riley, Pop Lever and Bill Horrocks all fiercely committed to that cause, the lad was never going to lack support, or belief in his future. Now, every time Tommy played a game his grandfather was joined on the touchline by the two teachers. The unlikely trio never missed a match. "They're your Three Musketeers, Tommy," laughed his uncles. "One for all and all for one!"

Over the next three years, Tommy's progress on the field of play served only to strengthen the rock-solid determination, total commitment and unshakeable faith of the Three Musketeers. Their protégé was going to play for England, absolutely no doubt about it, but Jim Riley was never going to tell his grandson that. "'E'll get an 'ead like Birken'ead if I do!" he told the others.

Under Bill Horrocks's enthusiastic stewardship, the Folds Road team won every competition it entered and the goalscoring achievements of its centre forward now bordered on being unbelievable: Tommy Lawton scored literally hundreds of goals. His success for Bolton Town Schools led to his selection for Lancashire Schools at 13. And a coveted red rose badge joined his medal on the Rileys' mantelpiece.

His mam, along with the rest of the Rileys, was even more proud of the lad now. Though her self-effacing style would not permit her to concede the fact, she had herself provided the family with another great source of pride. There had been huge excitement all over Bolton when a film starring Lancashire's nationally adored singing star and comedienne Gracie Fields was filmed on location at the Denvale Mill. And Lizzie was among the mill girls chosen to appear as extras.

The film, *Sing As We Go*, written for Gracie Fields by J B Priestley, was designed to lift the spirits of a seriously depressed Britain when it was made in 1933. It was the story of a mill girl, Gracie Platt – a girl just like Lizzie Lawton – who had to leave home for Blackpool when the mill at which she worked was closed by recession, causing misery, gloom and doom to beset the town.

After a series of misadventures by the seaside, our Gracie returned to persuade the bosses to re-open the mill and lead hundreds back to work. When Gracie marched back to the mill at the head of the throng of ecstatic returning workers, while belting out the film's title song as only she could, there was not a dry eye in the house.

> *Sing as we go, and let the world go by*
> *Singing a song, we march along the highway*
> *Say goodbye to sorrow*
> *There's always tomorrow*
> *To think of today*

The song became a huge hit record. The film became a blockbuster.

And right alongside Gracie in that final tear-jerking scene of the musical march of triumph back to work at the mill was Lizzie Lawton. "Our Lizzie the film star!" her brothers teased, more in pride than mockery. "Don't be so daft. It were nowt," she scolded – but secretly she was brimming with pride, knowing that she was appearing on cinema screens watched by millions of people all over the country.

Meanwhile, her Tommy was also keeping the family's flag flying high. Bolton Schools (Centre forward: T. Lawton) played Liverpool Schools in the final of the Lancashire Schools Cup at Goodison Park, home of Everton

FC, in front of a crowd of 22,000. Bolton lost an exciting contest 3-2 but Tommy scored both their goals and was only prevented from scoring a hat-trick and levelling the match when Liverpool's goalkeeper, George Burnett, pulled off a marvellous save – parrying the centre forward's fierce drive with five minutes to go.

That impressive performance led to a trial for the England Schools team. The North (Centre forward T. Lawton) played the South in the trial match in Manchester. Tommy had a great match, scoring a hat-trick in a 7-0 victory for the North but, astonishingly, the selectors did not pick him for England. Instead, they chose as England Schools centre forward, the centre half who had been marking Tommy when he slammed in three goals!

Two more trial matches followed, at Durham and Rotherham: again Tommy scored goals; again the England Schools selectors snubbed him.

For the first time in his exciting embryonic football career Tommy Lawton was devastated. And for the first time (but by no means the last!) his opinion of 'the stuffed shirts' was 'as low as a snake's belly!' What the short-sighted selectors had failed to do, however, was to dent his self-confidence. "I were best player on the pitch; not once, not twice, but *three* flippin' times," Tommy told Bill Horrocks, who, along with Jim Riley and Pop Lever, had been at all three trial matches and didn't need telling. "Call 'emselves selectors," said Jim over a pint with Bill and Pop, "they couldn't pick their own bloody noses!" The teachers gazed dolefully into the froth on their ale and nodded in agreement.

Tommy's anger – he had far too much self-belief to be disappointed for long – at the selectors' slight soon subsided. Undaunted, he carried on smashing in the goals – and not just in schools football. He was also playing on Saturday afternoons for Hayes Athletic in the Bolton League. Again, the boy's precocious talent was pitted against fit, hefty men. Again, just as in those tanner-a-man games with his uncles at the pit top, the age difference meant nothing to Tommy. But now, it was not just his skills that ensured that age gap didn't matter.

"By 'eck, 'e's a big 'un for a young 'un!" flat-capped spectators would observe as Tommy rattled in the goals for Hayes. At 14, Tommy Lawton was nearly six feet tall and weighed almost 12 stone. This was not surprising. Poor as they were, Jim Riley's mission to make his lad a top footballer included ensuring that he always got "plenty inside 'im."

Every meal put in front of Tommy had an abundance of potatoes, boiled, mashed or chipped, and a couple of times a week the dish of the day would be Jim's potato pie, mashed potatoes and onions stuffed into an inch-thick pastry tomb. Tripe and onions were a family favourite and as a special once-a-week treat they had sausage and mash. They could afford no waste so any leftovers would be saved, mixed together, fried into a crispy brown nondescript hash and re-served on a thick slice of bread. Now and again, the household budget, still almost entirely reliant on Lizzie's wages, would stretch to an egg each.

After every game, Jim, who never missed a match, insisted on sitting down with the lad to analyse every aspect of his performance and after every game Tommy was ravenously hungry, so the after-match inquest was accompanied by a slice of bread and dripping.

This almost entirely carbohydrate diet, the muscle-building training and the regular competitive matches had turned Tommy Lawton, who had always been a big lad, into a fine, fit, strong and healthy 'man' even though he was still just short of his 15th birthday. Already, few players could live with this lad on the field of play and his goal tally for Folds Road and Hayes Athletic reached an astonishing 570 in three seasons.

On Saturdays, after playing for Hayes, Tommy and his mates ran to Burnden Park, when Bolton Wanderers were at home, to watch the last few minutes of their League matches. The gates were always opened around 15 minutes before the end so that spectators who needed to leave early could get out – and that's when the local lads, who had no money to pay for the pleasure – could sneak in to watch their heroes.

High on the list of Tommy's favourites was Wanderers' captain, Harry Gosling. Gosling had been signed from Boots Athletic in Nottingham and, Nottingham being the home of Raleigh, he had brought an inherent interest in cycles with him to Bolton, where he'd opened a cycle shop. Tommy often went to that shop to stand and gaze through the window with the dual purpose of seeing one of his football heroes at close quarters and drooling over the smart new bike he couldn't possibly afford.

The irony of this scenario was that, unknown to the lad, Bolton Wanderers were also watching him. News of this local schoolboy with the phenomenal goalscoring record had reached Bolton Wanderers, mainly through one of their amateur players, Alf Thompson, who was a teacher at Folds Road. Walter Rowley, a coach at Burnden Park, asked Alf to invite Tommy along for training every Tuesday and Thursday.

Suddenly, Tommy's distant dream of becoming a professional footballer was a significant step closer to reality – and, what's more, with his own hometown club, the top-drawer winners of no less than three FA Cup finals in ten years.

Back home to relay the news to Jim, Mam and the uncles, Tommy jumped up and down on the spot with excitement.

Jim, though delighted deep down to hear of Wanderers' interest, was cool and circumspect. Tommy was soon to be 15, the age at which he would leave school. The rules of football dictated that he could not turn professional until he was 17. How was he to earn a living and contribute to the family's meagre income in the meantime? "Just 'ang on a minute, lad," he said, "This is not as simple as you think. I need to speak to Pop and Bill."

Now all three friends gazed into the froth on the pints of ale over which they had called their summit. "I see what you mean, Jim," said Bill Horrocks. "Not easy, is it?" said Pop Lever. "Wants thinking about," said Jim. "Why don't we go and see them at Wanderers and ask about the options?" suggested Pop. "That's it. That's what we'll do," agreed Jim and Bill.

In the meantime, Wanderers, anticipating a foregone conclusion, jumped the gun. Manager Charlie Foweraker presumptuously and prematurely announced that they had signed the star of Bolton schools football.

"The cheeky bugger!" exclaimed Jim. "Dad, just let me sign. Please!" pleaded Tommy. "Leave it to your elders and betters, lad," said his grandfather, in that tone which Tommy knew accommodated no argument. Waiting outside Charlie Foweraker's office the three 'elders and betters' were having a last-minute chat before being summoned to enter. Tommy sat alongside them on the big leather couch, respectfully silent.

"Look, I don't want our Tommy signing for the first club that comes along – even if it is Bolton Wanderers. I know 'e can't make money playing football till 'e's 17 but they've got to put something on our table," said Jim Riley. "I agree," said Bill Horrocks, "We all know your lad's going to be a top player. We don't need to rush it." "Right. We take our time," said Pop Lever.

Inside Foweraker's office, Jim came straight to the point: "What sort of job can you offer the lad?" "Oh," said Foweraker, "we'll get him a job in a butcher's shop." Tommy thought, "Oh, please. I'll do anything." But he could tell that his grandfather was seriously underimpressed.

"A delivery boy! 'Ow much is that going to pay?" Jim asked rhetorically. "It'll be about seven shillings and sixpence a week," replied Foweraker. Jim Riley immediately got to his feet. And Tommy knew the discussion was over.

"I can get 'im a job like that, anytime," said Jim. "Good morning, Mr Foweraker. You'll never see us again!" With that, Jim Riley walked out of the manager's office, followed by Pop Lever, then by Bill Horrocks and finally, reluctantly, by young Tommy. "Not good enough, Mr Foweraker," said Pop. "Not nearly good enough, Mr Foweraker," said Bill. "S-s-orry, Mr Foweraker," stammered the boy.

Charlie Foweraker watched the procession in disbelief. And when the door slammed shut, he asked himself, "What the bloody 'ell was that all about?"

Jim, Pop and Bill were convinced that they had made the right decision. After all, Lancashire, the spiritual home of football, was full of good clubs. As well as Bolton, there were Preston North End, Blackburn Rovers, Bury, Blackpool and Burnley. Close by were Manchester City and Manchester United. And not far away were Everton and Liverpool. Soon, they'd all be queuing up to sign a future England centre forward who scored goals for fun.

But they weren't.

There was no interest from Preston North End; nor from Manchester City; nor from Manchester United. Everton weren't showing any interest, either; nor Liverpool. None of them. Not even Accrington Stanley!

It was time for some more froth-gazing. "Wanderers' offer were an insult!" said Jim. "Oh, absolutely," said Pop. "Derisory," said Bill. They had all invested far too much time in their prize asset to allow him to be under-valued, they confirmed. One day, all those clubs would want the lad. And they'd offer more than a butcher's bike.

But in the meantime, what to do?

It was Bill who broke the long unproductive silence that ensued: "Hayes Athletic are not bad, but I reckon Tommy needs to step up a class in non-league football. That way, he's more likely to get noticed by the big clubs. I know them well at Rossendale United. I'll have a word."

That word saw 15-year-old Tommy Lawton playing centre forward in the royal blue shirt of Rossendale United against Bacup in the Lancashire Combination. It was a dreadful afternoon: the game was played in an unrelenting deluge of rain. The pitch was a sea of cloying mud, which coated the players' shirts so that you couldn't tell one side from the other as they struggled to wade through the quagmire into which they sank up to their ankles.

All, that is, bar one of them.

Rossendale United's new forward glided over that swamp with strength, pace and grace. He was vastly superior to any other man on the pitch. He scored a hat-trick and contributed directly to four more goals as Rossendale thrashed Bacup 9-1.

After the game, Rossendale's manager, Mick Tollman, sought out Tommy's grandfather and told him, "This lad's something very special. But I can't possibly sign 'im. 'E's too young. If 'e were 17, I'd 'ave 'im . . . then make bloody thousands out of transferring 'im!"

Even though their plan to expose the boy to top clubs as a Rossendale

United player had foundered after one incredible appearance, Tommy's Three Musketeers were well pleased. His performance and Mick Tollman's assessment convinced them that their judgment in rejecting Bolton Wanderers' butcher's bike had been impeccable!

But still they had to wait.

Liverpool heard about Tommy and invited him, along with Jim, Pop and Bill, to watch a game against West Bromwich Albion. Afterwards, a move to Merseyside was seriously discussed. Liverpool said they would be in touch. They weren't. Then Bury expressed a supposedly 'keen' interest that didn't materialise. Blackburn invited them to Ewood Park to watch Rovers play and to 'discuss the lad Lawton' but took it no further.

The mission of the Three Musketeers was hitting the rocks.

Tommy was a schoolboy no longer and that meant he had to earn his keep. He went to work at Walker's Tannery in Bolton. It was a boring, mindless job, polishing the heads of golf clubs which were to be sold to rich folk. To a working-class lad who had grown up with miners and mill workers it seemed utterly pointless work but at least it brought a few shillings home while his indefatigable mentors continued their passionate pursuit of his real destiny.

The lad's reputation had crossed the border to Yorkshire and they were invited to visit Sheffield Wednesday where manager Billy Walker came up with a firm offer and a clever compromise solution to the underage problem: "I'll sign the lad as an amateur, get him free digs and give him ten bob a week pocket money until I can find him a decent job." Tommy was elated. "I want to sign, Dad," he told his grandfather.

Jim Riley wasn't too keen on the offer at first, but the teachers thought it a fit and fair one. The Three Musketeers and their young protégé went back to Hillsborough and a deal was agreed.

Back home in Bolton, the Riley menfolk were delighted. "Grand news, our Tommy!" they all enthused, patting the lad on the back and shaking his hand vigorously. And grandfather was quietly content.

Then Lizzie came home from work. And her reaction was entirely different: "You're doing *what?*" she said when Tommy, thrilled to bits, broke the news to his mother. Then she delivered her verdict: "Over my dead body!"

Angrily, Lizzie Lawton confronted her dad and her brothers: "'Ave you all gone daft?! Don't you know 'ow far it is to Sheffield? Are you all forgetting 'ow old this lad is? 'E's *15*. 'E's only a boy. 'E can't be packed off on 'is own all the way to Sheffield. Who's going to look after 'im? I'm not letting 'im go and live all on his own in a big strange city miles from 'is 'ome – and that's an end to it."

Jim and his sons sat in silence, their heads bowed in contrition. They knew there was no arguing with Lizzie in this sort of mood. Just like her mam, she was, a real chip off the old block. You never argued with her, either. You just said nowt.

Only Tommy stood up for the Sheffield scheme: "Mam. Please. I'm grown up now. I'll be all right." "You aren't. And you won't be. You're not going." Thus did Sheffield Wednesday and the astute Billy Walker miss out on Tommy Lawton.

No setback was too much for Tommy's Three Musketeers. Just days after Lizzie vetoed the Sheffield Wednesday plan, Bill Horrocks contacted an old pal, Wilf Hopkinson, who was a director of Second Division Burnley FC:

"Wilf, you'll have heard about young Tommy Lawton, no doubt?"

"Too right I 'ave, Bill. A real good young 'un."

"Aye. Well he's available, you know."

"Really! We all thought the lad would go to a First Division club."

"No. He could sign for Burnley if you play your cards right."

Bill told Wilf Hopkinson all about Jim Riley's demands for a decent job for the lad to put money on the family's table until he was 17, about the rejected offer from Bolton Wanderers, about the lad's mother digging in her heels over Sheffield Wednesday and about the failure of Liverpool, Blackburn and Bury to pursue their initial interest.

"So there you have it, Wilf. It's hard to believe, I know – but the lad's still not got a club."

"It is 'ard to believe. Leave it with me, Bill. I'll see what I can do."

Within 48 hours, Wilf Hopkinson was sitting in front of Jim, Pop and Bill in a quiet, discreet pub, four pints of frothing ale and an extremely attractive offer on the table . . .

"We'll take the lad on as an amateur and we'll give 'im a good job in the office as assistant to our club secretary, Alf Boland. Alf will look after 'im well. We'll pay the lad two pounds, ten shillings a week. There'll also be a job for you, Jim, as assistant groundsman at Turf Moor and for that you'll get three pounds, ten shillings a week. And your family will be given a rent-free house in Brunshaw Road, just up the road from our ground. Now 'ow does that sound?"

Jim Riley thought it sounded pretty damned good. The teachers concurred. This time, there was no contemplative froth-gazing over their pints, but there was rather a lot of celebratory quaffing.

Back home and a little the worse for wear, Jim sat Tommy down at the table: "Now lad, it's to be Burnley. And this is the deal . . ." Tommy's mouth opened wider with every detail as Jim relayed the offer and when he'd done, Tommy jumped from his seat with a whoop of delight: "Oh, Dad. I can't believe it. That's wonderful!"

Jim tried to appear unmoved: "It's only Second Division, mind." "I don't care about that," said Tommy. "It's my big chance. I'm going to take it. And I'll make you all so proud of me!" "Just see that you do, lad. Just see that you do," said Jim placidly. But deep inside, his heart was leaping as joyfully as the boy's.

They came to see young Lawton

Chapter Three

TOMMY — THE BOY WONDER

Tommy Lawton, aged 15, walked into Turf Moor, home of Burnley Football Club in May 1935 feeling ten feet tall.

Not only was he now officially a Burnley player, but thanks to the deal struck between the club and his Three Musketeers his mam's wage packet was no longer going to be the only regular one coming in for the Rileys. Now, he was to get a decent weekly wage, his 'dad' was getting an even better one and in due course, when they moved into their new home, they would no longer have to pay rent.

And all because he was such a good footballer.

Tommy was filled with an intense feeling of happiness: he'd never felt anything like this before, this sense of excitement, anticipation and immense pride. It was to stay, etched into his soul, for the rest of his life.

For the first three months in their new jobs, Tommy and his grandfather travelled from Bolton to Burnley and back every day by bus. Burnley was different, smaller than Bolton. There were mill chimneys everywhere you looked, it seemed, but somehow, it had more space, more fresh air. It was a 40-mile round trip and the buses were very slow. It made a long day for them both but there was never a word of complaint from either of them because Tommy was beginning to fulfil the wildest dream of just about every working-class boy in Britain.

Football was massive. Football captivated and inspired millions. Football raised spirits and defeated drudgery. Football, for lads like Tommy Lawton, offered hope of a much better life.

On the pitch, it was a simple game but it was that very simplicity that provided the poetry in motion: the exquisite passing patterns, the thrilling pace, the pulsating excitement. Each player knew precisely what was required of him in the position he occupied on the pitch. The formation never varied: one–two–three–five . . . goalkeeper, right fullback, left fullback; right halfback, centre half, left halfback; outside right, inside right, centre forward, inside left, outside left.

The role of the centre forward was to lead his team's attack; to collect the ball from his own defenders, halfbacks or inside forwards; to keep possession under physical pressure from the opposing centre half or right or left halfbacks, before laying it off for his inside forwards or wingers or beating defenders and heading for goal himself, creating scoring chances for his teammates but, above all, scoring goals – his prime purpose. Centre forwards were mostly tall, strong, athletic men, fine physical specimens, with superb shooting skills and heading ability. They tended to be the most popular and glamorous players because they were frequently the match-winning heroes. But they could very quickly become villains if the goals were not forthcoming.

The games were played in all weather conditions: inches of snow would not force abandonment – merely much hard work by willing volunteers with shovels; frost and ice meant no more than rock-hard pitches with unpredictable bounce; torrential rain was a relatively minor inconvenience, even when the ball was stopping dead in deep puddles and ploughing through mud which was literally ankle deep was routine.

The only on-field treatment for injuries, other than broken limbs, was the application of a sponge soaked in bitterly cold water. The primitive cold-sponge treatment was delivered to whatever part of the anatomy appeared to require it, this operation often being accompanied by hoots of derision from distinctly unsympathetic supporters, especially if the discomfort was in a particularly sensitive area. Then the mocking cry of "Don't rub 'em, count 'em" added embarrassing insult to the eye-watering injury. Only very serious injury resulted in the removal of a player from the action because substitutes were not permitted and it was common practice to move an injured man who was barely able to walk, let alone run, out onto the wing, where he could at least be of nuisance value.

The players' clearly defined positions in their team were virtually set in stone and very rarely did any of them stray from their allotted roles. The symmetry thus produced was, for the enthralled spectator, a beautiful blend of athleticism, skill, speed, strength and courage and woe betide any non-believer who dared to suggest that football was merely 22 men kicking a ball around a field!

Off the pitch, even though football was a business supported and consequently funded by millions of working-class spectators, its administrative structure was riddled with elitism, status-consciousness and snobbery. Professional players, limited to a rigidly applied maximum wage (which, even when it included a couple of pounds in win bonuses was less than £10 a week) were treated as chattels, to be bought or sold at will, quite frequently against their own.

Football had a distinct class system, with the directors of clubs at the very top of the pile and the players, without whom there would have been no football, right down at the bottom. Attendances at matches were astronomically high and many hundreds of thousands of pounds were made, especially by the top clubs. But the players who, through their skill and dedication, their blood, sweat and tears, were responsible for generating those vast profits saw next to nothing of the huge amounts of cash they raised. The directors ruling over these serfdoms, who were sometimes self-made men treacherously exploiting their own working-class brethren, had to be treated with forelock-tugging respect, the players who called them *sir* being addressed in return only by their surnames.

This social and moral injustice in football was a reflection of the times in general, a mirror image of the inequity in industry and commerce. It did nothing to deter working-class lads with the ability and dedication from craving a career in professional football. For all the iniquities of its pay structure, the game still offered a better wage than they'd get down the pits or in the factories. Thus, footballers were relatively well paid for playing a game they loved and for being heroes idolised in their own communities, from which they rarely moved.

Not a bad alternative to digging coal or toiling in sweatshops!

On Saturdays when Burnley were playing at home, there was only one place Tommy Lawton and his grandfather wanted to be – Turf Moor. Match day in Burnley was something very special. Everybody who had a job worked until 1 pm. That's when the weekend began and that's when a sudden sense of freedom soared in the breasts of all those who worked so long and so hard for so little. The mills and other factories would disgorge thousands of temporarily liberated workers, many of whom would be going to the match.

Some arrived by bus, most walked from their homes or their local pubs and the narrow streets around Turf Moor became a seething mass of cloth-capped heads, above which the air was dense with smoke from ubiquitous pipes and cigarettes. The constant hum of expectant chatter was accompanied by the clip-clop clatter of police horses' hooves on the cobbles and the merry, mesmerising click of dozens of turnstiles, while above it all rose the sporadic ear-piercing cries of programme sellers, panicking lest they were left with their wares. This was an atmosphere electrified by anticipation and bolstered by camaraderie. For those caught up in it there was absolutely nothing better.

Inside the ground, only the 'lah-de-dah buggers' – the directors and their guests and the club officials – sat in the stand; most of the spectators stood on the huge, uncovered, gradually rising man-made mound of cinders and ash which was the Spion Kop. The roar that went up from that hill of humanity when their heroes emerged from the players' tunnel was spine-tingling, so moving that the cheers from many of these tough men were stifled by the lumps in their throats. Then for 90 minutes, the cares, the woes, the unremitting toil of working-class existence were banished as every tackle, every run, every dribble, every shot was instantaneously played vicariously by thousands of pairs of hobnailed boots on the Kop.

How desperately Tommy Lawton craved a role in this thrilling theatre.

Meanwhile, his weekday routine was well established: office work in the mornings; training in the afternoons. And when the family moved into their new house in Burnley, he was able to train in the evenings as well.

Of all those intense feelings of achievement which Tommy was experiencing, paramount among them was the fact that, having moved to the rent-free house and with those two new wages coming in, the family was now sufficiently well-off for his mam to give up her job at the mill, the job which had kept the whole Riley family going for much of the last 13 years of hardship.

Now, he could throw himself with great glee and gusto into the opportunity that Jim Riley, Pop Lever and Bill Horrocks had won for him and in next to no time, there emerged another man who, like those three, would have a huge input into the development of Tommy Lawton.

Ray Bennion was a Welsh international halfback who had spent 12 years at Manchester United. By his own modest description, Bennion was never a star, but one of those tough, solid, utterly dependable team players whose names were always the first to be written on the team sheets. When he retired from playing, Ray moved to Turf Moor as Burnley's coach.

Soon after joining the club, young Lawton was thrown in at the deep end one afternoon to 'make up the numbers' in a training game with the Reserves and 'A' team players. Ray Bennion stood watching on the touchline with Burnley's manager Tom Bromilow: "Tom, that kid can play!"

Bennion remarked to the boss. "Yeah. And just look at the size of him, Ray!"

Ray Bennion knew that he'd seen something exciting that afternoon and he started to take a special interest in Tommy. Throughout his first summer at the club, the lad worked one-to-one with the coach every day.

On the first of those days, Bennion went into goal, tossed half a dozen balls to the kid and told him, "Right, just keep hitting 'em at me. Both feet. 'Ard as you like. And aim for the corners." Tommy remembered those sessions with Bunny Lee at Tonge Moor School when he was only seven years old and he thought, "Easy. I've done this before!"

As quickly as Ray could return the balls, Tommy was belting them back at him – hard, both feet, into the corners, just as he'd been told. Soon, Bennion's back was aching from picking the balls out of the back of the net. It wasn't long before the coach needed a break, so he chalked a spot on the wall of the main stand and told him, "Now then, lad – you've got to hit that spot nine times out of ten. First right foot, then left foot and so on. And I won't accept less than nine out of ten. Got it!" Leaning up against the stand to rest his back, Bennion counted each successful effort out of ten . . . "Only seven that time. Not bloody good enough. Now, do it again!"

Never in all his years in the game had Bennion seen a kid with such promise. The accuracy with which Lawton could strike a football was unbelievable and he was so full of talent and confidence that it was impossible to push him too hard, so their training sessions became a good-natured contest between coach and youngster as Ray tried to make the exercises more and more difficult for him.

Even the self-assured Tommy thought the coach was pushing it a bit the day Bennion came up with a routine which he described to the lad with an impish grin that implied: "Right, you cocky young bugger. You'll never do this!" He said, "You're going to dribble the ball at sprinting pace around the touchline for full circuits of the pitch and every time you get by that sign over there on that advertising board that says 'Burnley Beer Is Best', I want you to turn, shoot and hit one of the capital Bs. Miss and you'll do it again and again until you get it right. OK?"

However, Tommy just smiled and asked cheekily, "Any particular one of the Bs?" The quick-witted coach didn't hesitate: "Yeah, since you've asked. The first time, it'll be the first B; the second time, the second B; the third time, the third B and so on. And you must keep that sequence going!"

Stifling a laugh, Bennion turned and walked to the centre circle to watch the lad's effort. Then he gasped – as Tommy hit the first B first time! But this was *really* testing the boy and from then on, Tommy's daily training sessions ended with that routine every day.

Then, just to make it a bit more interesting, Bennion added another routine. He took 12 shirts from the dressing room and laid them out to form a clockface in the middle of the pitch. As he threw the ball up to Tommy with a call of "one o'clock", "four o'clock", "two o'clock", "three o'clock" etc Tommy had to jump and head the ball to the left or the right and hit the shirt representing the correct time.

Not long afterwards Bennion was having a cup of tea with one of Burnley's senior players, the centre forward George Brown, and discovered that Brown hadn't yet seen Lawton play.

"George, you know that new lad in the secretary's office, young Lawton?" Ray inquired.

"Yeah."

"Have you seem him play?"

"No."

"Well, if I'm any judge, we've got somebody *very* special here. Come with me tomorrow afternoon and watch me put him through his paces. I'd like to know what you think."

Like everybody else at Burnley, Bennion had huge respect for George Brown. George was 33 but still very fit and all the players looked up to him. He had been in the famous Huddersfield Town team that won three consecutive First Division championships in 1924–26. Then he'd moved on to Aston Villa and, as he neared veteran status, to Burnley. He had won nine caps for England and on seven of those occasions he'd been inside forward to Tommy Lawton's greatest hero, Dixie Dean.

As George watched from the stand, Ray Bennion gave Tommy a particularly demanding training session. He wanted Brown to see the full range of the precocious talent this lad possessed – ending with the capital Bs routine.

George Brown looked on, lost in admiration. "I've never seen anything like that in a kid; how old is he?" he asked. "Only 15!" "You're joking! What have they been feeding him on?"

Like Ray Bennion, like Jim Riley, like Pop Lever and Bill Horrocks, George Brown knew he had seen something very special that day.

The next morning, he called into the secretary's office to see Tommy: "Hello lad, I'm George Brown. Pleased to meet you."

"Oh, I know who you are, Mr Brown, of course I do," Tommy stuttered, hardly able to believe that the firm hand he was shaking belonged to a man who'd played for England. And alongside Dixie Dean! "Come and have a word with me, any time you like. There's a lot to learn about this game," Brown told the boy, "and there's not much I haven't seen."

It wasn't an idle boast, but a mere statement of fact from a man Tommy came to idolise. His invitation to talk football with the lad had been sincere, too. They talked often, the seasoned veteran international and the 15-year-old who had only dreams. No question from Tommy – and there were hundreds – was too much trouble for George Brown to answer in detail. He was patient and considerate and the lad hung on his every word. After training, George often took Tommy to one side and showed him how to practise the special skills that had made him an international player. When he left, Tommy would stay on, alone, for hours – practising, practising, practising the latest skill that George had taught him.

At the start of the new season, Tommy Lawton was scoring goals regularly for the 'A' team. Ray Bennion continued to teach, train and encourage him and his scoring rate, which was now averaging a goal a game, was due in no small measure to one of the simplest but most effective pieces of advice the coach gave him: "As soon as you see the white line of the penalty box, hit the bloody thing. Hard."

In September 1935, manager Bromilow decided Lawton was ready to play for Burnley Reserves. He was still only 15 years old. It was a huge step up for a boy of that age and Tommy's usual confidence deserted him when he took the field against Manchester City Reserves at Maine Road. He had a poor game – and not just by his own self-imposed high standards. He was immediately dropped back into the 'A' team but his irrepressible spirit returned, the goals flew in, he was soon given another chance in the Reserves and this time, he held his place.

He was not scoring many goals for the Reserves; for the first time, he was finding that very difficult, but it was not surprising since he was regularly coming up against senior professionals, many with first-team experience. After 13 matches he had scored just three goals but Bromilow and Bennion were pleased with him, because his all-round play and contribution to the success of those around him were growing steadily and impressively.

By the time he turned 16 Tommy Lawton was doing well. But that was more than could be said for Burnley's first team. By late March they were at the bottom of the League, struggling to avoid relegation from the Second Division and time was running out. It was getting desperate. Time, Ray Bennion told his management colleagues, for desperate action. "We should play the boy Lawton," the coach told Burnley chairman Tom Clegg. "He can't do any worse – and he might just do better." "He's very young. But you could just be right," said Clegg. "I know I'm right. We're not scoring goals, so we've got nothing to lose," Bennion replied.

Tommy's tutor, George Brown, was now back in the top flight, having left Burnley for Leeds United. He'd been replaced as Burnley's attack leader by Ces Smith. And Smith hadn't scored a goal in the last eight matches. At the team selection meeting with his fellow directors, Tom Clegg made the case. And when the side for the next game was announced Lawton was at centre forward. He couldn't believe it. He was elated, excited and proud but so nervous that his stomach was in knots. The rest of the Burnley first-team players were surprised, but quick to support the lad. "You've got nothing to fear," the captain, Alick Robinson, told him. "You're a big, strong, fit boy – and we've all seen what you can do."

On 28th March 1936, Tommy Lawton, aged 16 years and 174 days, became the youngest centre forward ever to play in the English Football League.

The night before the game, to be played at home at Turf Moor versus Doncaster Rovers, he could not sleep. As he tossed and turned, one thought kept recurring: "Suppose I let everybody down?"

On the day, in the dressing room, surrounded by senior players thoughtfully encouraging, calming and reassuring him, the nervousness eased. Just before the teams were due to take the field, Ces Smith, the man the boy had replaced, came into the dressing room, strode up to Tommy, put a comforting arm around his shoulders and told him, "All the very best, son." This generosity of spirit delighted Tommy, but it did not surprise him, for when his debut was announced the first player to congratulate him had been Ces Smith. Now, the man's selfless dressing room gesture brought tears to the boy's eyes. "Thanks, Mr Smith," he replied. "I'll try not to let you down."

The selection of the youngster had captured the imagination of press and public in Burnley: "Burnley's Boy Leader" screamed the headline in the local *Express & News.* And an above-average crowd turned out to witness his debut. Among that crowd were three men with an extra-special interest. Jim Riley, Pop Lever and Bill Horrocks were more nervous than the lad himself and the 'Three Musketeers' had good cause to be anxious. Young Tommy's was not the only debut that day. Making his first appearance for Doncaster Rovers was burly centre half Syd Bycroft. His debut hadn't excited the papers and he was no emerging youngster, but this game was no less important for him.

The referee blew his whistle to start the game and there was a huge roar from the crowd as Tommy flicked the ball to Burnley's inside forward Bob Brocklebank, newly signed from Aston Villa, and dashed forward for the return pass – only to find his route unceremoniously blocked by the bulk of 'Big Syd', who sent him clattering to the ground. With the crowd booing and baying for the blood of Big Syd, the centre half offered his hand to the prostrate Tommy and, pulling him up on his feet, told him, "Tha's nought burra bloody amateur, lad. You'll get nowt outta me."

From that first minute on, Big Syd stuck as if glued to his young opponent and by occasionally fair but mostly foul means, ensured that the boy so many people had come to see hardly got a kick. On the few occasions that he did manage to get hold of the ball, the crowd's roar of encouragement for Tommy was silenced immediately as Syd, just as he'd predicted he would, made sure that it came to nothing. Tommy managed only one shot at goal in 90 minutes. It went wide. And when a corner kick found him, unmarked by Syd for the one and only time and perfectly placed ten yards from goal, he lost his composure, completely miskicked, missed the ball and ended up on his backside. The big centre half's huge hand was offered to assist Tommy back to his feet. "Unlucky, son," he said, with a smile that lacked something in sincerity.

Tommy just wanted the ground to open and swallow him up.

With just a few minutes of the game remaining Burnley were losing 1-0. When they were awarded a late penalty, the debutant centre forward wasn't invited to take it. It was, however, duly dispatched to earn a 1-1 draw for a Burnley performance which the *Express & News* reported as "puerile – the season's worst".

Battered, bruised and beside himself with an inconsolable sense of failure, Tommy limped home, telling himself over and over again: "You let everybody down. You were useless. It was so embarrassing. You might as well give it up. You're just not good enough." He went straight to bed and cried himself to sleep. He didn't hear the bedroom door open, or the tip-toed arrival at his bedside of Jim Riley. But he woke when his grandfather gently ruffled his hair as if he were a two-year-old. Jim said nothing. He didn't need to.

While the *Express & News* was brutal in its bashing of Burnley's performance, declaring it "not even worth the point they got," it was generously gentle in its review of the debutant centre forward, describing him as "keen and fearless", though conceding that Big Syd Bycroft had "stuck to him closer than a brother", and offering some sound advice on how he would have done better to have left the centre of the pitch more often, thus drawing the centre half out of position.

That 'keen and fearless' verdict was shared by Burnley chairman Tom Clegg, the management team and the directors, and Tommy's fears of a football career wrecked prematurely on the rock that was Big Syd Bycroft proved to be groundless. When the team sheet for Burnley's next game, away to Swansea City, was pinned up, T Lawton was still at centre forward and the typical resilience of youth had obliterated the memory of those debut tears. "This time," Tommy told Jim Riley, "will be different altogether. You'll see!"

Tommy had never been too far from home. His football had mostly been played around Lancashire. So the 500-mile round trip to Swansea was, for this naïve, working-class 16-year-old, the journey of a lifetime. He was wide-eyed and bristling with excitement when he joined the senior players at Burnley railway station early on Friday morning to catch the train to Manchester. At Manchester they changed trains to head for Shrewsbury. At Shrewsbury they joined another train for Swansea.

As the steam engine huffed and puffed its way out of Shropshire and into Wales, calling at every stop on the way, the lad sat with his face pressed up against the window, transfixed by the sights, the scenery and the utterly unpronounceable place names of another world. The journey took hours; Tommy's more experienced fellow travellers played cards or slept through it, but Tommy simply did not want it to end and when it eventually did it was dark.

At Swansea, another exciting new experience awaited him. The team was staying at a hotel! Tommy had heard of hotels: they were posh places where the 'lah-de-dah buggers' stayed and ate kippers for breakfast. His uncles had told him all about them. Now, he had *really* made it.

Perhaps it was the marathon journey to Wales that did it but, unlike the previous Friday night, Tommy slept soundly through to Saturday morning and woke refreshed and ready for the fray. No sign, this day, of the weeping boy who wanted to pack it all in a week earlier. It was the much more familiar, confident Tommy Lawton who marched out onto the Vetch Field pitch looking forward to his second game in League football.

A good game was evenly matched at 1-1 when, after 25 minutes, Burnley's Ronnie Hornby raced down the left wing and, spotting the matching run of young Lawton, hit an inviting cross into the Swansea penalty area. Tommy jumped high above the defenders and met the ball perfectly with his head. In a flash, the ball was beyond Swansea goalkeeper Stan Moore and rippling the back of the net.

He stood, rooted to the spot in shock. His captain, Alick Robinson, sprinted into the penalty area and grabbed him in a bear hug. "Tommy, lad! Brilliant!" he shouted. Captain and kid rushed to Ronnie Hornby, creator of Tommy Lawton's first goal in League football, to continue the celebration.

Tommy ran back to the centre circle, his head throbbing with emotion. The thrill he felt was overpowering. In the dressing room at half-time, he tried his best to be grown up, simply nodding a thanks to his teammates' congratulations, while repressing a childlike urge to jump up and down with joy.

He took the field for the second half with his confidence sky high. Midway through, Robinson caught a Swansea forward in possession, robbed him of the ball and slipped a perfect through-pass into space with an invitation to "Go, lad!" Tommy glided effortlessly onto the ball and – just as Ray Bennion had taught him – as soon as he saw the white line of the penalty box he hit it. Hard. The right-footed shot was so accurate and so fierce that goalkeeper Moore's despairing dive looked hopelessly late. The ball hit the back of the net like a bullet.

Burnley 3 – Swansea 1. The away victory the struggling Lancashire side needed so badly was in the bag, thanks to their amateur boy centre forward!

This time, the lad abandoned all pretence of handling the situation like a seasoned professional. He could not contain his excitement. He danced a jig of delight in the dressing room, singing, "I got two, I got two." This time, his captain did not join in the celebration. And his teammates ignored him. With the corrective air of a dutiful parent, Robinson told him, "You might think you're the cat's whiskers now, lad, but you won't do that every week, you know."

Jubilant Tommy was deaf to the cautionary common sense of his captain, blind to the studied indifference of his teammates. He carried on leaping around the dressing room, chanting even louder, "I GOT TWO, I GOT TWO!" Then trainer Billy Dougall, an elder statesman who commanded the respect of all the Burnley players, shouted firmly at the boy, "Just because you got two goals, don't go thinking you're a great player. Just sit down and shut up!" Tommy slumped down on the dressing-room bench, his euphoria swamped by a deep sense of injustice; "Miserable devils," he muttered under his breath.

As soon as the victorious Burnley team arrived at Swansea's Victoria Station for the long train trek back home, he dashed over to a vendor who was selling the *Evening Post* to buy a paper so that he could read all about his heroic performance. Suddenly, Alick Robinson was at his side: "Oh no you don't," he said, "Put your money back in your pocket and get back over there with the lads." Like the mere boy that he was, a sulking Tommy, shoulders slumped, face distorted in defiance, walked reluctantly back along the platform while his captain, like a resolute father determined to make his point, marched purposefully behind.

On the train, the centre forward, still sulking, fell fast asleep. "Just look at 'im," Robinson observed to his colleagues, "'E's nowt but a child." Back home in Burnley in the early hours of Sunday morning, Bill Dougall took the 'child' home to his grandfather and on the doorstep his instruction was unequivocal: "He's not to see the paper, Jim. Rip the sports page out and put it on the fire." Grandfather obliged. Determined not to be beaten, Tommy, who couldn't sleep anyway, rose extra early and ran downstairs to be first to the Sunday paper. He was foiled again. Jim Riley had beaten him to it. The sports pages were lighting the fire.

"I know," thought Tommy later, "I'll go down to the ground and see what everybody thinks of my two goals." Whistling and clearly very full of himself, he headed for the front door, only to find Jim barring his way: "Where do you think you're going, lad?" "Just down to the ground for half an hour, Dad." "Oh no you're not. You just want to show off. You're staying in all day."

This sent the boy into a sustained sulk. But Jim Riley wasn't shifting from his stance. He agreed entirely with Bill Dougall. They must not let yesterday's success go to the lad's head. It could ruin him. Jim reiterated the message the captain had given his young centre forward: "You're not going to score two goals every week." Less than a week later, Tommy discovered how true that was.

It was Good Friday and Burnley were at home to Manchester United. Burnley were still in desperate need of points to avoid relegation from the Second Division. United were equally desperate, because they stood on the brink of promotion to the First Division. The crucial importance of the match and the return to Turf Moor of the teenage conqueror of Swansea produced the best crowd of the season. There were 27,245 expectant spectators as Tommy trotted out to a hero's welcome from the home fans. But that was the last cheer he got that afternoon.

Manchester United's centre half, George Vose, shut him out of the game, just as Doncaster's Syd Bycroft had done. But this time, it was pure skill that achieved the desired result. Vose was not a big man. But he was a classy player who augmented superb positional sense with pace and clean, crisp tackling. He was far too good for young Tommy who was permitted no time or space to repeat the performance with which he'd thought he had made his name in Wales.

The boy was desperately despondent when one of his frequently futile attempts to go past Vose was foiled by a perfectly timed tackle followed by a long pass out of defence to United forward George Mutch which was so perfectly precise that even Burnley fans voiced their appreciation of the centre half's skill.

This was not the way it was supposed to be!

Fortunately for Burnley, others were able to hit the net that day. The match ended in a 2-2 draw, but not before it got even worse for Tommy Lawton. When Vose, for the umpteenth time, intercepted a pass intended for the centre forward, Tommy pulled up sharply – and immediately felt an excruciating pain in his groin. It was a bad strain. Back in the dressing room he was told to go home, rest and not to bother turning up for the remaining two Easter fixtures. His place would be taken by Ces Smith, the man he had replaced.

Tommy was intensely disappointed. But this time there were no tears. Instead, he reflected long and hard upon the contradictory experiences of his second week as a football league player. It was all very confusing. All right, maybe he shouldn't have got *so* carried away by his success at Swansea. And yes, he could appreciate now that he wasn't going to score two goals every week. But could he vow never again to indulge in what had seemed to others like big-headed behaviour but, to him, was just a natural reaction to having a brilliant game? That was a very difficult promise to make. He just didn't understand. They all wanted him to be keen and dedicated but not, it seemed, *so* keen and dedicated that he got excited when he scored goals! Why? Why did they expect him not to get excited when he only got excited because he was keen and he was only keen because they wanted him to be keen? He didn't know. He just didn't get it.

Ces Smith was unable to make the centre forward's shirt his own again. One of the Easter games Tommy had to miss was the return match with Manchester United, who thrashed Burnley 4-0 in spite of the absence of George Vose, also injured.

The teenager was recalled for Burnley's last four games and harsh lessons learned, he made the very best of the opportunity, scoring three goals to help Burnley avoid the dreaded relegation. When that 1935/36 season ended Tommy Lawton was still only 16 but he had started to make an impact in English football.

Tommy was never happy unless a ball was in close proximity. So he was delighted when Ray Bennion suggested that he should carry on with his training sessions throughout the summer. At this time of the year, Tommy discovered, there was very little for which he was required in the secretary's office and that left plenty of time for training. "Smashing!"

Bennion decided the boy needed more work on his heading ability so, inventive as ever, the coach hung a football by its lace from a beam high in one of the Turf Moor stands. "Now what you must practise until it's perfect is jumping so high that you are always above the ball: not under it, because then it will just go upwards; not level with it, because then you can't direct it so well; but over it. That way, you're in control of the ball and you'll be able to place it with your head. Got it? Get over it – place it. Right, left or centre, you place it."

Thus, hour after hour, day after day, found Tommy leaping like a salmon, striving to perfect the heading technique Bennion had taught him. This was extremely difficult. And at first, the lad simply could not do it. It required exact, almost exquisite, timing. Tommy was such a perfectionist that he carried on and on, long after others would have tired of this endeavour. Slowly, very slowly, he began to master the technique but he realised that one close season was not going to be enough to achieve the complete mastery he now craved. This, he resolved, was a training routine on which he was going to have to concentrate for years. His dedication and energy were inexhaustible, so much so that even the patient Bennion got bored and left him to it. With not another living soul to be seen anywhere else in that stadium, Tommy's grunts and (when he didn't get it right) groans echoed around the stand. This strange ritual was broken only by the occasional reappearance of Bennion at the boy's side: "'Ow's it going? All right? Remember up and over that ball . . . up and over."

For all his devotion to his training, the tireless youngster missed the competitive edge of matches and in the summer months, he could satisfy at least some of that desire by playing cricket. At school, he had been a more than useful batsmen and – just as incredibly precocious as he was as a footballer – he had played Lancashire League cricket in 1935. Burnley's Lancashire League cricket ground was next door to Turf Moor and in that summer of 1936, after a trial with the third team, Tommy established himself as a big-hitting batsman.

All the Lancashire League sides had a top professional. Burnley's was the West Indies' fast bowler Manny Martindale. For close rivals Nelson, it was another West Indies star, Leary Constantine. For most local Lancastrians, these were the first black men they had ever seen and kids would chase after them in the street shouting, "Hey, darkie, 'ave you been down t'pit?!" There was no such ridicule, however, when these two giants of their game took to the cricket field. There, they were revered.

Nobody admired Martindale and Constantine more than young Tommy Lawton and Martindale took a special interest in the lad. Manny and another top player, former Lancashire county professional Billy Cook who played as an amateur for Burnley, frequently took Tommy to the nets to teach him how best to play fast bowling, pace being a particular feature of Lancashire League cricket.

Every evening for two weeks before Burnley's needle match with Nelson, Manny prepared Tommy for the ordeal of facing Leary Constantine by imitating his West Indian comrade's bowling style, particularly the great man's famous slower ball, which had brought grief to many a Test player. When Manny bowled quick in the Constantine manner, Tommy coped well with it but the demon slower ball was an altogether different matter. By impersonating Constantine's style, Martindale hoped to teach Tommy how to spot that slower ball.

After one of these net sessions, Tommy – his mind never far from football – thought deeply about how these top bowlers could get a cricket ball to move in flight: "If they can do that with their hands, why can't I do it with my head? It's all about control and timing. If I can confuse a goalkeeper about which way the ball's going, he'll probably miss it – just like a batsman misses a clever ball from a bowler." This gave him a new dimension on his heading sessions with Ray Bennion. "If I can only stay in the air long enough, I can do it," he resolved. And he'd add that astonishingly tall order to his training routine from now on.

Meanwhile, the day that Manny Martindale had been preparing Tommy Lawton the batsman for had arrived. Burnley versus Nelson. Tommy was to bat first wicket down and that moment arrived much sooner than expected. As the 16-year-old boy left the pavilion to face the great Leary Constantine, Martindale told him: "Just remember what I've taught you. Watch his arm for the slow one."

Tommy did not have to wait long. The first ball Constantine delivered to him was the infamous slow one. Manny's uncanny description of the manner in which it would be sent had been entirely accurate. Tommy spotted it, moved out of his crease with speedy footwork befitting a footballer – and belted it into the football ground. Six runs!

Constantine looked surprised. Then, he grinned at the lad. "Oh, 'eck," Tommy thought. "I 'ope I 'aven't upset 'im!" The next ball was not intended to take any prisoners. This was emphatically not the slow one! Tommy swung at it wildly. Strictly speaking, he didn't hit it. But it did hit his flailing bat. Right at the bottom. And it went soaring. Six runs!

Tommy, his knees trembling, thought, "Now I *'ave* upset 'im!" Thereafter, the great man kept the cheeky youngster pretty quiet, but he carried his bat until the innings was declared closed. He'd scored a highly commendable 30 runs and cemented a regular place in the Burnley side.

Soon after came a Worsley Cup match versus Colne, who boasted the famous Indian international fast bowler Amar Singh among their impressive ranks.

The Worsley Cup had totally different rules, so comparatively complex that some said only pedantic Lancastrians could have come up with them. The first side to bat had to declare if they reached 130 with less than five wickets down. Then the second side went in and once its innings had finished or been declared closed, the first batting side resumed its innings if their suspended total had been passed, and chased the runs. It might have been unnecessarily complicated but it regularly produced a thrilling climax and the big crowds it attracted loved it.

Tommy opened the Burnley innings and rattled up 46 runs in less than 25 minutes, including a straight six off the bowling of none other than Test star Amar Singh, who sportingly applauded the shot as it soared way over his head.

Burnley declared but Colne left them a hefty run chase. Tommy resumed his innings and belted another 45 runs to help Burnley to an exciting victory which so exhilarated the crowd that a hat was taken round for donations of appreciation for the triumphant players. When the hat reached the dressing room it contained £20 in pennies, halfpennies and farthings.

Back in Lancashire League action, Burnley played Enfield at home. The visitors batted first and scored 112, leaving Burnley only 64 minutes to get the runs required to win. Burnley announced boldly, "We'll go for it," and their innings was opened by Martindale and Lawton. The game plan was for the youngster to go for the big hitting while Martindale kept the score moving with quick ones and twos. It was working brilliantly and when, with 90 runs on the board, Martindale was out Burnley were still up with the clock. But the scoring rate slowed when the partnership was broken and come the last over, they needed six runs to win. Tommy was 81 not out and facing Jim Bailey, a wily county standard left-handed bowler who played for Hampshire. The first five balls were too good to hit and Lawton required a six off the last ball to win the game.

"Neck or nothing, Tommy, 'ere we go!" the batsman told himself as Bailey ran in and delivered a ball of perfect line and length. Tommy opened his shoulders and threw the bat at it. The ball disappeared over the sight screen. Six runs! Ecstatic spectators stormed onto the pitch, lifted the young batsman off the ground and carried him on their shoulders to the pavilion.

A few months later, at the annual general meeting of the club, Tommy was presented with the ball which had last been seen flying over the sight screen. They'd had it mounted on a silver stand for him: another trophy for the Rileys' mantelpiece, which was beginning to get crowded. The presentation was to honour the achievement of topping the Burnley batting averages for 1936. Tommy had scored 369 runs in 15 completed innings for an average of 24.06. This was very impressive and there were those who believed the lad should pursue a career in top-class cricket, but that was not for Tommy Lawton. Football was his first love and his last. Cricket, however, had given him another target in his insatiable quest for improvement to his game . . . how to apply the science of flight and movement variation in bowling to the art of heading a football.

That summer witnessed a sporting extravaganza which, though its full implications were way beyond the comprehension of a 16-year-old Lancashire lad, carried early warnings of future events which were to have a massive impact on his career. The 1936 Olympic Games, which became known as the Nazi Olympics, were staged in Berlin against a backdrop of growing international fears over the expansionist militaristic ambitions of the German Chancellor, Adolf Hitler, who had turned his nation's fragile democracy into a fascist dictatorship which persecuted Jews, Roma (gypsies), homosexuals and political opponents. Hitler's regime did its best to camouflage its violent racist policies for the two weeks of the Games, temporarily removing official anti-Jewish signs and toning down the ranting rhetoric of its newspapers in order to present foreign visitors and journalists with a false image of a peaceful, tolerant country. Many were hoodwinked. Others were chilled by the Aryans-only selection policy for the German athletes and by the robotic Nazi salute given to Hitler by thousands of spectators at the extravagant opening ceremony.

In August 1936, Tommy reported back for training at Turf Moor and he was overjoyed when he was picked for the first game of the new season. Dare he hope that, at 16 years of age, he was now Burnley's regular first-choice centre forward? Well, why not? He was. And the goals came frequently and fluently. The helpful senior players were beginning to treat their young centre forward as an equal now and he no longer felt like a child in their company. His self-belief, never in short supply, was growing even stronger by the day. But he was still the amateur office boy and would have to remain so until his 17th birthday in October.

One day, his office boss, Alf Boland, confided that as soon as he turned 17 on 6th October, there was going to be a professional contract on the table for him. Tommy rushed home to tell his mother and his grandfather the great news and was perplexed, though much too pleased with himself to think any more about it, when Jim Riley's reaction was surprisingly grudging: "We'll 'ave to think about that, lad." he said. "Here we go again," Tommy thought, dismissing his grandfather's grumpy response: "Don't be getting too big for your boots, boy!"

His mother's happiness at hearing the news more than compensated, especially since he was able to tell her that signing a professional contract would mean that instead of his wages of £2 10s a week for working in the office, he would be paid £7 a week, plus bonuses of £2 for a win and £1 for a draw. This was very good money, a bigger wage packet than any of the Riley family had ever seen.

October 6th duly arrived and the birthday boy went into Alf Boland's office to sign his contract, along with his grandfather – and Mick Tollman, the manager of Rossendale United. Since they met on the day that Tommy played for Rossendale, Jim Riley and Mick had become firm pals and having followed the lad's progress closely, Mick was now even more convinced than he'd been when he first saw him play that Tommy's value in the transfer market would run into thousands of pounds.

"Make sure they give you a good signing-on fee, under the counter," he had told Jim. "Isn't that illegal?" Jim asked. "Well, strictly speaking, yeah," said Mick, "but don't worry. It goes on all the time, all over the place." Tommy had no idea that such a conversation had occurred and assumed that Mick was coming along just for the professional guidance he could offer.

The three of them walked into Boland's office, where the secretary sat on one side of a large, highly polished oak table with Burnley chairman Tom Clegg and directors Wilf Hopkinson, who had brokered Tommy's arrival at Burnley, and George Tate. Tommy, Jim Riley and Mick Tollman were invited to sit in the three leather-bound chairs that had been carefully placed on the other side of the table.

The seven participants in what Tommy thought was to be just a friendly formality faced each other across the table, on which the contract which was to make him a professional footballer had been placed for signing. The lad sat in between Jim Riley and Mick Tollman, bursting with pride and so happy. This was the moment he had dreamed of.

Then, the polite ceremony was suddenly shattered by his grandfather, who, before anyone else had the chance to speak, suddenly announced, "'E's not signing unless 'e gets five 'undred quid!" Mick Tollman nodded his head in exaggerated agreement. The Burnley directors looked horrified. Alf Boland, wide-eyed and open-mouthed, gasped. Tommy turned pale with shock.

An embarrassed silence ensued, to be broken by Tom Clegg: "Jim, that's outrageous. And what's more, it's totally illegal." "That's as may be, gentlemen. But tha can take it or leave it," said Jim. Then, with a gesture to Mick and Tommy that said 'Follow me', he rose from his seat and marched out of the office.

Outside, Tommy was stunned and furious. For the first time in his life, he shouted angrily at his grandfather: "What did you do that for?!" Jim Riley was unrepentant and adamant in his reply: "Look, lad. As soon as they've signed you they'll be out to transfer you for thousands of pounds and you'll see nowt of that. All you'll get is your accrued share of benefit – and that'll not amount to much, I can tell you."

Tommy was shocked and embarrassed by what his grandfather had done. He knew that the money being demanded was not for him. It was for Jim Riley. He wanted to go back in, apologise and sign that contract – but he had far too much love and respect for Jim to even contemplate defying him and making a fool of him in front of others. Not for the first time, he reminded himself of all that Jim had done for him. Hadn't he earned the right to make some money for himself? That thought calmed him. But it didn't comfort him. "What do we do now?" he asked his grandfather. "We both just go into work as usual, as if nowt ever 'appened. They'll come round, you'll see."

The next day's newspapers were much occupied with the impasse. "The Lawton Mystery," read one headline. "Lawton Still Not Signed," read another. And it seemed that everybody in Burnley, not to mention beyond, was bemused by the club's failure to sign its Boy Wonder.

Two days later, Tommy and Jim Riley were called back into Alf Boland's office. This time, the Burnley FC contingent had been joined by a VIP. Alongside Boland, Clegg, Hopkinson and Tate sat Charles Sutcliffe, Secretary of the Football League. Sutcliffe cut an imposing figure. A very tall man of generous proportions with greying ginger curly hair and a luxuriant greying ginger moustache, he wore a smart dark blue suit and a yellow checked waistcoat with two pockets into which he dug his thumbs, leaving thick sausage-like fingers dangling under a sparkling gold watch chain. He was a Northerner to the tips of those fingers. Not a man with whom to trifle. And he looked very angry as he opened the proceedings:

"Riley, I understand that your boy won't sign unless 'e gets five 'undred pounds."

"That's reet."

"Does tha know who I am?"

"Aye."

"Does tha realise, Riley, that your request is illegal?"

"Aye."

"And does tha realise, Riley, that your outrageous demand runs contrary to all the laws of football?"

"Aye."

At this point Tommy, cringing with embarrassment, suddenly recalled his grandfather's favourite *Old Sam* monologue and thought, "Oh no. It'll be ages before he picks up his flippin' musket!"

"Look Riley," stormed Sutcliffe, "we could suspend the lad *sine die* for these illegal demands." Jim Riley responded with a long, hard stare of defiance: "Fine," he retorted. "You ban 'im for life and I'll keep him an amateur for t' rest of 'is life – and there's absolutely nowt you can do about that!"

Sutcliffe got up from his chair and with white knuckles pressed hard against the shiny table top, delivered his assessment of the subject with the impatient air of a man who knew he was comprehensively right: "Look. I'll say this once and once only. If t' lad doesn't sign for Burnley, whichever club 'e does join I shall go through t' books with a fine-tooth comb and if there's so much as one penny discrepancy or t' slightest irregularity, I'll 'ave 'im suspended *sine die* and t' club as well. If 'e's going to turn professional he'll sign for this club. Got that, Riley? *This* club!"

With that, Sutcliffe lowered his large frame back into his chair, stroked his moustache and in a gentler tone concluded, "Look, t' lad's a good 'un. And if 'e gets any better, he'll play for England. But only if he toes the line. Understand?"

Jim Riley realised now that he had lost this argument completely. He knew there was absolutely no chance that he was going to get his 500 quid and he wished that he'd never listened to Mick Tollman, but he was far too stubborn and proud to admit to any of that: "And you understand, Mr Sutcliffe, that nobody tells me and my lad what to do!"

Sutcliffe turned to Tommy: "What have you got to say, lad?" The boy was tempted to reply that it had all been a mistake, that they appreciated Burnley's offer and they'd sign on the dotted line right now, but Riley family loyalty brooked no betrayal. Besides, he didn't like the way this bigwig was talking down to his grandfather. They weren't going to pick up their musket, yet! "Well, sir." Tommy told Sutcliffe, "Mr Riley's looked after me all my life and he's never let me down once. His decision is good enough for me."

Good-natured Tom Clegg intervened: "Can I suggest that we let Jim and the lad go away and discuss all this between them, in private, then come back to us when they're ready?" "Aye," grunted Sutcliffe, glaring angrily at Riley. "Aye," growled Riley, returning the glare.

For all his defiance, Jim Riley now knew he was in the wrong. No point in wrecking things for the boy, even if it did mean swallowing his pride and backing down. His own embarrassment would be fleeting, he reasoned, while Tommy had a whole lifetime in which to regret what he had done: "You'd best sign, lad," he told his grandson. "Only if you think I should," said Tommy. "Aye, lad, I do," he confirmed.

Then they went back in and signed Burnley's contract.

The next day, Tommy Lawton stepped boldly out onto the Turf Moor pitch, to a roar of approval from the relieved Burnley fans, for his first game as a professional. There could not have been a tougher match in which to come of age. The opponents were Tottenham Hotspur who, despite having to accept the temporary embarrassment of a spell out of the First Division, were a hugely admired club who put extra thousands on Second Division attendances wherever they played. This, plus the professional debut of Burnley's Boy Wonder, produced a bumper Burnley gate on a crisp, bright October afternoon which was just perfect for football.

The turf, still lush green and in fine fettle, felt especially good under his feet and Tommy Lawton, starkly aware of the significance of the occasion for him, was experiencing new heights of excitement and anticipation. His expectations, though, were mixed. He was going to be facing Arthur Rowe, who had played centre half for England. Tommy looked at Rowe as the teams lined up. "An international. He'll be a hell of a good player," he thought. It was a fleeting moment of self-doubt soon banished by the brash confidence of youth: "But, I'm a hell of a good player, too!"

Just 30 seconds after the kick-off, Burnley's Bob Brocklebank shredded a perfect ball through the middle for Tommy who gathered it elegantly in his stride, cut through the Spurs defence like the proverbial hot knife through butter and unleashed an unstoppable left-foot shot. Bang! Burnley were 1-0 up. Incredible! This was the stuff of fairytales. You could not have made it up. And 20,000 ecstatic Burnley fans could barely believe what they'd just seen.

But they'd seen nothing yet. Only minutes later Burnley won a corner through the persistence of Jimmy Stein, who took the kick himself and sent the ball high across the Spurs goal where Lawton, perfectly positioned at the far post, soared way above his markers and placed a powerful header perfectly and precisely to the left of the goalkeeper who had dived to his right. Goal! Burnley were 2-0 up. The 17-year-old playing his first professional game had scored twice in the first few minutes of a match they were expected to lose. Now this really was unbelievable. Tommy Lawton felt like the best player in the whole wide world. Nobody could stop him now. Arthur Rowe? Who's he?!

The centre forward chased, harried and fought for every ball, winning most of them. The seasoned Burnley pros, realising that the lad was having the game of his young life, looked for him every time a pass was 'on' and found him more often than not. But Tommy, over-anxious for his hat-trick, over-exuberant, over-confident and overdosed on adrenalin, lost his composure in front of goal. Not once, but twice, his pace and strength left him one-on-one with the goalkeeper. Not once, but twice, having dribbled skilfully around the diving keeper, he shot wide of an empty net. Not once, but twice, when perfect through-balls created chances just as good as the one he had buried after 30 seconds, he hit not the back of the net, but the front of spectators. Then, just before the half-time whistle, he out-paced Arthur Rowe, homed in on goal and shot high over the bar and almost out of the ground. But the Burnley fans could forgive the boy anything after that sensational start. When the players left the field at half-time, with Burnley still leading the mighty Spurs 2-0, Lawton received a deafening ovation.

Inside the dressing room, Alick Robinson sat on the bench beside Tommy and put a strong arm around the boy's shoulders. "Now, just calm down, lad," he said. "You're trying too hard to be the bloody hero. You're doing great, but settle down, take your time and just play your own natural game like you always do. Stop trying to be better than you are."

It was sound advice from the captain. Tommy did settle down. Even though they had tightened up considerably after the Burnley blitz of the first half, he knew he still had the beating of Arthur Rowe and his defenders but he started to think more about what he was doing. Instead of chasing frantically around he resolved to keep working hard but to wait patiently for the next scoring opportunity, which came when he ran onto another perfect through-ball, left Rowe trailing, flicked the ball over the head of the advancing goalkeeper then calmly thumped a right foot volley high into the net.

A brilliant goal! That was 3-0 to Burnley and the game was won. Spurs did manage a consolation goal but a memorable afternoon at Turf Moor ended in a fantastic 3-1 result for the home side and young Lawton had celebrated his professional debut with a superb hat-trick.

At the final whistle there was pandemonium around Turf Moor as jubilant fans stayed behind in their thousands to cheer a famous victory and to salute the teenage wonder who had secured it. Players, pressmen and supporters all wanted to shake the hand of young Lawton, who felt proud and privileged to oblige. He was truly the talk of the town. The veteran *Express & News* correspondent, known by the pseudonym of *Sportsman,* had watched the youngster since his early days in the Reserves and was prominent among those who believed Tommy Lawton to be a phenomenon in the making. The enthusiasm of his account matched that of the 20,000 fans who had witnessed something really special that afternoon: "Lawton was a sensation. Rowe could not hold him. It was a triumph well merited for the boy."

Tommy walked tall on his way home, reliving his three goals and telling himself, "One with the left foot – that was for Bunny Lee; one with the right foot – that was for Ray Bennion; one with the head – that was for Leary Constantine!" Then he started to sing as he strode along . . . "One with me left, one with me right – and one with the side of me 'ead!"

He burst in through the front door and into the parlour, ready to receive the accolade of Jim Riley. He should, by now, have known better. Jim sat on the sofa, with an unexpected guest at his side. Ray Bennion had left the Turf Moor celebrations early to seek out the boy's grandfather. "Sit down, lad," said Jim.

Then he and Bennion embarked not upon a euphoric eulogy of congratulation but upon a downbeat detailed inquest into every one of the chances Tommy had missed. "You should 'ave 'ad at least six," said Riley ruefully. "I want you in for extra training in the morning," said Bennion sternly.

And so, on the Sunday morning after the triumph of Tommy Lawton's sensational first Saturday afternoon as a professional, he was back inside Turf Moor, not in front of the cheering thousands but alone again in that eerie silence – practising, practising, practising.

When he joined the rest of the players for training later that week, Tommy was subdued. "What's up, lad?" asked Bob Bocklebrank, "You look down in the dumps." "It's nothing; I'm fine," Tommy replied. "Come on, lad; something's up," said the kindly Brocklebank, "You can tell me. What is it?"

"It's just that I thought I'd done really well on Saturday," Tommy confided, "and obviously lots of other folk thought so, too. But Mr Bennion had a right go at me and he's always right. The ones I missed were awful. I'm a professional now. If I'm going to be any good I shouldn't be missing chances like that, should I?"

Brocklebank chuckled and patted the lad on the back: "Look, Tommy, Ray's just looking out for you. He thinks the world of you and he doesn't want to see you waste your talent. Listen to him and take his advice because you'd be daft not to, but always bear this in mind . . . don't worry about missing so long as you're having a go. That's the important thing. Always have a go. Never be scared to have a go. It's the law of averages, you see. If you're going to score 'em, you're always going to miss 'em too. But you won't score 'em if you're not having a go. If you score one in every three chances you get, you'll get 30 goals a season. And that'll do. That'll do very nicely."

Bob Brocklebank's considerate and thoughtful words of advice, steeped as they were in simple common sense, made Tommy feel so much better that day and it was guidance he would never forget.

Such was his impact in that Spurs game that when Burnley played away to Blackpool the following Saturday no fewer than 10,000 supporters piled onto buses and trains to go and cheer Tommy Lawton on at the seaside.

This time, there was no hat-trick. In fact, Burnley lost 2-0. But young Lawton had had a go, a real go, plenty of them. Back in the dressing room after the game, Bob Brocklebank gave the lad a supportive wink. Tommy grinned. He hadn't scored but he'd played well and he didn't feel that he'd let those 10,000 fans down because not once had he been too scared to try. And there was always the next time.

Tommy didn't realise it. But the boy was fast becoming a man. That unavoidable fact of life was becoming evident in other ways, too. By now, the 17-year-old star of Burnley FC was beginning to appreciate that football was not the only pleasure to be savoured. He now thoroughly enjoyed walking the streets of Burnley and hearing folk exclaim, "Look! Over there! That's that Tommy Lawton!" And when that admiring recognition came from the local girls, to whom this handsome, strapping lad was rapidly acquiring heartthrob status, it was especially gratifying.

One lass in particular caught his eye. Sally was her name. She was as pretty as a picture, with rich brown hair falling in ringlets to her shoulders and deep brown eyes that danced as she smiled. Tommy was smitten. Sally lived in the village of Worsthorne on the outskirts of Burnley. It wasn't long before he was paying her clandestine early Sunday evening visits and while her mum and dad were in church, exploring the joys of extracurricular activities which weren't on the ecclesiastical calendar. Tommy knew enough to know that he had to be careful in pursuit of these pleasures, in more ways than one, so his arrival and departure from the scene of his dallying with the delightful Sally were planned with the utmost secrecy and discretion and an attention to detail that was military in its efficiency. What he didn't know was that there was a large group of small boys in that village who were so obsessed with Burnley FC and their goalscoring hero that his every move, before, after and during his lusty liaisons with his lovely Lancashire lass, was being closely monitored, keenly followed, avidly observed and exhaustively recorded in a grubby school exercise book which had his picture, stuck with flour paste, on the cover and "TOMMY LAWTON" scrawled with huge capital letters in multicoloured crayon underneath.

Fortunately for Tommy and Sally this dynamite document never found its way into the newspapers – but plenty was now being written about the Boy Wonder of Burnley and that was only to be expected. His story had *all* the ingredients. At home, his mother and his grandfather still went through the ritual of hiding the papers from him but it was becoming increasingly futile. Tommy didn't go looking for them but when he did spot himself in a paper it was only natural for him to want to read it and just as natural to feel flattered when he did.

The awesome potential of Tommy Lawton was now a talking point way beyond Burnley and the newspapers frequently carried stories linking him with moves to bigger clubs. By mid-November 1936 he had scored eight goals in nine appearances and First Division scouts were now among those drooling over his precocious power and pace, his ability to shoot so accurately with both feet and to head a ball with such precision. "Lawton to sign for Wolves," said the headlines, or "Lawton to join Manchester City," or "Lawton bound for Arsenal". "It's all just speculation," Jim Riley told him daily, "nowt but idle paper talk. Pay no heed to it."

But Tommy was to discover that this time, his grandfather was wrong. Despite being Burnley's first choice at centre forward, he still worked in Alf Boland's office. His assorted 'guardians' reckoned that would help to keep his feet on the ground. The secretary had issued a very strict instruction on how the boy should conduct himself in his absence: "Just say hello and take a message. No more." But mischievously, Tommy often ignored that, put on what he thought sounded like a posh accent and answered with "Assistant secretary here. 'Ow may I help you?"

On the morning of 16th November Tommy was feeling particularly full of himself, having scored both Burnley's goals in a 2-0 defeat of West Ham. This was definitely a day for perfecting the prank. The first call the assistant secretary answered in his extra-obliging manner that morning was from Wolverhampton Wanderers Football Club and the reply was, "This young lad, Lawton – we're interested in him." Tommy coughed, spluttered, then composed himself: "Mr Boland will call you back directly upon 'is return."

Then he fell down into Boland's capacious chair, thumped his boss's desk top and let out a whoop of delight. Almost immediately, the phone rang again: "Good morning, assistant secretary here. 'Ow may I help you?" This time it was Newcastle United: "The bairn Lawton. We want to know if he might be available." Then it was Arsenal; then Liverpool; then Manchester City; then Everton . . . all revealing their interest in signing the boy Lawton.

It was nearly lunchtime when Alf Boland returned to his office following a lengthy meeting: "Any calls, lad?" "Yes, quite a few," replied the assistant secretary as he handed Boland a list of the numbers to call back, "but I've no idea what they wanted!" "It'll be a private matter," said Boland as he inspected the list. "Best make yourself scarce while I ring them."

Every day for the next six weeks, Tommy waited anxiously for a call for him to go and see the chairman to be told about a dream transfer to a top club. Arsenal would do very nicely, he had concluded. But that call didn't come. What he didn't know was that Tom Clegg and his directors, contrary to what Mick Tollman had always surmised, did not want to sell their prime asset. Not yet, anyway. He was only 17 and they wanted him to score a lot more goals for Burnley first. The club was in serious need of funds and the bank was starting to get a bit pushy but they'd hang onto the lad for as long as they could.

So Christmas 1936 saw Tommy still a Burnley player, still banging in the goals and still revelling in every minute of every day. In the Riley household their best ever Christmas was celebrated with great gusto by all except the one member of the family who had made it all possible. He had to keep a clear head and a fit body for the next match. But there was more than enough enjoyment for him in seeing his loved ones gathered together in the rent-free club house, all so carefree after they'd lived through such hard times. "This really is a happy Christmas," Tommy thought as he took leave of the family party for a sensible early night. He lay in bed, humming along as his mam led the seasonal sing-song downstairs, with tears of sheer joy streaming down his face.

On New Year's Eve, the call Tommy had been expecting since November finally arrived. He was to go to the Burnley boardroom. The directors had decided they could no longer resist the money that was being offered for the lad Lawton. The club's need for cash was now paramount.

Around the boardroom table sat Tom Clegg, Burnley directors Will Cuff and Tom Percy, Alf Boland and Theo Kelly, the manager of Everton FC. Tommy knocked nervously on the huge door of the boardroom and waited politely for permission to enter. "Come in, lad," said Tom Clegg, "and sit yourself down. I'll come straight to the point. Everton Football Club want to sign you. And we've agreed."

Tommy interrupted the chairman's flow: "I'm sorry, but could you wait on while someone fetches my dad. He must be here for this." Summoned from his ground work, Jim Riley stepped gingerly into the imposing, highly polished, wood-panelled boardroom and stood before the expensively clad gathering, an incongruous figure in his grubby overalls, cap in hand.

"Sit you down, Mr Riley," said Tom Clegg. "There's business about the lad to discuss and he wants you here." Tommy and his grandfather exchanged mutually comforting smiles and the business commenced. It wasn't long before Jim Riley had made a typically forthright demand: "If our Tom's going to Everton, I'm going too, to look after t' lad." A telephone call to Everton soon settled the issue. Jim was offered a job as deputy groundsman at Goodison Park. The deal was done.

Tommy Lawton was bound for Everton FC, home of his biggest hero, Dixie Dean. The transfer fee was £6,500, an astonishing figure for a 17-year-old who had played only 25 League games, albeit with 16 goals. It was easily a record for a player under 21 and enough to ease Burnley's financial predicament with some to spare but Mick Tollman had been right about one thing – Tommy got only a comparatively tiny amount of that massive sum for himself, or more accurately for his grandfather. The player's accrued share of the benefit was £175 but that didn't concern the lad in the slightest.

He was to report to Everton the next day, New Year's Day 1937 and that left far too little time for him to say all that he wanted to say to so many good men at Turf Moor, men like Tom Clegg, Billy Dougall, Alf Boland, Ray Bennion, Alick Robinson, Bob Brocklebank. These men with their care, their compassion, their genuine interest, their guidance, their advice and so much of their time given so selflessly had set Tommy Lawton on course for a career in top-class football that only one boy in millions ever achieved. That would not have been possible without them. When you're only 17 you don't have the words to express so much deep gratitude anything like adequately and when Tommy tried they told him, "Shut up lad and bugger off to Everton!"

But as Tommy Lawton walked out of Turf Moor, there were some choked back tears among those outwardly carefree farewells to Burnley's Boy Wonder.

Chapter Four

EVERTON – THE 'SCHOOL OF SCIENCE'

I t was 7:30 am on New Year's Day 1937 that Tommy Lawton boarded the train that was to take him from Burnley to Liverpool and a tremendously exciting new phase in his young life.

Only one cloud marred the bright blue skies in his mind. Jim Riley was not with him as planned. His grandfather had been taken ill the night before. Tommy hoped it was no more than tiredness after the momentous events of New Year's Eve at Turf Moor but Jim had not looked at all well as he told him, "You get off, lad. I'll come along later when I'm feeling more like meself."

This was not like Jim Riley; not like him at all and it left Tommy entirely alone as he walked out of Liverpool's Exchange Station onto the streets of this strange city. He had expected somebody from Everton to be there to meet him and he stood on the station platform for several minutes, looking this way and that for a welcome that didn't come.

"How do I get to Goodison Park?" he asked a railway porter scurrying along with a trolley. "Practise!" he retorted and scurried on. "Thank you very much, pal!" Tommy muttered, while an elderly man who'd witnessed the unhelpful exchange tugged his sleeve and told him, "Go to Dale Street and catch a number 4 tram."

As he waited for the tram, Tommy felt lost and lonely. Liverpool was so much bigger than Burnley and so much busier with so many people bustling about. It made him feel small and unwanted, out of his depth. Aboard the tram, he asked the conductor for confirmation that it would get him to Goodison Park. "It will, lad," said the conductor. Then, staring at the young passenger, he asked: "Aren't you that Tommy Lawton?" Tommy perked up, pleased to be recognised at last: "Yes, I am." "Well, you'll never be as good as Dixie Dean!" Having delivered that encouraging welcome, the conductor rang a bell to stop the tram and gestured to Tommy: "You'll find the Everton School of Science at the top of that road."

Tommy walked up to the majestic football stadium, found a door marked 'Players' and a button to open it. "That's posh" he thought, pressing the button, upon which the door opened and as if by magic he was suddenly standing inside the great Goodison Park. This was like the eighth wonder of the world. He had been there before when playing for Bolton schoolboys, but he was staggered again by the breathtaking size and sheer magnificence of the place. As he stood, gazing in awe of his surroundings, an Everton player approached him. Immediately, Tommy recognised him. It was jovial Joe Mercer.

Joe, aged 23, came from a football family in Ellesmere Port. His dad, also named Joe Mercer, had played for Nottingham Forest and Tranmere Rovers. When young Joe was only 12 years old his father died from illness induced by having inhaled gas while serving in the Great War. Joe had had to grow up quickly and this gave him an air of maturity beyond his years. But he was also renowned for his good nature and his sense of humour.

"By 'eck, you're a big lad," said Joe. "Aye," said Tommy, stung into cockiness by the less than flattering way in which Liverpool had welcomed him so far. "And I can play a bit, too!" "Well then," said Joe, "You've come to the right place. They can all play a bit 'ere!" They were joined by Everton's trainer, Harry Cooke, a warm, friendly man: "Welcome to Goodison Park, Tommy," said Harry. "You're just in time to meet the players. Come with me."

Everton were playing Preston away that afternoon and the players had gathered before boarding the team bus. One by one, Harry Cooke introduced Everton's new signing to men of whom he'd only read or heard about: mythical men, legendary names, international stars. He could not believe he was shaking their hands. "Tommy White," said Harry Cooke, beginning the introductions . . . "Hello, kid." "Jackie Coulter . . . Charlie Gee . . . Albert Geldard . . . Ted Sagar . . . Joe Mercer, you've met . . . Willie Cooke . . . Tommy Jones . . . Alex Stevenson . . ."

But one man was missing: the man; the man Tommy Lawton had idolised since he was a young schoolboy; the man he had always wanted to be in those make-believe contests on the cobbled streets of Bolton; the man worshipped by millions of football fans all over England. "Where's Dixie?" Tommy asked.

The door behind him flew open, knocking him off balance. "I'm here!" said Dixie Dean. "And my name's not Dixie. It's William Dean. But you can call me Bill." He thrust out a strong hand and Tommy was speechless as it took hold of his own but the sight that met the lad's wide-eyed stare was not what he had expected.

His greatest hero looked a mess, like he'd just fallen out of bed. His thick black hair was dishevelled; he hadn't shaved and dense, dark stubble covered his chin. His clothes were crumpled and on his feet, those legendary feet that had scored so many great goals, were a pair of worn old carpet slippers!

Dean put an arm around Tommy's shoulders, took him to one side of the room, looked him straight in the eyes and told him, "They've bought you to take my place, you know." Tommy stuttered a genuine protest: "Oh, no sir, I mean Dixie, I mean Bill. No. No they haven't. I could never . . ."

Dean interrupted: "Don't be daft. Of course they have. Why do you think they paid all that money for you?" It was said without malice, but with grace and good humour, as the great man continued: "Look lad, anything I can do to help you I will. I promise, anything at all. Any time." Tommy tried to respond but the lump in his throat choked his words.

Then the great man added, "Just one thing. I mean what I say – don't call me Dixie!" Dean hated the name by which millions of football fans knew their hero. It was a nickname he had acquired because, though he was not of black origin, he had very dark skin, possibly the genetic influence of Merseyside's colourful, cosmopolitan seafaring traditions. 'Dixie' was a reference to the Deep South of America where so many black people lived. Dean, despite his boisterous manner, was an intelligent and deep thinking man and he thought that an insult – more to them than to him. He could not abide it.

He wasn't surprised that Everton had bought Tommy Lawton. He was just days away from his 30th birthday. His League career had started in 1923 and 14 years of brutal battles with countless centre halves determined to defuse the dynamite of his extraordinary talent had taken their toll, as had the long-term effects of a near-fatal motor cycle accident in 1926. The injuries he had sustained in that crash, which occurred when he took his girlfriend for a day out in North Wales, were horrific. Dean's skull was fractured, his jaw was broken, his right kneecap was shattered and he suffered multiple lacerations. At first he was not expected to live; then he was told he would probably never walk again, but with the bravery and determination which epitomised his football performances, he eventually walked out of hospital. He could not take more than a couple of steps unaided. Nobody thought it possible that he would ever play football again, but Dean and Harry Cooke, who became dedicated to the cause, had other ideas. They both refused to give in and against enormous odds he made an incredible comeback.

Defenders had always used every foul trick in the book to try to stop Dean. After he had scored in one game, a centre half told him that if he dared score again it would be the last goal he ever scored. Dean did score again and when the chance came, the defender kicked him so hard in the groin that he had to have a testicle removed. Other parts of his anatomy, less delicate but equally prone to pain, had been kicked, punched and pinched black and blue over the years.

Amazingly, despite this intense, unrelenting battering, intimidation and provocation, Dean never retaliated. He had never been booked, let alone sent off. But while his extraordinary mental strength could cope, there was only so much his body could take and it was starting to show. His pace had slackened; on the heavy pitches of mid-winter in particular, his movement off the ball was now restricted and he had become more injury-prone. But he was still deadly in front of goal and still played a classic centre forward's game better than most others in the Football League.

He was right in his judgment that Everton had seen in young Lawton another Dixie Dean in the making and from what he'd heard of the lad, he wasn't far off ready, but there were tens of thousands of Everton support-ers, to whom Dean was still the greatest player England had ever produced, who would testify in support of that tram conductor's assessment that his teenage heir apparent would "never be as good as Dixie!" There was every justification for that verdict, too. Since joining Everton from Tranmere Rovers in 1925 the boy from the back streets of Birkenhead had grown into a fearsome goalscorer of enormous national stature. He had scored well over 350 goals in nearly 400 games in all competitions for Everton, including an astonishing 60 league goals in one season in 1927/28, and he'd hit 18 goals, including two hat-tricks, in 16 games for England.

Sensing that they might witness a piece of sporting history, 60,000 spectators had packed into Goodison Park on the day Dean beat the previous record of 59 goals in one season. Everton were playing Arsenal in the last game of the season and Dean needed to score three goals to break the record. With less than five minutes of the match left to play, he had scored twice. Then over came a corner kick and up went Dean with one of his mighty leaps to crash a header into the back of the net. Those

60,000 supporters greeted their idol's 60th goal with a roar so rapturous, so loud that the grand old stadium had experienced nothing like it before or since.

Since that extraordinary record-breaking day, Dean had carried on banging in goals at the highest level of English football, season after season after season. So, Lawton, the Young Pretender, had some way to go!

Dean's heading prowess was particularly peerless. About a third of his goals had been scored with his head and he had an uncanny ability to leap several feet higher than his opponents then to hang in the air while directing the ball.

A party trick with which he often entertained his teammates was to jump from a cold standing start onto the middle of a snooker table, landing perfectly on both feet then powering himself back down to the floor with equally perfect two-footed precision before immediately springing up and repeating the feat.

Frequent challenges to his mates, young, fit and athletic though they were, to emulate his gymnastic snooker-room speciality invariably ended in embarrassing failure and many a wager was emphatically lost.

Dean's mighty reputation was such that no mere manager could tell him how to play so he'd also become Everton's unofficial team boss, thus hardly endearing himself to the real one, nor to the rest of the club's top brass. When Dean spoke, the rest of the players and all the staff hung respectfully on his every word. Though blunt, occasionally brash and outspoken, he was never an arrogant man but his aura was such that nobody else's opinion on the game, or on any other subject come to that, mattered one jot!

Outside the inner sanctum of Goodison Park, Dean was even more revered. Everton supporters had all but canonised him! They loved this man like no other. In particular, they appreciated the way he treated them. Dixie never forgot nor forsook his humble background and to him, those supporters were always his equals. Hundreds would line up outside Goodison Park just to catch a glimpse of him and when he spoke to them, as he invariably did, he was one of them. They shared the language of the proud Northern working class. Requests for autographs were never refused and on match days, he carried his complimentary tickets into the ground so that he could give them away, not to hangers-on but to real supporters who couldn't afford them. Often, when his complimentary tickets ran out, he went to the gates and bought more to hand out.

He'd never sought the crown but Dixie Dean was the King of Goodison. He realised that this made him unpopular with some of the Everton top brass, who were jealous of his standing and he knew that it would hasten his removal if they could find an adequate replacement for him. All of which made his genuinely warm welcome to Tommy Lawton even more selfless and commendable.

This first encounter between the two was a brief one, however. The original plan was for Tommy to travel to Preston with the first team to get to know his new teammates and to experience a match day in the First Division but manager Theo Kelly had changed his mind. Instead, Tommy was marched to the kit room, given his first Everton shirt and told that he would be playing at Goodison Park for Everton Reserves that very afternoon.

And Everton's opponents? Burnley Reserves! This induced a naturally strange feeling for Everton's new signing but in a way it made him feel more at home and before the kick-off he went into the visitors' dressing room to greet the former colleagues he'd left behind only the day before.

For the Burnley players, a bit of good-natured banter was irresistible . . . "All that bloody money – and you're back 'ere with us!" "They must think a lot of you 'ere then!" "Six and a half thousand pounds – for a reserve!" The leg-pulling barbs flew fast – as did a boot, accompanied by a cry of "Bugger off out of 'ere, you traitor!" Tommy laughed: "Right you lot. If that's the way you want it, I'll see you on the pitch!"

As the teams lined up, Tommy saw that he'd be marked by Bob Johnson, a tough centre half with whom he'd always had a good rapport. After the toss, the teams changed ends and as Johnson trotted past Lawton he taunted him: "I'll bet you five bob you don't score, Tom." "You're on," said Tommy.

And in the battle that ensued between the two, no quarter was asked or given. Lawton came out of a bruising battle on top, scoring both goals to celebrate his first game in the famous royal blue shirt with a 2-1 win for Everton Reserves, thus gaining the instant appreciation of a good Goodison crowd – and five shillings from his ex-teammate. After the Reserves' match, Tommy set off to find the digs that had been arranged for him in Liverpool feeling a very great deal more content and confident than when he arrived.

Jim Riley didn't take up his new job on the ground staff at Everton. The illness that kept him at home on Tommy's first big day got worse. Years of breathing filthy coal dust had caught up with him. His chest was giving up an unequal struggle. He never worked again. He and Tommy's mother left the Burnley club house in which they'd had such happy times and returned to Bolton, where Tommy visited them every Sunday.

In Jim's enforced absence, Dixie Dean became a father figure for the lad, of whom he was becoming increasingly fond. Tommy, still starstruck in the presence of his hero, could not believe that the man he had idolised for so long was now a friend and unofficial guardian. So much had happened to him in such a short time that his head spun whenever he tried to take stock of it all and it could all so easily have turned a young head in the wrong direction. But there had always been somebody there to keep his feet on the ground. And now that was none other than William Ralph Dean.

On Sundays, Tommy caught a train to Bolton to spend the day and night with his mum and grandfather. On Mondays, when his return train arrived in Liverpool, Dean would be sitting outside Exchange Station in his Morris car waiting to give the lad a lift to Goodison.

Dean saw so much of himself in Tommy; a poor working class kid making his way in a world in which the odds were so heavily stacked against him. This was a mirror image of his own fantastic rise to fame and comparative fortune and he was determined to help this engaging lad complete his metamorphosis from pauper to prince, no matter what the threat to his own exalted position at Everton Football Club.

A truly big man was William Dean – in heart, in soul and integrity.

Tommy thought his skills and techniques had come on in leaps and bounds under Ray Bennion's guidance at Burnley and so they had. But Dean helped him take them to a different level. "I'm no coach," he told Tommy "So just watch me and learn." This was not conceit – just the sound advice of a master craftsman instructing his apprentice. And when Tommy watched, he did learn – more than he had ever thought possible: the way Dean found space; the way he turned defenders; the way he used his strength to hold the ball until other players could join an attack; the way he found those players with deft flicks and controlled, accurate long passes; the way he saved his legs by making the ball do the work; the techniques of his lethal shooting, particularly on the volley. And above all, the way he headed a ball.

At five feet ten inches, Dean was actually shorter than Lawton. But the height he gained with the sheer power of his jumps had to be seen to be believed and the direction and flight he was able to execute with his head while hovering in the air was precisely the science that Tommy had sworn to study after playing cricket with Leary Constantine. "'Ow do you do that?" Tommy asked Dean during training one day. "Stay behind when we've done here and I'll show you," he said.

Thus, Tommy's extracurricular training sessions with Ray Bennion were replicated at Goodison Park, this time with England's greatest exponent of the art of heading a football imparting his knowledge then getting him to practise, practise, practise. The pair would play marathon matches of heading tennis. And it was *déjà vu* for Tommy the day Dixie Dean chalked two squares on the wall under the main stand, marked them *A* and *B* (shades of Ray Bennion) then stuffed a big, cased ball with wet paper to make it extra heavy and threw it time and time again (shades of Bunny Lee) for Tommy to head to the left or the right and hit whichever square he demanded. The sight of the old master and his young pupil going through that routine for hours after training became a daily occurrence at Goodison Park and they would move from that to a session on powering, timing and holding a leap.

In a matter of weeks, the lad learned more about skill and technique, not just from Dean but from watching and training with the other top class international players at Everton, than he'd ever thought possible. Now, Tommy knew what that tram conductor meant when he'd directed him to 'the School of Science' on the day he arrived.

Tommy's settling-in process was cemented when Everton offered a club house in Fazakerley so that he could leave his digs and his mother and grandfather could move to Liverpool to be with him. This house was not rent free and with no first-team bonuses coming in to augment the same weekly wage he'd been getting at Burnley, along with Jim Riley's incapacity for work, the celebrated, headline-making transfer to the top of the football tree meant that his family was significantly worse off financially! Ironic though this was, it was of little consequence to them. They were together and they'd managed on a hell of a lot less in their time – but it did bring home to them how extraordinarily well they had been treated by Burnley Football Club.

Though he was showing up well in the Reserves, Tommy was having to bide his time for a first-team place at Everton. Dixie Dean was playing well despite struggling, often, with the legacy of the many injuries he had collected in his time, particularly cartilage trouble which was terribly painful.

A significant part of the relationship that had developed between the 'King' and the 'Young Pretender' was a good-natured competitive spirit. In their games of heading tennis, both played to win. In their training sessions, neither let up for a second, lest the other looked superior. Secretly, Tommy was practising Dean's celebrated jump onto the snooker table, finding it incredibly difficult and failing dismally to succeed.

Close though he had grown to the boy and genuinely keen to see him do well, Dean was ruggedly determined not to give up his Everton centre forward's shirt without a fight. Tommy had to earn it; the hard way, just as he had done. And Tommy began to wonder if he ever would until a chance came when it was decided to rest Dean for the League match versus Wolverhampton Wanderers at Molineux on 13th February 1937. It was six weeks since he'd joined Everton but it seemed like a lifetime to a 17-year-old anxious to prove to the millions of football followers in England that he was worth the huge fee the club had paid to bring him into the big time.

Wolves were in tip-top form, developing a reputation as a potential glory team, while Everton, not having the best of seasons, were missing influential regulars Charlie Gee and Alex Stevenson as well as Dixie Dean. The contrasting fortunes of the two teams soon became evident. Tommy came up against Stan Cullis, a centre half who was not only tough and tenacious but clever. Cullis marked the high-profile debutant so tightly he was able to make little impact on the game and by half-time Wolves were 4-1 up. With 15 minutes to go, Wolves were winning 5-1 and coasting to a thoroughly well-deserved victory in the Molineux mud when Everton won a penalty. Acting captain Billy Cook decided that on such a boggy pitch, Lawton's strength might do the trick. It would also help boost the lad's confidence if he scored and if he didn't, well, it wasn't going to matter: "Have a go at it, Tom," he invited the youngster, who duly obliged, scoring his first goal in the First Division. Result notwithstanding – Wolves eventually won 6-2 – it was a grand feeling for Tommy.

A week later, Everton took on Tottenham Hotspur in a fifth-round FA Cup tie at Goodison Park. A rested Dixie returned at centre forward. Tommy was back in the Reserves, playing Bury in the considerably less impressive surroundings of Gigg Lane. Soon after the final whistle in that inconspicuous game, news reached the Everton players that the first team had only just pinched a 1-1 draw with Spurs thanks to a last-minute goal from Coulter and that Dixie had missed a penalty. It had been a poor, rough house of a game which at one stage had descended into a brawl. The Everton directors were not happy men. There must, they resolved at a meeting the following Sunday morning, be several changes in the team for the replay.

Tommy was at home that afternoon when a message was sent telling him to report to Goodison Park early the next morning for the trip to London. He got there and headed straight for the notice board to see if the team had been posted. His eye went immediately to the number 9 . . . Dixie Dean. Tommy looked again. At number 10 . . . Tom Lawton. He was playing inside left, alongside his hero and mentor. In an unbelievable 12 months, the kid from Bolton had gone from being an amateur at Burnley to standing next to the immortal Dixie Dean in the centre circle at White Hart Lane for the kick-off of a fifth-round FA Cup replay, just two games away from a final in front of more than 100,000 people at Wembley Stadium.

When the referee's whistle blew and the legendary centre forward rolled the ball to the feet of his inside left the touch sent an indescribable shiver of excitement down Tommy Lawton's spine. But that was nothing compared with what was to follow only two minutes later. Everton's Albert Gedlard – one of the changes from the first match and recalled after being dropped following a run of bad games that had seen him booed off the field by his own supporters – was a man with a lot to prove. And, boy, was he going to do it! The right winger picked up a pass in midfield, flicked the ball through the legs of the Spurs left half Ernie Grice, waltzed around him, raced to the by-line and hit a perfect cross to the near post. Fullback Whatley attempted a volleyed clearance which he mis-hit, straight to the feet of Lawton two yards out from the Spurs penalty box. Tommy hit a first-time shot, so fast, so fierce that the Spurs' keeper Jim Hall didn't see it and the inside of the net all but burst with its pace and power. It was a sensational goal! 1-0 to Everton.

As the rest of the Everton players danced with delight and rushed to congratulate Tommy, Dixie Dean turned to Joe Mercer and with resignation that harboured neither resentment nor regret, he told Joe, "Well, that's it. That's the end of me."

After 20 minutes, Geldard crossed for Dean to smash a first-time shot into the top right-hand corner of the Spurs net. 2-0 to Everton. Then Spurs' Morrison, who had been much involved in the brawl in the first match, beat Ted Sagar with a brilliant 20-yard drive. 2-1 to Everton.

Halfway through the second half, Everton were holding their lead and looking good value for a win and a coveted place in the sixth-round draw. And when referee George Mee gave a penalty against Spurs, Dixie Dean picked up the ball, placed it on the spot and prepared to give Everton the increased lead they deserved. The Spurs players, however, had seen the raised flag of a linesman and pleaded with Mr Mee to consult him. The Everton players were baffled. It had been a clear penalty, a blatant trip on left winger Torry Gillick well inside the penalty area. What was this all about? This, the linesman told the referee, was all about a foul throw to Gillick to set him off on his run into the box. And to Everton's disgust and dismay Mr Mee cancelled the penalty and gave a throw-in to Spurs instead.

After 66 minutes, Everton believed justice had been done when Lawton ran onto a pass from Mercer and hit a screaming shot from 25 yards out which looked to have been wasted when it hit Dixie Dean in the back, but the maestro spun round and, ten yards from goal, volleyed the ball into the net. 3-1 to Everton.

Surely they were safe now. But Spurs, technically inferior but full of

fighting spirit and roared on by a noisy home crowd, battled away and
Morrison met a cross from McCormick on the right wing with his head
to beat Sagar. Everton protested vehemently that Morrison had been
offside, but to no avail. 3-2 to Everton.

Everton were still much the better side. Geldard, having by far his best
game in that royal blue shirt, was teasing, tormenting and tying the Spurs
defence in knots. Only superb saves by Hall kept out first Dean then
Lawton as they met his perfect crosses. Then, after 86 minutes, an intense
period of Everton pressure was eased by a long punt downfield from
Hall, Spurs chased the ball in numbers, Sagar beat out a fierce drive
which fell to Meek at close range. The Spurs man belted it home. Spurs
3 Everton 3.

The White Hart Lane crowd was now roaring as one. The noise was
overwhelming and, re-energised, Spurs now took complete control for the
first time in the match. Sagar's goal was peppered but Everton were holding on for another replay until Spurs' winger Miller beat Cook and curled
a centre into Everton's box where it hit Gee on the shoulder and bounced
back to Miller who floated in another cross which eluded Sagar and his
defenders to find that man Morrison unmarked at the far post and grateful
to accept a header with which to complete his hat-trick and send White
Hart Lane into deliriums of delight. 4-3 to Spurs.

Seconds later the final whistle blew. The crowd surged onto the pitch;
the Spurs players were mobbed and carried shoulder high from the field
while the Everton team trudged off in disbelief. Tommy Lawton was weeping as he walked wearily to the dressing room. His experienced senior
teammates tried to lift his spirits but it was to no avail. He was devastated
by this defeat. Not even high praise for his cracking first-half goal from
the great Dixie Dean could console him. He didn't want to think about
the match; he didn't want to talk about the match; he didn't want to read
about the match, which was a shame because the *Liverpool Echo*'s
description of his goal was positively drooling: "Up stepped Master Lawton
to crack a shot so hot and fast, so rushing that goalkeeper Hall saw nothing of it. It was a crackerjack shot, taken with first time fury of pace."

The desperate disappointment of missing the chance to take a significant
step towards an FA Cup final at Wembley in a game his team should have
won comfortably overshadowed everything for the lad. But, in truth, that
game had marked the arrival of Tommy Lawton as a top-class
footballer.

Everton's season was to contain little of interest after that, apart from
the continued pairing in attack of Dean, the 30-year-old sorcerer, and
Lawton, his 17-year-old apprentice. Lawton's game improved with every

match and the partnership from which he was learning so much hit a peak of performance when Everton played Leeds United on the afternoon of Wednesday 3rd March 1937. It was one of those thick, cloying, mud and sand surfaces but while other players struggled to attain much more than pedestrian pace, young Lawton glided effortlessly and sublimely over it – just as he had done on that day he played for Rossendale United – and Everton supporters enthused over his strength, speed and shooting power. Tommy scored one and Dixie two as Everton cruised to a 7-1 victory.

When the season ended, Dean had scored 24 goals in 36 League games and Lawton, playing alongside him for seven of his ten appearances, scored three. Young Lawton was pleased enough with his progress and so, it seemed, were the Everton directors. They rewarded their protégé with a place in the Everton party for a summer tour of Denmark. The boy who had hardly ever left Lancashire before his incredible Everton adventure began was now sailing off overseas. At home, where they'd never believed a Riley would do such a thing, Tommy's mam had many warnings for her son of the evils that may befall a boy in a strange faraway land and of the temptations of foreign female flesh which were to be resisted no matter what, lest fatal maladies followed.

"Don't be daft, lass," his grandfather scolded. "The lad'll be just fine. He'll 'ave to get used to travelling abroad, you know, because 'e'll soon be playing for England!" It was the first time Jim Riley had ever paid Tommy such a direct tribute. Jim had always expressed enormous faith in his lad's potential but only to others, never to his grandson's face, lest he got too big for his boots and slackened off. Indeed, he hadn't meant to say it this time, but the immense pride he felt in Tommy's achievement had got the better of his customary control.

The moment was not lost on either of them. Tommy reached out and hugged his grandfather, feeling, as he did, how terribly thin Jim had become. They stood for a few seconds, cheek to cheek, clutching each other. For all their unspoken affection over the years since Jim accepted Lizzie's baby as one of his own they had never embraced in this way. "Let me go, you big Jessie!" said Jim. And turned his face so the boy could not see his tears.

It had been a year of immense self-discovery for young Lawton and on the voyage to Denmark he learned something else about himself . . . He was a lousy sailor!

Before the ship had even left Harwich for its trip to Copenhagen, its gentle stationary rocking made his stomach lurch. He found a seat and sat, as if glued to it, through most of the time on board. Even though it was an easy crossing he felt his head spinning whenever he stood up. The maiden voyage of Tommy Lawton could not end soon enough. But when it did and the Everton party disembarked at Copenhagen, Tommy's equilibrium was restored along with his great excitement.

Excitement had also got the better of the Danes that day. The arrival of the Everton party coincided with the jubilee celebrations of King Christian and when they got to the railway station in Copenhagen, where they were supposed to be met by an official welcoming delegation, there was nobody there.

There was, unsurprisingly, not a Danish speaker in the Everton party and little understanding of the English language among the natives at the station. "Is there anybody here speaks Scouse?" shouted Joe Mercer. For a while, chaos, panic and ill-temper reigned where there was supposed to be the calm, warmth and dignity of an official reception. Fortunately, unlike the English visitors, there were at least a couple of Danes with a basic grasp of the others' tongue and the party was bundled, unceremoniously and with neither explanation nor comprehension, onto a luggage wagon to complete the journey to their hotel, feeling like anything but VIPs. Tommy wasn't bothered. For him, this trip was all so new and invigorating, just like that train journey to Wales on the day he'd played at Swansea, but even stranger and much more fascinating.

Later, the Danish officials put in a belated appearance at the hotel. Profuse apologies were tendered and accepted, grudgingly at first, but with the friendly, flattering words of welcome flowing as freely as the drinks it was not long before the directors of Everton FC and the chiefs of the Danish FA were the very best of pals.

The players, not sure whether all of this should be above or beneath them, simply sipped lager – the flavour of which they thought rather splendid. Three whole days of leisure, the better to acclimatise the players it was said, but more likely to allow plenty of sightseeing time for the directors, had been built into the itinerary. Several trips were arranged and Tommy sat transfixed at the sight of the rolling meadowland, the windmills and the yellow brick houses, so different to the tight, narrow streets of terraced houses in which he'd grown up in Bolton. One day, they even crossed the frontier into Sweden. Two foreign countries. He couldn't wait to tell his mam and Jim how well travelled he now was. He was slightly disappointed to discover that his mother had exaggerated the extent to which loose foreign females would crave access to his naughty bits. In fact, it didn't happen at all. He saw some lovely Scandinavian lasses but, far from ravaging him, they showed no interest whatsoever. This, he told himself, was because he wasn't a lusty Viking like they'd be used to.

It was a very hot summer in Denmark and the Everton players were pleased that their first match, against a Combined Copenhagen XI, was to be played in the cool of the evening, possible because it remained light so much longer there. Tommy wasn't picked for that first match. Dixie Dean was at centre forward with Alex Stevenson at inside left and of course Dean was among the scorers in a 4-3 win for the tourists in front of an appreciative 20,000 crowd.

The next game was against a Representative Copenhagen XI. This time, Tommy replaced Dixie at centre forward. And this time the game was played in the scorching heat of the afternoon. The Danes, more comfortable with such conditions, ran Everton ragged in the first half but managed only one goal for a 1-0 half-time lead.

In the Everton dressing room, 11 large buckets of ice cold water had been laid out ready for the sweating, heat-exhausted men in the royal blue shirts. Torry Gillick plunged his head straight into one of the buckets and the other ten followed suit. Then they each picked up a bucket and poured what was left of the water over each other in what looked like a childish romp but in reality was anything but. They were seriously hot and dehydrated.

As the Everton team, only slightly refreshed, lined up for the second half, Tommy noticed something strange about the Danish centre forward: "Ey oop, Alex," he said to his inside left, "we didn't play against this bloke in the first half." "No, you're right, Tom. He's a new one." Then looking around the pitch, Alex said, "And so's he; and him; and him!" Tommy, also looking around the pitch, added, "And him; and him; and him! 'The buggers!" they chorused.

The Danes had put no less than seven new, cool, fresh, eager players onto the field of play on which Everton's scorched first-half 11 stood dripping with sweat and no longer with cold water! "They must have a bet on this!" said Tommy. "Right, so let's bugger it for 'em!" said Alex. Despite the blistering heat, the saturated duo kicked off with renewed vigour and determination. At the final whistle, Everton had won 4-1. Their scorers: Stevenson three, Lawton one.

The final match of the tour was against the full Danish international team. Dixie Dean was recalled at centre forward with Tommy switching to inside right. The attacking force of Lawton, Dean and Stevenson was exciting but, in another game played in intense heat, they didn't score. An excellent, highly competitive encounter in which some superb football was played ended honourably 0-0.

Everton had been unbeaten on the tour and mightily impressed with the quality of Danish football. Even more impressive was the Danish hospitality which, after that inauspicious start, had been absolutely splendid and Tommy was returning home the 'seasoned' traveller: "Now I've been to Denmark, Sweden, and Wales!"

On the homeward voyage, there was much drama. Shortly after their ship had left Esbjerg, on the Jutland coast, a group of the Everton players, sitting quietly on deck, were approached by a Lascar (East Indian) crewman who told them in broken English that he was being followed everywhere he went around the ship by a man who was out to harm him. The Everton lads calmed the agitated crewman and went to the dining salon for dinner without giving the incident another thought, but the meal was rudely interrupted by an almighty commotion on deck and suddenly the ship lurched off course and hove to. A Danish clergyman, like the Everton players, had tried to calm the stressed crewman but he promptly stabbed him, then jumped overboard. The poor fellow had, it transpired, gone stark staring mad.

A boat was launched and after a long search it returned with the East Indian lying in the bottom, safely trussed up. The Danish clergyman's injuries were serious – he'd been stabbed three times in the arm he had raised to protect himself – and the ship had to return to port in Esbjerg to hand the crazed crewman over to the authorities. It meant that the ship was severely late back into Harwich and instead of going on to London, which was the original plan, the Everton party returned direct to Liverpool after breakfast on board. One member of the party gave breakfast a miss, but at least the incredible episode with the poor, mad crewman had taken Tommy Lawton's mind off his seasickness for part of the voyage!

Back home in Fazakerley, Tommy's mother welcomed him as if he'd been away for years. His grandfather just said, "Back then, are you lad?" But both were delighted to see him safe and sound. "Tell us all about it, then," said his mam as she poured him a more than acceptable cup of tea. "Crikey," said her son. "Where do I start?!"

For the rest of that summer Tommy kept himself fit – and the puppy fat at bay – by playing cricket and golf, a new love he'd learned from the senior pros at Everton. In August 1937 he reported back to Goodison Park finely tuned and raring to go. But there was no first-team place for him on day one of the new season. Instead, he led the Reserves in the Central League.

Meanwhile, the First Division side were getting off to a depressing start, losing their first game at home to Arsenal 4-1. The following Wednesday they were beaten 2-0 by Manchester City at Maine Road. Then they lost 1-0 at Blackpool. Everton were bottom of the table.

Theo Kelly was trying desperately hard to impose the authority he believed to be rightly his. Everton had been one of the last senior clubs in

England to appoint a manager. Before Theo Kelly took over, team selection was the prerogative of senior coaches and directors sitting on committees with team captains like Dixie Dean. Kelly had been club secretary. The old pros, especially Dixie Dean, Charlie Gee and Tommy White, had no time for Kelly: "He's not a manager; he's just a secretary," said White. "What the hell does he know?" was the senior professionals' reaction to Kelly's attempts to wrest control of the dressing room from them. They were convinced that Kelly's plan was to freeze them out and bring in youngsters to replace them. The atmosphere was becoming hopelessly hostile.

Dixie Dean went to see Kelly to represent the players' viewpoint in this increasingly febrile conflict. He was intent on coming away with a peaceful settlement but the exchanges between the two became so heated that Dean punched Kelly. The man who had never once retaliated to fearful provocation on the field of play found that in an office meeting, his fist was the most effective method of getting his points across. This was not helpful. Tommy White then went to see Kelly in an attempt to broker peace. Again, the best of intentions fell foul of fury. This time, White smacked Kelly. This was even less helpful.

The impasse between Dean and Kelly then led to the unthinkable. Dean was dropped from the Everton first team. Shock and utter disbelief hit Goodison when the team sheet for the return match with Manchester City, to be played on 8th September 1937, was pinned up on the wall outside the dressing room.

No Dixie. Tommy Lawton at centre forward. This couldn't be right. The incredulity turned to an air of depression as it sunk in. This was no mistake. This was Kelly asserting his authority. Dean and his friends had been right in their suspicions. Kelly was intent on wielding a new broom to sweep away some of the old pros and bring in the promising youngsters. Stripped of the inevitable emotion, who could blame him? Everton had, after all, lost their first three games, scored only one goal and stood rooted at the foot of the First Division table. But that was not the way the majority of the players saw it . . .

Kelly had not only exceeded his limited knowledge, he'd taken leave of his senses! What a fool! The famous Everton team spirit was in tatters.

Tommy stood among the players as the buzz of discontent spread through them, feeling distinctly uncomfortable and beset by confused and conflicting emotions. He had been chosen to replace the great Dixie Dean! Here he was, a teenager, being preferred to his childhood hero.

He was elated, excited, honoured and flattered, of course he was; who wouldn't be? But he also felt genuinely sorry for Dixie, who'd been so very good to him, so sad to think that such a great career was coming to an inglorious end; it shouldn't be like that. But, this was his chance; Dixie had had his; and he was going to make absolutely sure that Dixie didn't get that shirt back.

He could sense that, for the time being at least, he was not popular with most of the players so he went home to break the sensational news to his grandfather. Jim was unequivocal: "Yes, Dixie 'as been a great player, lad; one of the greatest. But don't you go feeling too sorry for 'im. It's your turn now, so you look out for yourself and just make sure 'e doesn't get back in!"

Tommy knew that made sense. He would heed his grandfather's advice. But the uneasy sense of disloyalty would not go away and it marred what should have been the sheer joy of becoming Everton's first-choice centre forward. When he returned to the ground, it was with much trepidation over how the deposed King of Goodison might treat him now. He should have known better. Dixie Dean went looking for the boy, strode up to him and, just as he had done on the day they first met, shook him firmly by the hand: "Well done, Tommy lad," he said. "You've worked really hard and you deserve your chance. Just remember all you've learned since you came here and you'll do very well. I know you will."

Theo Kelly was nothing if not courageous. Everton were preparing to go into First Division battle with a very young side. Joe Mercer, now one of the 'veterans' at 23, joked, "It's not a trainer we need on the bench; it's a wet nurse!"

On the other hand, their opponents Manchester City were parading a thoroughly experienced and superbly talented team that had topped the table the previous season. A glance at their team sheet was enough to strike fear into the hearts of Everton's fledglings and despondency into the bosoms of the Goodison supporters, who thought Kelly was mad to leave out proven stars.

That formidable Manchester City line-up read: Swift; Dale, Barkas; Percival, Marshall (marking Lawton and playing his 495th League game to Tommy's 12th!), Bray; Toseland, Herd, Allmark, Doherty, Brook. But Kelly's faith in the youngsters was well rewarded when they beat Manchester City 4-1, with the vital first of the four coming from a sweet first time drive from the 17-year-old centre forward.

To score that, Tommy had to beat a giant in the Manchester City goal. Frank Swift was only 24 years old but he was a man-mountain, standing well over six feet tall and weighing 15 stones. His arms were abnormally long, giving him an amazing reach and his hands were huge. The span from the tip of his thumb to the top of his little finger measured an incredible 11 and three-quarter inches and he was able to handle and control a full-sized football in one hand as if it were a tennis ball.

Despite his intimidating size, Frank Swift was a gentle, caring young man, intelligent and blessed with an infectious sense of humour. He was already renowned in football for his exemplary sportsmanship. He had made his debut for Manchester City in 1933 but it was in the FA Cup final of 1934, when Manchester City played Portsmouth, that he first came to national attention. Manchester City had gone in at half-time a goal down, with a crestfallen Swift blaming himself for not having worn gloves to counteract the slippery ball on a wet surface. With only five minutes of the final to go, Manchester City's Fred Tilson scored his second goal of the second half to give City a 2-1 lead. Those last five minutes were tense in the extreme, with Swift repelling Portsmouth raids while repeatedly checking the time by the watch of an obliging photographer behind his goal. When the final whistle for which he'd been praying was blown, Swift was so overcome with emotion that he fainted. It took several minutes to revive him sufficiently to collect his winners' medal from King George V and the King had been so concerned about the young goalkeeper that on the following Monday he sent a telegram to Manchester City to check on his condition.

When Tommy saw for himself how impressively Swift filled the goal-mouth, he wondered how on earth he was going to get the ball past him if the chance came, but when it did his fierce shot was so impeccably well placed that the goalkeeper himself applauded it as he picked the ball out of the back of his net.

After the game and that shock, emphatic victory all the tension and hostility of the previous few days at Goodison was banished. It was a very happy band of Everton players who sang as they splashed merrily around in the communal bath. And none sang louder than Tommy Lawton.

Then, in spite of the disappointment of defeat, Frank Swift went into the home dressing room to congratulate Tommy Lawton on the successful way he had filled Dixie Dean's shirt. He grasped Tommy's own large, but now comparatively tiny, hand in his and shook it warmly, telling him, "Keep going like that, son – and you'll soon be better than all the rest." Tommy was so taken aback to hear such a sentiment delivered with such sincerity by an opponent he'd just beaten that he could only splutter a clumsy, incoherent reply. The giant goalkeeper, sensing the lad's embarrassment, gave him a friendly cuff around the ear and left the dressing room, laughing as he went.

Later, as he reflected on this incident, Tommy felt foolish. He had responded to the thoughtful kindness of Frank Swift's sporting gesture with the stuttering immaturity of the teenager he was and that bothered him. He was supposed to be a man now. He now wore Dixie Dean's shirt, for heaven's sake! And how would Dixie have reacted to such sportsmanship? He would have thanked big Frank fulsomely and politely with the right words – like a man. So that, Tommy resolved, was what he would do tomorrow.

It was not much of a journey from Liverpool to Maine Road, Manchester and not long before Tommy stood in front of the huge goalkeeper, this time finding the adequate words to thank him properly for his kind comments and good wishes. Swift, surprised and so appreciative of the trouble the lad had gone to, opened those long arms and grabbed him in a bear hug. Thus began a friendship between Tommy Lawton and the man he called 'Big Swifty', a friendship that was to prove deep, loyal and enduring.

Just a few days later Tommy was facing another goalkeeping Swift. Frank's brother Fred played in goal for Bolton Wanderers who were facing the new-look Everton at Burnden Park. But that coincidence was secondary, in the unfurling fairytale of Tommy's blossoming top-class career, to the opportunity to play against his hometown club, still containing a couple of the players he used to glimpse in action in the last few minutes of those matches he gatecrashed when he was a kid in short trousers.

His great pride in playing in front of friends and relatives, all willing him to do well, was bolstered when he scored the first goal in another win for Everton's vastly improving young team but their biggest test by far was to come on 2nd October 1937. They were to play Liverpool at Anfield. A curious kind of stalemate had gripped the derby games between these two great Merseyside rivals. For years, Everton had failed to record a win at Anfield and Liverpool had not won at Goodison Park.

The supporters of both sides, forever optimistic, always approached every contest between the two believing that this season would be the one in which the recurring pattern would be broken. And so it was with Everton supporters in the build-up to the big match of autumn 1937. Throughout the week, supporters gathered outside the ground shouting encouragement to the players as they prepared for the game: "Come on lads, we're going to beat 'em this time!" A youngster with less self-belief than Tommy Lawton might have been devastated the day he heard one of them add, "Not without Dixie, we won't!"

Walking out onto the Anfield pitch to a massive roar from more than 50,000 spectators made the knees of even the super-confident Tommy go weak. The teams entered that gladiatorial arena side by side, the only match in England in which that occurred, but that commendable Liverpool camaraderie was not shared by the Reds' supporters on the infamous Spion Kop, whose reception for the men in the blue shirts was intimidating, to say the least. This was an atmosphere beyond mere description. Tommy was frightened yet at the same time exhilarated. It was by far the biggest day of his young life.

With just 20 minutes remaining of another fierce derby battle in which neither side was taking any prisoners, the teams were level at 1-1. Then Everton inside left Peter Dougal, one of Kelly's Young Turks signed from Arsenal in the summer, was brought down in the Liverpool penalty area as the Blues attacked the Kop end. Penalty!

The damning prediction of that pessimist outside Goodison flashed across Tommy Lawton's mind. " So, we won't win without Dixie, eh?" he muttered to himself and imitating the purposeful air of the great master, strode forward to collect the ball for the spot kick. With the growling Kop willing him to miss and a goalkeeper who suddenly seemed bigger than Frank Swift facing him, he placed the ball on the penalty spot. Walking back for his run-up, he recalled Dixie Dean, feigning to send a penalty kick to the goalkeeper's right then hitting it hard to the left. He'd do that. Quickly, he turned, ran up and wham! The ball flew into the left-hand corner of the net as the goalkeeper dived to the right. Goal!

Everton held out. They had beaten Liverpool at Anfield for the first time since anybody could remember. And Tommy Lawton had scored the winner!

As the victors danced with glee in the dressing room, Dixie Dean came in. He was just seeing out his time until the end of the season now, playing in the Reserves and standing by to come in for Lawton should injury or other mishap necessitate it. He cast a forlorn figure as, looking much older than his years, he picked his way slowly through the steaming throng of exuberant, jubilant players. They, absorbed in their celebrations, ignored him completely as if he were some stranger seeking reflected glory.

Dean located his vibrant young successor and shook his hand: "See. I told you, didn't I, lad?" he said, "Just watch me and you'll learn." "Did you see it, Bill?" asked Tommy. "Did you see it? Did you? That keeper got nowhere near it! What a penalty! What a flamin' penalty!" If Dixie expected some expression of gratitude, none was forthcoming. Immediately, Tommy turned his back on his friend as a joyous teammate pulled him away for another embrace. As Dixie Dean walked alone out of that dressing room, nobody noticed, least of all Tommy Lawton.

A lesser man might have been offended. But Dean understood the elation Tommy was experiencing. He'd been there himself. The kid was entitled to savour moments like that. But he was concerned that it might all be starting to go to his head. That worried him. Tommy was too nice a lad to be going off the rails.

Dean invited Tommy to join him to watch the Probables versus the Possibles in an England trial match at Goodison. Suspecting that young Lawton's feet were in some need of contact with the ground, he told him, "You'd better come along. You might learn something." As the boy sat in the stand with Dean, his focus was almost entirely on the two centre forwards on trial. For the Probables it was Bobby Gurney, the hero of Sunderland. For the Possibles it was Ginger Richardson of West Brom.

Tommy watched their every move: every run, on and off the ball; every turn; every shot; every header. At full-time, he turned to Dean and told him: "They're both good players, Bill, but neither of them is as good as you." He didn't add what he was thinking: "And you're not even in our first team!" And if he'd told Dean what he now believed, it would have confirmed his fears about the way the lad's head was tending to expand: "I've seen nowt to say that I'm not going to get to the very top in this game." Dean's fears about his young friend were not without foundation.

Jim Riley's health and strength were deteriorating quite rapidly now, weakening his body, his resolve and his interest, even in Tommy. The lad no longer feared the lash of his grandfather's tongue when he got too big for his boots and the sage advice of his minders at Burnley – "Don't go thinking you're a great player" – was no longer heeded. Nobody stopped him reading the papers any more: he avidly consumed every word printed in praise of his burgeoning prowess – and there were thousands of them. Tommy Lawton, still only 17, now believed his own publicity.

When Everton drew 1-1 with Leeds United, their goal was Lawton's fifth in eight matches and it was an irritatingly cocky young centre forward who strolled into Goodison Park to join the rest of the Everton squad the following Monday. Hands in pockets, head nodding in time with the tune he was whistling, self-satisfied smile on his face, he called out to the players who were busily changing for training: "Morning, boys!" This was too much for Dixie Dean.

"Who the hell do you think you are?" he bawled at Tommy.

"What d'you mean?"

"I mean just who do you think you are with your 'Morning, boys'?"

"Pardon?"

"Who are you calling boys?"

With that, Dean turned to the players and told them: "Right. I want all the internationals to stand up." They duly stood and Dixie approached each of them in turn: "Ted's got 12 caps; Billy's got 14 caps; Stevie's got

15; I've got 16 . . ." When he'd completed the international roll-call, Dean turned to Tommy and demanded, "And how many have you got?"

Tommy said nothing. He felt every bit as humiliated as Dean had intended, but angry too. For the rest of the day he spoke only when he was spoken to. At home that night, he sat and reran the dressing-room exchange over and over in his mind. Dean, he thought, had been terribly unfair and unkind to him. He resolved defiantly, "Right, if that's the way the miserable devils want it, I'll keep my head down tomorrow and say nowt!"

The next morning, Tommy was in early and was changed before the rest of the players arrived. As he sat sulking on the bench, Dixie Dean turned on him again: "So we're not good enough for you today, then?" This time, it was too much for Tommy: "What the hell do you want me to do?" he shouted. "I've had enough of this. You can all bugger off and leave me alone!"

With that, the lad got to his feet to storm out of the room, but before he could get anywhere near the door, the senior players had grabbed him. They tossed him like a ragdoll, up and down in the air, higher and higher until his backside hit the ceiling. Then they carried him over to the bath and dumped him unceremoniously into several feet of cold water. As Tommy scrambled, shivering, out of the bath, Dixie Dean put an arm and a dry towel around his shoulders: "Point taken, lad?" "Aye, Bill. Point taken."

While the young centre forward continued to make excellent progress in the New Year of 1938, that of the new-look Everton as a whole was less impressive. Their results were erratic and after being knocked out of the FA Cup by the holders Sunderland in front of a Goodison crowd of more than 68,000 and losing away to Brentford, home defeats by Liverpool and Wolves prompted an emergency meeting of the directors and the management team at Goodison Park. This wasn't yet a relegation crisis but it was heading that way. What to do?

On the night of the defeat by Wolves, the Everton players were told to report to Exchange Station the next day: "They're taking us all on holiday to the seaside," quipped Welsh centre half T G 'Yanto' Jones. Jones, a player with whom Tommy Lawton was forging a good friendship, was 21. Everton had been so impressed that they'd paid Wrexham £3,000 for him after he'd made only six appearances for the Welsh club. Yanto was half right about that 'holiday'. The powers that be, acknowledging that the players had been through a lot of upheaval, a good deal of pressure and some morale-sapping results, had decreed that they should be taken away to Harrogate for a week-long training camp to refresh their appetites for the game and reignite team spirit.

Harry Cooke was in charge of the party and he had planned an enjoyable itinerary which included long walks in the keen Yorkshire air, fitness routines and the obligatory shooting and heading practice on a pitch provided by Harrogate Council. Harry also introduced an entirely new training experience, six-a-side matches. The players, particularly the younger ones, enjoyed these immensely. New techniques were required because dribbling was not allowed, for fear of injury. Instead, they had to perfect first-time passing, fast one-touch football. They loved it and Harry stood and watched with satisfaction as, day by day, they improved these new skills. Also much improved by the end of the camp was the team spirit which recent events had rendered so mercurial, bolstered here by plenty of leisure time to play table tennis, cards, billiards and golf. There was also a visit to the local repertory theatre, where they saw a particularly chilling production of a dramatic murder mystery.

Back at the hotel after watching that play, Tommy and Yanto, who were sharing a room, lay in their beds chatting when Yanto said, "Shush! Can you hear what I can hear?" He could. It was a clear, slow knocking on the wall of the room. They both left their beds and crept over to the wall to try and hear more, though they were desperately hoping there was no more to hear, when suddenly, from behind the wall, came a blood-curdling high-pitched scream! Tommy and Yanto ran so fast for the bedroom door that they fell over each other before sprinting down the stairs and into the hall where, convinced that their room was haunted, they spent the rest of the night huddled together on a leather sofa in front of the fire.

At breakfast, they relayed the horror of the haunting to their teammates, who dissolved into fits of laughter. The 'haunting' had been a jape involving Alex Stevenson, Wally Boyes and Norman Greenhalgh, who had discovered a 'secret' passage in the old hotel. Jones and Lawton, who had missed a night's sleep, laughed considerably less than the others and resolved to take their revenge the next night . . .

After all the players had retired to their beds following their assorted after-dinner activities, the pair sneaked downstairs and took a hollow white bust from the hall, stuck a candle inside it and covered it with a white sheet. Their dastardly plan was to creep into the room which Stevenson was sharing with Boyes, place the hooded bust on the dressing table, light the candle and depart, then to release a wolf-like howl and watch the effects.

However, their meticulously planned prank was thwarted. Stevie and Wally, anticipating a revenge mission, had locked and bolted their door. "Bugger!" whispered Yanto. "Tell you what, boyo. Let's do it anyway. They all had a laugh at our expense, didn't they." "Too right!" whispered Tommy.

The room next door was not locked. Inside, Torry Gillick and Stan Bentham were sleeping peacefully. The pranksters tiptoed in, executed the rest of the plan perfectly and crept out. Tommy put his head against the door of the room, cupped his hands to his mouth and let rip with the most fearful, evil howl. The door burst open and they were knocked flying by Torry Gillick, evacuating his room with the pace of an Olympic sprinter. The perpetrators doubled up with laughter. Revenge was sweet.

More laughter followed at breakfast, this time not shared by Torry, who responded with a stream of fierce Gaelic oaths. "Tell you what," said Yanto, "I might be offended if I could understand a word he's saying!" It was all a bit juvenile, yes. But it had been a long time since any of the players had laughed that much – and especially together.

'Holiday camp' over, the Everton party remained in Yorkshire for their next League game against Leeds United, a match in which the new training routines reaped immediate benefits. Soon after kick-off, Cliff Britton found Alex Stevenson with a neat pass; Stevenson to Jimmy Cunliffe; Cunliffe to Tommy Lawton; Lawton back to Cunliffe. Goal! It had taken less than 15 seconds from Britton's first pass to the ball hitting the back of the net. Harry Cooke stood on the touchline beaming from ear to ear.

This was fluent, fast football so brilliantly executed that Leeds didn't know what had hit them. Then Jimmy Cunliffe got another goal and Tommy Lawton hit two: four goals for Everton in a scintillating display of swift, one-touch passing football which was new to the British game.

Unfortunately, Leeds United also scored four – all of them from veteran international centre forward Gordon Hodgson. For all Everton's endeavour, goals and silky skills, they'd earned just one point, but the Harrogate therapy and Cooke's new training methods had worked wonders in establishing the foundations of what was to become a very good team indeed. And Theo Kelly's courageous, but controversial and perhaps selfishly motivated, move away from senior 'chiefs' like Dixie Dean and towards young 'braves' like Tommy Lawton was beginning to appear vindicated.

Then, Dixie Dean and the club he had served so fantastically and so faithfully since 1925 parted company.

He was transferred to Third Division Notts County, leaving behind an extraordinary record of 349 goals in 399 appearances and a bad taste in many mouths. Most Everton supporters and football writers reckoned it was shameful and spiteful that he had not been allowed to reach an even more historic landmark of 400 appearances. What harm could it possibly have done to give him one more game, they argued. That widespread suspicion of spite was not without some support in the events surrounding the great man's departure from Goodison, or at least in his version of them. Dean told Tommy later, "When I signed for Notts the only Everton official present was Theo Kelly. No chairman; no directors; nobody but Kelly and he said nothing, not even 'Goodbye', let alone 'Thank you' for all the years I'd given them, all the goals I'd scored and all the money I'd put across their turnstiles."

It might have been, of course, that Kelly and the directors had not taken too kindly to Dixie thumping the boss! There may well have been another side to this story, but it was as well that Dean, ever the professional, kept his feelings out of the public arena. Had he not done so, there might well have been a riot.

Dixie was also angry and disappointed because none of the Everton players had bid him farewell before he left. That had really upset him. "But that wasn't our fault," Tommy told him. "None of the players knew you were leaving until you'd gone!" That was true; indeed, the day before the deal with Notts County was signed and sealed, Everton had issued a statement which said that Dean would end his illustrious career at Goodison.

Tommy was too young, too wrapped up in his own blossoming career, too grateful for the wonderful opportunities he was being given and generally too naïve to grasp fully the deep sense of betrayal and injustice Dean must have been feeling as he left Goodison Park. But later in his life he would feel that pain himself.

Everton, meanwhile, avoided relegation – thanks in no small measure to seven goals in the last 11 games from Tommy Lawton, whose rightful place among the elite was well and truly confirmed when he ended the season as the First Division's top scorer, with 28 goals from 39 League games.

Good enough to see a teenage centre forward selected for England? Tommy thought so. And he wasn't alone. He had plenty of champions, particularly in the press. The selectors, however, were not convinced. When the England team for the summer tour of Europe was announced, two centre forwards were chosen: Arsenal's Ted Drake and Aston Villa's Frank Broome.

There was some immediate consolation, however, when he was told to pack his bags for Scotland, where Everton were among four English clubs – the others being Chelsea, Brentford and Sunderland – to take part in an Anglo-Scottish Cup tournament with Rangers, Celtic, Aberdeen and Hearts as part of the Glasgow Empire Exhibition of 1938. The matches were played at Ibrox Park and Tommy was among the scorers who contributed to Everton making it to the final, where they faced Celtic in front of 82,000 noisy, colourful and enthusiastic Scots.

The match, played on a balmy June evening, was a cracker. The sides were very evenly matched, despite an early injury to Cunliffe forcing Everton to play effectively with ten men. The English side played a lot of their newly perfected one-touch football and this was appreciated by a knowledgeable Scottish crowd which had, otherwise, electrified the atmosphere with its intense, deafening support for Celtic. At full-time, the score was 0-0 but that was no reflection on the superb quality of the football played by both teams in a match reckoned to be one of the finest ever seen in Scotland. In extra time, Celtic's Scottish international right winger Jimmy Crum finished a mazy dribble through the Blues' defence with a neat chip over Ted Sagar to give Celtic the lead. Almost immediately, Alex Stevenson netted for Everton, only to be ruled offside. Celtic held on to win the trophy but Everton had made many friends north of the border with their slick passing football and exemplary sportsmanship. They left the field to a standing ovation and those were hard to get in Scotland.

It had been a great experience for Everton's youngsters and this side was now blending and bonding into a very formidable unit with a very strong team spirit, helped on this trip, as at Harrogate, by a thoroughly enjoyable social programme, which took in trips to Arran, Dunoon and the Kyles of Bute and included a variety night at Barrfield's Pavilion in Largs. During that evening Tommy and Yanto fell instantly and madly in love with one of the 'turns', a beautiful raven-haired teenage girl with stunning legs who wore a red blouse and a short white skirt (Liverpool's colours – but never mind!) to dance divinely and sing as sweetly as a lark.

Tommy and Yanto cheered, whistled and clapped for all they were worth, hoping this gorgeous girl would notice them as she performed so exquisitely. She didn't, but undeterred, they made enquiries about her and discovered that she was a Lancashire lass: "Right, that's you out of the running, Taff!" laughed Tommy as the pair rushed to the stage door to introduce themselves in the earnest hope of winning her favours.

No such luck. The way to the young star's dressing room was barred by the fiercely protective presence of her large and very formidable mother, but at least, for future reference, the failed suitors now knew her name. It was Pat Kirkwood. She became a huge musical comedy star of stage and screen in the 1940s and 1950s. She was dubbed 'Britain's answer to Betty Grable' and her fantastic legs were described by theatre critic Kenneth Tynan as "the eighth wonder of the world".

Back in Lancashire, Tommy took up an invitation from Frank Swift to join him and his family by the seaside at Blackpool, where they ran pleasure cruises and fishing trips on their boat.

Blackpool was a magical place, a heady mix of sun, sea, sand and sin.

Millions of people descended on Blackpool for their annual holidays, particularly from the Lancashire cotton towns where the workers from the mills and factories took their Wakes Week, the one week of the year in which their hard lives were not regimented by the workplace clock. The origin of Wakes Weeks was shrouded in mystery. Some said it could be traced back to anniversary celebrations of churches, but nobody really knew, or cared. When early miserly mill and factory owners had tried to prevent Wakes Weeks, their meanness had backfired – people simply didn't turn up for work! Now, the bosses were resigned to it and the absence of the workers was seen as an opportunity to service machinery and restock supplies.

For the seething mass of humanity that would then hit Blackpool, only one thing mattered – enjoyment. Trains on which they had been packed into third-class carriages would disgorge excited, chattering holidaymakers by the thousands, all dressed in their Sunday best outfits – the men in their heavy three-piece suits which also came out for funerals, the ladies in the formal floral dresses which they wore to weddings and christenings.

The immediate first port of call for them all was the beach, where they sat in their striped deckchairs gazing in awe at the vast openness of the sea, their only sartorial submissions to the summer season being the removal of shoes – a savoured freedom, allowing liberated toes to dig deep into the cleansing sand – and for the men, the replacement of caps with handkerchiefs knotted at the four corners. The purpose of the knotted hankies was to keep the sun off their heads but they wore them, sunshine or nor, because that's what you did on the beach.

The crowds were so massive that Blackpool beach was blotted out by bodies.

Food was a special treat, the more so for being taken on the beach and welcomed by appetites whetted by the sea air: bags of cockles and mussels; fresh shrimps soaked in vinegar; fish and chips, wonderful fish and chips, deep fried in beef dripping and eaten out of grease-soaked newspaper.

"Fresh Air – and Fun" was what breezy Blackpool promised its legions of pasty-faced patrons and the latter attraction was well served by the irresistible temptations of the Pleasure Beach and the Golden Mile, where they piled onto hair-raising fairground rides like the Big Dipper, Noah's Ark, Sir Hiriam Maxra's Flying Machines and the Grand National (on all of which, concession to health and safety was confined to self-preservation and common sense!).

In their thousands, they toured the freak shows and peep shows, where a few pennies would reveal the dubious delights of the Headless Lady, the Moving Mummy, Zebra Man, Gloria the Half-Living Lady and the Girl in a Goldfish Bowl, which was little more than an excuse for the lads to ogle a pretty lass in a swimsuit – money well-spent, they reckoned!

Among the most bizarre of the freak shows was the chance to see Harold Davidson, the infamous defrocked Rector of Stiffkey, Norfolk, who could be viewed on hunger strike in a barrel to protest his innocence of having obtained carnal knowledge of prostitutes whilst saving their souls in Soho. The hapless Rector, still vehemently claiming injustice and campaigning for restoration to the cloth, later moved on from Blackpool to a fairground in Skegness where holidaymakers paid to watch him sitting in a lion's cage while pleading his honourable intentions towards those poor girls. Regrettably, the lion killed him.

That same fate befell young Albert, the fictional victim of a hugely popular monologue which was written by Marriott Edgar for Stanley Holloway in 1933. *The Lion And Albert* captured the essence and image of Blackpool and the working class millions who adored the brash resort were so fond of the monologue, heard incessantly on the wireless, that many of them knew it off by heart and could recite it as their front parlour party piece on family occasions:

> *There's a famous seaside place called Blackpool,*
> *That's noted for fresh air and fun,*
> *And Mr and Mrs Ramsbotton*
> *Went there with young Albert, their son.*
>
> *A grand little lad was their Albert*
> *All dressed in 'is best; quite a swell*
> *'E'd a stick with an 'orses 'ead 'andle*
> *The finest that Woolworth's could sell.*
>
> *They didn't think much to the ocean*
> *The waves, they were fiddlin' and small*
> *There was no wrecks; nobody drownded*
> *'Fact, nothing to laugh at at all.*
>
> *So, seeking for further amusement*
> *They paid and went into the zoo*
> *Where they'd lions and tigers and camels*
> *And old ale and sandwiches, too.*
>
> *There were one great big lion called Wallace*
> *'Is nose were all covered with scars*

'E lay in a somnolent posture
With the side of 'is face to the bars

Now Albert 'ad 'eard about lions
How they were ferocious and wild
And to see Wallace lying so peaceful
Well, it didn't seem right to the child.

So straight 'way the brave little feller
Not showing a morsel of fear
Took 'is stick with the 'orses 'ead 'andle
And pushed it in Wallace's ear.

You could see that the lion didn't like it
For giving a kind of a roll
He pulled Albert inside the cage with 'im
And swallowed the little lad – whole.

Then Pa, who had seen the occurrence
And didn't know what to do next
Said: 'Mother! Yon lion's eaten Albert'
And Mother said: 'Eeh, I am vexed.'

So Mr and Mrs Ramsbottom
Quite rightly, when all's said and done
Complained to the animal keeper
That the lion 'ad eaten their son.

So the manager 'ad to be sent for
'E came and 'e said: 'What's to do?'
Pa said: 'Yon lion's eaten our Albert
And 'im in 'is Sunday clothes too.'

Then Mother said: 'Right's right, young feller
I think it's a shame and a sin
For a lion to go and eat Albert
And after we've paid to come in.'

The manager wanted no trouble
'E took out 'is purse right away

And said:' How much to settle the matter!'
And Pa said: 'What do you usually pay?'

But Mother 'ad turned a bit awkward
When she thought where her Albert 'ad gone
She said: 'No! Someone's got to be summonsed.'
So that were decided upon.

Round they went to t' police station
In front of a magistrate chap
They told 'im what happened to Albert
And proved it by showing 'is cap.

The magistrate gave 'is opinion
That no one was really to blame
'E said that 'e 'oped the Ramsbottoms
Would 'ave further sons to their name.

At that Mother got proper blazing
'And thank you, sir, kindly,' said she
'What! Waste all our lives raising children?
To feed ruddy lions? Not me!

Tommy Lawton felt really at home in Blackpool. These were his kind of people. The plan was for him to earn his holiday keep with the Swifts by doing his bit with the boat-trip business and he was only too pleased to oblige . . . so long as it didn't mean putting to sea! So while Frank and the rest took the boat out, Tommy, looking very much the part in a jaunty sailor's cap, took the money off the customers, placing it in a biscuit tin for safe keeping. He loved seeing the odd mix of fun and fear on the faces of the holidaymakers as he helped them onto the boat and he chuckled often when they behaved as if they were embarking on a perilous voyage on the high seas!

That made him realise how much more he had seen of life since he used to sit around the table listening to the tall stories his uncles told, and when he and Frank went out on the town every night they made full capital of their worldly-wise personas. Smelling sweetly of shaving soap and Brylcreem, the pair sauntered forth in their smart flannels and blazers, clean pocket handkerchiefs protruding nonchalantly from breast pockets and, in Tommy's case, shoes polished so brightly he could see his reflection in them – *heels as well*, of course.

Blackpool was made for bright and breezy lads like these two. Big, strong, handsome, self-confident and capable of charming the birds from the trees, they hopped from one fun factory to another along the brash, bustling Golden Mile packed with people absorbed in earnest, yet banal and totally inconsequential, activity. At every stop they won new friends and what a dynamic duo they made.

The football fans among the working class lads revelling in the recuperative joys of Blackpool were so pleased to meet them, flattered that the two young stars found plenty of time to talk to them and hugely impressed that they treated them as equals. Many were those who returned to work in their home towns that summer with the proud boast: "Guess who we met in Blackpool? – and they bought us a pint!"

As the summer wore on, the friendship between Tommy and Big Swifty grew closer day by day. They were proper pals now. And when it ended, their only regret was that they were not both going back to the same football club. Next best thing, they resolved, was that whenever circumstances permitted, which they knew wouldn't be often but never mind, they would go to watch each other play and have a beer after the match.

Summer had been full of excitement for Tommy Lawton and the prospect of what lay ahead in the season of 1938/39 was even more thrilling.

Having spent so much time in Blackpool among lads of his own age who were going back to the drudgery of work down the pits or in the factories or, worse, to the soul-sapping misery of unemployment, he appreciated how privileged he was to have a job paying very good money for doing what he would happily do for nothing. While those other working-class lads got up every morning wishing they didn't have to, Tommy couldn't wait to jump out of bed and get to the ground.

"My job is playing football!" he reminded himself as he made his way to Goodison Park to report back for the first day. As he did so, he pictured in his mind's eye those other lads going off to their work. That wasn't hard for him to do, for he'd seen his uncles do the same, at least when they were able to, which, in those days of dreadful depression back in Bolton had not been nearly often enough. "What sort of a life is that?" Tommy pondered as he got close to the fabulous football stadium that was his workplace. "Having a job you hate but missing it like hell when you haven't got it." The question made him shudder. Dixie Dean had told him never to take what he'd got for granted. Now, he knew exactly what Dixie meant.

It was a much younger squad of players than Everton had been used to over the years that gathered at Goodison this time. Dixie Dean had gone; so had Albert Geldard, and Cliff Britton was now coaching.

The infectious excitement and enthusiasm of the youngsters; the great potential they carried onto the training pitch and the unique thrill of the anticipation of a new season was sufficient, for now, to overcome a nagging fear at the back of older minds at Goodison on that lovely, sunny day: could the manic activity of one Adolf Hitler possibly mean that Britain would go to war with Germany for the second time in 20 years? The Prime Minister, Neville Chamberlain, was doing his best to convince the population that the answer to that question, with all its horrendous implications, was 'no' but many were unconvinced.

Not so, however, the young bucks of Everton Football Club. They had only football on their minds. And young Lawton was chuckling at the destination for the Blues' first fixture. They were playing *Blackpool* at Bloomfield Road. Joe Mercer, who had been treated to a colourful first-hand account of the lad's escapades with Frank Swift at the seaside, couldn't resist a dig: "The crowd's going to be twice the normal size due to our centre forward's conquests!"

For Tommy it was just like going on holiday again, so it was a very relaxed young man who ran out to lead the Everton attack. But there was nothing relaxed about the Blackpool players after Everton picked up where they'd left off the previous season. Their fast, flowing, one-touch football bewitched, bothered and bewildered Blackpool. They won 2-0 with Tommy Lawton opening his goalscoring account for the new season. But the score did not reflect their superiority, which was described in one newspaper report thus: "Everton have hit the right blend right away. They played like a side ripe in the peak season of soccer. The forwards switched in and out and wandered with studied skill. They had confidence to move about and they left Blackpool's defence dazed, beaten and bewildered."

Everton took the confidence gained from that victory into the next match against Grimsby, who suffered similar head-spinning humiliation and a 3-0 defeat in which Tommy scored two brilliant goals inside three minutes from exquisite passes from Alex Stevenson. Thanking Stevie afterwards, Tommy told him, "You rolled those balls across like it was a billiard table. That was the hardest I've ever been able to hit a ball and it was thanks to you."

Next up were Brentford at Goodison Park: another good win for Everton, 2-1 with Lawton scoring both their goals. Then it was off to the Midlands to take on Aston Villa. Newly promoted from the Second Division, Villa were reckoned to be well-nigh unbeatable at Villa Park, where they had a superb home record. 'Impenetrable' was the word being used. But not by this slick Everton team. Lawton scored first – his sixth of the season already – and Stevenson added two more: 3-0 to Everton, who now stood proudly at the top of the First Division with a 100 per cent record.

Now it was time for a real test of the emerging credentials of this young side. The next match was against the mighty Arsenal at Highbury.

Convinced that the Harrogate experience of the previous season was the perfect recipe, it was decreed that Harry Cooke should take the boys to Bushey in Hertfordshire to prepare for this stern examination. So, three days before the game, the team met at Lime Street Station to board a special first-class carriage, courtesy of the railway company LMS, with a board above the windows bearing the club emblem and proclaiming the presence of Everton Football Club. These lads were going to a first-class ground to play a first-class football team. No way would Merseyside pride let them think they were second class!

Their hotel at Bushey was similarly first class: plush and sumptuously comfortable. The itinerary followed the Harrogate pattern: good, long walks and plenty of enjoyable leisure time mixed with tough fitness sessions and those six-a-side matches to which, on this occasion, Harry Cooke added a new ingredient, rubber shoes to facilitate extra pace. The demands of these matches were well understood by the players now: speed, quick thinking, accurate passing and positional anticipation. The ball had to be passed, first touch and at top speed, to the man in the best position to use it to most advantage. Simple enough. But it was proving devastating to teams not used to such tactics and Cooke was determined now to polish it to perfection.

Suitably primed, the Everton party arrived at Highbury by coach, singing their club song *McNamara's Band* as they edged through thousands of supporters making their way to the ground, there to be amazed by the luxurious dressing rooms built into the new state-of-the-art stand. For Tommy Lawton, this first experience of the incredible opulence of the grand temple that was Highbury Stadium was breathtaking.

Inside, all was marble and polished wood. It seemed most unlike a football club – more like how he imagined the interior of some potentate's palace would look. As they prepared to change in the posh new visitors' dressing room, Tommy suddenly felt an artificially warm glow in his feet: "Bloody 'ell, lads, have you seen this?!" he exclaimed. Running right around the floor under the area in which the players prepared was a steam-heated strip of wood panelling. "Crikey," said Joe Mercer, "I thought teams were meant to get *cold* feet when they played Arsenal!"

A terrific air of excitement filled the huge stadium as the teams took the field in front of 68,000 expectant spectators. The Arsenal fans had come in droves to find out just how good this new table-topping Everton team was, whilst believing that their own illustrious heroes were more than capable of ending the Blues' fantastic start to the season. The Arsenal team was packed with star players: Swindin; Male, Hapgood (captain of England); Crayston, Joy, Copping; Kirchen, Leslie Jones, Drake, Brynmor Jones (recently bought from Wolves for a record £14,500), Bastin. The Everton line-up, by contrast, had a mostly unfamiliar look, especially to the Londoners who'd flocked to Highbury hoping to see them brought down to earth: Sagar; Cook, Greenhalgh; Mercer, Jones, Thomson; Gillick, Bentham, Lawton, Stevenson, Boyes.

It took but a few minutes, however, for those Arsenal supporters to realise that this young team, far from being lambs to the slaughter, was something very special. By half-time they had witnessed what was later described as "some of the best football ever played in London". Everton, in that first 45 minutes, were like a finely tuned machine running at the very height of performance: every part in perfect harmony with the rest; the whole producing smooth, faultless precision; a gleaming new Rolls-Royce gliding effortlessly past Arsenal's spluttering old Ford.

After 14 minutes of mesmerising one-touch football from Everton, in which Arsenal had hardly touched the ball, Billy Cook took a free kick inside his own penalty area and instead of giving the ball the big boot which was customary in such circumstances, he tapped it gently and short to Joe Mercer. Joe slid a precise pass to Torry Gillick who, first touch, flicked it into the path of Stan Bentham. As Arsenal defenders rushed to block his path, Bentham cleverly jumped over the ball, knowing that Tommy Lawton would run onto it. With Arsenal players anticipating a run through the middle by the centre forward, Lawton fooled them by rolling a short pass forward for Alex Stevenson to run onto. Stevie picked it up, rounded Eddie Hapgood then slithered past Bernard Joy and, as Swindin advanced, tucked a neat shot past the goalkeeper into the empty net behind him. Goal! And one of such sublime collective artistry that the Arsenal supporters applauded in sheer admiration of their illustrious team's fresh-faced young opponents.

Twenty minutes later, following another sequence of precise passing and movement, Alex Stevenson turned provider when he played a through-ball for Lawton. Finding his path to goal blocked by a barrier of Arsenal defenders, Lawton forced his way across the Arsenal penalty area towards the left wing and with his body at right angles to the goal he hit a curling left foot shot. Swindin, shaping to deal with a right foot shot to the right-hand corner, was completely deceived as Tommy's sweet left-footer flashed inside the left-hand post for Everton's second. Another brilliant goal.

Everton's peerless first-half performance was, however, not without pain for Tommy. Minutes before half-time he went up for a header with Wilf Copping. Lawton met the ball perfectly. Copping didn't. His head made violent contact with the centre forward's face. Tommy's nose was broken. As Harry Cooke sponged the blood from the lad's nose, Copping trotted over to pat the injured player's head and enquire as to his health before telling him, "You're jumping too high, Tommy, lad. I'll have to bring you down to my level!"

It was with that same resolve to equalise this one-sided contest that Arsenal came out for the second half and threw all they'd got at Everton. The Blues were forced to defend for most of the half. Brynmor Jones pulled a goal back but Everton held out to record a superb 2-1 victory and stay top of the table. They had proved themselves capable of calm defence under intense pressure, but it was their first-half performance on that sunny September afternoon in the capital that had set them aside from the pack and had the nation's sports writers drooling with delight.

None of the soccer scribes was more impressed than John Macadam of the *Daily Express*:

This was vintage football. Cool, deliberate, rhythmic and planned. Every man on the Everton side had a duty to that ball – to play no matter what the risk. From Stevenson, best forward on the field, back to Cook and Greenhalgh, the backs, the ball was handled like a weakly child – wheedled, guided, fed and occasionally belted.

Roland Allen of the London *Evening Standard* was less colourful but equally enthusiastic, particularly about Tommy Lawton:

Lawton is more than a rusher and a finisher. He is a clever footballer, bringing his wing men into the game with shrewd flicks and widely flung and accurate passes. He is dangerous because he shoots from anywhere and for an 18-year-old he really is an extraordinary footballer.

And all were united in one prediction: "This boy will soon be leading England."

On the train back to Liverpool after that scintillating Highbury performance, the Everton players sat chatting over well-deserved bottles of beer when the chairman, Will Cuff strolled past, looked across at Tommy and asked, "Have you ever been to Ireland, Lawton?" "No, I haven't," Tommy replied. The chairman said no more. He simply nodded, smiled and walked on. "What on earth was what that all about?" Tommy asked his teammates.

"Dunno," they replied, equally bemused. "Perhaps he just wants to get you on a boat to watch you turn green!" said Joe Mercer.

Three days later, the chairman's question was no longer a mystery. "There's a letter for you, son," said Tommy's mother at breakfast, as she passed an official-looking envelope across the table. Inside was an invitation from the Football League to play for its representative team against the League of Ireland at Windsor Park in Belfast on Wednesday 21st September. Not quite a full cap, but the next best thing. Tommy knew that if he made the best of this opportunity it could be the start of an England career.

He was still only 18. Little more than three years had passed since Jim Riley, Bill Horrocks and Pop Lever struck the deal to get their promising boy onto the books of Burnley Football Club. What had occurred since – and the speed at which it had happened – was incredible, the stuff of dreams. Now he stood on the brink of international fame. He was bursting with pride, but in those three whirlwind years of success he had learned, sometimes painfully, to keep his feet on the ground. And what of the man most responsible for ensuring that he had absorbed that lesson? Jim Riley was so pleased and proud, too, but in his frail state of health he could not greet this wonderful news energetically, even if that had been his style. He didn't need to. Though Jim's debilitating illness meant he was no longer his grandson's guide and guardian, nothing could weaken the bond between them. Tommy knew intuitively how his grandfather felt.

The reaction of Tommy's teammates, however, lacked nothing in energy and enthusiasm, nor in genuine delight. He waited until training had finished before quietly informing them and the sincerity of their unanimous, fulsome congratulations brought tears to the lad's eyes. Such was the spirit of togetherness in this Everton team.

In his joy at reaching this international milestone at such a tender age, Tommy had fond thoughts, too, for an absent friend who had played such a major part in his development as a player and as a person when he joined Everton and he knew that if Dixie Dean and his mates had not dumped him in a cold bath of humiliation one day he would now have been celebrating in a much less self-effacing and endearing fashion!

Before he could concentrate on that Belfast date, however, Tommy Lawton had another First Division fixture to complete. Everton were playing Portsmouth at Goodison Park and if they won, it would establish a new record of six consecutive wins from the start of the season. Initially, it did not go according to the script. Portsmouth took a shock lead after just seven minutes, but Everton's young thoroughbreds found another gear and banged in five goals without further reply. Tommy Lawton hit one of them, bringing his total to eight goals in six matches, scoring in every match. A phenomenal start to a season: no wonder international recognition was calling.

The following Tuesday, Tommy reported to the Adelphi Hotel in Liverpool to meet up with the rest of the Football League side for the trip to Ireland. After a mercifully smooth crossing, during which Eddie Hapgood and Stanley Matthews thoughtfully tried to calm his nerves so as to minimise the effects of his seasickness, Tommy got his first glimpse of Ireland – thus correcting the erroneous impression planted in his still impressionable young mind by Joe Mercer, that the Emerald Isle had no inhabitants because they were all in Liverpool!

Despite heavy rain, a good crowd turned out at Windsor Park. Before getting changed, Tommy went for a walk around the ground, just to get a feel for the place in which a hopefully long international career was about to begin. The pouring rain did not bother him one bit as he stopped to buy a programme to add to the growing collection of mementoes he was gathering back home. He opened it and read the team line-ups:

Irish League: McCurry (Cliftonville); Adams (Distillery), Fulton (Belfast Celtic); McIvor (Newry Town), Carlyle (Derry City), Walker (Belfast Celtic); Todd (Glentoran), McAlinden (Belfast Celtic), Shearer (Derry City), Duffy (Derry City), McCormick (Linfield).

English League: Woodley (Chelsea); Sproston (Tottenham Hotspur), Hapgood (Arsenal); Willingham (Huddersfield), Cullis (Wolverhampton Wanderers), Welsh (Charlton Athletic); Matthews (Stoke City), Robinson (Sheffield Wednesday), Lawton (Everton), Goulden (West Ham United), Morton (West Ham United).

He read through them again, this time dwelling on the name of the English centre forward . . . Lawton.

And that name was on the lips of all the soccer writers as well as the thousands of spectators present when the match ended in an 8-2 win for the English League, four of those goals being scored by the debutant centre forward!

It had, in truth, been an easy victory for the vastly superior English team but it was not without its drama, caused not by events on the field of play but by the weather. With 35 minutes to go the rain, which had continued to fall intermittently since kick-off, suddenly turned torrential. Around 2,000 Irish spectators, marooned on the uncovered side of the ground and getting drenched in the deluge, decided to take refuge on the covered side and took the quickest route – across the pitch! The English players stood, hands on hips, in utter disbelief as the pitch became a mass of Irish humanity while the referee blew, like a man possessed, on his whistle in a hopelessly futile attempt to restore order and dignity to these august international proceedings. The pitch invasion was over in a few minutes and once the fleeing fans were safely under cover the game continued as if nothing had happened.

The following Saturday, Tommy and his Everton teammates lost their unbeaten record. They went to Huddersfield, who tore into them right from the kick-off, scored two goals in three minutes, never let Everton settle into their passing game, chased and harried like terriers and finished comfortable 3-0 winners. In the dressing room after the match, young heads had dropped and glum silence replaced the post-match euphoria to which they'd all become accustomed. Goalkeeper Ted Sagar, the 'veteran' of the team, tried to lift their spirits with some wise words of consolation: "Come on lads, we were never going to win every game; it was getting to be a millstone round our necks. We can relax now and come back even stronger."

"You're just saying that because you let three in!" joked Joe Mercer, flinging a muddy sock in Sagar's direction. As Joe spoke, the disgusting, sweaty sock wrapped itself like a python around the protesting goalkeeper's neck. That sight was all the lads needed to restore their senses of humour and perspective and laughter made a swift comeback in that dressing room.

Ted Sagar was right. They didn't come any bigger than the next match – Liverpool, who were third in the table, in front of a Goodison Park crowd of 65,000 – but Everton did come back even stronger; there was no sign whatsoever of a hangover from the Huddersfield defeat as the Blues won 2-1. No goals for Lawton this time – but as the familiar sounds of celebration reverberated around the home dressing room, he didn't care a damn about that.

Everton supporters, along with the entire population of Great Britain, had more than a football match to cheer that day. Twenty-four hours earlier, Prime Minister Neville Chamberlain had returned from having agreed the so-called Munich Pact with Adolf Hitler, whose provocative action in unifying Germany and Austria in direct contradiction of the Treaty of Versailles and building up armaments in defiance of various other treaties, was frightening the life out of the rest of Europe.

Britain was now beginning to sense, seriously and with much justification, an inevitability about war with Germany and Chamberlain, along with the leaders of France and Italy, had attended a four-way summit with the German Chancellor, during which he and Hitler met privately. There were many in Britain who disliked Chamberlain's attitude of appeasement with Hitler, Winston Churchill most notable among them, but Chamberlain remained convinced that Germany had been badly treated in the aftermath of the Great War and that Hitler was a man with whom he could do business. On the day before the Everton v Liverpool match, Chamberlain disembarked from his plane at Heathrow Airport, waving a piece of paper on which were written the words of the 'peace pact' to massive cheering from a waiting crowd. Later, he stood outside 10 Downing Street before a crowd of onlookers and hordes of pressmen to read out his statement:

We, the German Führer and Chancellor and the British Prime Minister, have had a further meeting today and are agreed in recognising that the question of Anglo-German relations is of the first importance for our two countries and for Europe. We regard the agreement signed last night and the Anglo-German Naval Agreement as symbolic of the desire of our two peoples never to go to war with one another again.

At this point, the cheering that erupted was so loud and long that it was some time before the Prime Minister could continue:

We are resolved that the method of consultation shall be the method adopted to deal with any other questions that may concern our two countries and we are determined to continue our efforts to remove possible sources of difference and thus to contribute to assure the peace of Europe.

Chamberlain then looked dramatically up at the crowd and declared:

My good friends, for the second time in our history a British Prime Minister has returned from Germany bringing peace with honour. I believe it is peace for our time. Go home and get a nice quiet sleep.

At which most went, not for a 'nice quiet sleep' but for a good stiff drink!

As the fans gathered for that Merseyside derby match, there was a huge sense of relief pervading the whole country. Before kick-off at Goodison Park, 65,000 spectators fell silent for 'prayers of thanksgiving for peace in Europe' then joined in hearty community singing of *God Save the King*. When Everton then proceeded to beat the Reds it completed a day of unbridled joy on the Blue side of the city and young Tommy Lawton could look forward to his imminent 19th birthday with the threat of war removed from his horizon of hope.

It was a fitting continuation of the celebration for Tommy when in Everton's next game against Wolves he scored the only goal of the game to secure yet another win for his table-topping team and increase the clamour for his selection for the full England team – a popular cause championed by so many football writers, including Charles Buchan, who wrote in the *News Chronicle*:

Lawton is undoubtedly England's centre forward. His great head work, moulded on the pattern of Dixie Dean, and his clever foot-work stamps him as England's leader for many years to come.

England's next international fixture was to be against Wales at Cardiff's Ninian Park on 22nd October 1938. And the team was due to be announced on the Sunday after Everton's defeat of Wolves.

"Do you think I might have a chance?" he'd asked his teammates in the dressing room after the match. "Don't get your hopes up, Tom." said Alex Stevenson, who as an Irish international, was used to this anxious waiting game and to the gut-wrenching disappointment on the occasions when he wasn't picked. "Try not to expect it – then it doesn't hurt so much when it doesn't happen," added Billy Cook. Ted Sagar was more full and thoughtful in his response: "Tom, I reckon you'll definitely get an England cap but perhaps not yet awhile. The selectors have hardly made a habit of picking 19-year-olds!"

All the same, it was a pent-up Tommy who set off for Burnley to visit his girlfriend on the fateful Sunday. She did not, to say the least, enjoy his undivided attention that afternoon and when she concluded that he might just as well go home, Tommy was too preoccupied to disagree. Making his way to the railway station, he suddenly had an idea. He stopped at a telephone box, put twopence in the slot and rang the *Burnley Express & News*.

"Hello, could you put me through to the sports desk, please?"

"Sports desk, can I help you?"

"Yes, I'm a regular reader and I wondered if you could tell me if the England team for the Wales match has been announced yet."

"Yes, it has. Would you like me to read it over to you?"

"Oh, that's so helpful. Thank you."

Tommy's hand was shaking so much that he could hardly hold the receiver as the obliging sub-editor read out the team: "Woodley, Sproston, Hapgood, Willingham, Young, Copping, . . ." His breathless excitement was mounting as every name got closer to that crucial centre forward position: "Matthews, Robinson, Morton, . . ."

"Morton? Morton? Who's Morton?"

"Not Morton, you loon. You're not listening properly! I said Lawton, Lawton – our Tommy. You must be the only bloke in Lancashire who's never heard of him!"

Tommy dropped the receiver and left it dangling on its wire as he leapt out into the street. A passing lorry driver looked on in amazement, the only witness to the astonishing sight of a big, well-dressed young man dancing an abandoned Highland fling outside a phone box early on a quiet Sunday evening!

In the week before his international debut, Tommy trained extra hard and as the big day approached, the tension he felt became almost unbearable, making sleep well-nigh impossible. He lay awake, all sorts of little worries and trivial questions assuming wildly exaggerated importance in the dead of night . . .

"How do I travel to Cardiff? How do I get to the hotel? What do I do when I get there? Will I do anything daft when I book in? How do I get to the ground? I'd better not be late! Suppose I oversleep? What bus do I catch to the ground?"

Then on the eve of the game, in a hotel bed with a stranger for a room-mate, he tossed and turned all night – this time his mind tortured by doubts about the game. Wales was a tough team against which to make your international debut. "Will I play well? Will I do anything silly? Am I good enough? Am I ready for it? I must do well. I must prove myself. I can't let everybody down. I can't!"

When morning came he had, in a totally sleepless night, burned up as much nervous energy as he would in six matches. Confident though he was for most of the time, it was easy to forget that Tommy was just a 19-year-old kid from an impoverished background, Football star, yes but man of the world he wasn't and that hotel room had seemed a desperately lonely place all night.

The first thing to strike Tommy Lawton as he peeped out from the players' tunnel at Ninian Park just before the teams were due out for Wales v England, was the naked emotion of the 40,000 Welsh supporters.

Sospan Bach and *Men of Harlech* the Welsh sang as one enormous choir, massed voices almost sobbing and everywhere Tommy looked there were leeks, real leeks but so huge he couldn't believe they were real: leeks being waved like flags in the crowd; leeks standing upright and looking vaguely obscene against the railings around the pitch; leeks suspended by string from the goalposts; leeks strewn around the goalmouth. His nan could have made enough soup to feed the whole of Lancashire with that many leeks. What a waste!

"Look up there," said Eddie Hapgood, who, as a good captain should, was keeping an eye on his young centre forward. Tommy peered up in the direction of Hapgood's pointed finger: "Crikey. How did he get up there?" Perched like a seagull atop a ship's mast, high above the ground on a pillar supporting the stand, a Welsh supporter sat festooned in the barbed wire meant to prevent such idiocy, blissfully oblivious to the perilously precarious nature of his position, waving his massive leek in the air.

The fervently patriotic support of that crowd soon transferred itself to the action on the field of play as a very strong and talented Welsh side attacked England from the off. That pressure never relented. Battered England lost 4-2. There was a debut goal for Lawton, a penalty kick which Hapgood insisted he should take. Tommy took it calmly and well, sending the Welsh goalkeeper Roy John the wrong way, but it was the only chance he got to make an impression on the game. His Everton teammate Yanto Jones, policing his young pal as Wales's centre half that day, saw very effectively to that. "Blimey, you're a hard bugger!" Tommy told his Welsh friend, more in admiration than complaint, when he whacked him from behind for the umpteenth time. "What do you expect, boyo?" said Jones with a wide grin. "Your shirt's the wrong colour today!"

It was with bleak feelings of disappointment and anticlimax that Tommy sat in the England dressing room after the match. His worst nightmare had come true – he *had* let everybody down. The senior international players counselled him not to despair; he'd done his best and worked very hard, they told him and nobody could ask for more: "It was just not our day," they reasoned, "and Wales were a damned good side." But Tommy feared that the unsuccessful sortie into this hostile land of fearsome footballers, sobbing singers, ludicrously large leeks and high-wire acts had been his last for England.

He did not have to wait long, however, before discovering that his fear was groundless. The England Selection Committee met immediately after the game to choose the team to represent England against the Rest of Europe in a game to be played at Highbury Stadium four days later to celebrate the 75th anniversary of the Football Association.

Meanwhile, Tommy had the opportunity to enjoy the night out of his young life. Like most youngsters, he was a great fan of swing music and like most youngsters – in fact, like most people of all ages throughout Britain – he was whistling and singing a tune that had got inside the heads of the whole nation:

> *Any time you're Lambeth way,*
> *Any evening, any day,*
> *You'll find us all,*
> *Doing the Lambeth walk,*
> *Oi!*

The Lambeth Walk was a hit song and dance routine from a massively successful London musical, *Me and My Girl* starring Lupino Lane.

The song and the jaunty, strutting, walking dance had its origins in the Limehouse district of London, where Lambeth Walk was a street frequented by lovers of the Cockney delicacies, pie, mash and liquor (liquidised peas) and jellied eels. *The Lambeth Walk*, performed by a cast of Pearly Kings and Queens, with chests out, thumbs in lapels, elbows protruding, led from the front by Lupino Lane, was a show-stopper as they left the stage and danced through the aisles with the audience joining in.

Both the song and the dance were incredibly infectious and soon, people were doing *The Lambeth Walk* all over the country. The craze had even swept across to Nazi Germany, where swing music was strictly *verboten* and a clandestine version, sung in German, was secretly recorded. The England players were invited to see *Me and My Girl* at the Drury Lane Theatre, where they had a wonderful evening, culminating in an impromptu performance of *The Lambeth Walk* for the benefit of the press cameras back stage with Lupino Lane and his leading lady.

For the match versus the Rest of Europe, there were victims of the Welsh defeat but they didn't include Tommy: centre half Alf Young and inside forward Jackie Robinson were dropped to be replaced by Stan Cullis and Willie Hall, but the rest of the team was unchanged.

This was going to be some match. There had never been one like it before. England were undefeated by any Continental team on home soil, but this was different. The national team, with 19-year-old Tommy Lawton leading the attack, was to be pitted against the cream of the greatest footballers from the rest of Europe – 11 stars chosen from no less than two million players from 25,000 clubs in the International Federation of Association Football. The build-up to this 'match of the century' in the national press was feverish. This was the strongest opposition ever to be faced by an England team: Olivieri (Italy); Foni (Italy), Rava (Italy); Kupfer (Germany), Andreolo (Italy), Kissinger (Germany); Aston (France), Braine (Belgium), Piola (Italy), Zsellenger (Hungary), Brustad (Norway).

On the day, all was pomp and circumstance with visiting dignitaries from all over the world assembled among a huge Highbury crowd, but despite all that ceremony and pre-match excitement, it was a much more relaxed Tommy Lawton who lined up with the rest of the players to shake what seemed like an endless parade of bigwigs' hands. He'd had no trouble sleeping this time: the Welsh willies he'd suffered had been a one-off. Now he felt like he belonged. It was a good feeling.

All the dignity and decorum of the opening ceremony evaporated, however, when the match kicked off and the visiting Continentals proceeded to punch, kick and hack at the England players: jerseys were pulled, feet were stamped on, ribs were elbowed, arms were pinched, ankles were tapped and ferocious foul tackles flew in. Tommy and his teammates had experienced nothing like this. It made the often brutal treatment meted out to Dixie Dean look like the genteel exchanges of a game of croquet on the vicarage lawn. And it was unrelenting. The referee, Mr (later RAF Squadron Leader) Jimmy Jewell, normally the strictest of officials, did his best to control the game and apply the rules but he was so conscious of the special nature of the occasion and the need to avoid upsetting all the visiting overseas top brass that he allowed a lot of the indiscretions to go unpunished.

One or two of the more robustly inclined English players, notably Wilf Copping, imposed disciplinary measures of their own, particularly after Andreolo had reacted to a free kick being awarded against him for flooring Ken Willingham by spitting at the referee. "Ey oop, Ken," said Wilf, "that's disgusting. I'll not 'ave that!" He then ensured that appropriate corporal punishment was administered every time he could get anywhere near to Andreolo, which fortunately for the Uruguayan-born Italian centre half, was not nearly so often as Wilf would have liked!

The rest of the England players, particularly the forward line of Stanley Matthews, Willie Hall, Tommy Lawton, Len Goulden and Wally Boyes, kept their heads under the intense provocation and exacted the very sweetest kind of revenge: a 3-0 victory with goals from Hall, Lawton and Goulden.

Protocol dictated that all hostilities should be forgiven and forgotten when players, officials, distinguished guests and the gentlemen of the press attended a posh post-match banquet at the Holborn Restaurant.

This was an occasion young Tommy Lawton from Bolton could never even have dreamed of and he had to stop himself staring, wide-eyed and incredulous, throughout the grand order of proceedings lest he looked 'a poor relation' out of his depth and out of his class, which he knew he was.

With help and advice from Joe Mercer, Tommy had hired evening dress and he cut a handsome dash in black tie, with a smart dinner jacket fitting snugly across his broad young shoulders. He had polished his shoes (*heels as well* for Jim Riley) till they shone like mirrors. He might have been from poor working-class stock but he'd made sure that his immaculate appearance was a match for any man present – including them 'lah-de-dah buggers' on the long top table.

Before the banquet commenced, the flags of 24 nations were unfurled. The Union Jack – which was then used rather than the Cross of St George – was left to last and the effect was dramatic; the National Anthem being sung with great gusto as the flag fluttered open. Tommy felt an intense sense of pride at that moment; he swallowed hard and fought back tears as he joined in the singing.

On the top table sat the FIFA delegates of Italy, Belgium, Germany,

Hungary, Holland, Yugoslavia, Norway and South America. The proceedings were led by Monsieur Jules Rimet of France, President of the Federation, whose full title was recited every time the red-coated toastmaster bellowed frequent invitations to various dignitaries around the room to "take wine" with "your President" – upon which they had to stand and raise their glasses to Monsieur Rimet. The wines the entire gathering were 'taking' were very special. Some of the best money could buy. They were strong wines, too and every sip Tommy took removed a little more of his uncomfortable inhibition until he was perfectly relaxed and enjoying every minute of this grand affair as if he were to the manor born.

A sumptuous meal of turtle soup, lobster cocktail, roast sirloin of British beef, meringue glace and cheeses was followed by brandy and cigars and speeches, each speech followed by yet more toasts.

The glittering evening was brought to a climax by none other than Gracie Fields, who was accompanied for her concert by top tenor Webster Booth. Gracie was now the whole nation's sweetheart, a massive star. Webster Booth, a brilliant operatic singer who made many popular records, often appeared with his wife, Anne Ziegler, with whom he formed a duo. But for this event it was Webster Booth and 'Our Gracie'. Their brilliant performance was received with rapture and concluded to a standing ovation, with no one clapping or cheering louder or longer than Tommy Lawton. As he stood applauding her, Tommy wondered if he should approach Gracie Fields and tell her that his mam had been an extra in one of her films. Best not, he thought. Might make him look a twerp, that.

The whole evening had been a new and fantastic experience, the memory of which would remain with Tommy for the rest of his life.

As Gracie Fields and Webster Booth performed, he thought back to the party the Rileys gave him for his 11th birthday, just before his nan passed away. Fish-paste butties they had eaten that day, not fine lobster and roast beef and it was his mam, not Gracie Fields, who sang for him. It had meant the world to him, that party with its impromptu family concert and in fond and grateful memory it still did. But this dramatic contrast brought a sudden realisation of how fantastically his life had changed since those fairly recent days in that tiny, overcrowded house in the back streets of Bolton. Thick, collarless, striped working shirts the Riley men had worn for his birthday party, not sparkling white dress shirts and black ties; Mam and Nan had worn pinnies over their faded floral dresses, not magnificent gowns like the one Gracie Fields wore tonight. But Our Gracie had not let fame ruin her: she was still a working-class Lancashire lass and proud of it and thanks to the wisdom and guidance he had been given (though not always welcomed!) fame had not ruined Our Tommy either. He was still a working-class Lancashire lad and proud of it and whatever life had still in store for him, Tommy vowed as he rolled an extremely expensive brandy around in its enormous glass, that's what he would always be. Then, as he sat so proudly in that plush London venue, surrounded by international dignitaries but alone with his thoughts, he raised his huge glass and proposed a toast all of his own . . . "My family."

Fame was now guaranteed. The international football career of Tommy Lawton, aged 19, was off to a flying start. Two full international caps and one Football League cap were soon followed by selection for the Football League versus the Scottish League (3-1 to the English) and for England versus Norway (4-0 to England) and then for England versus Ireland at Old Trafford on 16th November 1938.

Three of Tommy's Everton teammates joined him in this match — Alex Stevenson and Billy Cook for Ireland and Joe Mercer, making his international debut, for England — but the match was one in which all the headlines and plaudits were won by Stanley Matthews and Willie Hall, England's outside right and inside right respectively.

Stanley Matthews, aged 23, played for his local team Stoke City. He was the third of four sons born to Potteries boxer Jack Matthews, billed as 'the Fighting Barber of Hanley', who had brought his lads up to a strict code of discipline, determination and sportsmanship. Matthews had a deceptively languid style — betrayed when he left defenders standing for speed after mesmerising them with his dribbling skills.

Willie Hall, aged 26, played for Tottenham Hotspur. They paid Notts County £2,500 for him in 1932. Born in Newark, Nottinghamshire, Hall made his international debut against France in 1933. A players' player, he was highly respected for his clever approach to the game but he was used only intermittently by England.

During this match, Matthews produced a magnificent display of wing wizardry which so bewildered the Irish that he frequently beat up to four of them on one mazy run. And Hall, working in perfect harmony with his right-winger partner, scored five goals during a 30-minute period either side of half-time.

Matthews was unstoppable as he weaved his magical patterns down the wing to the corner flag from where he either cut into the penalty area to provide a perfect pass or flashed over a precision cross, one of which was gratefully received and faultlessly despatched into the back of the net by Tommy Lawton. But it was Willie Hall, brilliantly anticipating Matthews's service and playing superbly timed return passes with his winger, who reaped the maximum benefit. England ran out 7-0 winners (Matthews got the seventh goal himself) over an accomplished Irish side which was by no means a pushover.

As the teams left the pitch at the final whistle, Alex Stevenson, for all his experience and talent, told his young Everton colleague, "Tom, after that I'm only just starting to learn." Matthews had made everything look ridiculously easy, as described by L V Manning in the following day's *Daily Sketch* when, describing Matthews's goal, he wrote, "Matthews ran the ball up to the Irish goalkeeper, looked as if he was going to shake his hand, changed his mind and slipped the ball into the net."

It was the first of many occasions on which the Matthews magic was to work wonders for England but, full of admiration for him though he was, Tommy confided to Alex Stevenson, "Stan can be a difficult bugger to play with: when he goes off on one of those mazy dribbles you never know what he's going to do next and he sometimes leaves you fuming. Then, he'll hit an absolutely perfect pass and all is forgiven."

Back at Goodison Park, all thoughts of international football were put on hold as the realisation dawned that Everton could win the First Division title. For such a young team to become champions would be truly remarkable, but it was now looking achievable and Merseyside, or at least the blue sector of it, was alive with excited anticipation.

All the talk, the speculation and expectation, was the last thing the Everton lads needed. Nerves took hold and over the Christmas period they slipped up against their nearest rivals, Derby County. A quirk of fate decreed that the fixture list had Everton playing Derby twice over Christmas. The game at Goodison was drawn 2-2. At the Baseball Ground, Derby won 2-1. In five games during that spell Everton won only once and Tommy Lawton lost his goal touch, scoring none. Derby went top and the talk around Merseyside now was that it had all been too much for the youngsters of Everton. They had thrown it away – but never mind, there was always next season when they'd be an even better side for the experience.

The lads in the blue shirts, however, had other ideas. Their form returned and by Easter they were back on top of the League. Three wins and six points over the Easter holiday would possibly be enough to win the title.

But that fixture list had again thrown a huge spanner into the works. Their Easter holiday programme could not have been harder. On Good Friday, they had to play Sunderland at Roker Park – arguably the toughest away match of the season – then travel overnight to London to meet Chelsea at Stamford Bridge on the following day and back to Liverpool for the return match with Sunderland at Goodison Park on Easter Monday.

Sunderland were the powerhouse team of recent times, winning the

First Division title in 1936 and the FA Cup a year later. They hadn't had their best season in the League, but they remained the team to beat. They were captained by the brilliant England international inside right, Raich Carter, reckoned by many to be the best player in the country.

Horatio Stratton Carter, to use his somewhat pretentious proper name, was 26 years old. The son of a professional footballer (Robert Carter, an inside forward who played for Port Vale, Fulham and Southampton and was best remembered for being a tiny man), Raich was born in Sunderland, for whom he signed in 1931. He won his first England cap in 1934. He was a supremely skilful player, clever, creative, a bewildering dribbler and a brilliant passer of the ball. He could also be lethal in front of goal. Now, Raich Carter and his formidable, experienced Sunderland team stood between the emerging young guns of Everton and the Football League championship.

It could not have been better scripted. The national press, licking its lips in anticipation of the contests, built huge public interest in the Easter battles and sent all the top scribes to bring every detail of the story to millions of readers.

The Everton lads left Liverpool in high spirits, greatly excited at the prospect of the immense challenge that lay before them, and this time there was to be no repeat of the nerves that ruined their Christmas. They took the game to Sunderland, played their swift passing game to breathtaking perfection and for periods of the match mesmerised their illustrious opponents. In attack, Alex Stevenson and Tommy Lawton were absolutely outstanding, as was Joe Mercer at right half and Yanto Jones in defence, but it was one of those days when it was gratuitous to pick out individuals for plaudits because the whole Everton team produced a truly memorable performance. Sunderland did not play badly and battled well but the great Raich Carter was forced to take something of a back seat on the day, which he sportingly conceded after Everton won 2-1 with goals from Torry Gillick and Tommy Lawton.

It was a very buoyant Everton team that then boarded a sleeper train at Newcastle to take them to London for the next leg of their Easter mission. In fact, the lads were so keyed up that none of them could sleep. As the powerful steam train roared through the night towards London, Yanto produced a pack of cards: "Come on, you lot. We're not gonna get a wink of sleep so we might as well play!" And play they did, for most of that very long journey.

As the train rested in a siding at Euston the next morning, a railway steward boarded with a tray of tea for the team to find them fast asleep. Several of them were snoring loudly. "Blimey!" the steward exclaimed as, one by one, the players stirred from their deep, delayed slumber, "You lot are supposed to be playing Chelsea this afternoon. I wonder if I can get a bet on!"

With just 15 minutes of the match at Stamford Bridge remaining, the steward's bet looked pretty safe. In a tight game, Everton had looked the better side but could not find the goal they needed. Tommy Lawton's usual composure deserted him when a brilliant cross from Alex Stevenson, Everton's best player on the day, dropped temptingly at his feet just a few yards from Chelsea's goal. He snatched at his shot and much to the loud amusement of the Chelsea fans the ball soared high up into the Shed End. Then Joe Mercer hit a brilliant first-time drive which was screaming towards the corner of the Chelsea net until their England international goalkeeper Vic Woodley turned it brilliantly round the post.

It looked as if Everton were going to have to settle for one point in their quest for the championship. Then, little Alex Stevenson took matters into his own hands. The diminutive inside left, often called 'Mickey Mouse' by his mates who towered way above him, decided to do the centre forward's job. He soared way above big Chelsea centre half Bobby Salmond to meet a cross from the left and crashed a spectacular header past Woodley. 1-0 to Everton!

The goal amazed Stevie's teammates as much as it delighted them. They could hardly ever recall their little Irish imp ever heading a ball – let alone with such power and direction that it had the net bulging. As they gathered around him to congratulate the scorer on his 'miracle' goal, Tommy Lawton told him, "Blimey, Stevie, that was like Bud Flanagan dancing in a Sadler's Wells ballet!" The Irishman laughed: "I just thought I'd remind you how it's done, Tom. You seem to have forgotten!"

Minutes later, Torry Gillick scored a second and two vital points were in the bag for Everton. Their latest nearest challengers, Wolves, were still technically in with a shout so the Everton players were not celebrating yet. But the national press was doing it for them. On Easter Monday, the day they were to meet Sunderland at home, the *Daily Sketch* was pronouncing prematurely "Hail Everton" and its football writer L V Manning summed up their season thus: "I never saw Everton play without getting the impression that, from Lawton to Sagar, every man was enjoying a game of football and not making a job of work of it."

Well, they certainly enjoyed the return match with Sunderland at Goodison Park. They resoundingly beat Raich Carter's men 6-2, with a hat-trick from inside right Stan Bentham. The final whistle was the signal for ecstatic celebrations for the Goodison fans, hundreds of them leaping over the wall onto the pitch where they chaired every Everton player off the field.

For all the fans' rapturous response to the Easter Monday trouncing of Sunderland, results elsewhere ensured that Wolves continued to keep in touch. Everton needed to win their next match, at home to Preston North End, to confirm the championship on the same day that third-placed Charlton Athletic had to beat Wolves at Molineux to end the West Midlands club's challenge. Neither happened. Everton drew 0-0 with Preston; Wolves beat Charlton 3-1.

The following week, Everton needed to beat Charlton at the Valley to finally secure the title while Wolves needed to win away to Bolton Wanderers to stay in the hunt. The Everton lads had another attack of the nerves and were not at their best when they lost 2-1 at Charlton. However, Wolves lost at Bolton and that meant Everton could not now be overhauled.

The 1938/39 Football League championship had been won by Everton in a season in which, with so many youngsters in their team, they had been completely unfancied at the start.

With a mixture of clever planning, superb team spirit and good fortune, Everton had, in fact, produced a cracking side. In goal, Ted Sagar's experience had been crucial; Joe Mercer at right half had grown in stature with every game and T G Jones at centre half had been an inspirational revelation. In attack, the tiny trio of wingers Torry Gillick and Wally Boyes and the irrepressible Alex Stevenson, all of them under five feet four, were too quick, nimble and skilful for most of the big defenders who tried to contain them. But it was the young centre forward, now an established England international, who had made the biggest impact of all. Tommy Lawton had scored 34 goals in 38 League games.

The Everton directors decided that a gesture of generosity should be made to the lads who had won the title for them. They were rewarded with a day trip to Morecambe!

Tommy Lawton was every bit as delighted as was to be expected by the great progress both he and the Everton team had made in the 1938/39 season, but he had one regret: Everton had not won the FA Cup. Victories over Derby County (1-0), Doncaster Rovers (8-0) and Birmingham City (2-1 in a replay after drawing 2-2 in front of a 67,144 crowd at St Andrews) took them to the quarter-final in which they were drawn away to Wolverhampton Wanderers.

Wolves were the last opponents Everton wanted. Their League match at Molineux just two weeks earlier had been a disaster. They were thrashed 7-0 by Wolves in a match preceded by a national controversy which the papers dubbed 'the Monkey Gland Scandal'. The scandal erupted when it was claimed that Wolves manager Major Frank Buckley had injected his players with a potion made from monkey testicle in order to enhance their strength and staying power!

Major Buckley was an extraordinary man and an even more extraordinary manager. He had been a serving soldier but bought himself out of the Army in 1902 to become a footballer with Aston Villa. He went on to play for Brighton, Manchester United, Manchester City, Birmingham City, Derby County and Bradford City, winning one England cap, before the 1914–18 War interrupted his playing career. He went to war with the Middlesex Regiment and despite being wounded in the Battle of the Somme, rose to the rank of major.

The Major became manager of Wolverhampton Wanderers in 1927, taking Army discipline with him. He was feared and highly respected as a manager who didn't suffer fools and insisted on the game being played with power and simplicity. He was also enigmatic and enjoyed toying with pretentious people, particularly members of the press, whom he regarded as his intellectual inferiors.

The Monkey Gland Scandal alleged that in 1937 Major Buckley had been introduced to monkey-testicle therapy by a disciple of Serge Voronoff, a Russian surgeon who had developed the treatment at a Mediterranean monkey farm and it was said that, in typical Army-officer style, the Major had insisted on trying the therapy himself before administering it to his team. He had found the results so beneficial that he then gave it to his players. It was alleged that the monkey testicles (aided and abetted by heavy watering of the pitch to create mud bath conditions) induced the superior strength and stamina for which the Major's big, strong team of 1938/39 was renowned.

After the scandal broke, shortly before the League match with Everton, Major Buckley craftily refused to confirm or deny the story, teasing the press and deliberately fuelling the national speculation. The Wolves players had all been given injections, about which they were sworn to secrecy. Many among the press, and consequently the public, believed these did contain monkey testicle; some said they were just flu jabs; others that the syringes contained nothing more than water.

Before the Wolves versus Everton League game at Molineux, Tommy Lawton saw Stan Cullis, an England international teammate, walking down to the dressing rooms and called out, "Hello Stan – aren't you speaking to me, then?" Cullis ignored him completely and Tommy told his Everton teammates, "His eyes were glazed and he walked straight past me."

At half-time, Wolves were 5-0 up. And the Everton dressing room was deep in monkey gland discussion: "They've walked all over us and they're not even flippin' sweating!" exclaimed Joe Mercer; "I'm convinced they're on something," said Tommy, reiterating his earlier account of the encounter with Stan Cullis; captain Jock Thomson told his team, "Don't worry, lads. They were playing with the wind that half." To which Alex Stevenson replied, "Some bloody wind!"

So, with that experience and the 7-0 drubbing only two weeks behind them the Everton players would, all in all, rather have been anywhere than Molineux for the FA Cup quarter-final.

Before the kick-off they felt it was not going to be their day – not because of monkeys' testicles or mischievous pitch-watering but because, after a week of fine, dry weather, Mother Nature conspired on the Friday night to conjure up a torrential downpour of rain which continued relentlessly on through the Saturday morning of the match. It stopped raining at midday but by then the pitch was a mud heap. This was much more to the liking of the big Wolves team and their robust, direct style of play than it was to the Everton lads, with their slick one-touch passing game.

There was added spice to this match, should any be needed, in that Wolves had a centre forward, Dennis Westcott, who every football fan in Wolverhampton believed was better than Tommy Lawton and should have been playing for England instead of the Everton youngster. This belief was bolstered by the local newspaper, the *Express & Star*, which campaigned constantly for Westcott's selection, often extravagantly staking his claim while rubbishing Lawton's. This assessment by the paper, while owing infinitely more to commendable commitment to its local community than common sense, was avidly consumed and accepted without question by supporters who had only seen Tommy play on one previous visit to Wolverhampton!

The game was evenly matched until just before half-time when Westcott collected a clearance from Wolves' goalkeeper Bob Scott, forced his way past four Everton players and hit a superb low drive beyond Ted Sagar into the right-hand corner. 1-0 to Wolves. Just 15 minutes into the second half, Westcott went past three Everton defenders and hit another unstoppable shot past Sagar. 2-0 to Wolves. So ended Everton's interest in the FA Cup of 1938/39.

The Wolverhampton *Express & Star* was ecstatic: "Westcott's Wonder Goals Won It" screamed its headline and its breathless report described the goals scored by the man they wanted to see in Tommy Lawton's England shirt as "two of the most dramatic and picturesque goals imaginable" then went on to declare to its less-than-impartial readership: "There is no comparison between Lawton, the Everton and England centre forward, and Westcott." In an otherwise glorious season, this was a day for Tommy to forget.

And the great Monkey Gland Scandal? It remained neither proved nor disproved and that was just the way the canny Major Buckley wanted it.

On the way to Everton's championship triumph, Tommy Lawton had missed their League match on Saturday 15th April 1939 for the very best of reasons.

He was away turning a dream he had cherished since he was seven years old into incredible reality, leading England's attack against the old enemy, Scotland, in front of 150,000 spectators at Glasgow's Hampden Park. It was his fifth international cap and to Tommy, still not 20, this represented the greatest prize of all.

In the England team's hotel on the Friday evening before the big match, time hung heavily for the young centre forward. He was excited and couldn't wait for Saturday afternoon and the kick-off to the match of his life. At the same time, he was secretly fearful of letting England down and wondered if the world-famous, fearsome Hampden Roar would upset his game.

The Hampden Roar was first heard when Scotland were playing England in 1929. The home side had been reduced to ten men through an injury to Alex Jackson in the first half and were losing 1-0 when Aberdeen's Alec Cheyne scored a dramatic equaliser direct from a corner kick.

The terrifying Roar – an astonishing bellow, which rose to a crescendo before being held at a constant deafening level – began spontaneously among the crowd of well over 100,000 Scots as a way of inspiring their team to hang on until the final whistle. It was so effective that Hampden crowds supporting Scotland had used it ever since to terrify visiting players and, with the thunderous Roar so loud that it could be heard several miles away from the stadium, it often did!

Tommy was even more nervous than he had been on the eve of his England debut and he lay awake for most of that night, just longing for the day of the match to dawn.

At last, the moment came for the England team to enter that fiercely intimidating arena. They were facing a massive challenge. England had not beaten Scotland at Hampden Park for 12 years and Tommy was not alone in his nervous anticipation of the dreaded Hampden Roar: Only three of the team – captain Eddie Hapgood, goalkeeper Vic Woodley and right half Ken Willingham – had faced it before and outside left Pat Beasley was also making his international debut.

The England team, lining up in the tunnel ready to walk out and face that Roar from the throats of nearly 150,000 fanatical Scots, was: Woodley (Chelsea); Morris (Wolves), Hapgood (Arsenal); Willingham (Huddersfield),

Cullis (Wolves), Mercer (Everton); Matthews (Stoke City), Hall (Spurs), Lawton (Everton), Goulden (West Ham), Beasley (Huddersfield).

Waiting to go into battle with them for Scotland were: Dawson (Rangers); Carabine (Third Lanark), Cummings (Aston Villa); Shankly (Preston), Baxter (Middlesbrough), McNab (West Brom); McSpadyen (Partick Thistle), Walker (Hearts), Dougal (Preston), Venters (Rangers), Milne (Middlesbrough).

As he walked into the seething cauldron of that hostile arena, Tommy Lawton knew immediately why the Hampden Roar was so infamous. He couldn't believe that such a noise was possible. It echoed and eddied around the vast bowl of the stadium then smashed back into his eardrums with such force he feared they would burst and he felt his legs go weak. It quietened down a little during the kick-around and while the toss took place in the centre circle then abruptly stopped altogether as a pipe band suddenly skirled into the national anthem. The chilling sound of those bagpipes wailing in the now eerie silence brought a lump to Tommy's throat. Then, immediately, when the pipes stopped the Roar returned – this time, even louder.

Tommy looked around at the England players. Some looked extremely tense; one or two had turned pale; but Joe Mercer was laughing! As Tommy caught Joe's eye, his Everton teammate nodded and gave him a huge wink: "Now, that's the way to deal with this," thought Tommy and as soon as they kicked off, he felt no fear, no anxiety – just immense pride to be wearing the three lions of England on his shirt and an intense desire and determination to stuff that mighty Roar back down the throats of those thousands of baying Scots.

By now, it had started to rain heavily. The pitch soon became drenched and slippery and England looked a shaky side. The Hampden Roar seemed to be having much more effect on some of the other players than it was on Joe Mercer and Tommy: some of them looked completely overawed by the enormity of the occasion; some were making frequent mistakes, none worse than when, after 20 minutes, right back Bill Morris intercepted a pass intended for the Scots' centre forward and instead of booting the ball safely downfield, hesitated then played a poor back pass to his goal-keeper. Vic Woodley had advanced from his line; the pass from Morris evaded him and the fleet-footed Dougal seized gratefully on the loose ball and tapped it into the net. 1-0 to Scotland. That huge crowd went absolutely berserk!

Poor Morris sank to his knees in utter dejection. Eddie Hapgood and Joe Mercer, who were both playing well, particularly the latter, tried to lift the England players: "Come on, lads," urged Hapgood. "There's plenty of time." But as the rain continued to lash down incessantly and the Scots, inspired by Dougal's goal, grew ever more confident and determined, England looked beaten.

During the half-time interval, the Scots changed into a fresh new set of blue shirts, discarding those saturated by the rain. England had not brought spare kit and it seemed they would have to go out for the second half in the same soaked shirts they were wearing, until the Scots (with their only magnanimous gesture of the day!) offered them a set belonging to amateur club Queens Park, who also played at Hampden.

So it was a more comfortable and dry, if somewhat unfamiliar-looking, England who took the field for the second half, with a half-time pep talk from Eddie Hapgood ringing in their ears: "They think this game is won," he told them. "Well, let's get out there and show them it damned well isn't!"

It wasn't just the borrowed shirts that made England look a different side in that second half. Hapgood, Morris and Cullis were breaking down attack after attack by the Scots with tough tackles; Mercer (easily the man of the match) and Willingham were prompting and encouraging the forwards, sending pass after pass through to Hall, Goulden and Lawton; Beasley and particularly Matthews were troubling the Scottish defence with their pace and trickery. Gradually, it was the home team that began to look the shaky side.

With 25 minutes of the match remaining and the rain still beating down Stan Cullis broke up a Scottish attack, brought the ball out of defence and passed wide to Len Goulden, who hit a low first-time cross towards Lawton. Right back Jimmy Carabine raced to cut out the cross but Tommy beat him, turned and controlled the ball in one movement then played a perfect pass for the consequently unmarked outside left Beasley to run onto and smash a shot past Dawson from 12 yards. A dream goal on his England debut for the Huddersfield winger. Scotland 1 England 1.

And all to play for in the last quarter. The minutes ticked away. Chances came and went for both sides but, inevitably in the strong wind and driving rain, players tired and both sets of defenders were settling for safe kicks into touch rather than passes which might go astray on the treacherous wet surface and set up the opposition for a late winner. A draw looked certain.

But Stanley Matthews had other ideas. With just 70 seconds of the game left, Matthews picked up a loose ball and set off on one of his bewildering mazy runs. He swept past a lunging tackle from left half McNab and with left back George Cummings in hot pursuit, headed for the corner flag. There, Matthews stopped and impudently waited while Cummings got into position to block him. Then he slipped the ball through Cummings's legs, jinked past him and looked up to see Tommy Lawton powering through the mud in the middle with Goulden and Mercer pounding up in support.

Matthews's high cross was exquisite in its timing. Tommy rose majestically, the sinews in his neck bulging as he strained to reach the full height of the ball. Hanging in mid-air, the centre forward shouted, "Get in there!" Then he headed the ball so powerfully that it flew into the back of the net in a flash, sending thousands of rain drops cascading down onto the Hampden turf as if in surrender. It was a sensational goal! 2-1 to England.

Tommy dashed over to Stan Matthews who was simply standing, as if waiting for a bus. Tommy picked the winger up in a huge bear hug and lifted him off his feet, joking as he did so, "For God's sake, man I'm six foot tall, not six foot three!" The enigmatic Matthews blew on his fingers, a habit he frequently displayed (no one knew why) and replied nonchalantly, "Oh, all right. I'll put that right next time."

Now the entire England team, including goalkeeper Woodley, surrounded the scorer and creator of this wonder goal, dancing like mad mudlarks and hugging each other in delight. One commentator described deliriously happy captain Eddie Hapgood as doing "some crazy Maori war dance!"

Hapgood and his men were so abandoned in their celebrations they didn't hear the final whistle blow to end the game. The Scottish players did, though. One by one they slumped to the ground where they sat on the drenched turf, heads held in stunned disbelief, tears flowing. Of the Hampden Roar there was no sound.

For England, the Hampden bogey had been laid to rest at last . . . by Tommy Lawton, aged 19. England's beaming 30-year-old captain said after the match, "I've played all these years and this is the win I've longed for. I could jump over the moon!"

Scotland's right half Bill Shankly later delivered an eloquent account of the fantastic goal that had ended 12 years of Scottish home rule over the Auld Enemy and deprived his country of the Home International Championship:

I sensed the danger as Matthews took on George Cummings by the corner flag and I positioned myself to tackle him if necessary but the ball was lifted over and beyond me, arrowed at Lawton's forehead. I heard him shout "Get in there!" The ball went home like a bullet and the swish and ripple of the soaking net made a sound that frightened me. 'Wuishhh' it went, 'wuishhh', while 150,000 Scotsmen gasped in horror. It was like a knife going through my heart. I turned and saw Lawton with such a look on his face. I could have shot him!

The English press was rightfully fulsome in universal praise of England's brave, battling heroes.

George Allison of the *Daily Express* wrote, "It is a very long time since I saw an England side play with such united enthusiasm. They clustered around each other as they ran wet, dirty and bedraggled from the scene of a great triumph."

Jack Harkness of the *Sunday Post* wrote that England had produced its best team since the Great War and, with tongue firmly in cheek, evoked the heated political debate over international fears of another looming conflict by concluding, "Now I know why Mr Chamberlain told Hitler he could have Austria, Rhineland, Czechoslovakia and perhaps his colonies – almost anything except Stan Matthews."

All of the papers published a quote, which their reporters had waited patiently in the pouring rain to get, from the scorer of England's winning wonder goal. He told them, "I shall remember that goal when I am 70, when the name of Lawton is just another entry in the record books of this great game of ours."

That was a carefully considered comment. Off the field, as well as so dramatically on it, Tommy Lawton had come of age.

"Football's buggered!"

Chapter Five

MR HITLER INTERVENES

There were other stories in those papers reporting England's 1939 Hampden triumph, stories proving that sport was too tied up with politics for the liking of many and that the bellicose belligerence and transparent territorial ambitions of Adolf Hitler continued to cause great concern across Europe.

It was reported that the French FA had cancelled France's match against Germany at the behest of its Ministry of the Interior and that England's game with Italy, scheduled for Milan in May was likely to be the next one called off.

Tommy Lawton had a special interest in such stories. He had been selected for England's tour of Italy, Yugoslavia and Romania for three weeks in May.

After much discussion and diplomatic negotiation with the Foreign Office the FA was eventually given the all-clear to go ahead with the trip, but it had been touch and go before a final agreement that, given the universal appeal of football, the English party could actually fulfil a useful ambassadorial role in this time of international tension.

The merry band of footballers, under the charge of Arsenal trainer Tom Whittaker, who boarded the Balkans Express at Victoria Station bound for Dover were more interested in the games they were to play and the sights they were to see than the crisis which was mounting in Europe. Concern on that front was left to Stanley Rous, the FA Secretary, who carried the heavy burden of diplomatic duty and responsibility for conduct on the tour. This was no easy task. The voices which had been raised against the wisdom of making this tour had been strident: many believed it was wrong to go and that the safety of the players was being compromised. Stanley Rous was passionate in his belief that sport, especially football, could build bridges over troubled waters and that much good could come from the trip. Now he had to test that belief in circumstances that were, at best, fraught with risk. Rous had to smooth the way; to make sure that the touring party did not get into trouble, that nobody did or said the wrong thing.

The footballers at the centre of it all chatted happily away on the Channel crossing to Calais, oblivious to the enormous pressure Rous was under and for Tommy Lawton the biggest concern at this stage of the adventure was that the crossing would be a smooth one, for while his football career had developed brilliantly since he last went to sea his aptitude for sailing had not!

When the train taking the England party to Italy entered the border station of Stresa there was a prolonged delay for a customs check and for the first time since they left London, a vague sense of foreboding filled the carriages in which they sat. The England players exchanged nervous glances as, in dry-throated silence, they watched armed men in imposing uniforms approaching them and suddenly the reasons for the political disquiet which had preceded this tour became apparent.

Italy was a disturbing destination. Ten years earlier, it had become a one-party country, suppressing political opponents and its expansionist conduct under fascist dictator Benito Mussolini was causing almost as much international concern as that of Hitler. In 1935, Italy, which already controlled Eritrea and Somalia, occupied neighbouring Ethiopia, having failed at several attempts to colonise it. The League of Nations condemned Italy's aggression and imposed trade sanctions, including an arms embargo. Some political leaders in Britain and France opposed sanctions, fearing that it might persuade Mussolini to form an alliance with Hitler, who was known to admire the Italian leader.

Since then, Germany and Italy had both presented an escalating fascist threat to the rest of Europe. Mussolini's regime imposed racial purity laws similar to Germany's in 1938 and after Hitler annexed Austria and moved against Czechoslovakia, without previously consulting with Mussolini in advance, the Italian dictator, not to be outdone, decided to proceed with his own annexation of Albania.

Just days before the England team's triumph at Hampden Park, Mussolini's troops invaded Albania, shelling its towns and despite some brave resistance the Albanians soon fell to the Italians' vastly superior force. Albania's King Zog, Queen Géraldine Apponyi and their infant son fled in exile to Greece (and eventually to London) and the Italians set up a fascist government.

Such were the ruthless tendencies of the military regime governing the country to which the FA had sent its footballers, and for those lads Stresa this day was a far cry from the nonchalance and cosy ambience of an English railway station! It was with considerable trepidation that they waited quietly and deferentially for customs clearance. Not even the normally wise-cracking Joe Mercer had anything to say. Suddenly, the tense silence of the atmosphere was shattered by the clatter of advancing footsteps and the noise of agitated foreign voices, distant at first, then closer and closer, louder and louder, until it was a raucous racket. The players looked anxiously at each other. Joe Mercer broke the chilled silence – not with a jovial quip, this time, but with a nervous question: "What the hell is that?"

Then the doors of the train flew open and into the carriages came dozens of Italian civilians, all armed . . . with enormous bouquets of flowers! In no time, those carriages, filled with the fabulous fragrance of all manner of exotic blooms, began to resemble the crammed marquees of some fantastic flower show, the previous drab greyness of the surroundings now transformed into a glorious Technicolor extravaganza. "Benvenuto! Benvenuto!" the excited Italians shouted again and again, shaking the players' hands warmly and vigorously and slapping them on their backs.

"They are saying welcome," one of the beaming flower bearers explained. "You are most very welcome to our country!" "He speaks English!" exclaimed Ken Willingham, as if such an accomplishment was the eighth wonder of the world. "Of course he does," said Joe Mercer (comic inclinations restored to normal service). "He runs an ice cream parlour in Blackpool . . . you'll know 'im, Tommy!" Even worse jokes followed – a sure sign of the relief they were all feeling.

That was to be just the start of an extraordinary welcome from the Italian people. At each wayside stop on the journey between Stresa and Milan dozens more had gathered, including beautiful girls waiting to present pretty posies and sprays of carnations to the England players, who were now beginning to feel like visiting royalty.

At Milan, they were overwhelmed to find that a welcoming crowd of several thousand had gathered and the England party had to fight their way through it, taking more than half an hour to complete what would normally have been a very brief walk from the station to their hotel in Piazza Duca D'Aosta. As they struggled to find a path through the masses of cheering Italians, Joe Mercer shouted to Tommy: "These all friends of yours, Tommy?" "I can't believe it," Tommy shouted back. "I feel like a film star!" To which Mercer replied, "Wait till you get to your room; they've probably provided one for you!"

Settled, at last, into their hotel, the players sat in the bar and reflected, over a much needed drink, on the complete surprise, scale and genuine warmth of this incredible reception and discussed the bizarre contradiction of the hero worship with which they'd been greeted with the warlike intention of Italy to march with Adolf Hitler's forces in a crusade for "European peace and justice" as Mussolini had expressed to a worried world that very week. "Just goes to show," they agreed, "that politicians and people don't always think alike!"

The warmth of the welcome was matched by the weather when the tour party arrived to beautiful blue Italian skies and brilliant hot sunshine. They loved that and nobody more so than Tommy, who thought it just a little more balmy than Blackpool! But when thoughts turned to the business in hand, of taking on World Cup holders Italy in the newly opened San Siro stadium, they were less pleased about the climate, dreading a bone-dry, sun-baked pitch. They need not have concerned themselves with that. The night before and the day of the match brought a heavy downpour of rain, creating comfortably familiar conditions for the English.

As they took the field in front of a crowd of 70,000, Tommy was taken aback by the sight of high wire fences separating that huge crowd from the pitch. He'd seen nothing like this in his life. In England there was no need for such security; the only weapon the average English supporter took to a match was heavy sarcasm fired from a sharp tongue and when fans invaded the pitch it was only for good-natured celebration. Italy was different. Bottles and other deadly missiles were frequently used to record disagreement with referees' decisions and to express dissatisfaction with the perceived misdemeanours of opposing players; when pitches were invaded, here, it was with serious intent to inflict grievous bodily harm upon the hapless recipients of the crowd's discontent.

The chilling presence of those high fences gave the 70,000 people behind them an aura of mass menace which was alien in the extreme to the lads from England, as were the frightening ranks of armed Italian police. British bobbies at football matches were friendly-looking chaps in comforting helmets. When they weren't intently watching the game with everybody else they were called into service for the convenience of the crowd, not for combat and the numbers deployed, unarmed of course, were a tiny fraction of the masses of Carabinieri who, wielding their machine guns with a flourish which made them appear disturbingly trigger happy, were lined along every inch of the touchlines in Milan.

"Blimey, has war started already?" thought Tommy, as he looked nervously at the massed machine guns while sensing that the 70,000 caged Italians gathered here were not likely to be repeating the warmth of the greeting the English players had enjoyed on their arrival in this bewildering country.

Before the kick-off, the players lined up for the national anthems in the normal manner then had to perform a ritual which they knew would cause huge offence back home. They had been instructed to give the raised-arm fascist salute to the representatives of dictator Mussolini's regime, including his son Bruno, sitting up in the royal box. A year earlier, the England team had been ordered to give the same salute to Hitler's Nazis before they played Germany in Berlin and when pictures of that reached Britain, the FA officials' decision to capitulate to the Germans' demand had been vehemently condemned.

Six of the team who had to perform that sickening gesture in Germany (Eddie Hapgood, Vic Woodley, Stan Matthews, Frank Broome, Len Goulden and Ken Willingham) were on this tour. They and the rest of the players now ordered by FA officials to give the Mussolini salute, were informed in no uncertain terms that they had no choice in the matter. The tense situation in Europe was such that the slightest incident could set the whole thing off, they were told.

So teenager Tommy Lawton was one of 11 English footballers who stood to rigid attention in the pouring rain inside that massive, hostile foreign arena, surrounded by high wire fences, massed ranks of heavily armed police and 70,000 fanatical Italians and raised their arms in a fascist salute, turning in military precision until they had done it to all four corners of the stadium. At home, the British public later reacted with anger and disgust.

Just as there was no warm welcome from the Italian crowd, Italy's players gave the visitors a torrid time on the pitch. Right from the kick-off they had to contend with illegal pushing, shoving, shirt-tugging, elbowing and ankle tapping. Fouls galore were going unpunished by the referee, a German (what a surprise!) by the name of Dr Bauwens.

The Italians had no need to descend to the rough stuff. They fielded ten of the side that had won the World Cup, for the second consecutive time, less than a year earlier. This was a very good team indeed, considered, with a great deal of justification and proof, to be the best in the world.

England, who disdainfully shunned the World Cup, reckoned they were the best because . . . well, because they were England! They played eight of the team that had triumphed at Hampden Park.

England knew what to expect and had been warned not to respond to provocation; to be, out of diplomatic necessity, on their very best behaviour.

No one in that white shirt was being bashed and battered more than Tommy Lawton. He was up against centre half Mario Andreolo, his opponent in the FIFA representative game in London, a man of might and muscle who took no prisoners and was well equipped, Tommy thought, for Mussolini's mission!

Andreolo was shadowing the centre forward everywhere he went, bumping and pushing him every time they competed for a ball. But he was outdone by the same lethal Matthews–Lawton combination that had destroyed Scotland. Matthews's perfect lofted cross into the Italian penalty area hung invitingly in the air for Tommy to leap and direct his header across Andreolo into the far corner of the net. As he ran, without celebration, back to the centre circle, his goal greeted with absolute silence, Tommy wondered briefly if, while Bill Shankly had felt like shooting him at Hampden, Andreolo might actually do so!

The tension of the hostile atmosphere in the San Siro stadium was relieved slightly when Italy's centre forward Silvio Piola, who had scored twice in the World Cup final, hit a brilliant shot past Vic Woodley to equalise just before half-time.

During the interval, the England players, confident that they had the beating of the world champions, were encouraged to go out and do so by Eddie Hapgood, while stressing again how vital it was that they did not respond to the provocation that surely awaited them in the second half.

Hapgood's warning was timely. Soon after the break, Italy went ahead with a 'goal' which, had England reacted in the manner it deserved, would have caused a riot. Piola darted in brilliantly to meet a cross from the left but, seeing the ball agonisingly out of reach, punched it into the net. That was bad enough, but, following through, he also whacked fullback George Male ferociously in the eye, flattening him in the process. No one in the ground thought it was a goal. Except Dr Bauwens!

After he'd given it, the England players, though inwardly seething, stayed quietly where they stood while Eddie Hapgood alone went over to protest, calmly, to the referee and to invite him, politely, to consult his linesman about the legitimacy of this 'goal'. The referee, accompanied courteously by the England captain, walked over and did so but to the astonishment of everyone in the stadium, the linesmen declared the 'goal' legal and the crowd greeted the desperately dubious decision with ecstasy, shouting "Viva Göring; viva Ribbentrop."

This was an immense test for the diplomatic skills of Stanley Rous and the other FA officials sitting in the royal box and having to accept such blatant cheating while being mercilessly mocked by 70,000 Italians, but there was considerable consolation for them to see that Crown Prince Umberto (evidently untainted by the worst manifestations of Mussolini's Italy) was absolutely furious that the 'goal' had been allowed and, jumping up and down with incandescent rage, had to be restrained by Mr Rous from storming onto the pitch to order that it be annulled by royal decree! It was yet another example, of so many witnessed by the England party on this trip, of the crazy contradictions of Italy.

Down on the field of play, the England players heeded the warning they had been given ("You must behave like gentlemen at all times, in all circumstances") and simply got on with the game, with just ten men – George Male having been concussed by Piola's deliberately flying fist. It wasn't too long before justice, at least so far as the score was concerned, was restored. Matthews delivered another of his immaculate crosses and this time Willie Hall got on the end of it.

The game finished a 2-2 draw, following which the commendable English restraint was retained for the after-match dinner, despite the players being subjected to the additional, if this time unintended, provocation of being told by some of the Italians that they were paid £30 a match, nearly four times the weekly wage of a professional in England. Later, the FA officials formally thanked the players for their good conduct and professionalism, telling them it was to be admired and applauded, but the subject of the huge pay discrepancy did not come up.

The touring party left Milan for a day of sightseeing in Venice, where the delights of this romantic city soon removed the vexatious aftermath of events in the San Siro. For Tommy Lawton, visiting Venice was the most captivating and enthralling experience of his young life and how he wished that his family, especially his mam and grandfather, could have been there with him to share in it.

In the evening, the players were taken by gondola to an island casino, some way from the centre of the city. They were stunned by the extreme luxury of this extraordinary establishment and stood transfixed in the lavishly decorated main gambling room watching exquisitely attired punters at the roulette wheel.

Their attention was drawn to an attractive, beautifully dressed girl nonchalantly flipping stacks of blue and white chips from the pile at her right elbow. Tommy was particularly absorbed in the compelling ritual and felt drawn like a moth to the flame of this fascinating female. "Ey oop, lads," he whispered to his teammates, "those chips are in Everton colours. That's got to be an omen. We can break the bank 'ere!" The coincidence of chips in Tommy's team colours, the lure of the roulette wheel and the allure of the pretty girl playing it with such aplomb, not to mention the heady effects of the fine Italian wine consumed over dinner, were an irresistible combination.

"Right," said Tommy, "let's have a whip round for a kitty." All the lads emptied their pockets of loose change into Tommy's cupped hands and he carried the bounty confidently over to the cashier. The immaculate white-suited cashier looked down his nose as Tommy's cash cascaded onto his highly polished desktop. "Give us enough chips to cover this," said Tommy, with the assured air of a man about to risk thousands of pounds on the spin of the wheel. The cashier, nose aloft, pushed the coins away from him as if he was removing a cat's indiscretion from a carpet and with affected disdain he informed the young Englishman: "Sir, there is not enough here for one."

Somewhat less boldly than the manner in which he had approached the cashier's desk, Tommy made as discreet a retreat as the acutely embarrassing circumstances allowed back to where he'd left the eager England players to explain, red-faced, that they were going to need another whip round. They mustered enough to buy five chips, with which Tommy, brash confidence restored, strode to the roulette table, stood next to the pretty girl, gave her a nudge and a cheeky wink, told her "Just watch me, love" and began to play for the fortune he was convinced he was about to win. Alas, the kitty vanished in a flash and the England lads were left to watch in envy as the girl continued to play. Their ill-luck then appeared to transfer to her and they gazed in awe as her huge pile of chips became smaller and smaller until, without a trace of emotion, she had lost them all and, smiling gracefully, she retired from the table. Such style! They had all fallen instantly in love with this cool, dignified beauty.

Later, they discovered why this girl of their dreams could afford to lose all that money. She was the fabulously wealthy Woolworth's heiress Betty Hutton. For the rest of the tour, the England centre forward acquired a new nickname, having to endure the frequent taunt of: "Hey Betty. How are your lucky colours doing?"

The next leg of the trip for the England party was across the border to Yugoslavia where they were to play the host country in Belgrade. Again, they were met by the ominous sight of ubiquitous armed troops but, unlike the Italians, this lot looked poor and rather pathetic, wearing shabby uniforms and carrying obviously old-fashioned guns. Again, they were overwhelmed and deeply moved by the scale and warmth of the unexpected welcome they received, many thousands of people crowding the railway station to greet them when their train pulled in . . . at 1:30 in the morning!

The players were invited to spend the next afternoon at the official residence of the British ambassador where they were delighted to be served with a "proper, decent" cup of tea. Seeing the enjoyment the lads got from their cuppa Lady Campbell, the ambassador's wife, very thoughtfully gave them a gift of a pound of tea so that they could enjoy the occasional brew on the rest of the tour. Eddie Hapgood, custodian of this much-prized bounty, gave the precious parcel to the head waiter at their hotel, asking him to make "a real cup of tea" for them. The waiter duly obliged . . . by putting the whole pound of tea into one pot!

There were three days until the match, providing the opportunity for more sightseeing and while the breathtaking beauty of the scenery in Yugoslavia was a match for Italy, there was none of the style and opulence they had enjoyed in Milan.

Some of the players, including Tommy, decided to take up the offer of the restorative delights of a Turkish bath, presented to them by a pushy guide in Belgrade. The finest and most modern Turkish bath, he had promised – and just around the corner. Following the guide around the corner they were led to a tin bath, about ten yards in length, out in the open and occupied by fat old men who appeared to be having their annual wash and brush up. As the guide stood proudly at their side, Frank Broome whispered in Tommy's ear, "I'm not getting in there. It's bloody filthy!" "Yeah," replied Tommy, "and just look at the state of those old fellas!"

The problem was how to extricate themselves from this predicament without offending the guide, who was clearly a bit touchy. A long debate ensued, with Tommy and the rest of the lads trying to sound respectfully polite while determined to avoid the perils of the bath, before they felt able to depart the scene.

Another guide told the players that he was Maltese, which was doubtful; that his name was Joe Palooka, which was even more doubtful; and that he was *the* most expert guide in the whole city. Then he set out to prove that claim by escorting them on a walking tour which was so long and arduous that, when it finally ended hours later, it left even these fit young men exhausted. Before taking his leave of them, Joe Palooka offered the players certain services provided by some ladies of his acquaintance – services which, even if they had been reckless enough to accept, they were far too tired to receive. "My mam warned me about people like him," said Tommy. "I reckon he was hired by the Yugoslavian FA!" said Joe Mercer.

Five days after the match in Milan, England got back down to the real purpose of the tour, this time playing a very accomplished Yugoslavian team in front of a fiercely partisan crowd on a hard, parched surface in extreme heat.

The hosts, playing fast, flowing football with the ball kept almost entirely on the ground, were too good for England and their 2-1 victory didn't really do justice to the supremacy they enjoyed over their visitors, who struggled in the heat.

These had been difficult conditions for the English, but there was little sympathy from the powers that be on the tour. This was supposed to be the strongest England team ever to leave its shores and in two games so far they had drawn one and lost one. This was simply not good enough. Captain Eddie Hapgood called the team together for a serious pep talk. Five days later they were to play Romania, the third country on the tour, in Bucharest and nothing but a win would be acceptable. Hapgood could be a strict disciplinarian when required and clearly he had been instructed to read his team the riot act. The brainstorming session analysing 'weaknesses' in the previous two games lasted more than two hours.

Romania provided yet more fascinating, historical sightseeing and Tommy was able to reflect on how much he had learned, as well as enjoyed, on this trip. Hapgood's pep talk had not been wasted and faces were duly saved with a fairly comfortable 2-0 win in Bucharest, the goals coming from Len Goulden and Charlton Athletic's Don Welsh.

Meanwhile, England's League champions, Everton, were heading for Holland to play an exhibition match in Amsterdam. In order not to disappoint the hosts, it had been decided that Everton's two England international stars, Lawton and Mercer, would travel from Romania to Holland to join up with their clubmates and play in the match.

So, after leaving Romania with the touring party they bade farewell to their England colleagues in Basle and travelled from there to Amsterdam. This incredible journey from Bucharest to Amsterdam took the pair 15 minutes short of 54 hours. They had left Bucharest at 11:15 on Thursday morning, reaching Budapest in Hungary by 7:15 am on Friday; after a two-hour stop to be greeted officially by Hungarian FA officials they travelled on through Hungary and Austria, reaching Basle, on the borders of France and Switzerland at 3 am on Saturday; after just two hours' rest, they then travelled on to Amsterdam, reaching their Dutch destination at five o'clock on Saturday evening, only an hour and a half before kick-off for the match in which they were due to play!

Tommy was willing to play, but it was decided that the lad was simply too exhausted. The indefatigable Joe Mercer, on the other hand, *was* deemed fit to play. Tommy took a seat in the stand but saw little of the match. He fell asleep, so he didn't see his fellow travelling companion produce another all-action man-of-the-match performance. "You're not human!" Tommy told Joe later, "What's the secret?" "Eat slowly and avoid fast women!" said Mercer.

Lawton and Mercer joined their Everton teammates for the start of the 1939/40 season full of excited anticipation for another successful campaign. This Everton team, so young in average age, could only get better and their enthusiasm was shared by a full house which gathered at Goodison Park for the first match. Brentford were the opponents and a good, evenly contested game ended in a 1-1 draw with Tommy Lawton getting Everton's goal. Next came Aston Villa at Villa Park. Everton won 2-0, with goals from Tommy Lawton and Stan Bentham. On Saturday 2nd September 1939, Everton went to Ewood Park, Blackburn, where they drew 2-2 with Rovers, both Everton goals coming from Tommy Lawton.

It was to be the last game played in the Football League until 1946.

With war against Germany now looking immediately imminent, the Blackburn match had been preceded by orders to evacuate children from Britain's big cities and when the Everton team made the short journey to and from Blackburn it had been against a chilling backdrop of roads jammed by frantic traffic, most of it military. All around, the preparations for war were proceeding apace. These had been going on – the digging of trenches, the installation of tank traps, the issue of gas masks – for several months before but they had been accepted by the stoic people of Britain as 'just in case' measures. This day it was different. This day it was for real.

Players and supporters alike had tried to put the worries of war behind them for that match but, in truth, there was little appetite for it. The German invasion of Poland had begun. Now, even sublime optimists were fearing the worst.

On Sunday 3rd September 1939, the Everton players reported, as instructed, to Goodison Park but they didn't bother with the usual routine of changing into their training kit. Instead, they stayed in their Sunday best suits and gathered around the wireless in the dressing room.

At 11:15 am, Prime Minister Neville Chamberlain, his voice choking with emotion, delivered his grave broadcast to the nation. The Everton players sat in line on their bench, gas masks on their knees, arms around each other's shoulders to hear the Prime Minister announce:

This morning the British ambassador in Berlin handed the German government a final note saying that unless we heard from them by 11 o'clock that they were prepared at once to withdraw their troops from Poland, a state of war would exist between us. I have to tell you now that no such undertaking has been received and that, consequently, this country is at war with Germany.

As the Prime Minister finished his speech, the shrill wail of air-raid sirens reverberated around Goodison Park and the players rushed outside onto the pitch to see if German planes were coming.

One of the training staff ran outside after them shouting, "Get back in! Get back in! The boss says you've got to get back in!"

The players obeyed the frantic instruction and had dashed back into the dressing room when Joe Mercer challenged the wisdom of the boss's orders: "Hold on, lads. If they're going to drop bombs on us, how can it be any safer in here?"

Typically, Joe had broken the tension. One by one, the players looked at each other and started to laugh. But this was nervous, hollow laughter. They all knew that, really, there was nothing to laugh about now. They sank back into their places on the bench, staring at the floor and a grim silence descended, to be broken by a voice which spoke the truth none of them wanted to hear: "Well, football's buggered now."

Football was 'buggered'. But that was the very least of the country's concerns. It was at war with Germany for the second time in a generation. It was little over 20 years since the last war ended, a war in which millions of lives had been lost. People were going to die again, many thousands of them. Possibly, if not probably, your own loved ones would be among the dead. The country might fall under the march of Hitler's armies and what unspeakable horrors would follow if everyone was forced to live under fascist oppression?

Football? How could that matter any more?

Young as he was, Tommy Lawton grasped the harsh reality of this quickly and absolutely. That night he sat silently at home, deep in thought. His grandfather – now a weak, sick man – and his mother knew this was a time for the lad to be left alone. Nothing they could say could possibly make things any better for him.

He was convinced that his football career, which had been his dream, his life, his all, was over. This bore a huge, painful hole into his heart and soul but at the same time he knew that to dwell on that, to feel sorry for himself at a time like this, was selfish and stupid. He cursed Hitler for taking away all he had worked so hard to achieve and the cruel injustice of it all made him weep but he knew he had to choke back those tears and behave like a man. If it was all to end now, at least he had those wonderful achievements to comfort him. He had a Football League championship medal, won by scoring all those goals for one of Britain's biggest and best football clubs; he was England's centre forward; all over the country football fans idolised, admired and respected him; he had thrilled and entertained hundreds of thousands of people who shared his love of this great game; kids kicking balls in the street wanted to be Tommy Lawton, just as when he was a boy he had wanted to be Dixie Dean. Football had taken him to places most people could only ever dream of seeing – to Italy, Romania, Yugoslavia, Holland, Denmark. He had seen so much, experienced so much, learned so much; he'd played in front of royalty, sat at lavish banquets with the rich and famous. Not bad for a poor kid from the back streets of Bolton, a thought which brought him to the achievement that meant more than anything to him: his football had made a much better life for the caring family who had taken him to their hearts and given him so much love. Maybe, just maybe, there was a chance that this crazy world would one day be restored to sanity and football would matter again. But if not, nobody could ever take away the glorious memories of five fantastic years.

Now, Tommy had to prepare himself for a different calling. He was a very fit, strong young man. His country would need him. He'd played for England; now, he would fight for England; now, if he had to, he would die for England.

As the people of Britain prepared fearfully for the worst ravages of war, young Tommy Lawton went calmly to bed, strangely contented and ready to do his bit.

Among those war preparations was a ban on the assembly of crowds. The FA and the Football League immediately cancelled the 1939/40 season and suspended all the players' contracts. The Everton directors decided to pay every one of their players their accrued share of benefit. This was a warm-hearted act. They didn't have to do it. In fact, only a handful of football clubs did. Some of the Goodison playing staff were given as much as £650. Tommy, less than two years an Everton player, got £300. While he picked up that welcome sum, he learned that he was losing the money which was to have come from contracts he had recently signed for advertising porridge oats and shaving soap. The contracts were simply cancelled, without compensation

These events served chillingly to confirm that football was, indeed, 'buggered'; that Tommy's career was finished; that all his prospects of fame and fortune, which had been set so fair, were now well and truly shattered. Again, he cursed Hitler and all his evil works. But, again, he resolved not to indulge in self-pity and comforted himself with the knowledge that in the frightening, life-changing aftermath of the outbreak of war, there were many thousands of British people who were going to be a bloody sight worse off than him.

Gradually, it dawned on Britain that the panic which followed Mr Chamberlain's announcement on 3rd September had been unnecessary; that there was to be no immediate German invasion, no instant fighting in the streets of our towns and cities. Rather, this was going to be a long haul and a semblance of normal life could be restored. Indeed, the government concluded, given that the nation's morale was going to be a crucial weapon in this war, the more normal its life the better.

And what could be more normal than continuing to enjoy football matches between top players? On 14th September it was announced that while normal League competitions could not possibly be retained, games could be played on a different basis. The ban on assemblies at football grounds was relaxed and it was decreed that regional matches could be played between clubs within a 50-mile radius of each other. Regional competitions were set up. Crowds were restricted initially to 8,000 and then to 15,000. Admission for the wartime matches was set at a maximum of £1 10s ('30 bob') which was also what players were to be paid for appearing.

Everton wasted no time in using the new rules and on 16th September, Tommy Lawton was scoring goals again as they beat Blackpool 2-1 away. They went on to play against Preston, Liverpool and Burnley before the more formalised regional competitions began on 21st October. With so many players being called up for military service, these games could never replicate the Football League proper. With no contracts, players who were available could and would make 'guest' appearances for other clubs and the matches had nothing like the tribal atmosphere and excitement of the Football League, but they were games nonetheless, played to the same high standard of quality football and they were to provide an escape from the misery of life in wartime.

There were even international games and in November 1939, Tommy, now aged 20, played in the first of these, scoring in a 3-2 win for England over Wales at Wrexham. These matches were regarded as semi-official and the FA chose, pedantically, some thought, not to award full caps to those selected even though they were played to the same high standard and eventually attracted as many spectators as they had in peace time.

In December, he was on target again as England beat Scotland at Newcastle. He then played three games for Leicester City before returning to Everton and smashing four goals past Tranmere Rovers in a Christmas fixture. Tommy was enjoying these games, not least because on that awful morning of 3rd September he and his mates had believed they would not play football at any level while Britain was at war, but this could not last because his own call-up was imminent.

The break from the demands of the Football League had provided time for Tommy to renew and strengthen his friendship with Frank Swift. Frank was also waiting in anticipation of his call-up and in the meantime, he had joined the police force, with singular lack of success. With what he considered to be hopelessly inadequate instruction, he had been sent out on traffic-control duty in Manchester and made such a hash of it that confused drivers of cars, vans, buses and lorries got completely stuck in a dreadful snarl-up which was entirely of Big Swifty's own making. Tommy laughed at his pal's colourful account of the fearful jumble caused by the long, waving arms which were used to stopping footballs, not traffic. "So what did you do about it?" he asked. "I just walked away and left 'em to it!" said the genial giant.

By coincidence, Frank and Tommy both got their call-up papers on the same day and both were ordered to report for duty with the British Army in Aldershot on the same day in January 1940. The fact that these firm friends could make the journey down south and into the unknown together lessened the tension of the 13-hour train ride considerably but to say that neither was looking forward to what lay ahead was a huge understatement. Both cheered up, however, when they were told that they were being posted to a 'footballers' battalion' in the Army Physical Training Corps. Tommy's England international comrades Joe Mercer and Don Welsh were already in this battalion, as was Bob Pryde, the Blackburn Rovers centre half, against whom he'd played in that last match before war was declared.

When he walked into the depot at Aldershot, Tommy heard a shout in his direction: "Excuse me. Excuse me. Over here!" The approach was from an Army officer, a captain, and Tommy dutifully obliged.

"You're Tommy Lawton, aren't you?" the officer enquired.

"Yes. Yes, I am."

"I saw you play for England and I've seen you play for Everton. You are a brilliant footballer, It's such a privilege to meet you," said the captain, smiling broadly and shaking Tommy's hand vigorously.

"Likewise, I'm sure," replied Tommy, somewhat taken aback by the effuse welcome.

"I say," said the captain, "would you think me frightfully rude if I asked you for your autograph?"

"Of course not," said Tommy, "pleased to oblige." He signed the piece of paper proffered by the officer, who thanked him several times before turning and marching away.

"GET IN THERE!"

"That was nice," thought Tommy. "If all the officers are as friendly as that, me and the Army are going to get along just fine." Big Swifty had watched this encounter with great amusement and he ribbed Tommy: "There must be something about you, mate. He didn't ask for my autograph!" Tommy retorted, "That's because he only remembers you as that berk who buggered up the traffic in Manchester!" Then, laughing loudly, the pals entered the point of no return to be formally enlisted and kitted out as British soldiers.

Tommy Lawton, fashionably attired international football star, emerged from this process as 1548031 Private Lawton T, clad in rough, thick khaki uniform and clattering along in huge heavy boots. With a similarly de-individualised Big Swifty and several other raw recruits he was marched straight to the parade square where he was met by a monstrous pop-eyed sergeant major and the captain who had earlier given him such a hero's welcome to Aldershot.

"How do I look in my uniform?" Tommy asked his new-found 'friend' the officer. "You, there! SHUT UP!" bellowed the sergeant major and the captain told Private Lawton T in no uncertain terms, "When you meet an officer, the first thing you do is salute him. Got it?" Standing to attention in the row behind and sticking out like a huge sore thumb, Big Swifty was trying desperately hard to suppress a laugh. Tommy didn't have to turn around to know his pal was doing precisely that!

Tommy, Frank and the rest of the new recruits were scheduled for a seven-week course of drills, gym work and general toughening up. They despised it. They particularly hated the rigid discipline, the interminable parade-ground drill, the demeaning floor scrubbing and obsessive polishing of anything and everything that wasn't moving. Their treatment was humiliating, they thought. And not just because they were football stars. They reckoned this institutionalised bullying and harassment was dehumanising for any man, no matter what his civilian trade.

For the recruits who had come to those Aldershot barracks from 'ordinary' life, the news revealed by one of the sergeants, that "that Tommy Lawton is coming 'ere" spread around the camp like wildfire. They were all in awe of the world-famous new arrival and the gossip was rife . . .

"'Ave you seen 'im yet?"

"Yes. He's a big lad."

"But he looks so young."

"Like a bleedin' choirboy!"

"'Ave you seen his wristwatch?"

"Yeah. It's a bleedin Smith's!"

"You don't see many of those about."

130

"They cost a flippin' fortune!"

"'E's a good-looking lad, ain't 'e?"

"Like a bleedin' film star!"

"And so smart."

"'E's always polishing 'is boots."

"Yeah. More than 'e 'as to. Wonder why."

"Nice lad, though. Very friendly."

"'E ain't full of 'imself."

"Not at all. 'E's just a normal bloke."

Like all the 'normal blokes' at Aldershot, Tommy was struggling to come to terms with his new life but, for him, respite came when he was detailed to report to London to join the British Army football side bound for France to play three games against the French Army in order to entertain the lads of the British Expeditionary Force. When he joined the party, he saw that there were 17 more ex-professional players, including Andy Beattie (Preston), Matt Busby (Liverpool), Denis Compton (Arsenal), Stan Cullis (Wolves), Joe Fagan (Liverpool) and Don Welsh (Charlton). It felt great to be among First Division footballers again but the best morale boost of all for Tommy was to discover that two of the Everton players, Joe Mercer and Billy Cook, were also in the squad. The three Blues hugged each other, with a genuine intensity, as if they had been parted for years.

There was only one downside of this joyous occasion for Tommy: the party was to sail from Dover, so more excruciating seasickness awaited him. On the train from Victoria, he sat with another notoriously bad sailor, Matt Busby, and they were soon joined by another with the same affliction, Stan Cullis. The latter had some good news for his fellow sufferers: "Now then, lads," he said as he rooted deep into the breast pocket of his uniform, "I have been able to obtain for us a seasickness remedy which I am assured positively cannot fail. Expensive, mind. It's cost a guinea for just three tablets. But they work, so it'll be worth it, don't you think?" Tommy and Matt concurred enthusiastically: "If they're that good, they're worth a guinea each!"

The sea-legless trio waited until they got on board before swallowing the pills and then settled down in a quiet corner below deck to play cards. After several games had passed, their stomachs were calm and impeccably well behaved, their apprehension had decreased and their spirits had risen accordingly:

"Stan, you're a life saver!" chortled Matt.

"An absolute hero!" agreed Tommy.

"Don't tell anybody else," said Stan, "Let the buggers suffer like we used to!" And they laughed, loud and long.

An hour and a half later, with stomachs still in perfect working order and spirits sky high, Stan Cullis observed, "We ought to be there by now. Let's go up and look at France." Up on deck, they could see the shaded lights of a blacked-out harbour. "Calais," said Tommy with a smile of smug satisfaction. "No!" exclaimed a voice from the darkness. "Dover!" The ship's departure had been delayed and it was with some glee that their informant added, "We haven't bleedin' left yet, you berks!"

Soon after they did leave, the hapless trio were bent over the ship's side depositing the expensive pills, along with the rest of the contents of their stomachs, into the churning waters of the Channel. And there on deck, in a pathetic line of three, they stayed, heaving and retching over the side, through the entire crossing. When, mercifully, they did reach Calais and the misery finally receded, Tommy turned to Stan Cullis and with a look which, this time, was most certainly not one of appreciation, he told the Wolves man, "You should have brought those bloody monkey glands!"

In the matches that followed in Paris, Lille and Rheims, Tommy, with the debilitating effects of the crossing compounded by a persistent heavy cold, had what he reckoned were his worst games ever. The rest of the British Army team were not much better, apart, inevitably, from Joe Mercer, who secured a 1-1 draw in Paris with a spectacular goal-line clearance two minutes from time.

However, the trip served its purpose in providing welcome relief for the troops from the unremitting boredom of manning their trenches, aerodromes and gun sites while nothing was happening in what had become known as the 'Phoney War'. That Paris match was enjoyed by 35,000 British and French servicemen.

There were enjoyable elements, too, for the men from the footballers' battalion, not least a splendid evening of entertainment at the British Officers' Club in Paris, which, despite being blacked out, was a city of feverish gaiety with thousands of British and French making the very best of their leave. But, in truth, this whole trip was a very strange, contradictory and disturbing experience for Tommy Lawton, knowing that he would, himself, soon be back to the repressive, regimented routine of his Aldershot initiation and that this Phoney War was almost certainly just the lull before a fearsome storm. It was with that awful assumption that those thousands of young men were milling around Paris, desperately determined to sample every delight that this liberal city had to offer before they faced the inevitable conflict, in which there was a very good chance they would die.

The Phoney War did end on 10th May 1940 when Hitler launched his

Western offensive and invaded France. Fierce fighting ensued, leading to the dramatic evacuation of British troops from Dunkirk between 26th May and 4th June. A flotilla of 900 naval and assorted civilian craft crossed the Channel under Royal Air Force protection and performed the amazing, heroic rescue of 338,226 retreating troops. During the evacuation, the German Luftwaffe attacked frequently, reducing the town of Dunkirk to rubble and destroying 235 vessels. More than 5,000 soldiers were killed. British ships rescued 220,000 more Allied troops from other French ports and the total number of Allied troops evacuated during the ten-day operation was a staggering 558,000. The evacuation had succeeded against tremendous odds, epitomising the British bulldog spirit, boosting morale and enabling the Allied Forces to fight another day.

With the need to keep the spirits of the people as high as possible now an even stronger priority for the wartime government, football continued to be played and just days before Dunkirk, the Football League War Cup final was staged at Wembley. The Football League War Cup competition had been introduced to spice up the restricted wartime football for the spectators and on the way to the Wembley final, 137 ties were played in nine weeks. Despite genuine fears of Luftwaffe attacks on London, a crowd of 42,300 watched West Ham United beat Blackburn Rovers 1-0 in an exciting final.

By September 1940, Britain was, fully and fearfully, a country at war. The dreaded Luftwaffe began to bomb London and other major cities and by the following May had made 127 large-scale night raids – 71 of them on the capital, the rest on Liverpool, Birmingham, Plymouth, Bristol, Southampton, Coventry, Hull, Portsmouth, Manchester, Sheffield, Newcastle, Nottingham, Cardiff, Glasgow and Belfast; 60,000 civilians were killed and 87,000 seriously injured. Two million homes were destroyed.

By the time Tommy Lawton got his first posting, to the 8th Cheshires at Birkenhead, it had become clear what his own part in this war was to be. As an Army physical training instructor he had to bring soldiers to a peak of fitness for the fray, but there was more. As a top footballer his job was also to play for England, the Army, his Area Command team and other unit sides to raise morale and much needed money for the war effort, the British Red Cross and other service charities. Rationalised, it was an important role and one to which many of the country's best professional players were deployed. Tommy felt that he should be fighting but he was in the Army now and had to do as he was told. He was to stay in England, at least for the time being and do his job. So, he resolved to just get on and do it to the best of his ability.

He was pleased to be posted next door to Liverpool. It meant he could play regularly for Everton in the Regional League competition. Not all in the footballers' battalion were so fortunate. Enlisted players appeared for their own clubs when they could but that depended upon where they were stationed and whether they could get leave. Mostly, they had to obey a rule that they were only to play at grounds within easy reach of their units. So for Tommy, Birkenhead was a perfect posting.

It also meant that he would be able to spend more time with his new girlfriend, Rosaleen, with whom he was having a typically whirlwind wartime romance. Tommy met Rosaleen, a Liverpool lass who worked in the jewellery department of a local store, just before he was called up. She was a stunning girl, petite and doll-like with a complexion like fine porcelain, full, sensual lips and shining auburn hair cascading in ringlets. Tommy was immediately smitten – and she with him. The War was having a stimulating and liberating effect on the conduct of relationships. There was a feeling that there was no time for conventional conformity, for the patient ritual of 'proper' courtships. Couples were cementing and consummating their partnerships in haste, for fear that the War would split them asunder. It was easy and commonplace, in these frenetic circumstances, to mistake lust for love. And so it was with Tommy and Rosaleen.

As 1940 drew to a close, Tommy, now a temporary sergeant instructor, learned that in just a couple of months he was going to be transferred back to Aldershot, so he proposed to Rosaleen and they were promptly married early in January 1941. The bride looked as pretty as a picture in her wedding dress of white organza, with a big bow at the neck, her lovely hair set off by a halo-shaped Tudor-style lace headdress. The groom looked strikingly smart and handsome in his uniform, with shiny brown leather belt; boots polished to gleaming, *heels as well*; his luxuriant black hair slicked back and meticulously parted down the middle.

The newlyweds snatched a short honeymoon on the Clyde (briefly interrupted for Tommy to turn out as a guest player for Greenock Morton and bang in a goal in a 3-3 Scottish League draw with Hamilton Academical!) and their marriage got off to a very happy start.

By now, the Battle of Britain was well and truly joined but football carried on defiantly, if not entirely regardless. The grounds were shabby from inevitable neglect of maintenance; aircraft spotters, with strict instructions to watch the sky, not the game, sat high in the stands with powerful binoculars to detect the approach of German Heinkels, Dorniers and Stukas and air-raid sirens sometimes wailed over the games, sending players and spectators scurrying for shelter. But Mr Bloody Hitler was not going to stop the British playing football . . . By God, no!

Despite the enjoyment and morale-boosting release from tension that these games provided, the players who were making it possible had to contend with hostility from some people who thought they should be fighting for their country, not 'kicking a football around'. The women among these detractors were particularly vehement and volatile in their condemnation. They thought it wrong that fit, able-bodied young men were playing football in England while their husbands, sons and sweethearts were fighting in the sun-baked deserts of Libya and the Middle East, getting shot down over Europe or perishing in cruel seas. And they said so. When confronted with this, Tommy sometimes thought that his answer should be that he was doing his war job; that he was providing crucial, top-quality and potentially life-saving physical training for the fighting soldiers and raising vast sums of money for the war effort and that, in any event, like everybody else in the services, he had to do what he was told. But he didn't, because harsh though the criticism was, he understood this reaction and sympathised with it. He had a simple stock reply, which he always tried his best to give courteously: "I'm not going to defend myself. I have nothing to defend myself against." He could do no more than put the hurt the hostility caused to the back of his mind and get on with that job.

Back in the South, Tommy played eight times for Aldershot, scoring ten goals, mostly with the skilful assistance of Sheffield United's inside forward Jimmy Hagan, who was also stationed at the local barracks.

In the spring of 1941, Tommy took a week's leave to go back to Merseyside to visit his mother and grandfather, who was slowly and painfully dying in his 64th year. Tommy's heart was breaking as he sat at Jim Riley's bedside, holding his hand and gently stroking his cheek. This was an overpowering feeling for the young man, an intense mix of love and sorrow. Jim was too ill to recognise from whom these comforting gestures came with their unspoken love and that upset Tommy even more. He owed so very much to this man and he wanted to tell him, one last time. He thought Jim couldn't hear him, but he told him anyway. The love he felt for the man who so unselfishly became his 'dad' when the real one deserted him was stronger now than ever. He leaned forward and gently kissed Jim's forehead. This time there was no resistance, no rebuke, no "Get off me, you big Jessie!" How desperately Tommy wished there could have been. Then Jim Riley quietly slipped away.

This was the worst time of Tommy Lawton's young life. Not only had he lost the 'dad' he loved so much, but his marriage was not working out. Now that the first flush of passion had subsided, Rosaleen seemed to have little or no interest in her husband, a failing that he was beginning to reciprocate already. These two had next to nothing in common, very little of mutual interest about which to talk to each other. Both were headstrong, proud and opinionated, both independently minded. Rows broke out almost as soon as they got together which, owing to the demands of the Army, was infrequently, anyway. Barely six months had passed since their wedding day and this marriage was turning out to be a huge mistake. But there was something from Tommy's upbringing which told him he had to work at it, that it would be terribly wrong and cowardly to walk away from it.

He found solace in the companionship of Army life, which he otherwise hated, and particularly in the faithful friendship of Frank Swift. The bond these two had formed was strong and unshakeable. Big Swifty knew intuitively when his pal needed cheering up and just as instinctively when he was best left alone. When the former was required, Frank's zany sense of humour never failed to make Tommy laugh. Impromptu mimes such as a girl taking a bath, a man trying unsuccessfully to sew a button on his jacket or a Blackpool holidaymaker eating a pennyworth of hot chips from an imaginary newspaper were all delivered with dumb drollery, the hilarious charades and facial expressions rendered even funnier by the giant size of the man. No matter what the subject under discussion, Frank could create a new mime to turn it instantly into a joke. And when he felt that clowning was not the answer to Tommy's problem, he sat in considerate silence and listened before offering words of invariably sound advice or comforting consolation. Nobody ever had a better friend and while the unspoken rules of male friendship prevented expression of his fondness and appreciation, Tommy hoped that he was just as important to Frank as the big fella was to him.

In September 1941 Tommy was in an Army team sent to play three matches in Ireland and his predictable seasickness was compounded when, as the party crossed a rough Irish Sea in a totally blacked-out ship, a huge bang pierced the night air, sending the football party scurrying to find the lifeboats, convinced that they had been shelled, bombed or torpedoed. The panic rescinded when they discovered that one of the crew, on spotting a mine in the water, had disabled it with a gun!

After disembarking at Larne the Army team's matches were interspersed with some generous Irish hospitality from a wealthy friend of Ralph Birkett, one of the party. Ralph's friend, Albert White, had a fabulous home by the sea and he gave the visitors the run of the place, doing everything he could to make them feel that there was still some pleasure and comfort left in the world. The footballing soldiers returned as if from a welcome holiday.

Ever since he sat, as a child, at the Rileys' table in that little terraced house in Bolton listening in awe to his uncles' tales of Wembley Stadium, Tommy Lawton had cherished an ambition to play there. But never did he even remotely imagine that this ambition would be realised in the middle of a war!

He was called up to play for England versus Scotland at Wembley on 17th January 1942. This was a special match, the proceeds going to the Aid to Russia Fund, headed by wartime Prime Minister Winston Churchill's wife Clementine and as the day of the big game approached that began to look like a particularly appropriate cause . . . It snowed heavily all week.

With the Wembley pitch under a blanket of frozen snow it looked certain that the match would have to be cancelled but there was great reluctance to lose such a prestigious occasion and after sterling work by the ground staff it went ahead. Wembley might have been in mid-winter Russia as the teams emerged from freezing cold dressing rooms, deprived of heat by fuel rationing, onto a pitch resembling an ice rink. The only way the ground staff could produce effective lines on this surface was to paint them not the usual white, but blue, and this created a strange, alien scene.

The players of both sides lined up to be introduced to the fur-coated Mrs Churchill who, after greeting them pleasantly and shaking 22 freezing hands, was led to a microphone to address the crowd, while the players broke away to their respective goalmouths for the pre-match kick-around.

Intent on that ritual, the players could not hear what Mrs Churchill was telling the crowd but she was making an announcement about an historic event which was to have a major impact on the War. Her husband, the Prime Minister, was flying back to Britain after the successful conclusion of a conference between 26 nations which had led to the Declaration by the United Nations, an agreement which would see Britain, the USA, the USSR and China, nine American allies in Central America and the Caribbean, the four British Dominions, British India and eight Allied governments-in-exile combine military resources under one command in order to defeat Hitler's Germany. This was hugely significant and a great boost to morale in Britain where the War had become a desperate struggle amid frequent rumours of a Nazi invasion.

Mrs Churchill's proclamation was greeted with a huge roar of delight from the spectators, though the dramatic impact and momentous importance of it were wasted on one drunken Scotsman who was diving around the goalmouth into which his team was kicking in, attempting to assist goalkeeper Jerry Dawson in saving the warm-up shots. The inebriate Scot thought the cheering was for him and bowed extravagantly, doffing his Tam o' Shanter to the crowd!

As if in immediate celebration of Mrs Churchill's announcement, England scored 50 seconds after the kick-off, Jimmy Hagan taking a pass from Wilf Mannion then sprinting past Scottish defenders, who were struggling on the slippery surface, and smashing an unstoppable shot under Dawson's diving body.

If anyone needed confirmation of the wisdom of football being used to raise morale through this appalling war, it was there in the reaction of the Wembley crowd at that moment. The joyous cheer was deafening and gleefully discarded hats filled the air as Hagan accepted the congratulations of his teammates. Then Tommy Lawton took centre stage, beating Dawson to a low centre from left winger Denis Compton to prod home the second and soaring to meet a Stanley Matthews corner with his head for the third.

England had crowned a great day with a 3-0 win, but Tommy's dream debut at Wembley was tinged with sadness as he sat in the dressing room, thinking how much Jim Riley would have enjoyed seeing his lad score two goals against Scotland in that superb setting. If only he could have lived long enough. Jim would have been so proud.

Then, Tommy's day was marred by a mean-spirited FA official, Treasurer Mr Ewbank, to whose snooty presence the centre forward was summoned after the match. As he entered the office in which the Dickensian, wing-collared Mr Ewbank sat with a copy of *Bradshaw's Rail Guide* in front of him. Tommy thought how much like a screwed-up little bird this fellow looked, with his sharp darting eyes and hook nose and decided this was most definitely not his sort of chap. Without even the courtesy of an invitation for Tommy to sit down, Ewbank snapped, "Now look here, Lawton. The train fare from Aldershot is only seven shillings and fourpence."

"So?"

"So why have you claimed twelve shillings and sixpence?"

"Well, there's five bob for food – or aren't I supposed to eat?"

"That's still only twelve and fourpence."

"Beg your pardon?"

"What about the other twopence?"

This infuriated Tommy. He had already been told that, after all expenses were accounted for, the proceeds from the match had raised £26,500 for Mrs Churchill's fund. His pay for playing 90 minutes of international football was a mere one pound, ten shillings and this beaky little berk was quibbling about twopence!

"I'll tell you what happened to the twopence," he told Ewbank. "I was taken short twice on my way here. And it's a penny a shit!" The supercilious Ewbank looked up, pushed his thin, rimless spectacles higher up his bird-like nose and looked at Tommy with deliberate contempt: "There is no need for rudeness, Lawton." "Oh yes there is!" Tommy retorted. "And I'll tell you what you can do, Mr lah-de-dah bloody Ewbank. You can take my expenses and my match fee and put it all in the fund for Mrs Churchill. And don't you dare talk to me like that ever again!" As Ewbank gasped in disbelief at such insubordination, Tommy stormed out of the office, slamming the door so hard behind him that it shook on its hinges.

On the train back to Aldershot, Tommy, less angry now and pleased that he had stood up against such arrogant officialdom, whispered to himself with a satisfied smile: "That was for you, Jim Riley!" Back at the barracks, Tommy told Big Swifty about his encounter with Ewbank: "Bloody hell, mate," said Frank. "That's the last time you'll play for England!"

A week later, Tommy was playing representative football again, not for England, but for a strong British Army side, including Jimmy Hagan, Denis Compton and Stan Cullis, against the Belgian Army at Aldershot. That was followed by another British Army fixture against a Football Association XI, at which the distinguished guest of the day was King Peter of Yugoslavia, who graciously sent a note around to the dressing rooms to say how much he had enjoyed the game, which the Army won 3-1 thanks to two more cracking goals from Jimmy Hagan.

Then they played the RAF and with these representative fixtures now coming thick and fast, almost to the point of congestion, Tommy reflected on how all the players had thought the outbreak of war would mean they would not be able to play football at all!

However, with Big Swifty being so rarely wrong about anything, Tommy was more or less resigned to the belief that his row with Mr Ewbank might well have meant the end of his England career . . . until an invitation arrived for him to represent his country against Scotland at Hampden Park.

Either the powers that be reckoned his two goals against the Scots at Wembley three months earlier were more important than a bust-up over expenses or Mr Ewbank had decided to keep the altercation to himself, but that coveted centre-forward shirt with the three lions on it was once again to be in the possession of T Lawton, who was as pleased as punch. So, too, was Big Swifty who greeted his pal's news with a hearty slap on the back and the wry observation that he was "a lucky sod to have got away with that!"

When Tommy Lawton last travelled to Hampden to play for England it had been in luxury: first-class train coaches segregated from the rest of the passengers, equally first-class hotel accommodation, the best food money could buy, every conceivable comfort, every little requirement met. In short, he was pampered. What a difference a war made! The Football Association notice advising him of his selection, told him he had to make his own way to Scotland:

Players will make their own travelling arrangements and report at the Central Hotel, Glasgow, not later than 10 pm on Friday evening. Members of the party are advised to obtain a meal prior to travelling and to provide themselves with any necessary refreshments for the journey.

That comparison with Scotland v England on 15th April 1939 was not lost on Tommy as he was leaving the barracks, kit bag over the shoulder of his uniform, to head back up to Scotland in the spring of 1942. He was deep in thoughts of his first Hampden experience when a familiar voice shouted after him, "Tom, wait!"

It was Big Swifty: "You'll be needing this," he said, thrusting twopence into Tommy's hand. "In case, you're taken short!"

Huge contrast though it was to that same trip in 1939, the comparative discomfort of the wartime journey mattered not one jot to Tommy Lawton as he sat in third class on the over-crowded train which was to take him out of England. He was playing for his country again. And there was no better feeling in sport.

The match turned out to be one of the best games ever played between the two nations. Despite all the wartime restrictions, there were 91,000 spectators in Hampden Park and they managed to make the infamous Roar sound like it was coming from the pre-war 150,000 as Scotland won a real thriller 5-4. Tommy had a great game, scoring a hat-trick. And Scotland's late winning goal was scored by Bill Shankly, affording him a considerable degree of satisfaction after Lawton's winner in 1939. "Stick *that* in yer pipe and smoke it, big fella!" Bill joked as Tommy shook his hand at the final whistle and the pair left the pitch side by side, arms around each other's shoulders in a spontaneous gesture of mutual respect.

In June 1942, the football powers that be met in Nottingham and decided that for the following season, they should revert to the small localised competitions they had introduced when war broke out, but to compensate for this more parochial level of interest for the faithful fans, an even busier programme of representative games was to be arranged.

Tommy (now Company Sergeant Major Instructor Lawton in recognition of his value and dedicated service as a PTI) had no trouble keeping fit himself in the summer months because that was an occupational necessity, but if proof of his supreme physical condition was required it was there for all to see when, having been persuaded to compete in the Aldershot District Military Athletic Championships, he won the 100 yards and the long jump in great style, the latter earning him a new nickname, 'Leaping Lawton'.

On 5th September, he appeared in the first of the big representative matches, leading an FA XI against a Civil Defence side at Brentford. Then he travelled to play in Services matches against Ireland at Windsor Park, Belfast and Scotland before being selected for the first of the season's internationals, against Scotland, to be played at Wembley on 10th October. Among a crowd of 75,000 for this match, a wartime record, were seven Cabinet Ministers, including Ernest Bevin and Clement Atlee and watchful Spitfires circled the sky above the stadium, but it was a poor game ending disappointingly in a 0-0 draw.

A fortnight later there was another international, this time versus Wales at Wolverhampton. The selectors rang the changes for England, dropping Jimmy Hagan, Maurice Edelston and Denis Compton and bringing in two centre forwards, Ronnie Rooke of Fulham and Jackie Gibbons of Spurs, as inside forwards alongside Tommy Lawton. Jimmy Mullen, replacing Denis Compton at outside left was chosen to make his England debut at Molineux, his home ground.

After the uninspiring goalless draw with Scotland, the selectors reckoned they'd picked a side full of firepower; everybody anticipated a convincing win over the Welsh and it looked like that would happen when, after 11 minutes, Tommy finished off a fast, incisive attack by the English forwards to put them 1-0 up. But England, looking disjointed and top heavy and sorely missing the creative guile of Hagan, could not build on their promising start and Wales, full of typical fight and fervour, won 2-1. No one demonstrated that fierce Welsh pride and British wartime spirit better than Horace Cumner, playing at outside left for Wales. Cumner was in the Navy and only five weeks before the match he was seriously burned on his hands and face when a hydrogen container exploded. Nobody expected Cumner to be out of hospital so soon after this accident, let alone playing football for his country and scoring both goals in their well-deserved victory.

Back on League South duty, Tommy then figured in two remarkable games for Aldershot. Leading 3-0 against Arsenal with 35 minutes to go a strong Aldershot side with four internationals, including Lawton and Hagan, looked comfortable winners. When Arsenal pulled one back it seemed just a consolation and Aldershot were soon back on top at 4-1. Then, in an astonishing, whirlwind fightback which had their opponents reeling, Arsenal rattled in *six* goals to win 7-4! Following that, with Jimmy

Hagan at his brilliant, defence-splitting best, Aldershot rammed nine goals past Luton, Tommy Lawton scoring *six* of them!

Tommy's extraordinary six goals didn't impress the England selectors, however. When, early in 1943, they chose the team to play Wales again, this time at Wembley, they blamed Lawton, Rooke and Gibbons (rather than the real cause, which was their own error in picking three centre forwards) for the defeat at Molineux and dropped all three. There was no place for Tommy in the next England match, versus Scotland at Hampden, either, so he showed them what they were missing by scoring four goals for the British Army against the Belgians.

Soon after that match, Tommy left Aldershot, having been posted back to Birkenhead and was delighted to be able to play for Everton again. Sadly, there was no such homecoming joy on the marital front where his incompatibility with Rosaleen remained unresolved and the rows were frequent and increasingly unforgiving.

On 4th October 1943, two days before his 24th birthday, Tommy Lawton learned that he had won back his place in the England side to play Scotland in Manchester on 16th October. He had never been entirely convinced that his year in international exile did not have more to do with his verbal assault on the FA Treasurer than events on the pitch but he was delighted to be re-called for two reasons: England had scored eight goals against Wales at Wembley in the previous international (hardly the harbinger of a change at centre forward!) and selected in goal for the game at his home ground of Maine Road was Frank Swift. Big Swifty had been almost as busy a footballer as his best mate since the day he and Tommy joined the Army, playing for Manchester City as often as he was able, guesting for Aldershot, Charlton, Fulham, Reading and Liverpool and playing in several representative games, but there was something very special about the prospect of playing for England against Scotland at Maine Road and both of them approached the game with great excitement.

So, too, did thousands of English supporters lucky enough to get tickets – provided they were genuine, since many forgeries were discovered prior to the match. The day before, hundreds of servicemen who had hitchhiked from all over the country arrived to find that, under wartime conditions, the limited accommodation in Manchester was heavily taxed and out of their reach. Ever willing to show gratitude to 'our boys' who were fighting for King and country, the local authorities and Civil Defence got together, opened up a huge shelter which had been empty since the Manchester blitz and made sure that the lads all got a bed for the night, preceded by a free meal.

As kick-off neared, the excitement grew to fever pitch among the huge crowd inside Maine Road. Tommy hung his uniform on the dressing room peg and pulled on the white shirt of England again with renewed pride – and determination not to let it go this time: "This is where I belong," he told himself, "among the best players in Britain."

In the players' tunnel, Big Swifty and his pal shared an embrace which needed no words. The atmosphere of tingling tension and anticipation which always preceded these Anglo-Scottish battles was as electric as ever as the teams lined up:

England: Swift (Manchester City); Scott (Arsenal), Hardwick (Middlesbrough); Britton (Everton), Cullis (Wolves), Mercer (Everton); Matthews (Stoke), Carter (Sunderland), Lawton (Everton), Hagan (Sheffield United), Compton (Arsenal).

Scotland: Crozier (Brentford); Carabine (Third Lanark), Miller (Hearts); Little (Rangers), Young (Rangers), Campbell (Morton); Waddell (Rangers); Gillick (Everton), Linwood (St Mirren), Walker (Hearts), Deakin (St Mirren).

After just 15 minutes Tommy seized on a miskick by Young and cleverly back-heeled the ball, knowing that Jimmy Hagan was close behind. The fleet-footed inside forward raced through, drew Crozier and slotted home. 1-0 to England. That was the signal for Stan Matthews to produce another dazzling display of wing wizardry. He ran the Scottish defence ragged time and time again and in the process, Tommy Lawton scored three goals in ten minutes. 4-0 to England. With Matthews continuing to bewitch, bother and bewilder the Scots, Raich Carter got a goal – then missed a penalty. Half-time: 5-0 to England.

The England team left the field for the interval to a standing ovation. The crowd felt the match was already won. They'd witnessed something very special. Man of the match Matthews, along with Carter, Lawton, Hagan and Compton, had produced 45 minutes of the most sensational attacking football ever seen in an England international match. They had torn the Scots apart. Frank Swift, so keen to impress in front of his home crowd, had hardly touched the ball.

In the second half, however, Big Swifty got his chance to shine . . . Scotland's left half, Campbell picked up a loose ball and struck a fearsome long-range drive which was beaming into the top left-hand corner of England's goal until Frank leapt like a salmon and tipped the ball over the bar. He landed to thunderous applause from the crowd, got up and performed a theatrical bow!

Then Jimmy Hagan and Tommy Lawton scored Matthews-assisted goals in rapid succession and the already overjoyed supporters were ecstatic.

7-0 to England. Coasting now, England were so much on top and Scotland so demoralised that the main objective of the men in white shirts was to create a goal for the incredible Stan Matthews so that he could cap his scintillating performance by adding his name to what was surely to become an historic scoreline.

Carter, Lawton and Hagan all strove to set the enigmatic wing wizard up with a goal when they were perfectly placed to score themselves but it seemed it was not to be until Matthews, apparently frustrated by the 'inability' of his fellow forwards to create a good enough chance for him, decided to go it alone. He picked up the ball deep inside his own half then weaved his way through a succession of tired Scottish players, fooling them by feinting to pass *four* times. With defenders not having a clue what he was going to do next, he dribbled the ball right up to the goal-keeper then stopped and waited insolently for Crozier to make his move before casually side footing it past him and into the back of the net. 8-0 to England.

Bedlam broke out! Maine Road rocked and shuddered to sustained cheering, shouting and stamping; those of Matthews's England teammates who were near enough, instantly mobbed him while the rest stood rooted to the spot as if in shock, clapping their hands in wide-eyed acclaim; even Scotland players joined in the applause. Matthews merely ducked his head shyly and loped nonchalantly back to the middle, blowing on his fingers, looking for all the world like some inconsequential bloke walking slowly back to work after a tea break.

Some ten minutes later, the England team left the Maine Road pitch at the final whistle, knowing they had produced one of the greatest international displays ever seen. They walked very slowly, the better to absorb the crowd's continuing acclimation. This was a truly memorable sporting moment, the like of which occurs rarely in any generation. And for that moment, for all those present, the War was forgotten.

The magnitude of England's achievement that day was summed up by Mr Charles Wreford Brown, one of the England selectors and himself a great player 40 years earlier, who, in congratulating the team, said, "This England team, which has won such a magnificent victory, showed perhaps the greatest combination and team work in the whole history of international football. I myself have never seen anything like it before."

Tommy Lawton and Big Swifty, both becoming increasingly rebellious as their adult personalities took shape, usually greeted the "condescending" comments of "the big wigs in blazers" with studied indifference. But they listened intently to the carefully chosen words of Mr Wreford Brown – and they truly appreciated them.

As they came down from this incredible high and headed back to the realities of Army barrack life, Frank turned to Tommy: "Of course, you know what Wreford Brown was talking about, don't you?" "What?" "My save, of course!" "Bugger off!"

The breathtaking brilliance of England's 1943 Maine Road team won universal tribute from the press and one journalist, Ivan Sharpe, offered an interesting, if understated, theory for its excellence: "This is, perhaps, England's best team since 1907 and there is a reason. Services football has brought them into action more frequently than is possible in normal times. They have developed understanding."

Tommy Lawton continued the season in a rich vein of form, prompting the *Daily Mail* to observe, "Lawton is the best centre forward for 20 years."

Tommy had been well taught never to let such eulogies go to his head. He chuckled to himself as he recalled how Jim Riley would throw complimentary newspaper reports on the fire rather than let him read them. But he wished more than he wished for anything else in the world that Jim could still be there to read them for himself, and try as he might, he just couldn't understand why Rosaleen seemed to have no interest whatsoever in his achievements. That hurt.

By 1944, Tommy Lawton was being sent all over the country to organise the Army's gyms and training quarters and he never missed an opportunity to play football with the starry-eyed soldiers who idolised him. One of these, George Edwards, was awestruck as he walked out onto the field alongside 'England's best centre forward for 20 years' and asked the great man the first daft question that came into his mind: "Excuse me, sir. How should I cross the ball? Where would you like it?" Smiling, Tommy told him. "Well, Stan Matthews always manages to do it with the lace away, son . . . lace away."

The soldiers laughed aloud at that joke and it broke the ice; they went on to play comfortably alongside him as if he was just one of their mates and that's just what he wanted. On the basis that you never waste a good joke, Tommy used it often after that, leading to a place in football folklore for the apocryphal story that Matthews was so skilful at crossing the ball that he always ensured the lace, which could cause a nasty cut, never made contact with Tommy's forehead!

In February, Lawton's England again beat Scotland at Wembley, 6-2 this time. This victory was watched by King George VI, which gave Tommy another lifelong memory to store away when he was introduced to the King and shook his hand before kick-off. Then when April 1944 brought the chance for the Scots, who hadn't beaten the Auld Enemy since 1942, to gain their revenge at Hampden Park, the match assumed massive importance.

No fewer than 14 members of the Scottish FA sat down to spend as much time as it was going to take to pick a team capable of bursting the Sassenach bubble and after a marathon of deliberation they came up with: Crozier (Brentford); McDonald (Celtic), Stephen (Bradford); Macaulay (West Ham), Baxter (Middlesbrough), Busby (Liverpool); Delaney (Celtic), Walker (Hearts), Dodds (Blackpool), Duncanson (Rangers), Caskie (Everton).

The England selectors chose: Swift (Manchester City); Taylor (Wolves), Leslie Compton (Arsenal); Soo (Stoke), Cullis (Wolves), Mercer (Everton); Matthews (Stoke), Carter (Sunderland), Lawton (Everton), Hagan (Sheffield United), Smith (Brentford).

As the England players gathered in Scotland, they were thrilled to be told that the guest of honour for the big day was Field Marshal Montgomery, the hugely popular Commander of the Allied Forces – and even more so when they learned that 'Monty' was to address them at a luncheon before the game.

There was now a growing feeling of optimism in the country that the worst of the War was over; that the Allies were gaining the upper hand and the battling, no-nonsense Monty epitomised that spirit of hope. When he spoke to the pre-match gathering, Monty asserted this positivity by revealing that now, for the first time, he felt confident of beating Hitler. He then paid tribute to football for its contribution to sustaining public morale through the darkest days of the War, telling the players:

Those who fight overseas and those who work on the home front are members of one and the same team. One cannot do without the other. There are two things to be done – to fight the Germans and keep the mass of people at home from worrying.

The match had really captured the attention of the people of Scotland and attracted a crowd of 133,000 – astonishingly large under wartime circumstances and the biggest paying attendance at any event during the War.

The Hampden Roar that day was louder and more spine-chilling than ever and, suitably inspired, Scotland flew out of the blocks and totally dominated the first 20 minutes of play, England's new fullbacks, Frank Taylor and Les Compton, were having a torrid time trying to cope with the Scots' wingers Jimmy Delaney and Jimmy Caskie; centre half Stan Cullis was having to work overtime, halfbacks Frank Soo and Joe Mercer were pinned back in defence and Big Swifty was performing heroics to keep the marauders at bay. The intense Scottish pressure was rewarded when Jimmy Caskie's swerving shot bounced twice to deceive Swift and screw past him like a cricketer's leg break. 1-0 to Scotland.

Sensing the kill, the rampant Scots went immediately back on the attack from the restart and a battered England were penned in their own half until Swift's goal kick was picked up just over the halfway line by Raich Carter, who slipped a first-time pass through to Lawton. Tommy, 20 yards out, hit a fantastic shot which flew over the head of centre half Tommy Walker and whistled past goalkeeper Crozier on its way to the top right-hand corner of the net. A brilliant goal! Scotland 1 England 1. And for the first time since kick-off the Hampden Roar was silenced, that huge Scottish crowd stunned in disbelief.

That silence was all too brief and the Roar returned as, for the next few minutes, the game became an end-to-end classic of attacking football at its best. Then Stan Matthews drifted inside from the right wing and pushed a precision pass past Baxter to Lawton. As Stephen lunged in on the centre forward and Crozier hesitated, it was Tommy's boot which got there first. Goal! Scotland 1 England 2. Less than a minute later, Jimmy Hagan played a lovely ball into space for Carter to race onto and smash a cracking drive past Crozier from 25 yards. Goal! Scotland 1 England 3. After being on the rack for the first 20 minutes, England had scored three goals in ten minutes and Tommy Lawton had hit two of them.

This match had been tough and uncompromising in the first half. In the second half, it was brutal. Scotland charged at England as if their lives depended on it. Roared on by a frenzied, fanatical crowd, the rules of the game frequently playing second fiddle to Scottish passion, the blue-shirted fighters, aided and abetted by a swirling wind, mounted attack after attack on the English goalmouth. Crosses, shots, headers rained in but, with Swift having the game of his life, Cullis strong and resilient and Taylor and Compton now settled and competent, England were holding onto their 3-1 lead after half an hour. The Scottish tackling was taking no prisoners, England were giving as good as they were getting in the strong-arm department and the blood and thunder nature of the match was serving to make the volatile Scottish supporters even more vociferous and partisan than usual. When Raich Carter went to have a few words with Caskie for flooring Matthews the howls of Scottish protest raised the roof and the mass personal abuse heaped upon the England inside forward suggested that (with the possible exception of a certain little German with a black moustache!) he was the most unpopular man alive.

It was only a matter of time before the English defence was breached and it happened when Caskie lifted a cross into the middle, Dodds beat Cullis in the air and the ball skidded off his head past Swift. Scotland 2

England 3. A fierce and frenetic finale ensued but England held out for an epic victory.

It had been a ferocious fight – fit, perhaps, to lay before Field Marshal Montgomery, the master of combat, who said he had thoroughly enjoyed every minute of it. 'Monty' captivated everyone with whom he came into contact at Hampden and nobody knew what secrets he was carrying with him . . . just weeks later, the greatest armada of all time hit the shores of France in the Normandy landings on the day that went down in history as D-Day. Nobody knew, either, that football played a part in that historic triumph.

On 15th April 1944 General Dwight D Eisenhower, Supreme Commander of the Allied Forces in Europe, attended the Football League War Cup final at Wembley between Charlton Athletic and Chelsea. The general was introduced to the players on the pitch before kick-off and presented the cup to Charlton's captain Don Welsh after their 3-1 victory. Eisenhower's appearance in front of 85,000 spectators at the Cup final was highly publicised in newspapers and on Pathé News in order to fool Hitler into thinking that the Allies were on the back foot because such an important war leader would never have been wasting his time at a football match if anything major was about to happen. It was carefully planted disinformation designed to throw the Germans off any scent they might have had because it was absolutely crucial to the success of D-Day that the Nazis did not receive any intelligence about the enormity of the operation, which was to take place on 6th June and involve 175,000 troops, 195,700 Allied naval and merchant navy personnel and 5,000 ships. Plans to invade Normandy had been going on for 18 months, but the critical time was precisely when the Wembley match was being played and the cunning ruse clearly contributed to the success of D-Day.

In May 1944, Tommy Lawton was again on the scoresheet for England when they beat Wales 2-0 at Ninian Park and bagged another when they drew 2-2 in the return match at Anfield in September. After the Anfield match, Tommy went to a Liverpool restaurant where 24 wounded soldiers from a local hospital were being entertained by the chairman of Liverpool FC, Mr W H McConnell.

It was a deeply moving experience for Tommy as he sat with these lads, who were laughing and joking so merrily, apparently oblivious to the dreadful extent of their injuries. They were a pitiful sight, with their broken bodies, some of them with limbs missing, but they were great, convivial company and Tommy was thoroughly enjoying the evening. He did not feel in any way ashamed that he had not been able to fight for his country, but he couldn't help thinking that he could have been one of these lads, crippled for the rest of his life, if he had not been 'the famous Tommy Lawton' and this brought confused and contradictory thoughts and images to his mind.

As he prepared to deal from a pack of cards for a game with a young soldier in a wheelchair, the lad told him, "I can't believe this. You're my hero." Tommy filled up: "No, mate," he said. "You're the hero."

On 14th October, Scotland came to Wembley for yet another attempt to conquer England and it looked as though they would do it as, with just 34 minutes of the match remaining, they led 2-0. Then, with a strong wind blowing driving rain into the faces of the English players, Frank Soo whipped a long ball through to Lawton, shouting, "Yours, Tom." Lawton ran on, beat two defenders and smashed home a screaming shot. Then, he took control of the game, scoring two more goals himself and making two as England completed an amazing fight back to win 6-2. It was, in the eyes, of many observers, Lawton's best game for England and sportswriter Roy Peskett described it thus, for readers of the *Sunday Graphic*:

Tommy Lawton beat Scotland. England's dynamic centre forward, giving the greatest display of his life, pulled back a match which looked well won by Scotland thirty-four minutes from time. They say the occasion finds the man. It found Lawton all right. With the England forwards held in clam-like fashion by the sturdy Scots defence, it looked as if the match would run out with the Scots holding their well deserved lead. Then Lawton went to work. He fastened onto a pass from Frank Soo, eeled his way past Stephen, beat Baxter in his stride and with 93,000 throats roaring him home, smashed the ball past the Scottish keeper. The England team stood still and clapped Lawton back to the middle. Even some of the Scots patted him on the back as he made his triumphant way to the centre spot. It was more than a goal . . . it was a victory. Four minutes later Lawton scored again and from then on it was a rout.

As 1945 dawned, with the end of the War in sight and the nation collectively more relaxed, Company Sergeant Major Instructor Tommy Lawton was able to play properly for Everton again. He was 26 now and he'd gone from emerging youngster to elder statesman at Goodison Park.

Even though football had managed to carry on throughout the War, Adolf Hitler had blighted his professional career and deprived him of so much that would otherwise have been possible but, like all his generation, Tommy had grown up fast. He was rational and realistic and he bore no grudges for what the War had done to his life: "After all, what have I got to complain about," he told himself, "when some of my mates are not coming back at all?"

He was going to come out of this war alive, fit and able-bodied. The sight and plight of those 24 injured soldiers he met that night in Liverpool would stay with him forever, an indelible reminder, along with the deaths of so many, that he had been one of the lucky ones. So, he got on with his Army work and playing his football, not only for Everton but for England, for Western Command and for the Combined Services – and every day he thanked God for his blessings.

Recognising Tommy's huge appeal, the government and the BBC were using him frequently to speak to the troops via radio recordings. From a studio in Eaton Square, London he talked football to the front-line soldiers via steel records which were treated with a special acid to resist heat and cold then flown out to Italy and Burma. These radio broadcasts included a full eight-minute spot on the BBC's *Sportsmen's Corner* in which he gave a full and first-hand account of England's tour of Italy, Yugoslavia and Romania in 1939, including a description of how it felt to give the infamous fascist salute to Mussolini. This broadcast and many others made for the Army Radio Unit revealed a natural gift for communication and an ease in front of the microphone which much impressed the radio professionals and they were very popular with the troops.

Tommy also made frequent visits to military hospitals, where injured troops were thrilled to meet him and to listen, enthralled, as he told them 'secrets' from inside the world of soccer. One day, when he was taking part in a Brains Trust at an Army hospital, he was asked by a lad who had left both his legs behind on the blood-drenched battlefield of Caen, "Can Mr Tom Lawton please tell me who is the greatest footballer he has played with or against?" "Crikey," said Tommy, "I don't think I dare answer that!" Then he told the soldier, "Better still, I'll tell you of several. How's that?" The lad nodded in enthusiastic and appreciative anticipation. And Tommy began:

"I'll start with the little Scottish wizard, Hughie Gallacher, and I'll tell you about the advice he gave me when I was a raw lad of 16 playing for Burnley Reserves. Famous as he was, Hughie Gallacher was playing for Derby County Reserves that day and all the Burnley lads, me included, were in absolute awe of him. I was having a bad game and I was walking disconsolately off the pitch at half-time when Hughie Gallacher trotted up to me and said, 'Look son, you must learn to cover the ball with your body. If you are being tackled on your right, keep the ball at your left foot then your opponent will have to come across your leg to get at it. And it's the same when they come on your left . . . keep the ball at your right foot and they won't take it from you.' Well, I was overwhelmed that such a great player took the trouble to explain some of the secrets of his trade to a youngster just starting out. I stuttered, 'Thanks very much, Mr Gallacher' and d'you know, he will always be *Mr* Gallacher to me. A great centre forward with the heart of a lion making up for what he lacked in size.

"And talking of great centre forwards, there's William Ralph Dean. Now, is it true what they say about Dixie? I'll say it is! He was the best centre forward of his era. Strong, fit, powerful and dangerous anywhere near a 30-yard radius of the goal. Being so close to him, I perhaps subconsciously copied some of his methods but I've seen him do things nobody else has done or ever could do. Dixie Dean is a giant among footballers. We'll never see his like.

"Then there's that grand inside forward, Raich Carter. Raich is a perfect team player. I can't remember how many times, in the white heat of an international match, I've heard a quiet call from Raich, 'Yours, Tom', and the ball has come sliding through the backs, inviting a shot. So often, when I've jumped for high crosses and the goal's guarded I've had only to head the ball backwards and downwards, knowing that Raich will be there to latch onto it. He's not only a hard-working, scheming inside forward, he's also got one of the hardest shots in the game, with either foot.

"I've also got to choose wee Alex James, a weaver of spells who could change the whole course of a match with one wiggle of his foot. I've seen Alex move through at top speed, with two men coming in for the tackle, wave his foot over the ball to give the impression he was going to make a pass or back heel and the bewildered defenders have split leaving him to go triumphantly on his way. Genius! Alex could sell any sort of dummy and I learned, just by watching him playing for Arsenal or Scotland, the invaluable trick of making the false header. What do I mean by that? I mean feinting to head the ball towards one corner of the goal then when the goalie's made his move in that direction, heading it the other way. I scored a goal doing that against Scotland, when it was a wee Scottish fella who'd given me the idea! No justice, eh?

"When it comes to wing halves, Matt Busby comes straight to my mind. Matt would have made just as good a schoolteacher as a footballer because he has a touch of genius in passing on the skills, the crafts, the tricks of the trade to others. He is one of the hardest halfbacks to go past; he's a master of positional play and he has the natural ability to change the course of a game with a quick, shrewd pass. Matt has always had energy to spare, never knowing when he's beaten but when he is, he's the perfect, sporting gentleman in defeat. Yes, a very special man is Matt Busby.

"Then, I've obviously got to name Joe Mercer. I've known Joe ever since I joined the Goodison staff and he's always been the same: even-tempered, good-humoured and funny but also a great, hard-working footballer and one of the shrewdest judges of a game. To hear Joe describe a game is something special and he's a fine skipper. Joe's awkward bow legs hide his deceptive speed; he's a great man to play in front of and a devil to beat. He tackles hard, yet never unfairly. Joe's always alert to the opportunity to help his forwards and he's popped in many unexpected goals himself. I'll never forget a grand goal he got for the FA XI against the RAF at Stoke. It was only a few minutes from time and the score was 3-3. Joe suddenly ran through, beat four men, slid the ball out to the wing, then carried on to crack in the return for the winning goal. Wonderful! I was talking to the goalkeeper, who shall be nameless, after the match and he said, 'There he was, shouting 'Inside, inside' and the ball came in, hit him on the leg and went in. How could I stop it? He runs three different ways at once!'

"And of course, nobody could leave out Stanley Matthews! What a player! The elusive 'Prince of the Potteries', the only man I've ever seen who can take the ball right up to the fullback, show him the maker's name, then flick it away like a hypnotist clicking his fingers. Like Old Father Thames, Stan never seems to hurry but gets there just the same. Stan's shuffled his way to international stardom and I honestly believe, he doesn't know how he does it!

"I'll stop there because there are so many great players of this great game that I might talk for ever," said Tommy. His audience at that hospital, spellbound and hanging on his every word, would not have minded one bit if he had.

Naturally eloquent and now so confident and assured, Tommy Lawton's inherent ability to reach out to people and make them feel good was valuable indeed to the morale builders and he felt professionally fulfilled, despite the War.

He had only one big regret: that his hasty wartime marriage was proving so unhappy. His relationship with Rosaleen was so rocky now that he wondered if it was ever going to get any better, but still he could conceive of no other solution than to persevere and hope that it would.

On 27th January 1945 Tommy reached a milestone when he scored the 400th goal of his top-class career. It came in the 53rd minute of a game against Stockport County at Goodison Park. February saw another England win against Scotland (3-2) and another goal for Tommy at a bomb-scarred and shabby Villa Park, where there was a welcome indication of the imminence of the War's end. All the stand seats, which had been commandeered for use in Birmingham's communal air-raid shelters, were returned and refitted and a peacetime capacity crowd of 66,000 watched England's victory.

Tommy Lawton, the bad sailor, didn't know if he would be any better travelling by air because he had never flown – until March 1945 when the RAF provided a big Dakota to take 13 British international footballers to Belgium for two matches to entertain the troops. It did little for his understandable anxiety when, just before take-off, a helpful RAF steward told him, "Put your Mae West [life jacket] on tight, otherwise it'll strangle you when you come down in the drink!" In the event, he discovered that this mode of travel suited him very well. Indeed, he really enjoyed it.

Before landing, the pilot flew low over the Belgian coastal towns so that his passengers could see some of the war damage. It was a shocking sight, which the players observed in silence, shaking their heads in sorrow. Arriving in Brussels was an even more moving experience. Everywhere they looked there was evidence of the Belgian nation's huge gratitude to the Allied forces for delivering them from the cruel oppression of Nazi rule. They were given a fond and warm welcome but while that cheered and uplifted them, they were distressed and humbled to see the strain that the terror and undernourishment of German occupation had etched into the faces of the gallant Belgian people.

Thousands of British servicemen piled into the ground for the first game, in Bruges against the famous *Diables Rouges* (Red Devils) and not all of them legally, some tearing down wooden fences to get in. The strong British Combined Services team, which included Joe Mercer, Stan Matthews and Matt Busby, comfortably won 8-1. The servicemen, starved of quality football for so long, all came hoping to see the great Tommy Lawton score and he didn't disappoint them. To their delight and raucous appreciation he smashed in four.

Before scoring the last of his four goals, Tommy was getting into position for a corner kick to be taken by Brentford's Leslie Smith when his attention was attracted by the gesticulating hands of a British soldier who was sitting on the grass to the left of the goal, beckoning the centre forward towards him. Tommy duly obliged, to be told by the soldier, "Hey, Scouser. Make it four. I've got 300 francs on you scoring more than three!" "OK, son!" replied Tommy.

The corner came over, Lawton leapt to meet it, stretched that powerful neck and headed the ball like a bullet into the back of the net. "That do for you?" he shouted to the soldier, who was himself now airborne, arms outstretched, cap abandoned in wild celebration!

The British 'Tommies' were just as excited the next day in Brussels when they saw their famous namesake score a hat-trick as his team beat an impressive Belgian Representative XI 3-2.

Two weeks later, the trip was repeated by the Combined Services and Tommy, was honoured to be made captain for the tour but this time there was no Dakota to take them to Belgium. Air space was limited, the FA was told (because, it later transpired, their flight coincided with the airborne landing on the other side of the Rhine, a landing which effectively ended the war in Europe) so the tour party was flown across in several smaller Ansons. This meant fewer players could go, so the squad was augmented by ex-professionals who were stationed in North-West Europe.

Road transport was similarly in short supply and for the journey from Brussels to Bruges for the first match the players had to pile into a clapped-out bus with wooden seats, which the retreating Germans had left behind, while (typically!) the officials travelled in comfortable RAF cars. The bus journey was eventful. Twice, the driver got hopelessly lost and three times the tired old vehicle spluttered to a steaming halt and had to be coaxed slowly back into life by its long-suffering custodian, his face by now black with oil and his equilibrium seriously disturbed. When the old boneshaker broke down for a fourth time, on this occasion resolutely resisting all the driver's mechanical skill, pleading exhortation and Anglo-Saxon admonition, the players had to be transferred to a couple of RAF cars. As they disembarked from the bus, Charlton Athletic's Bert Brown did little for its driver's severely stretched composure by telling him, "Old Jerry knew what he was doing when he left you that pile of junk!" To complete the trials and tribulations of the journey, the RAF car drivers then both lost their way . . . twice.

When the worn-out travellers eventually pulled into their destination at Bruges, the old German bus was standing in the car park and alongside it its driver, whose two-fingered gesture to the players, or at least to Bert Brown, was intended to signify something other than victory!

The match at Bruges and the following one at Brussels were a much sterner challenge for the weakened British team, which drew both, scoring only one goal (by Bobby King, late of Wolves and Manchester City) in the process and being hugely impressed by the speed and athleticism of the Belgians, if less so by the Brussels pitch, which had been used as an exercise ground for German tanks.

Captain Lawton was certainly impressed (not to say slightly embarrassed, for such customs were not familiar in England) by the size of the spectacular bouquet of flowers presented to him by his Belgian counterpart before kick-off in a little ceremony accompanied by the wolf whistles of 40,000 British troops! That slight embarrassment was no impediment to him nursing the massive bouquet all the way back home where, having been reposed and refreshed overnight in the bath at the Great Western Hotel, Paddington, it was divided into two between him and Big Swifty and carried in triumph to their respective wives – Frank's spouse being considerably more responsive to the gift than Mrs Lawton.

On 14th April Tommy Lawton and England were back at Hampden Park to play Scotland again. A vast crowd of 150,000 observed a minute's silence in memory of President Roosevelt, whose death had shocked the whole world that very morning: the players stood, heads bowed, in a line across the centre of the pitch as the strains of *The Last Post* echoed eerily around the huge stadium and not another sound disturbed the incongruous quiet; the crowd, with every head bared respectfully despite the pouring rain, sang *Abide with Me* as the flags of Britain, America and Russia were lowered to half mast and a passing bomber dipped low in the sky above the ground to acknowledge the tribute.

With tears hardly dry from that incredibly moving pre-match ceremony and only 40 seconds into the match, Tommy Bogan, a 22-year-old Hibernian inside forward making his international debut for Scotland, chased enthusiastically after a long ball which had eluded the England defence. As Frank Swift advanced, Bogan was moving so quickly across the treacherous surface that he couldn't stop, somersaulted involuntarily over the big goalkeeper and landed, with a sickening crash, on his head. As the young forward lay motionless, unconscious and clearly badly hurt, Swift picked him up gently and carried him, cradling him like a baby in his huge arms, off the pitch then laid him tenderly onto a stretcher. As the lad was being taken to the dressing room Frank Swift ran back to his goal to an ovation from the Scottish supporters who had earlier greeted the unavoidable collision with loud booing.

England won 6-1 and Tommy got two more goals but, with the War drawing to a close, for once in these normally fiercely tribal Anglo-Scots contests the result didn't seem to matter all that much. It was to be the last of 15 wartime matches between the old rivals. England won 11 and Scotland two. Two were drawn. England, thanks in no small measure to Tommy Lawton, scored 53 goals to Scotland's 20.

On 4th May 1945 Tommy, along with Frank Swift and Joe Mercer, reported to the Great Western Hotel at Paddington prior to the following day's international, England versus Wales at Ninian Park. As they sat in the hotel lounge with teammates Stanley Matthews, Bert Williams and Frank Broome and the FA's Stanley Rous, the clipped tones of a BBC news reader announced, with matter-of-fact understatement, the surrender of the German forces in North-West Europe.

Immediately, the Great Western Hotel resounded to the sound of loud cheers and the manager ordered that the floodlights outside the hotel must be switched on. It was just the start of an impromptu celebration that was to last all night. The England players joined in the party, at which the double act of Swift and Lawton brought the house down with an impression of the 'sweethearts of song', Anne Zeigler and Webster Booth; Big Swifty's 'Zeigler', his huge frame draped in a hotel towel doubling as an evening gown, being declared the high spot of the whole event.

It was with happy hearts, hangovers notwithstanding, that the England party boarded the eight o'clock express to Cardiff on 5th May for a match played before tens of thousands of Welshmen who were all so carried away in continuing celebration of the previous evening's wonderful news that they were performing even more extraordinary feats than usual with their ubiquitous leeks.

They sang, cheered, clapped and danced through 90 minutes of unrelenting heavy rain. Neither that, nor a 3-2 England victory, with Tommy Lawton scoring the winning goal ten minutes from time, could dampen the spirits of the Welsh crowd that day. And their joy was being shared all over Britain.

It was a day of double celebration for Tommy, who that morning had received an official letter from the War Office informing CSMI T Lawton APTC that he had been selected for a British Army football tour to Italy. His delight was even greater when he read that among others making the tour were his mates CSMI F V Swift APTC and QMSI J Mercer APTC.

Immediately after the match in Cardiff, Tommy, his England teammate Joe Mercer and Welsh goalkeeper Cyril Sidlow, had to dash to catch the 5:30 pm back to Paddington to meet up with the rest of the 20-strong party for the flight to Italy from RAF Lyneham. "This is madness – but don't we all love it!" Joe Mercer exclaimed as they raced into the station. No one disagreed and that 'madness' was epitomised by the curt military notification of the tour contained in the letter:

Reporting: All players will report to the Great Western Railway Hotel, Paddington, London W in time for dinner early on Saturday evening, May 5th. This is the greatest importance as very little notice of airlift is given in advance. Separate instructions will be given to anyone playing for England or Wales at Cardiff on this date.

Returns: Will Officers Commanding please furnish this office by return with regimental number, next of kin and address, religion and vaccination and typhus inoculation up-to-date of players under their command.

Dress: Uniform will be worn by all ranks and AB 64 will be carried. If necessary arrangement will be made for a temporary issue in Italy of khaki drill. Baggage is limited to 55 lbs per man and provision should be made for an adequate supply of towels, soap, razor blades, tooth paste, etc. Players will also supply their own football boots.

Duration of tour: The tour will begin on May 6th and will end on June 2nd, with the proviso that any player selected to play for England at Wembley on May 26th will be flown back on May 23rd or 24th in time to take part in this match.

At eleven o'clock on a beautiful sunny morning, the party took off in a big RAF Warwick and as they looked down over Bournemouth, their last sight of England was of bathers gathering for a day on the beach – a day that was going to be all the more enjoyable with the momentous news of the German surrender. They flew down the Channel, across the Bay of Biscay, sighting Corsica and Elba, Rome, Anzio and the Bay of Naples and finally, after five and a half hours' flying, they reached their destination, Pomigliano airfield.

On 8th May, after settling in and being fitted out with khaki drill uniforms, they ventured forth to see the sights. First, they visited the extraordinary and unforgettable Pompeii, the ancient Roman city buried during a catastrophic eruption of the volcanic Mount Vesuvius in AD 79 and excavated to provide a fantastic insight into life at the height of the Roman Empire. This sort of experience was way out of reach to people from Tommy's sort of background and as he absorbed one amazing sight after another, he wished that he could have been sharing it with his grand-father. "My, how Dad would have loved this!"

Then, they went on to the breathtaking Church of the Madonna. Tommy was immediately struck by the pomp and extravagant worldly wealth of this magnificent, awe-inspiring place of worship and couldn't help thinking that such opulence was ill-becoming; out of place and at odds with the teachings of Christ, with which he'd grown up in an infinitely more modest church in Bolton, but at the same time he was transfixed, enthralled by the breathtaking beauty of these exquisite surroundings and filled with a sense of serenity and peace.

How appropriate that was, for on this same day the Allies formally accepted the unconditional surrender of the armed forces of Nazi Germany.

This was the end of the despised Third Reich, the end of Adolf Hitler, who had committed suicide during the Battle of Berlin, and the end of the War in Europe.

Nearly 400,000 Britons, military and civilian, had died in that war.

In the holy silence of that beautiful church, Tommy Lawton and his pals offered up a prayer for them all and for all of their loved ones now left to rebuild war-shattered lives without them.

The War is over!

Chapter Six

THE START OF THE REST OF MY LIFE

On the evening of Victory in Europe Day, the Combined Services football touring party listened to a moving broadcast by King George VI on the radio but there was no riotous celebration of VE Day for them. They were confined to camp, under canvas, for 72 hours. Nobody knew why, but such was life in the Army.

At least, they were treated to an ENSA show at the camp, with Cicely Courtneidge topping the bill. ENSA, the Entertainments National Service Association, an organisation set up in 1939 to provide entertainment for British armed forces during the War, served up first-rate shows. Gracie Fields, George Formby, Wilfred Brambell, Joyce Grenfell, Paul Schofield, Rebecca Cantwell, Laurence Olivier and Ralph Richardson were among the top entertainers who volunteered their services, Olivier and Richardson being created honorary Army lieutenants in ENSA after they performed Shakespeare's plays for the troops in a six-week tour of Europe.

Actress and comedienne Cicely Courtneidge was a particular favourite of Tommy Lawton. Apart from being renowned for her versatile talents, she was well known for her enduringly happy marriage to her equally famous husband, Jack Hulbert. They wed in 1916 and whenever they appeared together in public, the loving bond between them was evident.

As Tommy joined in the acclaim which greeted the end of Cicely's performance, he found himself wondering what Jack Hulbert's secret was!

That night, he lay awake making resolutions, as if the end of the War
was the end of an old year: "Tomorrow," he resolved "is the start of the
rest of my life." It was a thought being shared by millions of war-weary
Britons back home.

As the footballers gathered on the morning of 9th May to discuss what
lay ahead, Frank Swift revealed that he had lost his precious football boots,
a heinous happening for a player on a military tour. He'd inadvertently
left the bag containing them behind in England, a mishap greeted by
merciless mickey-taking from his mates.

After lunch, they all took refuge from the searing heat, resting under
mosquito nets, until it was time to leave for the first game of the tour, to
be played at the Vomero Stadium in Naples against No 3 Army District,
a side selected from players serving with units stationed between Bari and
Gibraltar. On a very hot night, the game attracted an excellent crowd, the
biggest ever gathered at the stadium. As was to be expected, the visitors
were too strong for the opposition and, winning comfortably, were putting
on an exhibition of skills much appreciated by the spectators when, with
half an hour of the match remaining, Bradford's Joe Hoyle, who was
keeping goal for No 3 District, injured his hand and had to leave the field.
The tourists' captain, Joe Mercer, sportingly offered his opposite number
(Notts County's Jack Reid) the services of Frank Swift, who, with Welsh
international Sidlow in goal for his team, was sitting comfortably in the
warmth of the evening idly enjoying the game.

Reid was pleased to accept Joe's generous offer and the enormous cheer
which greeted Frank Swift changed to hysterical laughter when he ran onto
the pitch. Big Swifty was wearing Hoyle's jersey, which was ludicrously
too small for him, a pair of long khaki shorts and huge, Army-issue boots.

Never one to waste the opportunity for a good laugh, Swift proceeded
to clown his way through the rest of the match while still producing acro-
batic saves which brought the house down and finding time to chat to the
troops behind his goal, signing dozens of autographs as he did so. As the
match neared its end, the Combined Services were awarded a penalty and
Mercer handed the ball to Tommy Lawton while Frank Swift paced up
and down his goal line on all fours, giving a very passable impression of
an enraged caged gorilla. "I can't do it. I just can't do it," Tommy told his
captain. "I mean, just look at the big daft bugger!"

Swifty was swinging by one hand from his cross bar while feverishly
scratching under his armpit with the other, his jersey up around his neck,
baggy khaki shorts hanging from his naked midriff, massive Army boots

dangling in mid-air. Tommy Lawton, England's feared centre forward and undisputed master of the penalty kick, was so helpless with laughter that he could hardly stand. "Anyway," said Tommy. "I don't want to take a penalty against my mate. At home, yes – but not out here."

"Give it 'ere," Mercer said, himself rocking with laughter, and invited Duggie Hunt to take it instead. Duggie duly obliged and in so doing, completed a hat-trick. The Combined Services won 6-0 but the result was a matter of complete indifference to the thousands of servicemen who had not only been treated to a scintillating display of top-class football but thoroughly enjoyed a brilliant comedy routine from Big Swifty. They'd cheered, clapped and roared with laughter on an evening they would never forget. What better way to celebrate Victory in Europe?! For the lads who'd put on that show for them all, there was a show of their own to enjoy later – more ENSA entertainment following dinner at the Officers' Club.

The next morning, they were all up early for the 150-mile journey to Rome. The transport (they all piled into an Army lorry) not being entirely conducive to sightseeing and scenery, Tommy, Frank Swift and Maurice Eddleston climbed up onto the roof for a better view.

En route, there was much evidence of the savage fighting which had been needed to take Italy and at Cassino, scene of some of the worst of it, they were stunned to see the famous hill, with the smashed-up ruin of the monastery, the airfield littered with shattered planes, the roadside remains of wrecked tanks and the town itself, virtually reduced to a pile of rubble. The wholesale destruction at every turn was devastating to behold. Then came the most tragic sight of all – three cemeteries containing the bodies of the British, American and German war dead. Line after line of them: the crosses on the British and American graves white; on the Germans, black.

They journeyed on through Valmontone, another town ravaged by war, where bombed-out civilians were living in caves or in the pathetic shells of their ruined homes, some of which still bore beautifully carved religious figures over the gaping windows and torn roofs. Italy, a country of such confusing contrast when Tommy last came here just before the War, was even more so now. And so bloody tragically.

The awful images of that journey still vivid in his mind's eye, Tommy took it easy the next morning, as did the rest of the party – either engaging in a little light training or watching those who were – but the afternoon had a fantastic experience in store. They were going to the Vatican, where they were to have an audience with the Pope.

After a good lunch and some souvenir hunting, the party's mood, which had been quite low after that harrowing journey, soon lifted and it was an excited bunch of lads who entered the Vatican by sweeping marble steps, to be enthralled by the breathtaking splendour of the intricate architecture and the indescribable atmosphere pervading this unique place. As at the Church of the Madonna, Tommy could not help comparing the richness and grandeur of the Papal palace with the poverty and squalor he had seen on the way there but, again, he was overwhelmed by its sheer beauty.

The footballers, overawed by it all, were on their very best, respectful behaviour as they stood nervously waiting for their audience with the Pope. Except, that is, for one . . . Big Swifty leaned across to his best mate and whispered in Tommy's ear, "I don't care who he is. I'm not kissing any man's ring!" "Behave!" whispered Tommy, trying desperately to suppress a laugh.

Then the Pope appeared, carried in by his Swiss guards, magnificent in his exquisitely embroidered robes and proceeded to bless them, one and all.

"Didn't you tell 'im you're Church of England?" Swifty asked his pal.

"I told you. Behave!"

"And that you come from Bolton?"

Despite Frank's irreverent mickey-taking, Tommy felt immensely proud to have been blessed by the Pope. Swifty was right about one thing. That didn't happen to many lads from Bolton!

From the Vatican, the party went on to visit an absolutely magnificent hotel, now a temporary leave centre for troops, which boasted a huge Roman bath, a fantastic communal facility epitomising the decadence of the empire. This was irresistible to the travelling footballers who were soon splashing around. All around the bath, marble slabs rose in tiers from the water and on those stood majestic 16-feet-high marble statues of Roman figures indulging in various poses favoured by sculptors of that time.

Swifty chose to pose alongside one of these statues, a particularly well-endowed naked Roman wrestler, thus providing his pals with a sight they thought they'd never see: the big fella dwarfed into insignificance. "This bloke's got nothing on me!" bellowed Frank but, since he had nothing on himself, they could attest to the extravagance of his claim! Suitably refreshed, they went on to complete their day with a visit to the Opera House for a performance of *La Bohème*. Now, this was living.

The next day, however, they were brought back to earth with a military bump when they took the field in front of another large crowd of service-men to play an Army in Italy XI. The teams were lined up, side by side, to be literally marched onto the pitch where, on the barked instruction "INWARDS, TURN", they faced each other to be introduced to the British

17 year-old Tommy Lawton pictured in 1936, shortly after signing for Everton after playing just 25 League games for Burnley.

COLORSPORT

Tommy warms up before an away match during his first season with Everton.

GETTY IMAGES/HULTON ARCHIVE

The great Dixie Dean, Tommy's hero and mentor who coached him by hanging balls from the Goodison Park stands for heading practise.

Tommy (right) with Dixie Dean (centre) and George Jackson on an Everton tour to Denmark.

Everton's League Championship winning team of 1938/39. Tommy is in the top row, first on the left.

"Football's buggered." Everton players Joe Mercer, Tommy Lawton, Jimmy Caskie, Gordon Watson and TG 'Yanto' Jones wonder what the future holds on September 3rd 1939, the day war was declared.

Company Sergeant Major
Instructor Lawton pictured
on the day of his wedding to
Rosaleen in January 1941…

… and on duty knocking new recruits into shape at Aldershot barracks in the same year.

"Get in There!" Tommy beats Scotland keeper Dawson to the ball to score in a wartime international at Wembley in January 1942.

Football rivals and comrades in arms – Scotland sriker Tommy Walker (second from right) gets together with Joe Mercer (left), Frank Swift (centre) and Tommy.

Tommy in action for Chelsea.

Beating his man in the snow against Charlton in front of a massive crowd at The Valley…

… and thumping in a trademark header against Derby in August 1947.

PA PHOTOS

Crunch! Tommy wins yet another aerial challenge playing for England against France at Highbury in 1947.

Scotland's Willie Woodburn pokes the ball away from Tommy during the 1-1 draw at Wembley in the 1947 Home International Championship.

FA Secretary Stanle Rous looks on as Tommy is introduced to Field Marshall Montgomery. Next to Tommy on his right are Stanley Matthews and Frank Swift. To his left Stan Mortensen and Billy Wright.

Walking out with England to face Switzerland at Stamford Bridge in 1948, Tommy is closely followed by his great mate Frank Swift.

England line up before the famous international against reigning World Champions Italy in Turin in 1948, the England team featuring the likes of Billy Wright, Stanley Matthews, Tom Finney and Tommy Lawton (fifth from the left).

England won 4-0 with a performance judged by many to be England's greatest ever on foreign soil, and thanks in no small measure to Tommy's 23rd minute goal which put the visitors 2-0 up.

Tommy leads out Notts County before their match with Millwall in October 1948. The England star's record £20,000 transfer to Third Division County had sent shockwaves through the football world.

In action in the same match, Tommy went on to score 90 goals in 151 matches for County.

Tommy rubbed shoulders with the rich and famous frequently but never lost touch with his working class roots. Here he chats to young County supporters outside the club's Meadow Lane ground.

And he would often frequent the local 'greasy spoon' café for a cup of tea and a chat.

Tommy signs for Brentford in another unexpected twist to his career in March 1952, to the obvious delight of manager Jack Gibbons (left) and the club's directors.

And pictured at Griffin Park in Brentford kit.

Following his divorce from Rosaleen, Tommy married Gay in London on September 23rd 1952.

Happy days! Tommy and Gay loved London life, but also loved to get away from it all to Devon.

Proud father Tommy, with the newly arrived Tom Junior.

The family – Gay, Tom Junior, Tommy and Carol – arrive at the Church for Tom Junior's christening.

The christening party: Tom Junior is being held by Susie Barna, wife of his Godfather Victor Barna (far right), a five-time world table tennis champion.

PA PHOTOS

Gunner Lawton. In 1953 Tommy signed for the mighty Arsenal, the club which arguably suited him best of all.

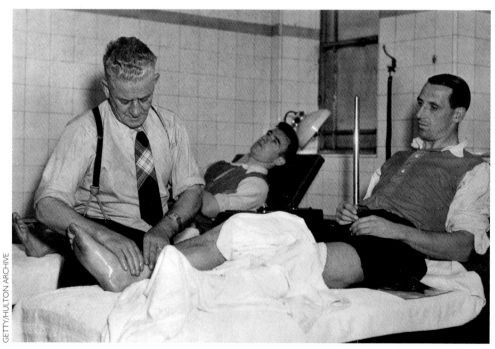

GETTY/HULTON ARCHIVE

Tommy receives treatment on his injured ankle from from Arsenal physio W Milne.

"Get in there!" Tommy scored 13 goals in 35 league games for the Gunners and was led to believe he was being groomed to take over from manager Tom Whittaker when he left to take the reins at non-league Kettering Town in 1956.

It was when Tommy took over as manager at Notts County, against his better judgement, that things started to go wrong.

Tommy (back row, second from right) is pictured with his Notts County team before the start of the 1958/59 season, which would end in bitter acrimony and would be his last job in football.

After the failure of numerous business interests, Tommy is a broken man as he arrives at Nottingham's Shirehall Court in June 1972 to face charges of obtaining money by deception.

Having found himself in the headlines for the wrong reasons, the football world rallied round Tommy. A testimonial was arranged at Goodison Park featuring the likes of Bobby Moore (who missed his train wwbut still drove all the way from London) and Bobby Charlton.

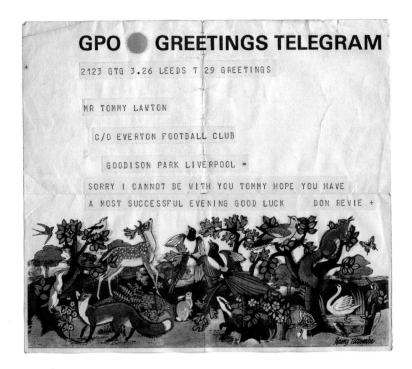

GPO ● GREETINGS TELEGRAM

2123 GTG 3.26 LEEDS T 29 GREETINGS

MR TOMMY LAWTON

C/O EVERTON FOOTBALL CLUB

GOODISON PARK LIVERPOOL =

SORRY I CANNOT BE WITH YOU TOMMY HOPE YOU HAVE

A MOST SUCCESSFUL EVENING GOOD LUCK   DON REVIE +

Legendary Leeds manager Don Revie sent a telegram apologising for not being able to make it.

But the testimonial barely raised enough to pay off Tommy's debts, let alone get his life back on track, and his problems with money continued. During these dark years he sold all of his England caps, medals and memorabilia for desperately needed cash. In November 2009 this inscribed watch, presented to him by the Football Association after he played for England against Italy in 1939, turned up at auction. The seller had obtained it in the 1970s. It raised £620.

NOTTINGHAM EVENING POST

NOTTINGHAM EVENING POST

Tom Junior, Carol, Tommy and Gay arrive at the 'This is Your Life' event organized by Williams to launch the publication of his life story in the *Post*.

Nottingham Evening Post editor Barrie Williams befriended Tommy and the paper ran a series of articles on the ups and downs of his life in 1984.

NOTTINGHAM EVENING POST

The event also coincided with Tommy's 65th birthday and he showed he'd still got plenty of puff as he made short work of blowing out the candles, ably assisted by Tom Junior (right).

The national press immediately picked up on the story and as a result a new testimonial for Tommy was organised by Brentford FC on May 20th 1985.

Here he is introduced to legendary Arsenal, Spurs and Northern Ireland 'keeper Pat Jennings before the match – between Brentford and a London All Stars XI - while Gerry Francis looks on in the background.

On December 12th 1986, Tommy was presented with a beautiful inscribed cut glass goblet when he was officially described as a 'Living Legend' by the Variety Club of Great Britain. The next day, Tommy sneaked into Barrie Williams' office, left the goblet on his desk and refused to take it back.

Tommy with three of his pals from the *Post* sports desk: from left to right Nick Lucy, David McVay – who was a Notts County full-back in the 1970s – and Duncan Hamilton, now a successful author who has twice won the *William Hill Sports Book of the Year* award.

Tommy jokes with former Bolton Wanderers and England centre forward Nat Lofthouse in 1989.
Both sons of Bolton, Lawton and Lofthouse attended the same Castle Hill School. Lawton was young
Nat's schoolboy hero, just as Dixie Dean had been Tommy's.

Tommy and Gay with a bowling award that Tommy won as a young cricketer in Bolton – one of the few sporting mementos he didn't sell during the dark years.

Tommy and Barrie Williams remained close friends for the rest of Tommy's life.

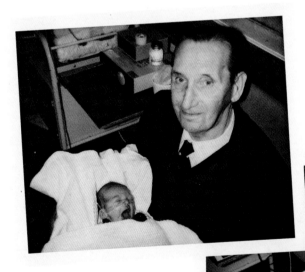

A proud grandfather. Tommy with his first grandchild, Anthony…

…closely followed by the second, Anthony's twin sister Zoë.

Tom Lawton Junior and family. From left to right, wife Gillian, Zoë and Anthony.

A floral tribute left on the gates at Nott's County's Meadow Lane stadium on the day of Tommy's death in November 1996.

Tommy's funeral cortege passes Meadow Lane on the way to his funeral…

…and members of the then current County team line up to pay their respects.

A happy Tommy pictured in 1988, four years after his resurgence.

Ambassador. Again, the Combined Services were too strong for the opposition, and won 10-2, the crowd being treated to five goals from their hero, Tommy Lawton.

Carrying memories to cherish for the rest of their lives, plus enough food for two meals (organised by Joe Mercer, who had been put in charge of rations) the party left Rome early on Sunday 13th May for a long, hot road trip by Army lorry to Ancona. The discomfort of the journey, with its debilitating heat and thick, choking dust, was relieved when they stopped for a nude swim at a wayside stream in the Apennines, which provided the opportunity for more banter with the 'victim' on this occasion, Matt Busby, being teased, "Is it the cold water, Matt – or are you starting to look your age?"

That cool dip, washing away the dust and chalk which, churned up by the wheels of the lorry, had left them resembling dusty millers, was so welcome: another of those memories which would be stored for ever. Indeed, though they couldn't know it at the time, this whole trip, with its team spirit, its spontaneous camaraderie, its fun and laughter, was cementing a relationship of true comradeship between this motley crew of footballers, a kinship which was to last for the rest of their lives.

That comradeship was tested, however, when the players, by now seriously hungry, stopped for their rations, only to find that all the food Joe Mercer had arranged for the trip was in cans – and he'd lost the tin opener! Frantically, they searched for a knife, a nail, anything that would get them into the cans for the food, mostly the inevitable bully beef, which they were by now craving, but it was all to no avail. "I know what we can do," said Joe, seeing his long-standing popularity evaporating amid the hunger pangs, "Let's put the tins on the ground and drive the lorry over them. That'll open them!"

In the earnest impromptu discussion that ensued, the real risk of puncturing the tyres, thus leaving them stranded, was subjugated to the hunger and the corned beef was laid out carefully in two lines so that the driver could roll slowly over them and pop them open. Regrettably, the theory did not stand up well to practice and the meat that was not flattened and buried deep into the sand was splattered all around in tiny, almost inedible fragments. The bits they could salvage from this wreckage did not go far; the rest of the journey was made on virtually empty stomachs and for once, genial Joe Mercer was not smiling broadly as his fellow travellers glared at him all the way.

When, finally, they reached Ancona, another town sadly disfigured by the deep scars of war, they were delighted to receive an unscheduled and genuinely warm welcome from the locals and an Army meal which, for all its customary culinary limitations, tasted absolutely wonderful. The whole afternoon of the rest day which followed was spent lazing on the beach, just lying, for much of the time, in the gently lapping shallow water of the sea, soaking up the brilliant sunshine. This induced an idyllic atmosphere in which it was impossible not to forgive Joe for the previous day's incompetence but 'Mess Sergeant' Mercer made sure he never lost his tin opener again!

After another comfortable victory, 7-1 against a District Services XI, the men of the Combined Services football tour party were treated to a sea trip from Ancona Harbour aboard Royal Navy minesweepers. *HM Minesweeper 2171,* the one carrying CSMI T Lawton, CSMI F Swift, Pte C Sidlow and Cpl J Bacuzzi, had a Liverpudlian second in command, Lieutenant Burrows of Crosby, who was a keen Everton supporter and he made sure that the four soccer stars on his ship had a marvellous time.

Three miles out to sea, the ship anchored for them to go overboard for a swim in the sparkling blue sea, after which they lay out on deck to sunbathe. The other three wondered what prank was coming when Frank Swift got up quietly and sneaked away. They did not have to wait long to find out. He had spotted a fire hose with which, having obtained the willing assistance of a couple of sailors, he proceeded to hose his teammates off the deck and into the sea! The startled trio had had enough of Big Swifty's japes. Revenge was nigh. They swam under the ship, boarded it unseen on the other side, charged at the unsuspecting big fella from behind, picked him up and threw him overboard. As he splashed around in the sea like a huge porpoise his pals let it be known that if he did not cease his practical joking from now on, a much worse fate would befall him. "OK, OK, I promise," spluttered Frank. They didn't believe a word of it.

On 17th May, the tourists met their stiffest opposition so far when they played the Naples Area XI in Rimini. This was a very good side which included Bryn Jones of Arsenal, Bob Pryde of Blackburn Rovers and several Welsh and Scottish players who had been top pre-war professionals but the Combined Services won a really hard fought game 2-0 with both goals from Billy Elliott and fine performances from Joe Bacuzzi and Billy Watson.

The next stage of the tour was to Florence and *en route* they stopped in Forli for lunch at the Dorchester Hotel, which, they were intrigued and amused to discover, had retained most of its top-class services and facilities, despite being commandeered as a NAAFI and offered the British lads there on leave luxuries like a shampoo and trim in the posh barber's shop and piano lessons in the plush lounge.

There was nothing remotely luxurious, however, about the journey which followed, over narrow, twisting roads, some barely more than cart tracks, across mountain passes 3,000 feet above sea level with sheer, unguarded drops on both sides of the Army lorry in which the players sat rigid with nerves, the occasional quips of bravado fooling none of them.

When a field service cap blew out of the lorry, Joe Mercer announced in a voice born to command, "Let it go. Whoever's lost it should be more careful." "But Joe", his mates chorused, "it's *yours!*" "Whoa there!" Joe shouted to the driver. Then, amid loud, ironic cheers, he ran 300 yards back down the track to retrieve his cap, returning, red-faced, to a resounding rendition of "He'll be coming round the mountain when he comes!"

Settling in at 54 Rest Camp in Florence, the tourists met 'Brazil Joe', an endearing member of the Brazilian Army, which was attached to the Allied Forces in this area. Joe equally attached himself to the touring party, who discovered that in peacetime, he was a cabaret acrobat and impresario. All the lads took immediately to Joe and his engaging patter, which included a solemnly presented offer to Tommy Lawton to play for £200 a game in Argentina after the War!

Joe took them down to the soccer pitch at the Rest Camp to show them four of his compatriots who were training for the match to be played the next day and stood with an air of vicarious pride as they demonstrated flashy tricks of the trade in which they were clearly master craftsmen. These 'red hot' South Americans were in the Fifth Army XI, the team to face the Combined Services for the game in Florence and if their inclusion added spice for the tourists, it was nothing compared with the thrill they got when they saw the stadium in which it was to be played. It was magnificent. The nearest thing to Wembley they had seen since leaving England. They went to their beds that night full of anticipation of a great occasion.

Regrettably, that was not to be. Among the big khaki-clad crowd were large numbers of British soldiers who were clearly angry that these 'over-protected stars' had spent the War safely at home playing football while they had been having such a tough time fighting and seeing so many of their mates killed or maimed. They had gone to the match prepared to give the visiting players as much abuse as they could throw at them.

It mattered not that many of them had idolised these same star footballers before the War. It was a repeat of the cold-shoulder treatment meted out to Gracie Fields, once adored and admired but now despised and ridiculed because she had followed her Italian husband, who would have been interned had he stayed in Britain, to his home in America and was safe in Canada while our cities were being blitzed. It was ill-informed, cruel, irrational but at the same time perfectly understandable and in that stadium in Florence, Tommy Lawton, Joe Mercer, Frank Swift, Matt Busby and the rest got the full abusive white feather contempt, hurled at them with real hatred and venom.

The mocking "Come on, you D-Day dodgers" aimed at the Combined Services team and the supportive 'Play up the real soldiers" for the Fifth Army side were among the least hurtful taunts and catcalls suffered by the tourists.

Stung by this, the Combined Services dropped all semblance of the relaxed, entertaining exhibition football they had served up elsewhere and tore fiercely into the opposition, annihilating them 10-0.

At a reception at the exclusive Riverside Club after the match, there were no hard feelings as both teams enjoyed two hours together, all present agreeing that, after all they had been through, the protagonists in that crowd were to be forgiven for their conduct: "Who can say, hand on heart, that he wouldn't do the same in their position?" said Tommy. His pals all nodded in agreement.

After Florence, Tommy and Joe Mercer left the tour party to fly from Rome back to London to play for England against France, while the rest went on into Greece, playing a series of matches.

Back home, Tommy and Joe heard BBC commentator Raymond Glendenning deliver an assessment of their contribution to the war effort which was in comforting contrast to their experience in Florence. Declaring the Combined Services tourists to be "our first ambassadors to liberated Europe" Glendenning went on to say of those players whose role had been to stay at home and play for morale: "On and off the field, they've done more for this country's prestige than is generally realised."

Lawton and Mercer arrived home on 25th May 1945, the day before the international with France and were told to go straight to Lancaster Gate to see Stanley Rous, who had an honour awaiting Tommy. He was to captain his country against the French in recognition of his great performances throughout the season.

"Tommy Lawton, captain of England," he recited to himself time and again as he looked forward to the match. He was bursting with pride when he experienced the tremendous thrill of leading England out onto the lush, green Wembley turf, with the flags of the United Nations fluttering in the sunshine and fighter planes roaring overhead, then shook hands with General Koenig of France before leading him along the line of English players, introducing them one by one. General Koenig became a celebrated war hero when he commanded a Free French Brigade at the Battle of Bir Hakeim in North Africa in 1942 and Tommy felt truly honoured to be in his presence.

Sadly, it wasn't a good game. England, who had been expected to win comfortably, never really got going, drew 2-2 and attracted a lot of criticism for an unsatisfactory display. The criticism was harsh in the extreme. England were football-weary after a long, hard season and two men upon whom they relied so much, Lawton (who scored one of the goals) and Mercer, were both shattered after an exhausting journey back from Italy. However, Tommy, mature beyond his years now, was not upset: "That's football," he said.

The war with Germany was over but in the Far East, victory against Japan had still to be achieved and that created transport problems for England's next away trip to play Switzerland. When the players reported to Paddington they were told that the Air Ministry had cancelled the plane in which they were to fly and withdrawn permission for air transport. It was too late to arrange train and boat transport across Europe and the match looked in jeopardy, until the Swiss government stepped in. On 18th July, a message was received at Croydon that a Swiss passenger plane, the first to leave Switzerland for England since 1939, wished to land. No notification had been received so the foresight and courtesy of the Swiss was repaid by refusal to land. The plane provided to help England out was then kept in the air until the Air Ministry had sent a message assuring all concerned that it was in order for it to land.

When, eventually, the England players clambered aboard, it was not just the borrowed aircraft which seemed strange: for the first time since 1939 they were travelling in civilian clothes. Switzerland had remained neutral throughout the war in Europe and a law of its devout neutrality was that 'uniforms of a belligerent nature' were banned. The English FA made a diplomatic decision that it might cause offence if our team arrived, as usual, in uniform so the players were provided with a special issue of ration coupons with which to buy personal clothing. It was a liberating experience for the England players to be wearing individual 'civvies' for the first time in six years and as they settled down for the flight to Zurich, Tommy turned to his travelling companion Big Swifty and observed, "Surprising how quickly you can get fed up with khaki!"

Surprising, too, how 'quickly' you can get used to food rationing. The players, gathered for dinner at the magnificent Hotel Gotthard in Zurich, could not believe their eyes when they saw the food laid out for them. Not only were massive sides of beautiful, succulent beef carved in such generous portions that it would have taken a year's ration coupons to obtain back home, there were huge, whole sumptuous salmon, chocolate cream cakes and other wickedly delicious desserts, the like of which had not been seen in England for six years, and – best of all – bananas, grapes, oranges, peaches, melons . . . a positive feast of forbidden fruit, all fresh, fat and juicy!

The players stood agog before this gastronomic nirvana, each telling the other what they were going to enjoy most and licking their lips in anticipation. "Just watch me murder that melon!" said Tommy. "Bugger the melon," said Big Swifty, "just let me at that beef!"

They had been surprised when, outside Zurich's Duebendorf Airport on arrival, they were mobbed by hundreds of enthusiastic Swiss soccer fans and when this happened again when they boarded the train for Berne, but neither of those warm welcomes compared with the scenes which greeted their arrival at Berne. It took 20 minutes for them to fight their way from the station through tumultuous crowds to their nearby hotel and it would have taken much longer even than that, had it not been for mounted policemen forcing a path through for them.

The next day, an expedition around shops, whose heavily laden shelves were a sight for sore eyes, was followed by a light training session and a civic reception in their honour before a trip to see the exciting night life of the famous Kursaal, scene of roulette, dancing and cabaret.

This whole Swiss experience was a fantastic release from the austerity of war-worn Britain and in the relaxed comfort of their civilian clothes, those players felt like visiting royalty when they arrived at the stadium for the match against Switzerland which, they had to remind themselves, was the purpose of this visit!

From their large squad, the England selectors chose: Swift (Manchester City); Scott (Arsenal), Hardwick (Middlesbrough); Soo (Stoke), Franklin (Stoke), Mercer (Everton); Finney (Preston), Brown (Charlton), Lawton (Everton), Hunt (Sheffield Wednesday), Smith (Brentford).

Before the game, that team joined 35,000 spectators packed into the tight little ground, to watch a dazzling display of massed coaching. Groups of boys, aged 12 upwards, were dotted around the pitch, all dressed in the colours of their own football clubs, giving demonstrations of ball control, trapping, heading, back-heeling and dribbling – all superbly synchronised, each skill being interchanged with perfect precision at each sharp blast of a whistle. This was an extraordinary sight, a blend of athleticism and theatre so beautifully choreographed that it brought lumps to the throats of the England players. They'd seen nothing even remotely like this in England. "Crikey," said Joe Mercer, "if the kids are this good, what's their team going to be like?"

The answer was too fit, too fast and altogether too good for England. The Swiss played an unfamiliar tactical formation, two speedy inside forwards spearheading the attack while the centre forward dropped back, roaming freely behind them. The centre half played well upfield while the fullbacks combined the dual roles of stopping their respective wingers and policing the middle. The whole team had a fluidity which facilitated inter-changing of positions and they were all good ball players, comfortable in possession. Above all, there was pace in every position.

Switzerland were so superior that the final score of 3-1 flattered England. But for a superb, heroic display by Frank Swift in goal (so impressive that he was carried off the pitch, shoulder high, by Swiss supporters) it would have been a humiliating thrashing for the team which had arrived in Switzerland all-conquering, feared and revered the world over.

Tommy and his teammates rationalised the defeat: it was a scorching hot day; the Swiss team had been away for three weeks' special training in the woods while England had come straight from Army camps or Air Force Stations – indeed, young Tom Finney, one of their few successes on his international debut, had arrived just before the match from Austria, where he was stationed with the Central Mediterranean Force; the England team was bound to feel the effects of a six-year war and they'd played so many games as part of their morale-boosting role that they were jaded, while the players from neutral Switzerland were fresh and focused on their football.

Legitimate reasons for such a sound defeat? Or was the rest of the world now perfecting football skills, new team tactics and fitness regimes to such great effect that England, inventors and for so long undisputed kings as well as custodians of this beautiful game, were beginning to be left behind? Did the brilliant Swiss performance and that breathtaking pre-match display by the boys of Berne, serve warning that the English crown was slipping?

Maybe Mr Stanley Rous thought so. Speaking at the post-match banquet he said, "Our men were beaten by the cleverer team. They played as well as they were allowed. The Swiss have made tremendous strides since we last played them."

Some pride was restored in England's next international – a 1-0 win against Northern Ireland in Belfast in September 1945. Tommy was part-nered up front by Stan Mortensen of Blackpool, who scored England's winner five minutes from time.

Football in immediate post-war England remained a serfdom. The play-ers, who earned hundreds of thousands of pounds for the clubs, were still paid a tiny fraction of the money they generated while wealthy directors lined their pockets. Discontent had simmered among the players since before the War and had resurfaced in 1943 when the Players' Union issued a 1,000-word report calling for: abolition of the maximum wage; establishment of a superannuation scheme; greatly increased bonuses in semi-final and final Cup ties and representative matches; alteration of players' agreements to run from 1st August to 31st July each year; increased compensation for injured players; player representation on committees affecting their well-being; and a revised transfer system.

With so many pressing priorities in wartime, nothing came of the demands in that report. But by the autumn of 1945 they were not only resurrected but a postal ballot of players at 86 clubs had secured a huge majority in favour of a strike if they were not agreed and implemented. The 'peasants' were revolting. And with every justification. The maximum wage had stood at £8 a week since 1921. Yet hundreds of thousands of paying spectators were putting increasing sums of money over the turnstiles and into the pockets of the directors every season.

The scene was set for a dramatic meeting of the Players' Union at the Grand Hotel in Manchester on (appropriately!) 5th November 1945. The purpose of the meeting, which attracted hordes of eager pressmen, was to discuss the players' demands in full and to formalise the strike vote.

Players representing 52 clubs packed the room, among them, Tommy Lawton. Tommy had always been a pay rebel; how could a lad brought up by Jim Riley be anything else? As one of football's biggest and brightest stars, people wanted to know where Lawton stood on the issue. And Tommy had plenty to say. Later he would describe it thus:

The present system is all wrong. A player who, by his skill, helps to draw a £25,000 gate and then receives, at the most, only £10 from this vast sum, as happens in a Wembley international match, is surely entitled to more.

What can a top-class player earn in a season? Let's look at my own case. Let's look at my earnings for the year before the War: May 1938 to May 1939 . . . I'm a reputed top-class player, centre forward of the League Division One champions, capped eight times for England and this is what I got:

Winter pay at £8 a week: £266.

Summer pay at £6 a week: £100.

Eight internationals at £8 per match, plus expenses: £74 10s.

Bonus for winning the League championship: £25.

Match bonus at £1 a point (League): £59.

Match bonus (Cup): £7.

That's a total of £531 10s for the year – and that's about £31 10s more than Tommy Trinder [a famous comedian] gets in one week!

Just like Tommy Trinder, we are top entertainers and I think top-class players should be paid a great deal more money weekly, or there should be a talent bonus scheme which would make certain the game's stars could take something out of all the money they bring in. And why isn't a player who commands a huge transfer fee for his club entitled to receive something for his own talent?

In most walks of life, if a man makes a success of his job and is persuaded to move to a better position, he doesn't go for less money, or even for the same money. No, he gets a rise. But there's no rise for the professional footballer. The only chance he has of making a nest egg for himself is if his club decides to grant him a benefit, which must not exceed £650, but the club can't be forced to do that. It's at the club's discretion. And the player is at their mercy.

I don't want people to misunderstand all that I'm saying. I don't want to sound bitter. I know full well that the professional footballer has a wonderful life compared with the lot of the average working man. Yes, I do know that. I'm truly grateful for all that football has given me and I'll never take that for granted.

I also appreciate that for those of us fortunate enough to be in the top flight there are compensations: overseas trips with the chance to see foreign countries under the very best conditions, first-class travel, top hotels, laid-on tours, souvenirs and all that. And in pre-war days there was always the chance to pick up advertising contracts by telling the world you use somebody's toothpaste, or wear somebody's boots, or patronise a particular tailor. And there's money to be earned from newspapers. Yes, I do know all that, but that's only for the lucky few. For the majority of players there's little else to be made out of the game other than a salary that an American baseball player, or an ice hockey player or a world famous boxer wouldn't even look at!

Views like those so vehemently expressed by Tommy held sway at that packed meeting and after much discussion of every aspect of the players' demands it was resolved to send the Football League an ultimatum that, unless the Management Committee agreed to meet the Players' Union committee to discuss these demands, no League football would be played in England and Wales after 17th November 1945.

Unknown to the great British public and most of the football world, Tommy Lawton had asked for a transfer away from Everton in July that year. He had no quarrel with the club which had given him the chance of that top-flight career. On the contrary, he loved playing for Everton and everything about the club – particularly the supporters, so knowledgeable and so appreciative of the fine arts of the game.

His problem was his marriage.

The relationship between him and Rosaleen had now deteriorated so badly that, he confided to Frank Swift, home was "hell" and something had to be done. The couple had been married for four years yet, owing to the War, had hardly seen anything of each other. All attempts to make the marriage work were failing so, Tommy believed, making a completely fresh start away from Liverpool might save it.

His first transfer request was refused but with no sign whatsoever of things improving with Rosaleen, he persisted and when it was finally granted, the news shook the soccer world to the core. Of course, numerous clubs were interested in signing England's best centre forward but why on earth was Lawton leaving Everton? They'd only had two seasons out of him before the War; the side that won the title were very young then and now they were well capable of becoming champions again. The papers were full of the mystery. Rumours were rife, but only his mates Big Swifty and Joe Mercer shared fully in Tommy's secret.

On 7th November, Tommy was transferred to Chelsea for a fee of around £14,000. He was stationed at Seighton Camp in Chester when the deal was struck and signed in a quiet back room of Dixie Dean's pub.

Press and public were stunned and mystified by the move. Tommy felt he couldn't tell the truth, couldn't 'wash his dirty linen in public', couldn't say that he really wanted to stay with Everton, so he told the clamouring reporters that his wife was ill and that doctors had said that a move to the South would be good for her. It was a completely fabricated 'explanation' and the first time in his career that Tommy had not been absolutely truthful to the press boys, with whom he had a brilliant rapport. He hated lying but his mind was in a turmoil of worry and confusion over his marriage and the strict adherence to doing the right thing, so deeply embedded in his nature from his upbringing, still dictated that he should strive to keep it alive despite all the evidence to the contrary.

So, on Saturday 10th November 1945 Tommy Lawton made his debut for Chelsea at Stamford Bridge in a Wartime Football League South fixture versus Birmingham City. Such was Everton's loss and Chelsea's gain from his transfer (and proving the point Tommy had made at that Players' Union strike meeting five days earlier) the attendance at Stamford Bridge was 53,813 – 22,000 up on the previous home game. Chelsea won 3-2 and Lawton scored two of their goals.

The arrival of Tommy Lawton was not the only cause of huge excitement around Chelsea Football Club that week. Four days later, Moscow

Dynamo were due to play in a friendly match which had captured the imagination of soccer fans all over the country.

Such was the interest in an unprecedented visit to Britain by the mysterious Russians that a crowd of around 100,000 turned up for the match: many broke into the ground and found unofficial vantage points; some perched precariously on the roof of the stand; others vaulted the pitch walls and stood on the greyhound track surrounding the touchlines. Estimates put the number of spectators inside the ground at something in excess of 85,000, with thousands more locked out. So great was the crush around the pitch that the police had to clear a path for the players to get through.

Before they took the field for the kick-off, the Russians did something never before seen on a British ground – going out onto the pitch in tracksuits and using several balls for a warm-up session. That huge crowd, intrigued by such a strange ritual, laughed, cheered and whistled as the visitors went through their routine.

They laughed even louder when, after the Band of the Royal Marines had played the national anthems, each Russian player, on command from their trainer, stepped solemnly forward to present every Chelsea player with a posy of pretty flowers. As the crowd jeered and wolf-whistled at what was, to them, an extraordinarily effeminate gesture, Tommy muttered under his breath, "What is it with these foreign players and their bouquets of bloody flowers!"

At least, having been given a similar floral tribute in Belgium, Tommy was not so flabbergasted as the rest of the Chelsea team who stood, holding their posies like reluctant bridesmaids, in extreme embarrassment until an even more red-faced Norman Smith, the Chelsea trainer, was despatched to collect them all before suffering the acute discomfort of having to walk off, looking like some mobile flower stall, to the unrestrained mirth and mockery of all those spectators.

As the teams lined up, the crowd's curiosity was further fired by the Russians' exotic kit – Baltic blue shirts with a large D on the left breast and darker blue shorts with a white stripe around the bottom. Just like the strange rituals, this Moscow Dynamo strip was like nothing they'd seen before.

Tommy was more interested in the players than their kit. Looking around them, he saw young, beautifully built athletes. "This lot are going to be quick," he thought. And so they were. With brilliant ball control, they tore into Chelsea from the kick-off and for the first 20 minutes, the hosts were left chasing swift shadows around the pitch. Chelsea, who weren't helped by being a bit disorganised, having had to solve an injury crisis by borrowing two players, Joe Bacuzzi and Jimmy Taylor, from Fulham, were so outplayed by the Russians that they could have been four goals down in that opening spell.

Then, after 25 minutes, Tommy Lawton made his mark. He went up for a cross with Dynamo goalkeeper Tiger Khomich, headed the ball out of his hands then tapped a pass to Len Goulden who stabbed it into the net. Six minutes later, Dynamo's left back Stankevich panicked under pressure from Chelsea's Reg Williams and, in trying to clear, crashed the ball against Williams, from whom it rebounded into the net. Well, they all count! 2-0 to Chelsea.

Just before half-time, Moscow Dynamo were awarded a penalty, only for left half Leonid Soloviev to be left burying his face in his hands after fluffing his kick – a mishap which might well have been precipitated by the proximity of the baying spectators who were surging around the goal! This distraction became more evident after the interval and on several occasions the police had to force the crowd back so that throw-ins and corners could be taken, but the patience, pace and skill of the Russians paid off with goals from inside right Kartsev and outside right Archangelski levelling the game at 2-2 to set up a great finish.

It looked like Chelsea's match when Lawton, with a typical leap, headed a long high ball past the advancing Khomich to make it 3-2. Then Dynamo's inside left, Bobrov, who was standing at least five yards offside, stabbed a loose ball into the net. The infringement was so blatantly obvious that both sets of players and every one of that massive crowd waited for the referee, Commander Campbell, to disallow the goal but to everybody's astonishment he signalled a goal and ran back to the centre circle, hotly pursued by Tommy Lawton.

"You can't give *that!*" shouted Tommy.

"It was for diplomatic reasons," replied the referee.

"Well, you've diplomatically robbed us of a win bonus," said Tommy. A friendly it might have been, but Chelsea's new centre forward was not amused!

This unique, ground-breaking match had created massive press interest and Tommy was asked to give his assessment of these strange visitors, as if they were men from Mars. His verdict:

The Russians do not dribble. They flash the ball from man to man in bewildering fashion, often while standing still. Only when there is a clear run to goal does the Dynamo really whirl into motion. Then, seven men converge like destroyers on the opposing goal. If the ball is blocked, back they all go to pack their own penalty area, the halfbacks and inside forwards as well. It's very impressive, yet there are flaws. A cool-headed side with two quick-moving inside forwards would shatter the defensive–offensive system, which is very similar to basketball tactics.

The match was just as big a talking point in Moscow, where, much to Tommy's amusement when he read it reprinted in the London *Evening Standard,* a radio broadcast declared:

Chelsea played with a strengthened team. Determined to beat Dynamo at all costs, the club had spent thousands of pounds to secure some of Britain's best footballers. For instance, Chelsea paid £14,000 for Tommy Lawton just so that he could play against Dynamo.

"Well," Tommy chuckled, "thanks for the compliment!"

After the game, Chelsea staged a party for the players and officials of both teams and despite the obvious inability to understand a word of the other's language, they all managed to make themselves understood and a good time was had by all, Tommy – a smoker like several of his fellow professionals – particularly appreciating the gift of a splendid inscribed lighter.

Moscow Dynamo went on to play Cardiff City, Glasgow Rangers and Arsenal, amid the same intense fascination and interest as they created at Chelsea.

In a rare burst of enlightenment, during the tour the Football Association invited the Russians to join selected English players and club managers for a round-table discussion on the differing interpretation of rules, the different tactics, training methods and philosophies. Among the English delegates for the meeting in London was Tommy Lawton, who not long afterwards published his thoughts on this historic gathering in a book:

Perhaps the biggest debating point concerned tackling. In their match at Stamford Bridge the Russians did not indulge in the sliding tackle, nor in fact did they do any hard tackling when the ball was in the possession of a Chelsea player. Instead, they preferred either to stand in our way to impede us with hand or body or often push us off the ball. Naturally, those tactics can be very annoying.

In turn, we found that hard tackling or charging the goalkeeper is not permitted in Russia. Heavy charging is forbidden so as to prevent accidents as far as possible. Whatever the rights and wrongs from both our points of view, the rules should be stabilised when next a British and Russian team meet. It will help to prevent any possible incidents.

Another difference is that substitutes are permitted under Russian rules. In deference to our requests, they kept down the reserves as much as possible. While substitutes are very welcome in case of serious injury to a player, particularly a goalkeeper, freedom to play substitutes ad lib *could lead to unfair practice.*

Tommy was also a guest at the Lord Mayor of London's Banquet at Mansion House held in honour of the Russian visitors; a grand affair, this, with white tie and tails and all the civic plate on view. On the same table as Tommy sat one of the Common Councillors; a very venerable old gentleman who'd imbibed rather too well, his spontaneous personal contribution in tribute to the Russians was to stand up on unsteady feet and in a booming voice, perform a recitation:

> *Caviar's the roe of the virgin sturgeon*
> *The virgin sturgeon's a very fine fish*
> *Not every sturgeon's a virgin sturgeon*
> *That's why caviar's a very rare dish.*

Tommy was not convinced that the old boy's offering was entirely appropriate to the pomp and circumstance of this august gathering, but *he* enjoyed it!

He was also invited to the farewell party for Moscow Dynamo at the Scala Theatre, London, hosted by the Russian Ambassador to Britain, at which guests were shown two films demonstrating the supreme physical fitness being demanded of participants in all Russian sports – another example of how foreign sporting nations were beginning to offer lessons to a country they had all once lagged behind.

With Tommy in fine form for his new club it was, perhaps, just as well that the threatened players' strike never materialised. Their union's demand for a meeting was agreed by the Football League which then made a few minor improvements, such as increasing the maximum close season wage to £7 a week. But the miserly main maximum wage remained intact and there was no significant change to the gross injustice of the massive gap between the vast amount of money football was making and the share the footballers were getting for bringing it in. This was an issue upon which the eloquent campaigning of Tommy Lawton was having no impact.

There was, however, no lack of impact on the fortunes of Chelsea FC from the Lawton goalscoring magic. In just four weeks following the Moscow Dynamo game he scored four in two games against Brentford, three against Swansea, two against Millwall and another three against Millwall in the return match at the Den, which Chelsea won 8-0! And the Chelsea fans were flocking to see their new hero. "Right," Tommy told

Big Swifty when they met for a beer one night, "I've repaid my transfer fee already – from now on, they've got me for nowt!"

Tommy settled into Stamford Bridge so quickly, helped by his England colleagues Vic Woodley and Len Goulden, and with players of the calibre of John Harris, Danny Winter, Dick Foss and Dick Spence this was a strong Chelsea team. Several of those players, Tommy included, were still in uniform and the 1945/46 season was still being played to the wartime structure. So, too, were England international matches against Scotland, Wales, France, Northern Ireland and Belgium, all of which Tommy played in – scoring three goals (two against Scotland, one against France).

The game against Belgium, at Wembley, attracted 85,000 spectators but they saw very little of the second half after a thick fog suddenly enveloped the stadium. England won 2-0 and, as they played on through a real London pea-souper, Frank Swift made a sensational save to keep out a blistering 30-yard drive. "How did you manage that?" asked Tommy in deep admiration. "Easy," said Big Swifty, "I heard it coming!"

CSMI Lawton T, then stationed at Kingston upon Thames, was demobbed later that season. For Tommy it was freedom, as well as full and final confirmation that the War in Europe was over. That war had robbed him of six years of his professional career but, unlike thousands of young men of the same age, he had emerged from it with life and limbs intact. And he thanked God for that.

As if there had not been enough tragedy during that war, soccer had one of its own in March 1946 – and it was very close to home for Tommy Lawton. Several of his relatives and friends were at the FA Cup tie between Bolton Wanderers and Stoke City at Burnden Park when a wall collapsed, crushing spectators and causing a stampede. Thirty-three people were killed and more than 400 were injured. Mercifully, none of Tommy's relatives were among the dead and injured but he was sickened and angered by the tragedy.

The football grounds of England had been badly neglected during the War; no money had been spent on them, even though huge sums had been made out of football and with the War over, fans were packing those creaking old stadia. Tommy and his Chelsea teammates had just played Arsenal when news of the carnage at his home town ground came through. They were stunned. Tommy sat with his head in his hands. "It needn't have happened," he said. "It needn't have bloody happened."

On 19th May 1946 Tommy Lawton played in England's last 'wartime international', away to France. They lost 2-1 but Tommy had scored 24 goals in his 23 of those internationals.

In the following close season, Tommy was asked to represent the

Football Association in Switzerland, coaching Swiss players and coaches. His ability as a coach had been recognised and much appreciated in the Army and – never lacking in confidence – he knew he was good at it but, even so, he was surprised and flattered to be chosen.

His exhaustive tour took in most of the Swiss clubs, including Geneva, Lugano and Berne and all the Swiss coaches gathered at the Tommy Lawton Training Camp at Magglinden, high up in the Alps. They all stayed at a large, first-class hotel and woke to an alarm call at 6 am every morning, upon which Tommy found it a joy to go immediately outside and breathe in the invigorating cold, crisp air before training against a backdrop of beautiful mountains and fir trees. Then they gathered back at the hotel for structured discussion in which they compared the English and Swiss styles of play, analysed the differences and pooled their ideas. The Swiss took cine film and recordings of Tommy's training sessions to circulate throughout their country. It was hard, tiring work for Tommy, his action-packed days often not ending until 11 o'clock at night but despite that, it felt like a tonic.

At the end of his tour he'd lost a stone in weight and had never felt better. When Chelsea players reported back for the start of the first full post-war season, with normal Football League service resumed after a six-year break, there was nobody fitter than the centre forward!

There was another milestone in English football that summer . . . England appointed the first full-time director of coaching and manager of its international team. Step up, Mr Walter Winterbottom.

Winterbottom was a schoolteacher, trained at Chester Diocesan Training College, who was playing amateur football when he was spotted and signed by Manchester United in 1936. He played 26 games for United's first team before his playing career was ended by a spinal ailment in 1938.

Tommy Lawton and Frank Swift, now to come under the control of the ex-teacher for internationals, rarely disagreed about anything. But they did disagree about Walter Winterbottom. Big Swifty thought the new manager was a fine coach, a first-class appointment. Tommy thought he was a berk!

What was to prove a less-than-perfect relationship with the new England boss got off to the worst of starts when Tommy withdrew from his first session with the squad, prior to a match against Scotland in aid of the Bolton Disaster Fund, because of a groin strain, probably not helped by the exhaustive itinerary on his summer trip to Switzerland. Thereafter, it gradually deteriorated. Fairly or not, Tommy thought there was too much of the 'lah-de-bloody-dah' about Mr Winterbottom, to whom he always referred as 'Old Summer-arse'. For his part, Winterbottom was not overimpressed with Tommy and Big Swifty habitually enjoying a half-time cigarette in the dressing room!

But Tommy, after a quiet start by his standards to the 1946/47 season, began to hit goalscoring form for Chelsea. He now had a wealth of experience, yet he was still only 26 years old. England could simply not ignore him. So Lawton was back, leading the line, for his country against Northern Ireland in Belfast on 28th September. England won 7-2, with all five forwards getting on the score sheet.

The next England international match, two days later, was to be an historic occasion: the first time England played the Republic of Ireland. During the 1940s there were two Ireland teams – the IFA in Northern Ireland and the FAI in the Republic – and both claimed jurisdiction over the whole island. Consequently, a number of top Irish footballers played for both! Ireland had been partitioned in 1921 and the Irish Free State was formed in 1922. In nearly 25 years since then, England had regularly played the IFA team, but never the one representing the Republic. So this game, to be played at Dalymount Park, Dublin, was special.

Just as special was the meal provided for the England party the night they arrived in Dublin. Britain was still suffering food shortages and in the iron grip of rationing so meals back home were almost as austere as they'd been in the worst of the war years. The Republic had no such problems, having remained resolutely neutral throughout the War. And the fare that greeted the English players at the Gresham Hotel was as mind-boggling as the feast they'd had in Switzerland the previous year.

"Have you really got all this?" Big Swifty asked an attentive Irish waiter as they ogled the extensive menu with its soup, fish, beef, lamb, chicken, turkey, cheese and fruit. "We have indeed, sir," said the waiter, "and it's all lovely." "Beats Spam fritters, eh, Swifty?" said Tommy. Then the footballers, normally noisy at meal times, worked their way meticulously through that magnificent mouth-watering menu in almost total silence.

The following morning the players went to Dublin's Government House to be presented to the man who had famously fought so hard for Irish independence, Éamon de Valera, the Taoiseach. Éamon de Valera, who had been born in America to an Irish mother, was a fascinating man who had dominated Irish life as a freedom fighter, hero, leader and statesman for 30 years. Much admired for his work with the United Nations, he had resisted intense pressure, sometimes even threats, from Germany, Britain and the United States over his policy of neutrality in the War. This had not endeared him to many in war-ravaged Britain but, the politics of that aside, Tommy Lawton considered it an honour to shake the hand of a man who had always demonstrated such determination to stand by his principles. He respected that.

Later, reflecting on how many famous people he had been able to meet, Tommy remarked to Frank Swift, "And all because I play football. Amazing!" "Ah, but look," said Big Swifty. You're famous, too!" Despite all his success, that had never really occurred to the lad from Bolton.

For the game with the Republic, England kept faith with players, such as Lawton, Carter, Mannion and Finney, who had done so well against Northern Ireland. For Tommy there was a reunion with his former Everton colleague, Alex Stevenson, who was in the Republic side, which also included two men, Johnny Carey and Bill Gorman, who had played for Northern Ireland two days earlier. The Republic offered stronger opposition and England won 1-0, the winner coming from Tom Finney nine minutes from time.

When the England players returned to Liverpool there was another encounter between Tommy Lawton and the parsimonious 'lah-de-bloody-dah' Mr Ewbank, the FA treasurer. Expenses for the trip to Ireland were being sorted out when Ewbank beckoned, "Lawton . . . over here." "Oh, bloody 'ell," thought Tommy, "now what have I done?" But Ewbank told him, "Here's the penny you're owed from the last game when we didn't have enough change to recompense you in full." "Oh, thank you very kindly, sir," said Tommy, tugging his forelock in an exaggerated gesture of mock humble gratitude, "Now, I'll be able to have a shit on my way home, if that's all right with you!"

Insubordination to the treasurer and half-time fags notwithstanding, the increasingly rebellious Lawton was named in an unchanged England team for the first official international match to be played at home since the War – versus Wales at Maine Road – and was able to make two more reunions. At centre half for Wales was his good pal and international adversary Yanto Jones, while at outside left for Wales was Swansea City's George Edwards – the same George Edwards who had so respectfully asked Tommy how he wanted the ball crossing in that Army game back in 1944.

How Tommy enjoyed a good natter with those two genial Welshmen but, as ever when England met Wales, there was no quarter asked or given when they got on the field of play. It was a terrific, hard-fought game with Wales, fast and skilful, giving their hosts a real battle. England won 3-0, thanks to what sports writers declared to be one of the best attacking displays ever seen in England by the powerful forward line of Tom Finney, Raich Carter, Tommy Lawton, Wilf Mannion and Bobby Langton and some superb goalkeeping by Frank Swift. Tommy scored one of those goals and laid on another for Wilf Mannion, who got two. Those enthusiastic press scribes were able to wallow in England's post-war strength in attack by pointing out that there was no place in this side for the great Stan Matthews or for the hugely talented Newcastle forward Len Shackleton – Preston's Finney and Blackburn Rovers' Langton keeping their places after good performances in Ireland and Lawton holding on to the number 9 shirt in spite of the burgeoning claims of Blackpool's high-scoring Stan Mortensen.

Impressed though they all were with that forward line against Wales they'd seen nothing yet. Picked again when England went on to play Holland at Huddersfield on 27th November 1946, Finney, Carter, Lawton, Mannion and Langton tore the Dutch to pieces. England won 8-2 with man of the match Tommy Lawton scoring four times.

Tommy's brilliant all-round performance that day prompted eulogies in the national press, including a fulsome tribute from his mate Frank Swift, who said, "That was, without doubt, the best display I have ever seen from a centre forward." It was a view shared by the President of the Dutch FA, Mr Karel Lotsy, who declared, "In 30 years of football on the Continent and in England I saw today a forward line such as I have never seen before." It was a forward line led superlatively by Tommy Lawton, whose command of every aspect of the centre forward's game was so complete that he was now reckoned by many well-qualified observers to be the best in the world.

Tommy's goals were flowing just as freely for Chelsea and he looked set fair for a great season. Maybe this would be the year in which he would gain the one honour still to elude him – an FA Cup final appearance.

In the third round, he played his full dramatic part in three magnificent ties with Arsenal, watched by a total of 180,000 spectators and culminating in a 2-0 victory for Chelsea on the neutral ground of White Hart Lane in the second replay on 20th January. Thousands of Chelsea fans among the crowd of 59,000 went wild with delight as their hero Lawton scored both goals, one with his head, one with his left foot, to put Chelsea into the fourth round.

Arsenal were captained by Tommy's old Everton buddy, Joe Mercer. The pair shared a taxi after the game and Mercer told his chum, "With this lot, you must have a chance, Tom." Tommy dared to hope that he was right. That taxi was taking Joe to Euston Station for his train back to Hoylake in Cheshire where he lived and Tommy to the club house in Kenton, Middlesex, where he lived with Rosaleen, who was not interested in whether or not her husband would make it to Wembley.

Then, on 22nd January it started to snow. This was the first day of the

Big Freeze of 1947 to which football (along with every other facet of life in Britain) was to fall victim. After that first snowfall on 22nd January, snow fell every day until 17th March. The unrelenting Arctic conditions, temperatures as low as -18 being frequently recorded, brought transport and industry to a standstill. Even the chimes of Big Ben were frozen into silence. The country was woefully ill-equipped to withstand the effects of the Big Freeze. The War had left Britain debt-ridden and on its knees. Food rationing was still, of necessity, rigidly applied and there were genuine, though suppressed, fears of famine. The abject misery of the vicious, enduring cold was compounded by severe rationing of coal.

Football? Well, believe it or not, some games were played, with sweat literally freezing in the players' hair, falling snow blurring their vision and obliterating the pitch markings, but the majority were wiped out and it was the middle of June before all the Football League fixtures could be completed.

On 25th January, it was bitterly cold but the Big Freeze was still in its infancy and Chelsea's fourth round FA Cup tie with the holders Derby County at Stamford Bridge was one of the games to survive. With just one minute left and Chelsea 2-1 up, Tommy's fervent hope seemed intact, until Raich Carter grabbed an equaliser. Four days later on a Baseball Ground pitch which was frozen solid, big centre forward Jackie Stamps scored the goal that won the replay for Derby and put Lawton's Cup final dream back on hold.

Another game to beat the Big Freeze was Chelsea's visit to the Valley to play Charlton Athletic on 1st February. Chelsea won 3-2 and Charlton's goalkeeper Sam Bartram later described Tommy Lawton's winning goal thus:

As Len Goulden was about to take a free kick, Tommy pointed at the top left-hand corner of my goal and told me, "That's where it's going, Barty!" The ball came over and Tommy was still climbing as his marker, Harry Phipps, was beginning to drop down. Lawton arched his neck, his forehead met the ball and guess where it went – top left! He headed it so hard and so accurately that I couldn't stop it, even though I knew where it was going!

When that weather-hit season finally ended in June 1947, Tommy Lawton was Chelsea's top scorer with 26 goals in 34 matches – a new club record.

With a scoring record for the season like that, it was no surprise that Tommy Lawton was an automatic choice as the best centre forward in Great Britain when an historic fixture was played in front of 135,000 spectators on 10th May 1947. In the game, which the press called the

'Match Of The Century' a Great Britain XI drawn from the best players in England, Scotland, Wales and Northern Ireland played The Rest Of Europe at Hampden Park. The match was staged to celebrate the return of the British Home Nations to FIFA, which they had left in 1920. That huge crowd produced gate receipts of £35,000 for FIFA, whose finances had been damaged by lack of competition during the war.

The Great Britain team, playing in navy blue shirts to honour their Scottish hosts, was: Frank Swift (Manchester City & England); George Hardwick (Middlesbrough & England); Billy Hughes (Birmingham and Wales); Archie Macauley (Brentford & Scotland); Jackie Vernon (West Brom & Northern Ireland); Ron Burgess (Tottenham & Wales); Stanley Matthews (Blackpool & England); Wilf Mannion (Middlesbrough & England); Tommy Lawton (Chelsea & England); Billy Steel (Morton & Scotland); Billy Liddell (Liverpool & Scotland).

The Rest Of Europe lined up: Da Rui (France); Petersen (Denmark); Steffen (Switzerland); Carey (Eire); Parola (Italy); Ludi (Czechoslovakia); Lemberechts (Belgium); Gren (Sweden); Nordahl (Sweden); Wilkes (Holland); Praest (Denmark).

Stanley Matthews and Tommy Lawton had both played for England versus the Rest Of Europe in that tetchy affair back in 1938 but there was to be no repeat of the foul play from the Rest Of Europe which had soured that bruising pre-war encounter. This match was played in a much better spirit on a bright, warm day which provided the 135,000 fans with welcome relief from the freezing winter. Matthews and Lawton shone for Great Britain with Tommy scoring twice in a 6-1 victory which had the Scottish *Sunday Mail* declaring whimsically: "Never have so many owed so much to these two!"

There has only been one other occasion on which a Great Britain team consisting of players from England, Scotland, Wales and Ireland has played an international match and that was in 1955, when they again took on the Rest Of Europe in a game to celebrate the 75th anniversary of the Irish Football Association in Belfast on 13th August 1955.

This time, there was no place for Tommy Lawton, Great Britain's No. 9 shirt being worn by Roy Bentley of Chelsea, but the evergreen Stanley Matthews was again at outside right. Great Britain lost 4-1.

The frozen winter had been one of discontent for England's professional footballers, who were still, through their union, striving to correct the injustice of their pay structure and in the spring an arbitration tribunal ruled in favour of the players and decreed that the maximum wage should be increased to £12 a week in winter and £10 a week in summer.

This was still almost criminally disproportionate when set against the massive profits top football clubs were making out of gates averaging 50,000 to 60,000; the judgment still failed to positively discriminate between players of Tommy Lawton's world-class calibre and those playing for small clubs in the lower leagues and it preserved the 'feudal' grace-and-favour benefit system, the proceeds of which, for those players lucky enough to get one, were taxed while professional cricketers' benefit receipts were not.

So Tommy continued to be a publicly prominent and outspoken critic of the footballers' lot, while never failing to appreciate and to point out the difference between the new wage and the £3 a week paid to a miner which, from his poor working-class background, he might well have become.

For one reason or another and rightly or wrongly, 'the world's best centre forward' was now firmly moulded as a rebellious troublemaker, adored by his millions of working-class fans but mistrusted and feared by soccer's establishment, who would much rather do without him but didn't dare to. They continued to pick him for England and between 12th April and 25th May 1947 he followed his four-goal performance against Holland with caps against Scotland, France, Switzerland and Portugal (against whom he achieved another extraordinary four-goal tally) and that two-goal appearance for Great Britain at Hampden Park.

He had been looking forward to the end of that long, hard season so that he could have a break and when Chelsea announced a summer tour of Sweden, that rebellious Lawton streak came to the fore again. He felt jaded. Because of his FA coaching trip to Switzerland in the previous close season he had not had a break from football for 18 months. And the interminable domestic troubles still plagued him, despite his belief that a new life in London might have cured his marital ills. One way and another, he needed a club tour of Sweden like a hole in the head. He'd never given anything but 100 per cent and he felt that to go on tour in that sort of physical and mental state wouldn't be fair to the club, or to one of the young up-and-coming players who could have the chance to go in his place. And that's what he told Chelsea manager Billy Birrell.

Birrell's response was "You'll have to go to Sweden and I'll have no arguments." Tommy replied, "There's nothing in my contract to force me to play in Sweden and I'm just not prepared to." "We'll make you go," stormed Birrell. "Have no fear about that." That was the worst thing he could have said to Tommy the Rebel. Shades of grandfather Riley's *Sam, Sam, Pick Up Tha Musket* shone through the red mist of his anger. Now, his back was well and truly up: "Wild horses won't drag me there!" he shouted at Birrell and stormed out of the manager's office.

That night at home in Kenton he had a visit from Chelsea chairman Joe Mears and another director, Jack Budd. They threatened to report him to the Football Association and to stop his wages unless he toed the line and went to Sweden. Not the right approach. Now, Sam's musket was definitely staying on the bloody ground! "Listen, you two," said Tommy, "I had enough of this sort of ordering around in the Army and I'm not going to tolerate it in Civvy Street. I might just have considered going on tour before you came round here with your big stick act. This is not a concentration camp. I've had enough. I'm not going. Got it?"

What none of the Chelsea top brass had told Tommy was that they had promised their Swedish counterparts personal appearances by the great Tommy Lawton as a crucial part of the deal for the tour. Had he known that, his attitude would have been different and, tired as he was, he'd have gone. Instead, their haughty, dictatorial approach incensed him. His heels were irretrievably entrenched. They were going to Sweden without Tommy Lawton.

And that was the beginning of the end for him at Chelsea FC.

The relationship between Tommy Lawton and the football fans of England was extraordinary. He was hero-worshipped throughout the country and in London he was treated like a film star everywhere he went. He was at his peak and in his prime, both as a player and as a handsome young man. Women adored his good looks and natural Northern charm; men admired his athleticism and skill. He wrote a column for a national newspaper and used it frequently to speak out for the players against the football establishment. His outspoken views on the 'lah-de-dah' hierarchy gave him a 'Robin Hood' aura and made him even more popular with the masses.

There were just two places, however, where he was not lauded and idolised: at home, where Rosaleen, now the mother of a baby girl, Amanda, appeared to prefer anybody's company to his, and in the corridors of power at Chelsea Football Club.

While the Chelsea players were understanding and sympathetic towards Tommy's stance, the tension over his refusal to tour led to a very strained atmosphere with the top brass when the 1947/48 season got under way, but it had no effect on his form, nor on his ability to fill Stamford Bridge. Having picked up an injury in training, he missed two League games but when he made his first appearance against Derby County at Stamford Bridge, the gate of 59,919 was 23,000 up on the previous home game. He didn't disappoint all those extra fans either, winning the game for Chelsea with a trademark bullet header.

In September, he was hitting the world's headlines again when he scored a sensational goal in just 12 seconds from kick-off when England beat

Belgium 5-2 in Brussels. In those 12 seconds there were eight passes and no Belgian player touched the ball. Lawton kicked off to Wilf Mannion; Mannion back to Lawton; Lawton to Tim Ward; Ward to Stan Matthews; Matthews to Lawton; Lawton to Mannion; Mannion to Matthews; Matthews to Lawton. Goal!

By then, Tommy, fed up with the strained relationship at Stamford Bridge, had handed in a transfer request to Chelsea. It was refused. He persisted until they put him on the list and dropped him to the Reserves the day after another England call-up!

The Reserves were playing Arsenal Reserves at Highbury and when Arsenal manager Tom Whittaker heard that Tommy Lawton was playing he increased the usual reserve game order of just a few thousand match programmes to 20,000. Meanwhile, over at Stamford Bridge, where Arsenal's first team were the visitors, the Chelsea directors were smugly content with a near-capacity crowd: "So who needs Lawton?" They were not quite so convinced of their own argument, however, when they learned that the reserve game had attracted a crowd of more than 22,000 and canny Tom Whittaker had sold all his programmes! Four days later, Chelsea reserve Lawton scored as England drew 2-2 with Northern Ireland.

Persistent marital problems aside, Tommy was happy in London. He had grown to love the capital and the warm, outgoing Londoners had taken him so much to their hearts that he felt he belonged there among them. His ideal choice for his next club was Arsenal, so much so that he had sounded them out and Tom Whittaker had expressed an interest in signing him. Tommy then spoke to Bill Birrell about the possibility of moving to Highbury. Birrell told him that Arsenal were not interested. "You're a liar!" Tommy raged. "I know full well that they are." To which Birrell replied, "Look, there's one club you're not going to and that's Arsenal," thus proving that Tommy's oft-repeated protests about soccer serfdom were well founded.

One club which Chelsea were happy for Tommy to move to was Sunderland. Before he was transfer-listed, Tommy had played very well in a 3-2 win at Roker Park and he was sitting on the team bus ready to return to London when Sunderland's manager Bill Murray invited him into his office. There, Murray told him, "Any player in dispute with his club who can play as well as you've just done is the sort of man I want here." He said he could promise that Tommy would not only be well looked after as a player at Sunderland but a business would be provided for him, assuring him of a steady income when he retired from the game.

It was a very good offer and Murray's complimentary words had moved him but he had convinced himself that he did not want to go back up north and still clung to the hope that he might be able to sign for Arsenal, so he declined. After he'd been put on the transfer list, Bill Murray rang him several times at home to try to persuade him but, politely and gratefully, he insisted that he must stay in the South.

One morning, Bill Birrell called Tommy into his office at Stamford Bridge and handed him a list of clubs, saying, "Cross out the ones you don't fancy." And among the names on that list was one most unlikely club: Notts County.

The back streets of Nottingham

Chapter Seven

NOTTS COUNTY? YOU'RE JOKING!

Arthur Stollery was the masseur at Chelsea and Tommy Lawton, invariably kicked black and blue by lesser soccer mortals trying in vain to contain him, was a frequent visitor to his treatment table. Tommy was a great admirer of Stollery and not just for his healing skills. Arthur was a strong, interesting personality, the sort of no-nonsense man that Tommy had always liked and the two very quickly became firm friends. They would talk football for hours and, what's more, Tommy felt this was a man he could trust so they also discussed personal matters. They became close confidantes.

One day, Stollery told him, "Guess what. They've sacked me!" "Never! Why?" "I dunno. But they want rid of me." "What are you going to do?" Stollery explained that he was actually quite pleased to be leaving. He had, for some time, believed that he was capable of managing a football club and this was the spur he'd needed: "I'm going to look for a job in management."

"Arthur, I wish you all the luck in the world," Tommy told him. "Nobody deserves to succeed more than you and if there's ever anything I can do to help, at any time you know you can rely on me." "Well, actually I was thinking," said Stollery, "If I do get a job as a manager and you're ever contemplating leaving Chelsea, will you sign for me?" "Yes I will. And that's a promise," said Tommy. The friends shook hands on that promise.

Neither man had dreamed at the time that the day for that promise to be kept would come so quickly and that Arthur Stollery, manager of lowly Notts County, would have the effrontery to be trying to sign the world's best centre forward, the great England international Tommy Lawton, to play for him . . . in the Third Division!

But when he saw the name of Notts County on Chelsea manager Bill Birrell's list, Tommy had little hesitation. Clearly, he was not going to be able to join Arsenal and paramount among so much that he'd learned from grandfather Riley was that a man must always keep his word. If Notts County could afford the transfer fee, he would sign for Arthur Stollery.

Bill Birrell was flabbergasted. "You are joking?" he gasped. "Never been more serious," replied Tommy. And nor had Arthur Stollery.

Yes, Notts County could and would pay Chelsea's asking price (a new British record of £20,000!) and, for his part, Tommy was able to rationalise the incredible drop into the Third Division: a promise was a promise and, in any event, football's feudal pay structure meant that he'd earn more or less the same money as he was getting at Chelsea. If a move to Arsenal had been possible it would have been different and anyway, if it had been, Arthur would not even have attempted to call in that promise.

A trip to Nottingham cemented Tommy's resolve to join County. He met vice-chairman Harold Walmsley who told him that, if he joined them, he would be very well looked after. Not only would Notts County treat him as well as any other club in the land but they would also guarantee him a job outside football to secure his future when his playing days were over. "Right," Tommy told a delighted Stollery. "I'm signing."

The news shook the soccer world to its roots. Tommy Lawton, still only 28, dropping into the Third Division! The newspapers could not print enough copies. They were selling out throughout the length and breadth of the country. In the pubs, where they consumed the headlines as avidly as their pints; in the factories, shops and offices there was only one topic of conversation: What on earth had Lawton done? And why?

The sports journalists were working as feverishly as their imaginations, criticising, theorising, speculating, boasting the 'exclusive inside story' of why Tommy Lawton was leaving the limelight for the 'sticks'. Some of the stories were bizarre, some were just fanciful, most were inaccurate. In Nottingham the garrulous gossip about 'the real reason' was as rife as the Notts County supporters' jubilation over the incredible signing was boundless . . .

He'd been given thousands of pounds 'in his back pocket'; he was being paid, illegally, well over the maximum wage; he was getting all manner of surreptitious extras; he'd be getting half the gate receipts for himself; there would be a 'Tommy Lawton turnstile' and he'd get all the cash from it; he'd been involved in some massive scandal at Chelsea that no one could talk about but it meant that no First Division club wanted to touch him with a barge pole!

It was all nonsense. There were three reasons why Tommy Lawton had signed for Notts County: discontent at Chelsea, loyalty to a friend and the promise of security. Not sensational and scurrilous, which is what some of the national press would have preferred and the gossip implied, but principled and pragmatic. And true.

Neither, contrary to the rampant rumours, was there a big share of that record transfer fee for the man whose peerless football prowess had created it. All Tommy got out of it was £300 in accrued benefit and a £10 signing-on fee.

Yes, he was wealthy by a lot of people's standards but most of that money came from writing for newspapers; royalties on a book, *Football Is My Business*, which he'd written in 1945, and personal appearances. His football earnings had always been limited to the maximum wage, meagre bonuses and paltry England appearance payments. (Plus the odd penny or two in expenses for visits to public toilets when he could get them past Mr Ewbank of the FA!)

Still, compared with Britain's average weekly wage of £4, he was doing very well indeed and this prompted top national newspaper journalist Frank Butler to write:

Twenty-eight year old Tommy Lawton became the first surtax-paying professional footballer yesterday when he was transferred from Chelsea to Notts County. His income from all sources will be nearly £3,000 a year.

For the transfer, Lawton got only £300, the accrued benefit, plus £10 signing-on fee. But he was also given a choice of four-figure salary jobs in Nottingham industry. With any job he selects will go a five-year contract.

He already has a four-figure newspaper contract. And he will still earn, in the Third Division, the standard £12 a week for winter playing, £10 a week in summer and bonuses when the team wins or draws. The resultant income will be higher than the Chelsea manager's salary.

He and his wife and baby have also been provided with a modern detached house in Mapperley, on the outskirts of Nottingham.

Lawton's grey sports car will become familiar in the neighbourhood.

That same day, 14th November 1947, the *Nottingham Guardian Journal* reported:

The ambitious plans of the Notts County directors who yesterday created a football record by signing Tommy Lawton, the 28-year-old England and Chelsea centre forward, include the spending of a large amount of money on players necessary to restore the club's fortunes.

Lawton's signature, which was obtained over a luncheon table in the Great Western Hotel, Paddington, cost Notts the equivalent of a £20,000 fee – £4,500 above the highest previously paid. In addition to a payment believed to be £17,000, William Dickson, an Irish wing half, was transferred in part exchange.

The County, for whom Lawton will appear at Northampton Town tomorrow, have already approached Everton for Tom Jones, the Welsh international centre half, who has been put on the transfer list at his own request. Other stars will be sought.

"We are prepared to spend to the limit to put this old club back where it belongs," stated Mr H J Walmsley, director and treasurer of the club after the signing. "Lawton is coming as player-tactician. We hope his presence will increase our gates but the financial angle is only one of many considerations which prompted us to seek him. Chelsea have been most helpful during the negotiations."

The Chelsea manager, Mr W Birrell, commented, "It is unfortunate that it had to take place but it was dictated by circumstances."

Lawton's decision to go from First Division to Third Division football was influenced by the welfare of his wife and baby daughter. According to Mr Walmsley, Notts County are finding Lawton suitable employment outside football in Nottingham and he has the choice of several business offers which will assure his future.

All the rumours and stories about his move to Notts County went over Tommy's head. He heard them, of course, but he considered himself to be way above such gossip, far too big a star to demean himself by letting them bother him. "Let the gossips say what they like," he said. "Why should I deny anything. It's their privilege to form their own opinions; it's my privilege to smile because I know that they could not be more wrong!"

So there it was. The football world was stunned; the gentlemen of the press were dumbfounded; the rumour merchants were working overtime, but the fact of the matter was . . . Tommy Lawton, 'the best centre forward in the world', was now going to be playing for Notts County in the Third Division.

Notts County was reputed to be the oldest professional club in the world. It had been going since 1862 and was one of the founder members of the Football League in 1888. If the name of its ground, Meadow Lane, conjured up visions of a leafy rural idyll, they were soon shattered when people saw it for the first time. It stood in the middle of an equally inaptly named, deprived inner city area of Nottingham, the Meadows. These Meadows were not filled with pretty buttercups, dainty daisies and sweet-smelling hay but with row after row of soot-stained back-to-back terraced houses, with tin baths and outside toilets, crammed into cobbled streets; a mirror image of the poor working-class area of Bolton in which Tommy had grown up.

Meadow Lane was no Highbury. The dilapidated old ground had been bombed during the War and patched up to be passable. Its antiquated facilities were frugal: fans took a half-time pee in troughs under flimsy tin roofs and visiting players would find no polished wood panels and under-floor heating in these dressing rooms.

But to the flat-capped, salt-of-the earth, no-nonsense men of the Meadows who made up the bulk of Notts County's supporters it was the only place to be when alternate Saturday afternoons allowed escape from the dreary toil in the huge Victorian-built factories where most of them eked out a meagre wage. Worn out it might have been, but Meadow Lane was the theatre in which they acted out their football fantasies and dreamed their shiny soccer dreams for 90 minutes before being sucked back into the squalor and drudgery of their everyday lives. These were hard men: hard working, hard drinking and very hard to please, testament to which could be given by many a hapless player who failed to measure up to their extravagantly exacting standards, which were sky-high, even though their team played in the lowest sector of the Football League, the Third Division South.

Set in the industrialised East Midlands, this lusty, combative city (the home of Players Cigarettes, Raleigh Bicycles, textile and lace manufactur-ers, assorted heavy industries and, in its environs, coal mines by the score) had much more in common with neighbouring Yorkshire and with Tommy Lawton's Lancashire than with the counties of the softer South, but because there were so many clubs in the football-crazy North those in the middle had to be bunged in with those from the South to make up the numbers.

Anyway, the Third Division South was where Notts County plied its soccer trade and hardly spectacularly, for on the day Tommy Lawton joined them they were languishing third from bottom of their division and looked set for the big drop out of the Football League – a parlous position which made the record transfer fee they paid for Tommy all the more breathtakingly brazen!

With his transparent nature, his honesty, his shunning of the pompous and pretentious and his anti-establishment reputation, Tommy Lawton's image as a hugely popular man of the people had grown and followed him from Chelsea. Soccer still drew its mass support mainly from the working class. His millions of fans knew all about his impoverished upbringing. He was proud of his roots and for that they loved him even more. They did not begrudge him his worldwide fame and his comparative wealth. Instead, they took vicarious pleasure in the success of one of their own.

So it was with immense pride and no surprise that thousands of Notts County supporters caught their first glimpse of England's centre forward, newly arrived among them: his impeccably groomed jet black hair swept back and precision parted; his gleaming white shirt and bright red tie sparkling under his beautifully tailored, double breasted, dark blue suit; brilliant shine (*heels as well*) on his top-brand shoes; expensive heavy overcoat on his arm. He looked, every inch of him, like a handsome film star and that's just how they had all expected 'their' Tommy to look.

It was much to their disappointment that he was to make his debut for Notts County not at Meadow Lane but away at Northampton Town and even if they had the means to travel, which the majority of them did not, County were being permitted to take only 150 supporters into the ground. Some, however, were far more privileged than others . . .

As he was about to get on the team bus to take Notts County to Northampton, Tommy, who had already been appointed captain, was appalled to see more wives and friends of directors than players on board. Waving in the direction of the fur-coated ladies and assorted hangers-on, he asked the chairman, Charlie Barnes, "What's all this?"

"What's what?" replied the chairman.

"This is the team bus, not a bloody wives' outing!"

"But this is how we travel to all our games."

"Not any more it isn't. Not if you want me on the bus."

"But it's not doing any harm."

Barnes was the wealthy owner of a big Nottingham printing business. He wasn't used to being spoken to like this, particularly not by a mere employee! "They're staying on the bus," he said, using his most authoritative tone. "You heard me. I want them on another bus or I'm not going."

The chairman realised he was not going to win this argument. He could see Tommy was determined not to back down. Sheepishly, Barnes boarded the bus and alighted a few minutes later followed by a procession of 'lah-de-dah buggers', each stopping to glare at Tommy Lawton as they got off. The team bus duly left for Northampton while the ladies and friends of the directors, red-faced and angry, followed in a separate bus of considerably inferior calibre. Tommy Lawton, outspoken as ever, had not yet kicked a ball for his new employers. But already, he'd made enemies.

In anticipation of Lawton's sensational arrival in the Third Division, Northampton Town's County Ground was packed to its 21,000 capacity, with several thousands more locked out, well before kick-off.

As that excited crowd awaited the big moment at which England's centre forward would run onto their uncelebrated pitch, the Notts County players with whom he was about to appear were in awe of him as they prepared in the dressing room. Stripped to his boots, socks and jockstrap Lawton cut a supreme figure of power and physical perfection as he limbered up, muscular frame rippling while his new teammates, sat in respectful silence, feeling unworthy, as if in the presence of some prince.

Sensing their unease, Tommy spoke to them in a quiet, casual voice full of friendly reassurance: "Now lads, don't panic just because I'm here. I'm no different to anybody else. Just play your normal game, relax and do what you normally do out on that field. Me? I'll be around. Just look up and you'll see me and let me have that ball whenever you can. Good luck. Now, let's get out there."

Get out there they did. Relax they did. Play their natural game they did. Except that, inspired by the presence of the legendary Lawton and coaxed by his deft distribution, they produced by far their best display of the season. The game was barely five minutes old when Tommy, jumping higher than anyone in that 21,000 crowd had ever seen any footballer jump before, put County 1-0 up with a textbook header and despite spirited opposition from Northampton, themselves stimulated by this great occasion, Notts ran out 2-1 winners.

Just two days later, on 19th November 1947, Tommy was back in more familiar palatial surroundings at Highbury as he became the first Third Division player ever to play for England. It was with mixed, conflicting feelings that he sat in Arsenal's stately dressing rooms preparing for the game against Sweden.

He felt he had been right to honour his pledge to Arthur Stollery and he had no regrets about leaving Chelsea but as he took his number 9 shirt from its peg and chatted away to his international teammates, he knew that this was the level of the game at which he belonged, along with his pal Big Swifty and the rest of the top-class players putting on those famous England shirts.

As if determined to prove the point, Tommy had one of his best games for England that day, scoring from the penalty spot and skilfully setting up Stan Mortensen for two of the inside forward's three goals in a 4-2 England victory.

Those mixed feelings flooded back when Tommy bid farewell to his victorious international friends as they left Highbury, bound for the first-class stadia of their top-flight First Division clubs, while he had to return to tired old Meadow Lane, Notts County and the Third Division. He felt terribly guilty about the dull, depressed feeling in the pit of his stomach. After all, it was entirely his own decision to become a Notts County player and he should surely give them nothing but his best, in enthusiasm for the club as well as skill and effort on the pitch. And yet . . .

Suddenly, he found himself thinking, "What would Jim Riley say if he were here now?" Then he answered his own question. "He'd say, 'Get back to Nottingham and make sure you do your very best for all the supporters. They're the ones who matter; they'll be putting all their faith in you and you have to repay their faith. But just make sure the buggers in the boardroom treat you right!' Yes. That's what he would say. And that's what I'll do."

When Tommy walked back through the gates of Meadow Lane it was with his head high, a smile on his face and a spring in his step. There were hundreds of happy, cheering supporters waiting to greet him and he was happy to sign so many autographs that his wrist began to ache. One old man shouted, "Thanks for coming here, Tommy." Tommy shouted back, "Glad to be here, dad!"

On the day Tommy made his home debut for Notts County against Bristol Rovers 38,000 spectators were glad to be inside Meadow Lane. Notts County's home gates had previously averaged 6,000 to 7,000. One man, Tommy Lawton, had put more than 30,000 football fans through those creaky old turnstiles.

The result was perfect: a 4-2 win for Notts with two cracking goals from Lawton. That record transfer fee was already beginning to look like a very sound investment. Tommy's share, meanwhile, was his weekly pay packet containing only £12, with an extra £2 for a win!

Other Notts County players were paid less, Tommy soon discovered. Some of them were getting £10 a week; some only £8. "This can't be right," he complained to the chairman. "Every player in the team should be paid the same wage. It's bad policy not to, bad for team spirit."

The directors weren't pleased: "Who's running this club – the board or Tommy Lawton?" they asked. But they realised that Tommy was now a prized and essential asset and had to be kept happy. So it was a pay rise all round at Meadow Lane, thanks entirely to the new skipper. But all *he* had earned for himself were more black marks in the boardroom.

Directors' feathers were well and truly ruffled by the new star of Notts County, but on the field the signing was paying huge dividends. The goals were coming. And the victories. And the crowds. And the cash. On Boxing Day 1947, when Notts played Swansea, there were 45,000 spectators inside Meadow Lane and another 10,000 locked out. When the season ended, Tommy Lawton had increased the average Meadow Lane gate to an astonishing 37,500.

In addition to all that revenue, Notts received 25 per cent of the gate receipts from away matches, at which the presence of Tommy Lawton broke each club's record Third Division attendance figure every time. Notts County had finished in a safe League position and that was thanks to Tommy Lawton, who had scored 18 goals in 19 games and given the players around him a new sense of belief and ambition. In every respect and in no time at all, Notts County's new record signing had made a fantastic contribution to the club – but, already, there were people within that club who resented his presence, his power and his pugnacious personality.

Tommy Lawton and Notts County picked up where they had left off and their 1948/49 season got off to a good start. His influence on and off the pitch was having a positive effect on all the players and none more so than inside forward Jackie Sewell. Sewell, a slight, skilful player, was 20 years old. He'd signed for Notts County in 1946 after playing as a youngster for Whitehaven Town in his native North-West. Like the rest of the Notts players he'd been awestruck, at first, in the presence of the legendary England centre forward but a strong bond developed between the two. Tommy saw great potential in the lad and took him under his wing. As a result, Sewell's game, as well as his self-confidence, improved enormously.

So did the team as a whole. Notts County were becoming an attractive and successful side, retaining great support, way above the level at which they were playing and with Lawton and Sewell banging in the goals their future looked set fair.

Unfortunately, the same could not be said for Tommy's friend, Arthur Stollery. The manager was falling out of favour with the Notts directors, some of whom thought he was merely dancing to Lawton's tune. Tommy was such a strong character, such a dominant force in the dressing room, that it was easy to jump to that conclusion, even though he had no intention or desire whatsoever to usurp Stollery's control.

Tommy was just being Tommy, straight-talking, opinionated and passionate about the game, while Stollery was a minnow to Lawton's whale in terms of experience, knowledge and tactical knowhow. For Tommy, it would have been a dereliction of duty not to impart that knowledge, so he had plenty to say about tactics and the players, subconsciously or otherwise, came to respect him more than they did the boss.

There were also, now, frequent differences of opinion between Stollery and the man he had brought to the club. Lawton thought Stollery a 'baby' where professional football was concerned: altogether too soft, too concerned with his own popularity and not nearly ruthless enough. Tommy, always an open book, told him so. Home truths had always been a stock in trade in the Riley household and that was the way Tommy was brought up: he knew no other way than to speak his mind. All this led to a belief around Meadow Lane that Lawton wanted to be player-manager. It was, in truth, the very last thing he wanted but the die was cast and when Stollery was eventually sacked there were many who thought it was Lawton's doing. Maybe the directors believed that if Lawton was running this team, they might as well let him do it and save the manager's salary. If they did, it was a measure of how much they misunderstood the man and his motives.

County finished the season in a comfortable mid-table position. They'd hit a phenomenal 102 goals and that was 15 more than champions Swansea had scored. Unfortunately, they had also conceded 68 goals, twice as many as Swansea. If that statistic told a story about the way Tommy Lawton liked to play football it also explained why Notts County continued to be by far and away the biggest crowd pullers in the Third Division and one of the best supported clubs in the entire Football League.

Tommy's contribution to that goal tally was 20, while Jackie Sewell got 26. Despite many of Sewell's being assisted by Lawton and vice versa, a good-natured duel over who would finish as the top scorer developed between the two and the rivalry was epitomised when Notts were in the process of thrashing Newport County 11-1. Sewell had scored four and Lawton three when Jackie went to meet a perfect cross from Frank Broome with the goalkeeper stranded. This was a 'sitter' for Sewell's fifth until, suddenly, he was sent flying by a push from behind. He looked up to see that his assailant was Tommy Lawton, who had finished the job himself and stood smiling broadly in celebration!

Meanwhile, Tommy's forthright and outspoken approach to the game had not gone unnoticed in the England dressing room, either. While Walter Winterbottom had continued to play the man from the Third Division against Scotland at Hampden Park, where England won 2-0, and against Italy in Turin, where Tommy scored in a 4-0 victory, the manager was growing increasingly impatient with Lawton's blatant disrespect for authority and his international days were beginning to look numbered.

Winterbottom's job with England was not easy. There were few forward-thinking men at the FA but some who were, like Stanley Rous, were sensing that other nations were now more sophisticated in their tactical approach to the game and that while England remained a dominant force there was no divine right to retention of that status. Winterbottom, therefore, was tasked with moving the country forward in its coaching techniques.

Some soccer writers, notably Charles Buchan, were appreciative of Winterbottom's efforts. After that 4-0 victory over Italy in May 1948, he wrote: "Never have I seen a better display from a British team abroad – perfect teamwork, footwork and co-operation." In fact, Buchan reckoned the team that triumphed in Turin – Swift (Manchester City); Scott (Arsenal), Howe (Derby County); Wright (Wolves), Franklin (Stoke City), Cockburn (Manchester United); Matthews (Blackpool), Mortensen (Blackpool), Lawton (Notts County), Mannion (Middlesbrough), Finney (Preston) – was the finest he ever saw.

But Tommy Lawton, typically, was to the fore of a few of the experienced international players who thought little 'Summer-arse', the schoolteacher, had nowt to teach them. And Tommy being Tommy, he didn't just think it. He said it.

He got so exasperated at one of these 'classroom sessions' that he let the unfortunate Summer-arse have it with both barrels, inviting him to place his "bloody blackboard" firmly up his fundamental orifice. "If you think you can teach Stanley Matthews how to play on the wing and me how to score goals, you've got another think coming!" he told Mr Winterbottom.

He'd also had another spat over his expenses when he'd taken the train from Euston Station to Glasgow for the Scotland match because he'd been in London on business the day he travelled. Called to account for why he was claiming travel expenses from London when he now lived in Nottingham he had suggested that the FA might care to deposit its money in the same place as Summer-arse's blackboard!

As if that were not enough, the enduring fondness of Tommy and Big Swifty for a dressing-room fag was now a major irritation for Winterbottom and his staff. Aware of this growing disapproval, the pals made just one concession to authority – they started going to the toilet, each locking themselves into a cubicle, to enjoy their cigarettes away from the glare of detection. This subterfuge led one day to an exchange, through the locked cubicle doors, between the trainer Jimmy Trotter, Lawton and Swift:

Trotter: "Now then, you two. I know what you're doing in there."

Swift: "Blimey, with powers like that, you should be in a theatre!"

Trotter: "I don't need to see through doors, wise guy. The smoke's coming over the top."

Lawton: "That's not smoke, mate. It's steam!"

Swift: "Yeah. It must 'ave been that lunch you gave us."

The matter came to a head when Winterbottom himself witnessed Tommy taking out the cigarettes and Swifty the matches from the pockets of their shorts as they came off the field at the interval, the quicker to affect their lighting up in the loos. He was furious and gave them a severe lecture, which might have been more effective had they not roared with laughter throughout the whole process. "It helps our breathing!" Swift told him.

On 26th September 1948 Tommy Lawton was in the England team which drew 0-0 with Denmark in Copenhagen.

It was his last game for England.

A month later, aged 29, he was discarded by Walter Winterbottom in favour of Newcastle United's Jackie Milburn and, despite the support of several prominent soccer writers who felt he was still more than capable of doing a good job for his country, he was never picked again.

Despite the rows over the half-time cigarettes, Tommy's best mate stayed more in favour. Frank Swift had captained England in the 4-0 win over Italy in Turin, the first goalkeeper since Alexander Morten in 1873 to achieve that honour, but he had already announced that he was going to retire from football at the end of the 1948/49 season and he played *his* last game for his country against Norway in May 1949. He was 36 and he'd represented England in 14 wartime and 19 peacetime internationals.

When he made his farewell appearance for Manchester City, the club to whom he'd stayed loyal for 16 years, against Huddersfield on 7th May 1949, there were emotional scenes culminating in a parade in his honour. However, the giant keeper was back at the start of the following season when his successor, Alec Thurlow, contracted tuberculosis and he kept goal for City four times until they could secure a replacement. When he finally hung up his massive goalkeeping gloves, Frank Swift had played 510 games for Manchester City. A number of other clubs, including Manchester United, tried to tempt Swift out of retirement, prompting the Maine Road club to hang onto his registration for several years, but his mind was made up and, after a spell as a director of a catering firm, he became a sports journalist.

Tommy reckoned that was an excellent career move and he told Big Swifty, "I'd like to do that when I pack it in." When the government had used Tommy for public relations purposes during the War, he'd enjoyed broadcasting and he was very comfortable writing star columns for the newspapers. "You should," said Frank, adding with typical modesty, "You'd be better at it than me."

In the week that Frank Swift made his farewell appearance for Manchester City against Huddersfield, the soccer world was stunned by an appalling tragedy when a plane carrying the Torino team home from a friendly match in Portugal crashed into a hill near Turin. There were no survivors. Thirty-one people – 18 players, five club officials, including manager Arnaldo Agnisetta, three journalists, four aircraft crew and trip organiser Andrea Bonaiuti – were killed. Torino had played in a farewell match for Xico Ferreira against Benfica in Lisbon before taking that fateful flight. Their plane flew into a thunderstorm as it approached Turin and when the pilot was forced to descend because of desperately poor visibility, it crashed into a wall of the Basilica on Superga Hill.

The crash wiped out a famous team which had won the last *Serie A* title before the War intervened then returned to win the title on three consecutive occasions and was again leading *Serie A* with just four games left to play that season. Only one first-team player, Sauro Toma, remained alive. He missed the trip to Portugal because of injury. Torino completed the *Serie A* programme by fielding its youth team. As a mark of respect, each of their four opponents, Genoa, Palermo, Sampdoria and Fiorentina, also fielded their youth teams and Torino won a fourth consecutive *Serie A* championship.

Ten Italian internationals were among the 18 Torino players killed in the crash. Seven of them – Mazzola, Gabetto, Loik, Menti, Grezar, Ballarin and Bacigalupo – were in the team that Tommy Lawton and Frank Swift had played against in England's 4-0 victory in Turin and knowing those seven men, as they did, brought the horror and tragedy of the Superga disaster closer to home for them.

For Tommy Lawton, six years younger than his pal Big Swifty, there was still much to be done with his playing career and when the 1949/50 season kicked off, the aim of Notts County Football Club was promotion to the Second Division.

With Arthur Stollery gone, the directors asked Lawton to take over as player-manager: "No thank you," he replied firmly. "I'm not ready for that sort of position yet. I just want to play."

He suggested they should approach Eric Houghton, a veteran winger who had played for Aston Villa for 17 years before joining Notts County in 1946. Houghton had been a legend at Aston Villa, having made 392 appearances and scoring 170 goals since joining them straight from junior football in his native Lincolnshire. He'd been a star performer in the celebrated Villa side of 1930/31 which set a Football League goalscoring record of 128 in one season. Houghton got 30 of those goals. He had also played seven times for England.

"Eric would be a very good choice," Tommy told the Notts directors. "He's got years of experience and his playing days are drawing to a close. He's the right man for the job – not me." The directors took Lawton's advice but before Houghton accepted the job, he went to see Tommy at his home: "I'm not taking this job unless I can depend on your support," he said bluntly. "Don't worry," said Tommy. "You've got my support. In fact, I recommended you. I'll back you all the way."

Thus, Eric Houghton became manager of Notts County for a season that held much promise. This was now a very good Third Division side. From goalkeeper Roy Smith, through defenders and midfielders Bill Baxter, Tommy Deans, Aubrey Southwell, Harry Adamson, Billy Evans, Harry Chapman, Norman Rigby and Fred Evans, to forwards Tommy Lawton, Tom Johnston, Jackie Sewell and Frank Broome, there was strength in depth, skill, goal power and above all, experience. Seven of that regular side were in their 30s and apart from the 'baby', 22-year-old Jackie Sewell, the youngest was Harry Adamson at 25.

But it was the partnership and the extraordinary telepathy between Lawton and Sewell, the lad he mentored, that was the most impressive aspect of this remarkable team. Sewell was quick-thinking and quick off the mark, and possessed deadly shooting ability – all the attributes that set the young Tommy Lawton apart from the rest when he first arrived on the Football League scene back in the 1930s. In the Third Division, Tommy deliberately changed his own style of play to bring the best out of his young partner, dropping back, scheming, fetching and carrying for Sewell while still being good enough to get plenty of goals himself.

It proved a devastating pairing in a high-quality attack which put Notts County in a different class to the rest of the teams in Division Three and as they set about the task of amassing the points needed to win the championship, Lawton and Sewell were both on the same scoresheet nine times. At the end of the 1949/50 season, Sewell had scored 19 goals and Lawton, incredibly given the deeper role he was now playing, hit 32. Notts won the Third Division South title, a comfortable seven points clear of second-placed Northampton Town and nine points clear of their local rivals, Nottingham Forest, who finished fourth.

The Nottingham clubs, whose neighbouring grounds were separated only by the River Trent, had battled for supremacy for years and the 1949/50 season was no exception. On 22nd April 1950, Meadow Lane was packed with 46,000 supporters, an astonishing attendance for a Third Division game, when County beat their neighbours 2-0 with goals from Lawton and Sewell to clinch promotion and send the black-and-white side of the river into deliriums of delight. It was a fabulous day for the old club and its supporters, a truly historic occasion.

Yet it was the earlier Nottingham derby match at the City Ground on 3rd December 1949 that was to endure even longer in the memories of both sets of supporters, thanks to a wonder goal scored by Tommy Lawton. This was a goal of such breathtaking power and beauty that it became part of Nottingham's football folklore.

Tommy, having a great game, was well outside the Forest penalty area when Frank Broome hit a high outswinging corner from the right. Lawton, running in at speed, soared in a majestic leap to meet Broome's cross, outjumping the red-shirted defenders by at least two feet. "Get in there," he shouted as he met the ball plumb in the middle of his forehead and smashed a header into the back of the net with such force and pace that it bulged as if from a ferocious shot. The Forest supporters, at first instantly stunned and silenced, then sportingly joined their rapturous rivals in sustained applause to acclaim a truly fantastic goal.

Frank Broome scored County's other goal in a 2-1 victory for the visitors from over the river that day but the details of a stirring local derby were lost to the indelible image of that goal.

Such was the impact of that stunning Tommy Lawton goal that Nottingham football fans were still describing it in awestruck admiration 50 years later. It didn't matter whether you supported Notts County or Nottingham Forest, if you'd been among the 37,903 spectators who were there to witness it, you were privileged indeed. It became one of those ever-enduring 'I was there' sporting moments. Crawford White, the venerable *Daily Express* soccer writer, was there and he described it thus: "This was the hardest header of Lawton's distinguished career. I have never seen anything like it. He made a spectacular leap, timed the flight of the ball uncannily and nodded his head. The next thing the crowd saw was the ball hurtling past the Forest goalkeeper. It was soccer sorcery!"

Wonder goal apart, this was one of the best all-round performances of Tommy Lawton's career and evidence of just how up for the game he was that day could be found in the Notts dressing room before kick-off. With County top of the League and unbeaten in 16 matches beforehand, this was a great game for Forest to win. It was the sort of soccer scenario for which the term 'banana skin' was invented. The tension in the visitors' dressing room was unbearable and the skipper, prowling the room like a caged animal, was as keyed up as any of them.

As the ground outside was filling up to capacity, the nerves were getting even more frayed when suddenly, Tommy announced, "Right lads – kit off!" "What?" they chorused. "You heard me," said Lawton and he proceeded to strip. The players looked at their skipper, then at each other: "What is he doing?" "Come on!" shouted Lawton, now completely naked. "I said kit off!"

The order was followed and soon 11 men of assorted shapes, sizes and appendages stood in the middle of the dressing room, resplendent in the nude! "Now, we're going to do a war dance," said Lawton and he started whooping and dancing, Apache-style, knees raised high, arms pumping up and down, hand to mouth to reverberate the hollering. One by one the naked players joined in until the whole team was circling the dressing room, emitting blood-curdling war cries as they danced behind their 'chief'.

After the game, the great victory and his own wonder goal, the lads asked Tommy why on earth he'd made them all dance naked like that. "I haven't got a clue," he confided. "But it worked, didn't it!"

On 30th April, all the Notts players gathered at Tommy Lawton's impressive house in Nottingham's prestigious Mapperley Park, for a promotion celebration party hosted by their celebrated captain and his wife. It was one of the few occasions that Rosaleen had anything to do with her husband's job. She never watched him play and took little or no interest in his achievements. Asked by the press if she was going to be watching that promotion-clinching game, she'd replied: "No, I shall be shopping, as usual." This sham of a marriage, doomed from the start, was now more fragile than ever.

Tommy found much solace from the ceaseless cold of his marital misery in the warmth of his relationship with the people of Nottingham, particularly the football fans. They adored him – and such affection did not come readily from these blunt East Midlanders who were rightly reputed to be mightily hard to please and even harder to impress. Tommy Lawton had pleased and impressed them.

Tough working men, who would never have admitted to hero worship of anybody beyond Keir Hardie, gained 'brownie points' over their pints of bitter if they could prove a sighting of Lawton in the city, usually resplendent in immaculate camelhair coat with huge shoulder pads which made him look even stronger than he was. Tommy Lawton was the bright, shining light at the end of a tunnel of hard relentless toil through their long weekday hours.

At work all week, they counted the days to the next home game: another chance to see their big handsome idol standing on the centre circle waiting to kick off, rubbing his hands together, as if relishing the prospect of the imminent annihilation of the mere mortals who opposed him; another chance to watch him burst into athletic action, frightening the life out of hapless defenders charged with the hopeless task of trying to stop him; another chance to stand in awe and admiration of his ability to run, turn, pass, shoot and best of all, to leap, hang in the air and power those peerless headers. "'Ow does 'e stay up in the air like that?" they asked each other. "Does 'e have wings?"

At school all week, youngsters did the same, eagerly awaiting their next chance to gather in the nine-penny Kids' Pen at the bottom of Meadow Lane's Spion Kop where they sang their own football anthem to their hero. In *Music, Music, Music*, a hit record about playing a jukebox, American pop star Teresa Brewer sang:

> *Put another nickel in,*
> *In the nickelodeon,*
> *All I want is loving you,*
> *And music, music, music.*

The adapted version sung by the lads in the Meadow Lane Kids' Pen went:

> *Put another ninepence in,*
> *In Notts County's turnstile tin,*
> *All we want is Notts to win,*
> *And Lawton, Lawton, Lawton.*

And for one of the kids to sight that famous camelhair coat out in the city and then to capture the great man's autograph was as good as it got!

Tommy had been around enough football clubs and enough football people to know that the environment inside soccer could be a cauldron of cynicism, deceit, jealousy, resentment, faked friendship and two-faced hypocrisy. Inside this rarefied atmosphere, you chose your real friends with great care and caution but outside in the real world of work-a-day Nottingham it was different. The 'ordinary' people of this vibrant city had taken Tommy Lawton to their hearts and he enjoyed nothing better than being among them in their own environment.

He looked an inappropriate intruder into the grimy inner sanctum of the cheap and cheerful café in the city centre that he frequented almost daily, his exquisite sartorial elegance standing out incongruously against the greasy plates and cracked cups as he enjoyed a bacon butty and a good natter with the locals but if, outwardly, he appeared out of place he was, inwardly, completely at ease with these folk and they with him. These were *his* people. He would never forget how a pot of scouse fed seven adults for a week in that tiny old house in Bolton that he'd loved so much as a kid and the plates of crispy bacon, sausages, eggs and chips that the honest working blokes devoured in that café would have seemed to him, then, like one of those seven-course banquets to which he'd now grown accustomed. He sat happily talking football over copious cups of tea with these men, willingly allowing them to pay their way for he knew that if he insisted on always paying it would be treated not with gratitude but with contempt for the superiority that such a gesture, however well-intentioned, would imply.

There was no misunderstanding of his generosity, however, the day that a tramp came into the café, shivering violently from the freezing cold outside, to accept his daily cup of tea on the house from the kindly proprietor. As he was leaving with Jackie Sewell, who often joined him on visits to the greasy café, Tommy took off his huge, expensive Crombie overcoat and placed it gently over the tramp's shoulders. "Here you are, dad," he said softly. "You need this far more than I do."

Tommy had executed the gift so discreetly that none of the customers in the café noticed until well after he'd left, while the old tramp sat beaming under his splendid new coat, unable to believe his luck and never to know if the money in one of the pockets had been left there by accident or design.

The 1950/51 season should have been one of continued enjoyment, success and satisfaction for Tommy Lawton, who had given so much to Notts County. But football can always kick you in the teeth – and it did.

This was a season, not of achievement through team spirit and togetherness but of unrest, bitterness and backbiting. Tommy confided, as he still did, to Big Swifty one day, "All of a sudden, the manager is great and the players are great. Some of these players have got big-headed because they're now in the Second Division and they've started telling me how to play the game and I'm just not having it." Swifty cautioned, "Calm down, Tom. Don't let it get to you. These things have a habit of blowing over."

But Tommy, tortured by the purgatory of his home life, was in no mood to calm down. For years, he'd been able to put his marriage problems to one side and concentrate on his football but now the stomach-knotting tensions were going into work with him. He was thoroughly miserable and this was not a good time to add the fuel of conflicts at Meadow Lane to the fire of his hopeless relationship with Rosaleen.

He believed that some of the Notts County players resented him, were jealous of what they thought was preferential treatment being given to him by the directors and were convinced that he was angling for the manager's job, even though he'd already turned it down and had not the slightest inclination for it. He did have the ear of the board but only because he had never yet been proved wrong in his outspoken views on club policy.

Far from being the directors' pet, he did not get on at all well with certain members of the board and never had done. In fact, he suspected that one or two of them hated the way he spoke his mind and refused to tug his forelock. And he knew, for sure, that they resented his massive popularity. He believed that having sought his opinions, as they always did because of his incomparable knowledge and experience, they were then often ignoring his advice or, worse, turning what he told them against him. He was convinced that is what happened when he expressed his view that some of the players were simply not up to Second Division standard. For some of the directors then to make sure that the players got to know what he'd told them was, for Tommy, unforgivably snide and unprofessional.

When the board decided to break up the successful partnership between Lawton and Jackie Sewell by selling Sewell to Sheffield Wednesday for a new record British transfer fee of £35,000, Tommy was disgusted. He believed it showed a distinct lack of ambition at Meadow Lane. It also split the board. After the deal had been signed, but before he'd left for Sheffield, Sewell was asked by a County director, George Cottee, to meet him the next day. In Cottee's chauffeur-driven car, they went to Hillsborough, where Cottee produced Wednesday's £35,000 cheque, offered it back and asked for Sewell's registration to be cancelled. Needless to say, his offer was refused but the transfer led to ructions in the Meadow Lane boardroom. Cottee and fellow director Jack Levy resigned and later joined the Nottingham Forest committee.

The big signings that Notts had promised publicly when Tommy joined the club had never materialised. His old Everton pal, Yanto Jones, was never signed and was now player-manager of non-league Pwllheli. Tommy implored the Notts board to spend some of the money that was still pouring through the Meadow Lane turnstiles on better-quality signings. He suggested Raich Carter and Wilf Mannion, veterans now but more than capable of making a huge improvement to the skills ratio of the team, and Manchester United winger Charlie Mitten, who was capable of providing the service which Lawton could convert into the goals that were much harder to score at this level. No significant signings were made and that frustrated him immensely.

Some in the Notts dressing room were convinced that Tommy was on a much better financial deal than them, which was not only completely untrue but flew in the face of the stance he had taken in getting them onto the same wages as him. That these players could so easily choose to forget what he'd done for them, not just in their pay packets but on the field of play, hurt him deeply.

Neither had this so-called special treatment produced the promised and much-publicised 'well-paid future outside soccer' for Tommy. In the event only one job was offered, with a local firm which manufactured typewriters, and that disappeared along with the company when it went bust.

There were honourable exceptions to the dressing-room snipers, young Jackie Sewell before he was sold notable among them, and in a different frame of mind, Tommy would probably have let the unpleasantness of the rest wash over him. And the directors? Well, he'd never really had any time for those 'lah-de-dah buggers' anyway, but this was all getting too much for him and his form was suffering badly, as was that of the rest of the team.

It was hardly surprising, then, that neither Notts County nor Tommy Lawton set the Second Division alight that season. They finished sixth from bottom with 39 points from 42 games. Tommy played in 30 of those games but scored only nine goals. By his standards, that was a famine.

Meanwhile, he had started to hear gossip around the city about the conduct of his wife. Every time he went home she was out. It was one thing to put up with this in private but when he felt that the whole of Nottingham was sniggering he could stand it no longer. He hired a private detective to trail Rosaleen.

On 14th March 1951, Tommy Lawton walked into Nottingham Divorce Court, the petitioner in an application for divorce from his wife, Rosaleen May Lawton, alleging that she had committed adultery with company director Adrian Van Geffen, whose address was given as Loughborough Road, West Bridgford, Nottingham. After hearing the evidence, Judge A C Caporn granted a *decree nisi* with costs against Van Geffen. "It is quite clearly a case of adultery," said the judge, "and there has been a good deal of deceit."

Mr M V Argyle, counsel for Lawton, asked that the question of custody of the child should be considered in chambers. Custody was given to Rosaleen and Tommy saw nothing of the child, Amanda, from that day on. Tommy had become consumed by his suspicion that the child might not be his, though he had no firm evidence to support that nagging doubt, which he was to carry with him for the rest of his life. He was never asked or ordered to pay maintenance for the child. Rosaleen went her own way and later re-married.

With the burden of his unhappy marriage finally lifted from his shoulders, Tommy started to rebuild his personal life. As he did so, he reflected on the career moves he had made as he'd tried to keep that marriage alive. His biggest regret, now, was leaving Everton. If it had not been for his marriage problems, he could still have been at Goodison Park, banging in the goals for those wonderful Scouse supporters and possibly still playing for England, too, for while his spats with Walter Winterbottom had hardly helped, it was widely believed that he would probably not have lost his international place so suddenly had he not dropped down into the Third Division.

Indeed, there had been much talk among England fans, still reeling from the shock of their mighty team's defeat by the soccer pygmies of the USA in the 1950 World Cup in Brazil, about how it would never have happened had Stan Matthews and Tommy Lawton been playing. The Americans were a scratch side and they'd been expected to have no chance of avoiding a crushing defeat by their illustrious opponents.

The pompous English FA had ignored the World Cup since its inception in 1930 but after they condescended to appear in the 1950 tournament they were one of the favourites to win, even though an England tour of Canada had been arranged at the same time. That Canadian tour deprived Walter Winterbottom of a number of players he would have picked for the World Cup and that meant that one of these, Stan Matthews, missed their opening game of the tournament when they beat Chile 2-0. Winterbottom had Matthews flown in for the USA match, but the selection committee overruled him and ordered him not to change a winning side.

Even without Matthews, England were still expected to annihilate the underdogs of the USA but after going ahead with a fluke goal in the first half, the Americans resisted everything England could throw at them and won 1-0. It was a result that stunned the whole world of soccer and brought ridicule and shame to England, for whom it was the lowest point in the country's international football history. At the end of the second half, England had peppered their opponents' goal with 20 shots on target to the USA's one and many a fan reckoned that with Matthews playing and Tommy Lawton on the end of his crosses their team would have won by at least 10-1!

Tommy didn't necessarily agree with that generous assessment but he wasn't going to argue with it and he did subscribe to the view that he would almost certainly have won more England caps if he'd stayed at Everton, where he was so happy. That move had been made purely in the futile attempt to save his marriage which, hindsight now proved, was doomed no matter where he and Rosaleen had lived: "I should have stayed at Everton and transferred the wife!" he told friends.

Though he was no longer playing a part in the England set-up, Tommy retained a close and keen interest in the international team and he was delighted when the number 9 shirt went to Nat Lofthouse of Bolton Wanderers.

Nat was a Bolton lad like Tommy and went to the same Castle Hill School. Lofthouse hero-worshipped Lawton and back in 1938, after playing in a Lancashire Schools trial match, he and a schoolmaster had a chance meeting with the great man. Young Nat was so overawed in the presence of his idol that he'd been completely tongue-tied but Tommy remembered that day and when Nat Lofthouse made his debut for England against Yugoslavia at Highbury in 1950 he received a pre-match telegram from Lawton. It read, "Go out and give them all you've got, Nat." Lofthouse certainly took his hero's advice. He scored both England goals in a 2-2 draw.

Nat Lofthouse went on to play 33 games for England between 1950 and 1958, scoring 30 goals. In 1952, he became famously known as 'The Lion of Vienna' after scoring England's second goal in a 3-2 win over Austria – despite being elbowed in the face, tackled from behind and finally brought down by the goalkeeper. That dogged bravery epitomised the rest of his career, as did his loyalty to Bolton. He played 452 games for Wanderers between 1946 and 1958, scoring 255 goals.

In May, 1951, Tommy Lawton was offered a lucrative opportunity from New York to spend the summer in the United States, coaching for a series of American National Challenge Cup games. The man who made the offer, Nick Moller, manager of the German-Hungarian team of Brooklyn, told him in a cablegram that if he accepted the offer it would "give a big boost to soccer in the United States." But Tommy declined. He told the *Nottingham Evening News* : "It was a very big offer, but I have turned it down because, during the close season, I want to combine the effort of getting really fit again with some other business transactions which I have in hand."

One morning as Tommy Lawton was driving down the hill at Mapperley Hall Drive, sitting low down in his AC Sport, he drew level with a fantastic pair of silk-stockinged legs emerging from number 18: "Wow, just look at those legs," he enthused and slowed down to get a proper sight, through his rear-view mirror, of the rest of the woman to whom they were attached. He was not disappointed. She was gorgeous!

This vision of loveliness was steering a pushchair containing her little girl and simply walked on by, head in the air, when Tommy, who was instantly smitten with her, stopped his car to say hello. He drove on, resolving to get to know her as soon as he could and asking himself, "They talk about love at first sight. Is this what they mean?"

The next morning, he made sure he was driving past number 18 at the same time. And the next morning. And the morning after that. Every time, he offered a cheery "Hello". Every time she ignored him. Finally, she relented and they spoke, only to talk about the weather but there was an immediate chemistry between them. She was as struck by this handsome, well-dressed man as he was with her beauty. "I'm Tom," he said, reaching out from his car and taking her small hand in his own. "And my name's Gay," she told him.

This was Gay Rose, *Mrs* Gay Rose, a glamorous 29-year-old lady on the upper-crust Nottingham social scene. She was married to Harry Reginald Rose, better known as Rex Rose, one of a very wealthy family which had made a fortune by selling its textile business. Rex Rose was popular and highly respected in the city. He had served in a tank regiment during the War, in which he lost a brother, Alan, who had been in the RAF. A second brother, Charles, was a prominent Nottingham solicitor.

Soon, the meetings between Tommy and Gay were becoming more than just polite conversations in the street. They were falling deeply in love. As that love grew, they started to spend clandestine nights away together, on the Lincolnshire coast where neither of them were so likely to be recognised. Their love remained hidden away for months but as they began to realise that they could not bear to be apart from each other and their secret nights became more and more frequent, Rex Rose grew simultaneously suspicious. A year after his marriage to Rosaleen ended, Tommy Lawton was back in that same Nottingham court, this time cited as co-respondent by Rex Rose in his petition for divorce from Gay. Adultery was not denied.

Being with the man she loved cost Gay dearly. Her own family, all devout Roman Catholics vehemently opposed to divorce, immediately ostracised her. The love affair between Tommy Lawton, the huge international soccer star and Gay, the beautiful wealthy socialite, was a big nationwide scandal and in Nottingham, often described as a small village in a big city, it was even more intense.

The furore provided Notts County with the perfect excuse to get rid of the star who had, to their increasing displeasure, become much bigger than the club. The directors decided he must leave Meadow Lane and Tommy, who was now thoroughly disillusioned with Notts County, was not going to regret it, though he did object to the way they went about it. They said that the troubles in the dressing room were caused by him and he learned from the club secretary, Wilf Fisher, that manager Eric Houghton had gone to Barnsley to sign Cec McCormack to replace him. It was the first he knew of the club's intention to freeze him out. Without telling him, Notts gave Hull City permission to approach Tommy but even though Hull were managed by Raich Carter, for whom he had such great respect, this was not a move he wanted. With the writing on the wall about his lack of a future at Meadow Lane, Tommy played alongside McCormack as the club tried to unload him while endeavouring to make it appear that they were not doing so.

He was still adored by the fans so the board, fearing a massive backlash, announced that because of his domestic problems, Lawton had insisted on a transfer. He hadn't, but he didn't care what they said. He felt desperately in need of pastures new, a fresh start with the woman he loved so much and her little daughter, Carol; a new family; a new life.

In March 1952, Tommy Lawton was transferred to Second Division Brentford for a fee of £15,000. So far in that season, he had scored 12 goals for Notts County in 29 matches to bring his total to 90 goals in 151 League games since moving to Meadow Lane in 1947.

In four and a half years, Notts County had done very well indeed out of Tommy Lawton. They were recouping 75 per cent of the £20,000 they paid to get him from Chelsea; he put tens of thousands of extra paying customers through the turnstiles, home and away, at every one of those 151 matches; he won them promotion from the Third Division; and he coached, nurtured and developed Jackie Sewell, for whom they received that princely sum of £35,000 from Sheffield Wednesday.

Excellent business for the board of directors. But what, Tommy pondered as he left Meadow Lane without ceremony, about the poor bloody fans?! And as for him? Tommy Lawton was in no doubt whatsoever that joining Notts County was the worst thing he'd ever done: "But if I hadn't been in Nottingham, I wouldn't have found Gay."

That thought comforted him as he headed back to London and filled his heart with a joy he'd thought he would never find in his private life.

Chapter Eight

LONDON CALLING

London in March 1952 was much changed from the city Tommy Lawton left in November 1947. The bright early spring sunshine greeting his return to the capital contrasted vividly with the grey autumn skies of his departure and reflected both the brightness of his mood and the optimism of this great city, whose indomitable spirit was captured in its determination to recover from those dark days of war. The energy of renaissance was all around as Tommy, Gay and little Carol arrived to start a new life of their own and there was a poetry to the coincidence of these converging circumstances which he couldn't put adequately into words but felt deeply inside.

He'd always loved London and tears welled in his eyes as he squeezed the hands of Gay and Carol on a walk around its exciting streets. He wanted Gay to know why he had missed London so much. He didn't need to explain. She could see it in his face. And she was so pleased for him.

By 1952, not just London but all of Britain was getting back on its feet after that crippling war. The reconstruction effort was in full swing: new houses, hospitals and schools were being built, manufacturing industry was beginning to flourish, the docks were booming and thousands of new white-collar jobs were being created. There was still a very long way to go, in London in particular huge bomb sites provided stubborn testament to the dreadful devastation of the blitz, but all around there was a positive sense of recovery; of a country on its way up.

Tommy Lawton felt that he, too, was back on his feet, the miseries of his failed marriage and the rancour of his final days in Nottingham behind him now.

As soon as he set foot inside Brentford Football Club, he felt at home and at ease in an atmosphere so very different from that he'd left behind at Notts County. This was a happy club; a friendly, family club. It felt a million miles away from the bickering and backbiting which blighted his latter days at Meadow Lane. There was a warm welcome waiting from the Brentford chairman Frank Davies and his brother Harry, the vice-chairman. Tommy was immediately impressed by their enthusiasm and sincerity, sensing a genuine concern for the welfare of the players. Manager Jackie Gibbons, too, was an open book.

That week, millions of cinema-goers all over Britain saw the story of Lawton's move to Brentford on the Pathé Pictorial newsreel. They watched a close-up shot of that famous signature going onto the dotted line while the clipped public-school tones of the announcer told them, with up-beat enthusiasm:

Tommy Lawton is always big news and he's hit the headlines again as Brentford, through manager Jackie Gibbons, secured his signature on transfer from Notts County. Tommy is still considered by many experts to be England's greatest centre forward and Brentford have their eyes on promotion. Enough said.

The camera then focused on the handsome face of Brentford's new signing as he told manager Gibbons, "Well, Jack, I'm very happy to be back in London and very pleased to be coming to Brentford." Then the focus shifted to a beaming Gibbons who replied, "Well, we're just as pleased to have you."

They had every right to be pleased when Lawton attracted a gate of 31,000 to Griffin Park for his debut against Swansea. This was 9,000 up on the previous home game and it was hats off to Tommy . . . Hats were an essential part of a man's wardrobe in these days. Rarely did a man go out without a hat on, usually a trilby or a cap, so most of the 31,000 heads at Griffin Park that day were hat-covered and when Tommy Lawton appeared all those hats were raised as one, as if choreographed, in tribute and welcome. It was a moving, if rather comic, sight.

Then Brentford won 3-1. It was the very best of starts.

When the 1951/52 season ended a few weeks later, Tommy Lawton was a very contented Brentford player and already on the scoresheet with two goals.

On September 23rd 1952, Tommy and Gay became Mr and Mrs Lawton in a quiet wedding ceremony at Caxton Hall. Married to the woman he adored, settled in the city he loved, playing for a club he liked and respected, Tommy Lawton was now a truly happy man.

A few months later, Jackie Gibbons left Brentford. His assistant Jimmy Bain took over but didn't do well and when he reverted to assistant manager, Tommy was invited by the board to become player-manager. He agreed.

This was not a good move. At 33, Lawton was not ready for management. As a player, he had always been an obsessive perfectionist. Now, he sought the same perfection as a manager, which was asking too much of himself, and he expected the same perfection from his players, which was asking too much of them. An older manager, more skilled in man management, would have demonstrated more patience, tolerance and understanding. Tommy, subconsciously managing the same way as he played, was too demanding. Some of the players thought him aloof; some were scared of him. One way or another, he was losing the dressing room.

Two of Brentford's best players had been transferred, Jimmy Hill to Fulham and Ron Greenwood to Chelsea, and it soon became clear that, having forked out for Lawton, there was no money for further significant signings. Brentford fell well short of their promotion ambitions, ending the 1952/53 season sixth from bottom of Division Two on 37 points, having won 13, drawn 11 and lost 18 of their 42 matches. Player-manager Lawton played in 34 of those games, scoring 13 goals.

Being player-manager wasn't working; splitting the role meant he was doing neither job to best effect and at home at their bungalow in Twickenham he told Gay, "I like it here, I really do. But this is an ulcer job!"

Meanwhile, there was some welcome light relief for Tommy Lawton when he got the opportunity to make his debut . . . as a film star. The film company making *The Great Game*, a British comedy/drama set in a fictitious football club and starring the gorgeous young actress Diana Dors, had asked if the film could be shot on location at Griffin Park and if some of the players could appear. Inevitably, at the top of their list of players was Britain's biggest soccer star, Tommy Lawton.

The film cast top actor James Hayter as 'Joe Lawson', the chairman of a football club whose love of gambling led to his involvement in the criminal underworld. It also featured Thora Hird, Glyn Houston and the luscious Dors as 'Lulu Smith', a young lady of somewhat suspect virtue.

The delectable 22-year-old Diana Dors was a huge star. She was Britain's version of America's blonde bombshell Marilyn Monroe, a comparison which had guaranteed the release of this film in the USA as well as in Britain, where, with its tempting recipe of glamour, comedy, crime and football, it was assured of great success.

Under the irresistible pin-up allure of the ample-breasted Miss Dors was a very fine actress and a natural comedienne. The film set was a fascinating new workplace for Tommy, who took to it like a fish to water and the lovely Miss Dors was genial and often hilarious company. Tommy's favourite story, which was confirmed in her autobiography, was the one she told about her real name. She had been born Diana Mary Fluck. "They asked me to change it," she explained, "because of what would happen if it was up in lights and one of the bulbs blew!"

Back home in Swindon, after she had become famous, she accepted an invitation to open a church fête. The vicar with the task of introducing her to the crowd fretted nervously before the event over the risk that he would mispronounce her real surname and he walked around for days practising: "Fluck, Fluck, Fluck." On the big day, the vicar got up on stage and announced, "Ladies and gentlemen, it is with great pleasure that I introduce to you our star guest. We all love her, especially as she is our local girl and I therefore feel it is right to introduce her by her real name: ladies and gentlemen, please welcome the very lovely Miss Diana *Clunt!*"

On 2nd June 1953, Tommy, Gay and Carol joined virtually the entire population of Britain to celebrate the Coronation of Queen Elizabeth II. The young Queen was succeeding her father, King George VI. The much loved King, who had reigned for 16 years and stood proud with his people throughout the War, had died in February 1952.

There were many who feared that the pretty 25-year-old Princess Elizabeth was too young to be Queen and that Great Britain and the Commonwealth were asking far too much of her. But for many others, her youth, her freshness, her energy and her optimism symbolised the country's rebirth and the spirit of hope for a bright new future. Tommy and Gay were firmly in that latter camp. They had come to London for a fresh start and the Coronation of the young Princess, heralding a new dawn for the country, reflected the excitement of their own new life together.

The Coronation captured the hearts and minds of the British people like no other event had ever done before. Three million of them packed the processional route, most of them having slept out on the pavements to be sure of a view. But for the first time, many more millions were able to watch such an historic event on television.

Several members of the government, Sir Winston Churchill among them, had cautioned against such 'intrusion', arguing that it was not right and proper to open up such a solemn occasion to television cameras. They tried to persuade Elizabeth that she ought not to expose herself to the strain and the heat and glare of the cameras, but the young Princess, in a determined stand typifying the conflict between old and new which was symptomatic of the time, refused to listen to their protests and insisted that as many of her people as possible should share in her great day.

So, all over Britain, families and friends gathered around 14-inch black-and-white television sets, which were to be found in only a few homes. The scarcity of sets meant that the front parlours of those lucky enough to own one were as tightly crammed as the streets; curtains were drawn, the better to see the grainy, grey picture, and cups of tea, sardine sandwiches and fairy cakes were consumed by the million as mums, dads, grandparents, children, uncles, aunts, nephews and nieces all peered through the gloom at those tiny screens in excited anticipation of a moment in history of which, thanks to that small box on the sideboard, they were themselves to be a part.

There was just such a Coronation gathering at Tommy and Gay's house. Several television-less neighbours piled in and the happy couple were pleased to entertain them. Along with the 8,000 VIP guests inside Westminster Abbey they were able to witness the dramatic ceremony in wonder at the magic of television and in awe of the pomp and majesty of the magnificent proceedings, during which they worried about the vulnerability of the slight, nervous youngster at the centre of it all.

When it was all over, they went to a nearby street party, with paper hats, more sardine sandwiches, fancy cakes and scalding hot tea from a huge urn while the kids tucked into jelly, ice cream and lemonade. It was a scene being played out by millions of people in hundreds of thousands of streets across the whole nation. They listened to the new Queen's radio broadcast in which she made a solemn pledge, all the more poignant coming from one of such tender years: "Throughout all my life and with all my heart, I shall strive to be worthy of your trust." And they shed a tear for her.

Despite their disappointing 1951/52 season, the Brentford directors were happy to persevere with their young manager. They had plenty of faith in his ability to succeed and they particularly liked the way he was bringing on promising youngsters like Jimmy Bloomfield, Ian Dargey and Gerald Cakebread. Tommy, just as happy with his employers and far too proud to throw in the towel, resolved to carry on. His plan was to mix the emerging Brentford youngsters with older players in the hope that a blend of youth and experience would produce the recipe for success.

In the close season, he took Gay and Carol for a holiday in North Wales to stay at an hotel run by his old mate Yanto Jones, still player-manager at

Pwllheli and enjoying that dual role much more than Tommy was. There was also a dual purpose behind Tommy's choice of holiday venue. He spent many hours of the two weeks trying to persuade Yanto to come back into League football at Brentford. It didn't work. Mr T G Jones was 'very happy, thank you boyo' where he was.

Tommy had more luck, however, in his pursuit of two more veterans. Frank Broome, the winger with whom he'd played at Notts County as well as for pre-war England was 38 and welcomed a move to Brentford. So did another winger, Ian McPherson, late of Glasgow Rangers and Arsenal. Ian was 33.

Lawton hoped that the two top-class wing men would provide the quality of service from which he could score lots of goals while the youngsters, playing alongside the three of them would benefit enormously from the experienced example they could set and the words of wisdom they could impart. This didn't work out either. Brentford got off to a bad start to the 1953/54 season, Broome and McPherson were shadows of their former selves and the Brentford fans began to vent their frustration with the veteran trio (combined age 104!) by singing *Dear Old Pals*. This was the first time in his illustrious career that the great Tommy Lawton had ever been ridiculed – and it hurt him deeply.

Tommy didn't want to let down the directors. He'd never had much, if any, time for the boardroom brigade elsewhere but he liked these men and he believed that if the club had been wealthier, their genuine commitment to Brentford FC could have made it one of the finest clubs in the country. But he was failing as player-manager; failure had never been a word in his vocabulary and carrying on like this was in nobody's best interests. At the next board meeting, he resigned as player-manager. He told the board he would be very happy to stay at Griffin Park but only as a player. That way, he could get back to his goalscoring best and Brentford FC would benefit by getting much more out of him. The directors agreed, but asked him to remain as player-manager until they could find a suitable boss to replace him.

Unlike Rosaleen, Gay Lawton took a very keen interest in her husband's career and she insisted that he should ring her after every away game with a report on how the match had gone.

After a 3-0 defeat by Doncaster Rovers, it was a despondent Tommy who rang his wife. Brentford had just lost their fourth game in succession; there was no sign of a new manager, nor of new players to pep up the pack; he had been injured and he was 200 miles from home in depressing Doncaster, where it was cold, wet and miserable. For the first time in his life, he felt that football had finished with him.

Gay, on the other hand, sounded upbeat and excited when she answered the phone: "Don't waste time, Tom," she said. "Go outside and ring me from a phone box where no one can hear."

"But why . . . what?"

"I can't tell you until you're on your own."

"Can't you give me just a hint? "

"Darling I can't. Just get to a quiet call box – as soon as you can."

Tommy was on tenterhooks as he fumbled with the coins in a phone box, wondering, "What on earth, is it?" It soon became obvious that Gay's excitement was more than a little justified. She had taken a telephone call from Tom Whittaker, the manager of Arsenal.

"He wants you to play for Arsenal!"

"Don't be daft, Gaye. I'm in no mood for practical jokes, love."

"No joke. He wants you to play for Arsenal. He says to phone him."

"Well if you're not joking, he must be."

"Tom, I promised you'd ring him. It can't do any harm, can it?"

Tom Whittaker was a man for whom Tommy Lawton had a lot of time and a lot of respect. He'd been trainer for the pre-war England team and they'd got on very well. Whittaker was a big man, physically and metaphorically. The offspring of a military family, he had fought in the First World War before becoming an Arsenal player in 1920, when Tommy was just one year old. Serious injury forced him to give up playing when he was 28 but he resolved to become a successful manager instead and he took over from George Allison in 1947. Strong in body and spirit, Whittaker was a rock at Highbury, a straight-talking man of abundant energy and great integrity. Tommy knew he could be honest with Whittaker and he with him.

From that same cold, damp call box in Yorkshire, Tommy rang the manager of the mighty Arsenal, the club he had dreamed of playing for. Could he possibly be serious about this? Tom Whittaker answered in the affirmative.

"But, Tom, I'm 33 years old," Tommy protested, "and I haven't played in the First Division for donkey's years! It's a great offer and a great opportunity and, believe me, I appreciate it more than I can tell you. But I think it's ludicrous for me to consider going back to that class of football at my age and I'd hate to let you down."

Whittaker answered calmly and thoughtfully: "Look, Tommy, I've given this a lot of thought and I know what I'm doing. I need a man with your experience and influence; a thinker; a talker; someone who will have the respect of all the players, who can pull the team together and inspire them."

Arsenal were certainly in need of inspiration. They'd lost their first seven matches, including a soul-destroying 7-1 thrashing by Sunderland, and were bottom of the First Division. After a few more minutes of discussion, Tom Whittaker's considerable powers of persuasion had done the trick.

"OK," said Tommy, "I'll be honoured to join Arsenal. And I don't think you know just how much I mean that."

Brentford had been good to Tommy and they were in need of a decent transfer fee. He knew they wouldn't want to stand in his way. Arsenal paid them £7,500 and gave them Arsenal reserve right winger Jimmy Robertson.

Incredibly, after Arsenal had first expressed an interest in signing him 17 years earlier when he was Burnley's 'Boy Wonder', after Tom Whittaker had tried unsuccessfully to sign him from Everton and six years after Chelsea had stopped him joining them, Tommy Lawton was at long last on his way to Highbury. He signed at lunchtime on Friday 18th September 1953, just before the Press Association rang Highbury for Saturday's team for the home game against Manchester City.

Soon, Tom Whittaker's phone was red hot. Calls from journalists were flooding in, all asking, "Who's this Lawton?" Mischievously, the Arsenal boss gave every one of them the same answer: "Oh, it's just a young lad I've signed." They soon saw through the jape, of course, and yet again, Tommy Lawton made the splash headlines in all the next day's national newspapers.

Many people thought Tom Whittaker had taken leave of his senses but, just as he'd told Tommy, he knew what he was doing. He'd done it to good effect twice before. He signed 35-year-old veteran Ronnie Rooke from Fulham in 1949 and got great service from him. And Joe Mercer, who was in his 30s and reckoned to be a spent force when he joined Arsenal, went on to become a successful captain of the Gunners. The barbed comments of the doubters were, therefore, water off a duck's back to the canny Mr Whittaker.

Having played so many crucial games in his long career, Tommy Lawton thought he had long since forgotten what it was like to be really nervous before a match but when he walked into the supreme soccer shrine that was Highbury Stadium to play his first match for Arsenal, it felt like his spiritual home and his stomach was in knots!

"It's good that you feel like this," he told himself. But he couldn't let it show in the dressing room because that would defeat the object of his signing. When he ran out onto the pitch to tumultuous applause he struggled to compose himself. This was a fantastic sight and an unbelievable experience. Nearly 66,000 spectators had gathered to witness his return to the top flight, almost 20,000 more than had watched Arsenal's previous home game. More than 18 years after he signed for Burnley and after hundreds of games for subsequent clubs and country, Tommy Lawton still possessed enough pulling power to put 20,000 extra soccer fans through First Division turnstiles. He was deeply moved by the size of that crowd and by the genuine warmth of its welcome and such emotion, heaped on top of already strained nerves, was not good for the concentration. Just as Big Swifty (who was there to report the story for the *News of the World*) and Joe Mercer always did, Tommy calmed the butterflies in his stomach by joking to himself, "Ey oop, Old Whittaker's got his money back already. That means he's got me here for nowt, the crafty old sod!"

The nerves evaporated completely when the match kicked off but it wasn't long before Tommy realised how foolish he'd been to drop out of this class of football. He felt out of place and out of touch with the much higher standard, the pace and the very different approach. Gradually, as the game progressed, he settled and began to feel much more comfortable, but at half-time he chastised himself: "You were a bloody idiot to go fooling around in the lower divisions. This is where you belong and you should never have left."

Unfortunately there was no warm welcome back from the Manchester City centre half Dave Ewing, whose job that day was to mark the returning hero. Tommy was already carrying an ankle injury from the game at Doncaster and when the tough Scottish defender clobbered him, it became serious. He managed to last through the 90 minutes of a creditable draw and a much improved Arsenal performance but the injury was so severe that it was to keep him out for the next six weeks.

Not being able to play did not detract from the other qualities for which Tom Whittaker had secured Tommy Lawton's services. He asked him to help with training and to be in the dressing room, home and away. "You're good for morale and team spirit," Whittaker told him. "I want your influence and advice around the players. They're responding to you already."

It paid off. The results began to improve and Arsenal started to look more like the reigning champions they were. Mr Whittaker was well pleased and so was Tommy. He was learning all about management at the highest level but, even more importantly, away from the pressures of being the manager, a responsibility he had accepted too soon at Brentford.

At the end of the 1953/54 season Arsenal finished in a respectable 12th position in the First Division with 43 points from 42 matches. Tommy had played in nine of those matches, scoring one goal, but his contribution off the pitch had been invaluable.

Now, at work and at home, Tommy's happiness was complete.

His marriage to Gay was proving to be as strong as it was successful.

They were utterly devoted; she was his lover, his friend, his advisor and, when it was necessary, his minder, too. The happy couple had a brilliant social life, mixing with top show-business personalities, most of whom they found to be warm and thoughtful as well as very entertaining.

Back at the top of the soccer tree, Tommy was now a much sought-after star on the London celebrity circuit. He was a regular broadcaster on radio and television, an authoritative voice on sports programmes hosted by Eamonn Andrews; he was a star panellist, alongside Isobel Barnett and the irascible Gilbert Harding on the hugely popular TV game, *What's My Line?*, in which the stars had to guess the occupation of contestants by asking them a set number of questions; he did several shows with boxer Freddie Mills; he had his own series on children's television in which he gave the kids top tips, not just on playing football but on how best to look after their kit and keep themselves fit through the right sort of exercise; he was invited to read the classified football results on the BBC's *Sports Report,* a role in which the producer, Angus Mackay, was able to overcome the Corporation's traditional resistance to regional accents, having broken the taboo with Eamonn Andrews's Irish tones. This, however, eventually proved to be a bridge too far for pools punters struggling to come to terms with some of Tommy's Lancastrian pronunciation, particularly of Scottish clubs like Alloa!

Such was Tommy Lawton's celebrity status that he was even offered a contract worth £10,000 to be the face of a nationwide advertising campaign for Guinness, but his club put a block on that, deeming it inappropriate for an Arsenal player to be promoting an alcoholic beverage.

Tommy's natural wit and intelligence also made him a popular guest on current affairs programmes, on which he never missed an opportunity to raise the continuing iniquity of the maximum wage for footballers. This was now £17 a week, which meant that his extra earnings from TV and radio were making a valuable contribution towards their London celebrity lifestyle.

Tommy and Gay did not live extravagantly, but they did live very well. They paid rent on a smart London house, which they furnished expensively. They ran an equally smart sports car, they ate well and they dressed well, keeping up appearances being important since they were frequently called upon to attend public functions, open fêtes and garden parties and present prizes at sports events.

Though they were quite often out by invitation to dinners and top social events they shunned the London nightlife, never went near the clubs or pubs and liked nothing better than spending their evenings together quietly at home with Carol. Tommy had grown really fond of Carol, to whom he had become an affectionate 'dad' but Gay longed to give him a child of his own to complete the happy family.

The Lawtons were unaware until much later that among their neighbours was a man who was to become famous for rather less acceptable reasons than the rest of their acquaintances. Carol was at home with measles and watching television when the signal was suddenly ruined by bad interference. Tommy went out and scoured the street to detect the cause of the problem but had to return without success. It happened on one or two occasions but it wasn't until much later that they discovered the offender was the infamous Russian spy Guy Burgess and that Carol's TV enjoyment was impaired because he was sending radio messages to Moscow!

Tommy now played golf so well that he was down to a handicap of two and often played with the famous Welsh Ryder Cup player Dai Rees. Other celebrated friends were the Welsh rugby star Cliff Morgan, singer Jimmy Young and cricketer Colin Cowdrey. Afternoons were sometimes spent on the racecourses with football mates and every Sunday that summer he played charity cricket matches with star players from Middlesex CCC.

Everybody, it seemed, wanted to know Tommy Lawton. Everywhere he went he was pursued by fans – as many women, who adored his film star looks and celebrity status, as men who admired his soccer skills and fantastic achievements.

He kept in touch with Big Swifty, whose career in journalism was going from strength to strength and they again discussed the possibility of Tommy one day following the same route into the press.

All in all, life didn't get much better than this.

At Arsenal, Tommy continued happily with the dual role of player and unofficial trainee manager under Tom Whittaker, from whom he was learning so much. Tommy was being given the opportunity to study the game he loved from the boss's perspective, which he now realised was an entirely different one. He learned just how Whittaker ran this huge football club, how he dealt with the daily problems, large and small, how he organised his staff and delegated authority. He watched and learned from Whittaker's man-management techniques, something at which he'd failed dismally at Brentford and he was taught the value, structure and routines of a good scouting system. In short, he was learning how to be a top football manager from one of the very best and most experienced in the business.

Tommy was doing much to bring on exciting young players like Derek Tapscott. The tried, tested, trusted and timeless training methods he'd learned from Ray Bennion and Dixie Dean were now familiar at Highbury, with footballs dangling from the stanchions in the stands and players hanging in the air while Lawton barked his instructions on how to head them. And the 'old master' was proving, whenever it was asked of him, that he could still be a match for the young 'uns on the pitch. When he played, the youngsters had the edge over him for pace but he was a peerless on-field tactician and his shooting and heading powers were as lethal as ever.

At Highbury and at major grounds across the country, floodlights were starting to be used, introducing night football to the fans. Floodlit football had been a long time coming, mainly because of the reluctance of the football establishment to accept it. Experiments in playing games under artificial lights had taken place as long ago as the late 19th century. At Bramall Lane, Sheffield in 1878, lamps were mounted on timber gantries and lit by dynamo machines powered by steam engines. Several games were played under lights like those but they were far too unreliable and too many games had to be abandoned when they were suddenly plunged into pitch darkness.

However, football club directors, driven (as ever!) by the potential extra revenue they could earn from charging spectators to watch games at night (without evening matches, the five-and-a-half day working week and religious sanctions limited football to Saturday afternoons only) carried on pushing the prospect and trying out different methods of illumination. One such experiment took place in 1895 when for a night match at London's Canning Town the pitch was surrounded by electric light bulbs attached to poles and the ball was dipped in whitewash to make it easier to see. This time, the game finished without technology failure and the local newspaper reported that "a big crowd paid at the gate to witness the contest".

Women blazed the floodlights trail, too. Ladies' football had become popular during the First World War and in December 1920 one of the best teams, Dick Kerr's Ladies, arranged a charity game against the Rest of England to raise money to buy food for impoverished ex-servicemen for Christmas. The game was played at Preston's Deepdale ground and Winston Churchill, then Secretary of State for War, gave permission for two anti-aircraft searchlights, generation equipment and 40 carbide flares to be used in order that the game could be played at night to attract a bigger crowd. The floodlights worked a treat, 12,000 spectators watched Mr Kerr's Ladies win 4-0 with goals from Jennie Harris (two), Florrie Redford and Minnie Lyons, a jolly good time was had by all and £600 was raised for the Unemployed Ex-Servicemen's Distress Fund. Such a satisfactory result all round that many commentators concluded that, should this whole floodlights issue be left to women to sort out, every major men's team in England could be playing night matches next week!

But instead, it was left to the menfolk of the Football Association who remained steadfastly unimpressed by the notion until, 30 years later, clubs like Wolverhampton Wanderers went ahead anyway, installed floodlights employing slightly more sophisticated technology than that used by Dick Kerr's Ladies, started playing floodlit friendly matches against attractive foreign clubs and attracted very large crowds to watch them.

In November 1954 Arsenal played Moscow Spartak under the new Highbury floodlights and were beaten 2-1. Much to Tommy Lawton's disappointment, he wasn't picked to play on this historic occasion and watched impatiently from the bench as Arsenal lost 2-1.

The previous month, Arsenal made history by becoming the first foreign club side to play behind the Iron Curtain. The Russians had specifically asked for Arsenal to be the opponents of Moscow Dynamo for a special exhibition match so, despite the rigours of such a long trip and the well justified fears of the unknown in Cold War communist countries, it was an offer which they could not, in the interests of diplomacy, refuse!

The first leg of the journey was to Prague. The pilots of the two BEA Viscounts in which they were flying were under strict orders only to enter Czechoslovakian airspace between 3:59 pm and 4:01 pm and they were escorted by eight Russian MiG fighters. After refuelling, the British planes had to leave and the Arsenal party was herded onto two elderly, noisy Aeroflots for a distinctly uncomfortable, bone-shaking onward journey to Minsk, via Warsaw for a refuelling stop. At Minsk they were delayed by bad weather and taken by shabby bus to a drab room tightly packed with beds, some of which were already occupied. After two hours, they were woken up and taken back to the airport for the two-hour flight to Moscow.

Throughout every stage of the flight they were accompanied by three mysterious Russian men in large overcoats, whom they assumed to be members of the KGB, a suspicion bolstered by the fact that they spoke to no one and kept the party under observation through darting eyes all the way from Prague.

When they eventually arrived at the Hotel Mockba in Red Square, the first thing the players did was to search their rooms for hidden microphones. They had convinced themselves that they would be bugged and kept under close observation for every minute they were there, for such was the tension between communist East and capitalist West and the papers back home abounded with stories of spies and their dirty deeds. They were, however, very pleasantly surprised. Despite their worst fears having been raised by the unfriendly discomfort of that marathon journey, they were given a warm and generous welcome by the Russians who provided first-class hospitality and shattered all preconceived images of cold-hearted, suspicious communist zealots.

The players were taken on a tour of Moscow and Tommy was enthralled by the beauty of the buildings. The Kremlin, Lenin's tomb and the university took his breath away. People with such a feeling for beauty, he thought, cannot be bad, and that served to strengthen his abhorrence of the repression with which the communist states ruled their lives. Even Moscow Dynamo's stadium had beautiful tapestries and carpets.

Tommy was amazed and deeply flattered to discover that he was a huge star in Russia. Crowds turned up just to watch him train and he was conscious of them pointing him out to each other and calling his name . . . *"Lowtoon"*

The game was a big disappointment for Arsenal and their followers. Moscow Dynamo won 5-0. The Gunners played well enough in the first half but tired badly, which was perhaps understandable considering the nightmare journey they had experienced, and four of the Russian goals came in the second half.

The following day, Tommy was deeply moved by a wonderful gesture from the Russians. It was 6th October, his 35th birthday. And Moscow Dynamo gave him a surprise birthday lunch at the hotel. There was caviar, followed by steaks, a huge ice-cream birthday cake, the special gift of a Russian camera and a little speech in broken English from the team captain, Mikhail Semichastny, who had been in the side that played Chelsea and Tommy Lawton nearly ten years earlier.

As the Arsenal players reflected on the 5-0 defeat on the flight home, Tommy shared their disappointment but he was not too concerned. He was just thrilled to have had the experience: "If anybody had told me that I'd play football in Moscow at the age of 35, I'd have thought them stark, staring mad!" he told his teammates.

At home, however, there was no such reasoning. The press panned Arsenal's performance, seeing it as further manifestation of the decline in English soccer standards, following two embarrassing thrashings of the international team by the 'Magical Magyars' of Hungary. The press boys were right about this. While football still packed the stadia of England with devoted fans, the old country's crown as the inherent ruler of the game was now well and truly tarnished, if not knocked from its head!

Back home in London, Tommy kept Gay entertained for hours with the story of his trip behind the infamous Iron Curtain, the many surprises it revealed and the mixed feelings it evoked. Gay was captivated: "And what about communism?" she asked him. Tommy drew a long breath, then told her, "Don't ever think that communism means all are equal. What it really means is that two per cent of the people have all the wealth and 98 per cent are equal only because they all have nothing."

As the season progressed, Arsenal were doing reasonably well and Tommy continued to be available for selection whenever required, with mixed fortunes, ranging from the wonderful high of Christmas Day 1954 when he scored the winning goal against Chelsea in front of 47,000 spectators at Highbury to the definitive low when he returned to Turf Moor, where it had all started for him 20 years earlier, to have a stinker in a 3-0 defeat by Burnley, thus sending the thousands of extra fans who had turned out to see him trudging home with the reluctant conclusion that their 'Boy Wonder' was now well and truly past it!

Another high came in January when he scored the winning goal against Cardiff City, who had the dashing Welsh international Trevor Ford at centre forward, in the third round of the FA Cup at Highbury. Ford, a brave, direct and dangerous front runner, had been tipped as the potential match winner but it was 'old man' Lawton who, having been marked out of the game for the best part of 90 minutes, nipped in craftily for a late clincher. Tommy's goal put Arsenal in the draw for the fourth round and he dared to dream: could this be the year that he finally made it to that FA Cup final at Wembley, the one honour still to elude him?

The dream did not last long. The Gunners drew League champions Wolves at Molineux, where, in front of 52,857 spectators, Lawton narrowly failed to beat Wolves' England international goalkeeper Bert Williams with a trademark header before Roy Swinbourne got a winner for the home side. Tommy Lawton's FA Cup final dream had gone for ever.

In March 1955 Tommy went to Hillsborough, the home of Sheffield Wednesday, to play in a very special match. It was to raise money for a trust fund set up to help Derek Dooley.

Dooley, a big, powerful red-haired centre forward, scored 63 goals for Sheffield Wednesday between 1950 and early 1953, an incredible 46 of those coming in his first season. Only 24 years old, he had a glittering career in front of him until the day, on 14th February 1953, he collided with Preston goalkeeper George Thompson during a game at Deepdale and suffered a double fracture of his leg. He was rushed to hospital in excruciating pain and the leg was set. As he was getting ready to leave hospital, two days later, a nurse noticed that there was no response when she touched his toes. The cast was removed and doctors found that a scratch on the back of his leg had become infected. Gangrene had set in and the leg had to be amputated.

The terrible fate of young Derek Dooley touched the hearts of everybody in football and united the rival 'Steel City' fans of Wednesday and United. A testimonial match was organised for Dooley, whose father and mother were both factory workers. A combined Sheffield team was to play a combined International XI, for whom Tommy was invited to play.

The teams were:.

Sheffield: Burgin (United); Martin (Wednesday), Graham Shaw (United); Jack Shaw (Wednesday), McEvoy (Wednesday), Joe Shaw (United); Alan Finney (Wednesday), Quixall (Wednesday), Cross (United), Sewell (Wednesday), Marriott (Wednesday).

International XI: Kelsey (Arsenal and Wales); Foulkes (Manchester United and England), Byrne (Manchester United and England); Farrell (Everton and Eire), Charles (Leeds United and Wales), Forbes (Arsenal and Scotland); Matthews (Blackpool and England), Quigley (Blackburn Rovers and England), Lawton (Arsenal and England), Hagan (Sheffield United and England), Eglington (Everton and Eire).

The referee was Arthur Ellis of Halifax, who had been officiating on the day Dooley suffered his dreadful injury.

Sheffield Wednesday chose this match to switch on their new £22,000 floodlights and 55,000 Sheffield football fans of both clubs turned out on a freezing cold night to raise £7,500 in gate receipts. Another £15,000 was raised by a public collection in the city of Sheffield and £2,700 was donated by local newspapers, *The Star* and the *Sheffield Telegraph*, making a grand total of £25,200 for young Dooley, who had also been given a job by a local firm owned by one of the Sheffield Wednesday directors.

Before the kick-off the two teams lined up in front of Hillsborough's main stand, the lights were turned up to full power and into their bright glare Derek Dooley limped out of the players' tunnel to a fantastic roar from the crowd which then stood in prolonged applause for two minutes to show the poor lad that Sheffield would never forget him.

Tommy could only imagine the feelings of young Dooley as he moved slowly along the line of players, shaking hands to thank each one of them, then turned and waved to all four sides of the ground to more thunderous applause. A great football career nipped so cruelly in the bud. Tommy stood, applauding with a lump in his throat and as he watched Derek Dooley limp off that pitch for the last time, he thanked God that good fortune had prevented his own career from ending in such a tragic way. "There, but for the grace of God," he thought. It could so easily have happened to him.

Tommy scored a goal that night in a game won 5-1 by the internationals, who put on a super show for the crowd. Jimmy Hagan got two, Stan Matthews one and Eddie Quigley one. Tommy's ex-Notts County protégé

Jackie Sewell scored for the Sheffield team, whose supporters gave the visiting stars a standing ovation for making Derek Dooley's night so special.

Arsenal finished the 1954/55 season in ninth place in Division One. Lawton had played in 18 League matches and scored six goals. But, again, Tom Whittaker was firmly of the belief that this man's positive contribution went way beyond those statistics. The bond between Lawton and Tom Whittaker had grown ever stronger. There was now an unofficial agreement between the two that Tommy was being groomed as the manager's successor and both were happy and content to start the 1955/56 season on the same footing.

Meanwhile, Tommy had an even better reason to be happy. The baby for which he and Gay had tried for so long was due in the summer. Gay reckoned it was a hat-trick, conceived on a night after Tommy had scored twice for Arsenal!

The expectant joy turned to serious concern, however, when the pregnancy became extremely difficult. Doctors at the Royal Northern Hospital discovered a large growth, the size of a football, just above the baby's head. This was removed, leaving fears that the baby might have been damaged during the operation. With this complication and the fact that Gay's blood pressure was very high, the imminent delivery was a cause for great concern and it was agreed that if it led to grave risk to mother or baby, it was the mother who was to survive.

Mercifully, it went well. At 2:15 am on Saturday 2nd June Gay gave birth to a healthy baby weighing 7 lb 8 oz. The baby's head appeared first, leading a nurse to exclaim, "It's a girl!" "Not with those shoulders," said the surgeon, a Welsh rugby fan by the name of Rees. "It's a rugby player – and he'll play for Wasps one day!"

The birth had come nice and early for the national Sunday papers, whose reporters and photographers were camped outside the hospital, waiting for news. The picture of lovely mum and beaming dad looking fondly and proudly at their bouncing baby, who was laid in a crib decorated in the red-and-white colours of Arsenal, was a cracker. The headline over the story on the front page of *The People* said "Twinkle Toes"!

The baby was named Thomas James Hugh, after his father, of course, and after the grandfather Tommy had loved so much. Bursting with pride and happiness, Tommy cradled the child tenderly in his arms and whispered, "Bet you're pleased, Jim Riley."

Baby Tom's christening at Barton Seagrave Parish Church on 14th October 1956 was a parade of the stars. Many of the guests, friends of his mum and dad, were sports or show-business celebrities. One of his godfathers was Victor Barna, five times world table tennis champion. Victor was an escapee from communist Hungary and was once engaged to actress Eva Gabor, sister of Zsa Zsa.

The arrival of Tom Junior gave added weight to Tommy's chats with Tom Whittaker about the possibility of a future in football management. And Whittaker told him, "Your best bet now is to move to a club at a lower level and learn the job from the rough. It's the only way to start. Do the lot yourself: organise your own office work; find your own players; do all the things we've got dozens of people doing here at Highbury. That way you'll get a really thorough grounding and there won't be a job to be done that you haven't done yourself."

This was sound advice and it wasn't just Whittaker who was prepared to help Tommy. One of the Arsenal directors was friendly with the officials of his hometown club, Southern League Kettering Town, and through him came the offer of a player–manager's job on a salary of £1,500 a year, plus 10 per cent of receipts from gates over 3,000 and expenses. Viewed alongside the maximum player's wage of £17 a week and with financial opportunities off the field of play now beginning to shrink proportionately with his prominence on it, this was a superb offer.

At home with Gay, the pros and cons were assessed. Financially, it was very sound. On the downside, it meant quitting Arsenal, where he was so happy, leaving London, which they loved and forsaking the limelight and trappings of fame to which they'd both become accustomed.

If he went to Kettering it would mean that, for the first time in 20 years, Tommy Lawton would no longer be in the national spotlight. But then, even though he felt he'd got at least a couple of top-flight playing seasons left in him, they were going to lose all that one day in the not too distant future anyway and if he could come back to Highbury as Tom Whittaker's successor they would be back in their beloved city eventually. Job done, then. Kettering it was. "Well done, Mr Manager Lawton!" said Gay. "Why, thank you ma'am!" said Tommy. And they laughed happily as they exchanged an exaggerated handshake, convinced that the future of Tommy, Gay, Carol and Tommy Junior was secured.

The 1955/56 season had got off to a flying start on the pitch for Tommy – he'd scored a hat-trick in a 3-1 win over Cardiff City – but a regular first-team place was looking increasingly unlikely and he played his last senior game for the Gunners in a friendly against Rangers at Ibrox. When he left Highbury he had played eight First Division games for Arsenal so far that season and scored six goals. It was a suitably impressive goals-to-games ratio with which to bow out of the top flight, but it was just a tiny drop in the ocean of a fantastic career spanning an incredible 20 years.

Tommy's record since 1935 read:

Clubs (League and Cup): 627 games; 510 goals.
International and Representative: 104 games; 125 goals.
Grand total: 731 games; 635 goals.

In every one of those 731 matches he had demonstrated such sportsmanship that his conduct on the field was held up as an example to all. Never once was he sent off, nor even booked. To mark the end of that amazing playing career, Tommy wrote a bestselling book, *My Twenty Years of Soccer.*

In that book he offered his thoughts on the future of football:

Soccer has a great past. What of its future? Well, I am convinced that soccer has a great future. It will never die. It is an international institution. No other sport has such a fantastic hold on players and spectators throughout the world.

I think it is in the international sphere that we are going to see the major changes in the future. Some of the suggested changes might seem Wellsian at the moment, but who would have thought that the whole of Europe would be able to watch the contest for the World Cup on television? Yet it happened.

Now, on top of the World Cup, we hear talk of a European Cup. The march to more and more international football is on. Air travel will play its part. The development of the aeroplane has contracted the world. A trip across the Atlantic to America is just an overnight hop. Even Australia and the Far East are almost on our doorstep. So there are bound to be more and more international matches, both at national and club level. As well as the World Cup every four years, a European Cup is a certainty, despite the opposition of certain sections of the footballing world.

We might also have international festivals of the leading clubs from each country as a forerunner of the European League. For the European League will come. Maybe it won't come in our lifetime, but it will most certainly come.

Not for a minute do I think that it will interfere with the purely national competitions at first, because these domestic leagues will always have their hold on the public, but I am convinced that we shall have a European League of, say, eight clubs to start with. That will be the start and the natural development will be to relegate the national competitions to the level of secondary competitions, with the leading European clubs taking part in a full-scale European League with its own promotion and relegation.

Maybe I am jumping much too far ahead but fantastic as this European League might sound, it sounds no more fantastic than some of the suggestions that were made years ago and are now fact. For instance, being purely parochial, who would have thought, say 20 years ago, that 100,000 people would watch the FA Amateur Cup final or a schoolboys' international match at Wembley? Yet now we accept those huge crowds as a matter of course.

So, in the years to come, we will have Arsenal supporters gaily beribboned in their red-and-white colours, hopping the regular air buses from London to Budapest to cheer the Arsenal as they play Honved in a game that will decide the championship of the First Division of the European Football League. Fantastic? But what is fantastic in 1955 can well be fact in 1965. And by 1984, who knows what? Can you imagine Big Brother as the England team manager?

Floodlighting will also become more and more popular, but the future systems will be much more brilliant than the present ones. By the time "it's grand to be alive in 1985" even the Sheffield Wednesday lights, easily the best in Britain today, will be made to look prehistoric.

Will all this international football be a good thing? Of course it will. Just because there was a riot at the World Cup game between Hungary and Brazil, the anti-soccer brigade tells us that sport can do nothing towards cementing international friendship. But if you take their stupid arguments to their logical conclusion, Britain and Australia should by now have broken off diplomatic relations. For does any sporting engagement cause so much bickering as the England v Australia cricket Tests? And remember that bottles were thrown onto the field at a cricket Test in the West Indies.

The more football that is played between the people of the world, the less fighting there will be. The trouble that sometimes follows sporting international meetings is caused not by the sportsmen but by the politicians and the misguided people. I have, for instance, heard people say they hope the Hungarians will lose because they are communists. Personally, although I am a long, long way from being a communist, I don't care two hoots about the Hungarians' politics. They are great footballers and that is what matters. The thing that causes the trouble in sport is phrases like 'Kuts, the Red runner'. Who cares a fig whether he is red, green, blue or sky blue pink in his politics? What matters is that he is a great runner and a great sportsman.

During my career in soccer I have made many great friends in various parts of the world. So have the other players. So have the spectators who have travelled abroad to watch our matches. Those friendships will be multiplied as international soccer increases and the world today needs bigger and better international friendships.

We can get to understand each other better by meeting on the sports field, a more pleasant and a more valuable meeting than meeting on the battlefield. Old prejudices can be forgotten as sporting prowess draws men and women closer together. If you think that is stupid idealism, remember the case of Bert Trautmann, the Manchester City goalkeeper. He was signed just after the War when we didn't take too kindly to the Germans. But by his brilliant work in the Manchester City goal, Bert has made himself a great favourite all over Britain. Sport meant more than the fact that Bert served during the War as a paratrooper – against us.

What has happened between Bert Trautmann and the British people can happen throughout the world. So many of the world's troubles are caused by the fact that the various nationalities do not meet often enough to understand each other's points of view. Regular meetings on the soccer field, with the constant mixing of the supporters, will change all that.

And that is why I say the future of soccer is set fair in the international sphere. And why the future of the world can be set fair, thanks to soccer.

In the same book, Tommy reflected on his playing career:

More than 20 years of soccer. What glorious years. Years that all the money in the world couldn't buy. I have been lucky. I have played with great clubs; I have escaped serious injury; I have played for my country; I have even captained my country; I have won many of the game's top honours.

Soccer has been good to me and I hope that I have repaid the game in some small way. I have had great experiences. I have met some wonderful people. I have memories that nobody can ever take from me.

If I could turn the clock back 20 years, I would still go into the game as a full-time professional and I can say to any lad who is contemplating a career in football: Go ahead, son . . . providing you are willing to work and work hard and providing you are willing to learn the craft thoroughly. You will meet some of the grandest fellows you could ever wish to meet and you will have a pleasant, healthy life and be quite well paid for it as well.

My own career in soccer has been a great experience. I only wish I could go through it all again. But as I cannot, may I tell all youngsters: Remember, it is what you put into the game that counts, not what you take out.

As if to throw a spotlight on Tommy Lawton's forthright public pronouncements, a recurring feature of his incomparable playing career, the dithering dinosaurs of the Football Association, for whom he had so little time and even less respect, finally relented and gave their official approval to floodlights. The first floodlit League game took place between Portsmouth and Newcastle United on 22nd February 1956, three weeks after he left the top flight. It was just another of so many changes the great game had seen since that cheeky lad signed for Burnley in 1935 and he chuckled at the irony as he pondered, "The lights are going up on football just as they're going down on me."

But what a career he'd had; what an example he'd set. And what an inspiration he was to all those youngsters avidly reading the advice he gave them in that book; advice that was as well qualified as it was sound and sensible, because nobody had ever put more into the game than Tommy Lawton.

Chapter Nine
TOMMY THE MANAGER

To Tommy Lawton, Highbury was not a stadium. It was a palace. And as the 'King of Soccer' walked out of his 'royal abode' he believed that, after he'd cut his managerial teeth at Kettering, he would be walking back through those palatial doors as Tom Whittaker's successor. He was convinced that he was going to become manager of the world-famous Arsenal Football Club.

This conviction was not shared by enough of the Highbury top brass. Less than a fortnight after Tommy left, they appointed a bright young Third Division manager, Alec Stock of Leyton Orient, as assistant manager and heir apparent to Whittaker. Stock was to stay only 53 days before resigning and returning to Leyton Orient but his appointment so soon after Tommy's departure for Kettering, a move he had so firmly believed to be a deliberately arranged stepping stone back to Highbury for him, was a huge blow for Lawton.

He was mystified by this development, which was clearly telling him that Arsenal did not see him as their future manager, despite the impression to the contrary that he had been given.

Was this snobbery at work? Was Lawton, despite his worldwide fame and popularity, too working class for some of the 'lah-de-dah buggers' at Highbury, where hyphenated surnames and old school ties were not uncommon? Were Lawton's Lancashire accent and direct down-to-earth Northern manner unacceptable to some in that oak-panelled palace?

Or did they think he was too big a star to do their bidding, too famous for them to be able to handle?

Tommy would never know. But he did know that he'd made his bed now and he had to lie in it; he had agreed to do a job at Kettering and he had to be true to his own code of professionalism and get on with that job.

Kettering were doing badly in the Southern League. They had narrowly escaped relegation. Manager Lawton knew that he faced a huge task of complete reorganisation and that he was in for an extremely busy close season. Although he'd joined the club only a few weeks before the season ended, he'd seen enough to realise that the right sort of team ethic was missing and that a number of players he reckoned were liabilities had to be weeded out.

He wasted no time with that, nor with scouring the country in search of free transfers; experienced players who were in the twilight of their Football League careers but could shine in the non-league environment. He signed Amos Moore from Aston Villa, Jack Wheeler from Huddersfield, Jack Goodwin from Brentford, Bob Thomas from Fulham, Norman Plummer from Leicester, Harry McDonald from Crystal Palace and Geoff Toseland from Sunderland. And of course he had a pretty useful centre forward – some bloke by the name of Lawton!

In goal, he went for Jim Standen, a young keeper at Arsenal. Tommy had thought him a good prospect: 'a bit chicken' but that could be cured with more match experience. Jim was Arsenal's fourth-choice goalkeeper. He was playing only occasionally for the 'A' team and this was stunting his progress. Playing regularly in the Southern League would do the lad a power of good. He reached a gentlemen's agreement with Whittaker that if Kettering could have young Standen on permanent loan he would be allowed to return to Highbury immediately if Arsenal needed him. Kettering had Jack Wheeler as more than adequate cover should that occur and in the meantime, Jack, a man whose knowledge of football impressed Tommy, could provide valuable assistance on the training ground.

With the exception of Standen, it was a bit of a 'Dad's Army' that started the 1956/57 season for Kettering, but they were all more than fit enough for the Southern League and they brought levels of skill and top-flight experience way above non-league standard. Meanwhile, with an eye on long-term development, Tommy was scouting for young talent and cleverly advertised in the local paper, offering young players "a week's free coaching under England international Tommy Lawton". Tommy's name and reputation were still absolutely top drawer and good youngsters from miles around were soon flocking to his sessions.

Non-league it might have been, but suddenly there was an air of top-class professionalism about Kettering Town. Lawton had assembled a cracking team for the present and was already planning thoughtfully for the future. Kettering, who had paid Arsenal £1,000 for Tommy's signature, had spent their money very well indeed.

While Tommy was throwing himself into his new job, there was sad news about his managerial mentor. In October 1956 Tom Whittaker suffered a heart attack and died. His death upset Tommy deeply. He was very fond of Whittaker. He owed that man so much for leading him out of the lower divisions and back to the glory of playing for Arsenal. He knew Whittaker thought the world of him, too and he felt sure that, if it had been up to Tom alone, his eventual return to Arsenal as his successor would have been a formality, but that was a matter of no consequence, now, compared with the sudden loss of a fine man and such a good friend.

The least he could do for Tom Whittaker now was to justify the faith he had shown in him by becoming a successful manager. He built a team entirely of his own making, playing the game the way he believed it should be played. Kettering Town were well and truly on the up.

By Christmas 1956 they were ten points clear at the top of the Southern League and still going strong in the FA Cup. Tommy, with all his charisma and charm to the fore, had become 'Mr Kettering' to the swelling numbers of supporters and he was manna from heaven for the local press, for whom he always found plenty of time. As well as grabbing the headlines in the local newspaper, Tommy Lawton's name was still magical nationally and that gave little Kettering Town positive national newspaper coverage the like of which they had never even hoped to experience.

Tommy Lawton, the manager, was doing very well indeed.

Meanwhile in the East Midlands, the fortunes of Notts County, so incredibly high thanks to Tommy Lawton from 1948 to 1952, had sunk into the doldrums. The team in red from the other side of the Trent was in the ascendancy while the miserable Magpies were looking doomed to relegation from the Second Division. They had sacked their manager, George Poyser and appointed the loyal Frank Broome, the winger from the Tommy Lawton team, as caretaker manager.

Broome was working hard to avoid relegation and had a lot of support in the corridors of power at Meadow Lane, but despite some vehement boardroom opposition, the Notts County chairman, powerful local textile manufacturer Len Machin, had decided he wanted Tommy Lawton as his manager and was determined to get him.

Early in the New Year, Tommy got a phone call at home one night from Albert Stapleton, a highly respected Nottingham sports journalist who had the ear of the Notts board. "Would you be interested in returning to Meadow Lane as manager?" he asked Tommy. Always respected for shunning the use of really bad language, Tommy was initially tempted to break the good habit of a lifetime with a two-word riposte! Instead, he replied firmly but politely: "Go back *there*, after all that happened last time? You must be joking, Albert. Anyway, I'm more than happy at Kettering for the time being, thank you very much."

Len Machin, fiercely single-minded in his pursuit of Lawton, was not prepared to take no for an answer. He rang Tommy personally and repeated the question, with its implied offer. Tommy was equally determined to decline: "Look, Mr Machin," he said, "I don't want to be rude to you but Notts County is a club that simply does not interest me. You know I left under less than happy circumstances and a really bad atmosphere and resentment still rankles on both sides I'm sure."

The following day, the local *Guardian Journal*, reporting Tommy's response under the headline "Lawton Rejects County's Offer", told the people of Nottingham:

Tommy Lawton is not coming to Notts County. The former England and Notts centre forward told the club yesterday that he does not want to be manager at Meadow Lane. This means that Frank Broome, the assistant trainer, who has steered the club through their last two games from which they collected three points, will continue to be in charge.

In a statement yesterday Lawton declared: "On the principle that my players must believe in me and my methods I feel it is only fair that Mr Broome should have the opportunity to provide the Nottingham public with a successful side. The Kettering players have always believed I could bring them success and I am determined that both they and myself shall reap the benefits from our labours." Speaking about the future, Lawton had this to say: "I will think about that when I have completed the job I am being paid to do, but I can say that my aim is to one day manage a Football League club."

The announcement was reassuring news for Frank Broome, who has rocketed to top popularity with Notts supporters for the gallant way he has rallied the team. "As far as I am concerned, the position is the same as before when I was told to carry on," Frank told the Guardian Journal *from his Littleover, Derby home.*

But Mr Machin was not a man to give in. A few weeks later, with

Kettering still storming ahead under Tommy's successful management, he called him again: "Let me come and talk to you, man to man. That can't do any harm, surely." "Oh, all right," said Tommy. "If only out of common courtesy. But I have to warn you again, Mr Machin, that you are almost certainly wasting your time. There's just too much bad feeling up there in Nottingham."

When Machin arrived at Tommy's home he brought with him a fantastic proposition: "If you come and manage Notts County we'll give you £2,500 a year, by far the highest salary in the Division, a house and unlimited expenses." The generosity of that shook Tommy. He had a wife and two children to consider and this was an amazing package. But . . .

"I know most people would jump at that, Mr Machin, but I am really concerned that if you appointed me, it just would not work out, for either of us," he said. "You've got the same board of directors there as when I left. They were divided over me then and they'll surely be just as divided if I go back. There are those who are for me and those who are violently against me. There are some people at Meadow Lane who would sooner see me in hell than back at Notts County. How could I work well in that atmosphere?" "I don't think it would be like that," said Machin, "and in any event, you'd always have my support, 100 per cent. And I'm the chairman!"

The conversation carried on in that vein for another half hour, Machin assuring Tommy all would be well, Tommy repeating his misgivings. Finally, Tommy agreed that he would at least give the offer some serious thought.

That night, Tommy and Gay talked long into the early hours, weighing the pros and cons of Machin's brilliant offer. The money was fantastic; Tommy was ambitious. If he succeeded at Notts he would be set fair for a top career in management and with all Tom Whittaker's guidance and his success at Kettering there was no reason to suppose he could not succeed. But on the downside, he would be walking into a cauldron of political in-fighting at Meadow Lane and on the domestic front, Nottingham had hardly been a haven of tranquillity for either of them. It was an agonising decision to make but by breakfast time, it was made.

If a formal offer was given, he would rejoin Notts County as manager.

In the meantime, that possibility was to remain under wraps because Tommy still had a successful first season in management to complete and Mr Machin had a mountain of opposition to climb. At the end of the season Kettering Town were runaway champions of the Southern League, having lost only four of their 42 games. Tommy played in 30 of those games and scored 15 goals. But much more importantly, he had proved himself as a manager. And he had done Tom Whittaker proud.

Over at Meadow Lane, Frank Broome had also done well, successfully leading Notts County to safety from relegation, but that hadn't shaken Len Machin's steely resolve to have Tommy Lawton as his manager and after inviting Lawton to his imposing home on Wilford Lane, West Bridgford, just down the road from Trent Bridge, to discuss a deal and meet other directors, the cover was blown.

The meeting was held at Machin's home because he was suffering from a chill and at 6:30 pm four directors, Messrs Edwards, Linnell, Sherwood and Hubbard, plus the club secretary, sat around the chairman's bedside discussing the issue while Tommy waited outside in another room. When Tommy was summoned to the bedside meeting at 8 pm, Alf Hubbard was leaving the room and said, "I am sorry, Tommy." Hubbard was, according to a report in the *Nottingham Evening News*, "in a distressed state" when he left.

At 10 pm, Lawton emerged and told reporters that he had been offered the job and that he would be conveying his answer to the board after he had spoken to his wife.

Tommy Lawton was still such a huge name that the news spread around Nottingham like wildfire and Frank Broome was, with every justification, deeply disappointed and upset. He told the press, "This is a big blow to me. I thought I was in with a very good chance of getting the job. I was told one thing and another is happening. I am very disheartened."

Some of the directors, all the players and many of the supporters were with Broome. They believed he was being shabbily treated and by saving the club from relegation, he had earned the right to carry on.

So, before Tommy Lawton had set foot back inside Meadow Lane, there were two conflicting camps in and around the club and feelings were running very high all over the city. Frank Broome had been very badly treated and the inherently argumentative Nottinghamians had a genuine injustice over which to disagree.

In the pubs, the clubs, the factories, the offices and the front rooms there was one topic of conversation. Should Nottingham welcome back the biggest name in British soccer and wish him well at Notts or should Frank Broome be given total public support in the interests of decency and fair play? The *Guardian Journal*'s readers came down heavily in favour of Broome and that was a reasonable barometer of feeling throughout the city.

When Tommy broke the news of his decision to Kettering Town chairman, Jack Nash, Mr Nash told him, "Tom, you're taking a very foolish step." This was merely confirming Tommy's own first thoughts and fears but the warning was to no avail. The fusion of Len Machin's superb financial offer, and all that it meant for him, his wife and two kids with the chance to get into Football League management and build a great second career, was a cocktail of golden opportunity which was just too strong to resist.

The author Graham Greene once wrote, "Nottingham is like a book you can't put down – like a woman you can't forget." It was a reference to the fact that so many people, having once experienced life in that great city, find themselves drawn inexorably back to it. So it was for Tommy Lawton. In a reversal of the fabled conundrum, his heart said no but his head said yes and his head won. Len Machin, stubborn to the end, had got his man at last.

On a sunny day in the early summer of 1957, Tommy Lawton was unveiled as Notts County's new manager. He stood in one of the goalmouths on the Meadow Lane pitch being photographed with Machin. The thick-skinned chairman, delighted to have won the battle and apparently impervious to the furore over his treatment of Frank Broome, proclaimed, "Notts County will be the Arsenal of the Midlands."

While the press cameras clicked, the boardroom resentment intensified. Alf Hubbard had told the local papers he was amazed that it had happened. He claimed the Lawton deal had been plotted between Machin and two of his fellow directors, Frank Sherwood and Bertram Edwards, while the rest had been expecting Frank Broome to be appointed as, he alleged, had been agreed at a previous board meeting. "Since that meeting, I have heard nothing," said Hubbard, "And I can't understand how this can be done without a full board of directors."

One way and another, Tommy Lawton was hardly starting his new job and beginning a crucial new stage in his life in perfect circumstances!

The task of transforming Notts County from Division Two strugglers into the chairman's promised 'Arsenal of the Midlands' was going to be difficult enough without all the political intrigue and boardroom in-fighting, not to mention having to attempt it with a squad of disgruntled professional footballers, most of whom didn't want to play for him and deeply resented the removal of Frank Broome. It wasn't made any easier when Tommy allowed himself to be persuaded by Machin to accept Broome as his assistant manager and keep Broome's backroom staff and club captain, Ron Wylie.

Machin obviously thought that a clear-out to bring in his own people, which is what Tommy should have done, would have been a bridge too far in the boardroom and in the court of local public opinion. This was not good advice for the new manager who should have had his own loyal and committed people around him. Tommy did, however, make one such appointment, bringing genial Jack Wheeler in from Kettering as his first-team trainer.

It was impossible for anybody to dislike Jack: a gentle man and a gentle-man he exuded genuine warmth and good humour. But he was nobody's fool. He knew the game inside out and he was a good judge of a player. Jack also had tremendous respect for Tommy Lawton; for his achievements in the game, for his class and for his tactical knowledge. He was convinced that, given time and experience, Tommy would make a great manager and happy though he was at Kettering, he was excited by the potential he thought Lawton was taking to Notts County.

Tommy Lawton's short spell in non-league football had not dimmed his appeal to the media. Back in Nottingham he was a magnet for the national press and television. He still carried the aura of a superstar and he had to suffer the gross gossip and ridiculous rumours that were always a heavy burden of such exalted status.

As soon as he arrived back in the city, all the old stories about his alleged illegal payments when he was there as a player began to recirculate and the passage of time had added even more spurious detail to the foolish fiction. Like a certain medieval bandit in Sherwood Forest, Tommy Lawton had become part of Nottingham folklore, except legend didn't have him robbing the rich to help the poor. On the contrary, Lawton had allegedly pocketed vast amounts of the hard-earned pounds, shillings and pence that working men had paid to watch him play!

The residual trappings of Tommy's celebrity lifestyle in London, the Jaguar car, the expensive clothes, the film-star persona, probably helped fuel the flames of these ludicrous stories but even if he rode around in rags on a rusty bicycle it wouldn't stop the gossip, he reasoned, and anyway, why the hell should he?

Now that he was a manager, with all the extra responsibility and financial propriety that went with the job, he considered making a full statement to the local press to clear his name. He could ask, for instance, whether he would ever have been appointed manager if there had been so much as a tiny shred of truth in the stories. But he decided that to dignify this nonsense with an official denial, which was bound to make big national news, would only serve to give importance and credence to the lies. Better, he resolved, to do as he had done before and just treat it all with the contempt it deserved.

The fact that some of the players who didn't want Tommy Lawton at Meadow Lane chose to believe the gossip because it served to bolster their own resentment wasn't exactly conducive to dressing-room harmony, either. For an underperforming Second Division team, Notts were way overstaffed, with no less than 33 professionals, and when Tommy then discovered that there would be no money to fund a clear-out and bring in the fresh faces that his dressing room so desperately needed, the wise words of warning from Mr Nash at Kettering came back to haunt him. He shouldn't have touched this job with a barge pole!

But there was no going back. He would never be a quitter and there was only one thing to do: plough on, do the best with what he'd got, bring on good youngsters, plan for the future; and with the loyal support, encouragement and hard work of 'Gentle Jack' Wheeler to help him, that's what Tommy did.

Despite the malevolence, inadequacy and laziness of some of them, Tommy treated the Notts County players as if they were Arsenal stars. On away trips they stayed at the best hotels; he made sure they got the very best facilities at Meadow Lane; he even had them all fitted out with tailor-made woollen suits and he fought their corner in the boardroom whenever the directors questioned his generosity towards them. He told Jack Wheeler, "I've always thought the maximum wage is a disgrace and giving the players the best conditions you can is one way of redressing the balance."

By no means were all these players impressed, however, and it was impossible to escape the conclusion that some of them were giving him nothing in return. "In a perfect situation," he told Jack, "I would move at least ten of them on. But they're all on good contracts and they're too comfortable. They're going nowhere." On the pitch, the results reflected the malaise.

Tommy found comfort in the rapid and exciting progress of his youngsters, particularly Jeff Astle and Tony Hateley, whom he'd signed as apprentices. They were both centre forwards and Tommy saw the young Lawton in both of them. Yet again, the training techniques of Ray Bennion and Dixie Dean came into play and they were as effective as ever. These lads looked absolutely first-class prospects. There was also young Terry Wharton and five exceptionally promising kids he had discovered playing Lancashire League football. Tommy and Jack Wheeler were as convinced as they were enthusiastic about all these boys: "They're the future of Notts County Football Club and the way they're coming on it's not too distant a future, either," they agreed.

Early in the New Year of 1958, relegation was already looking a distinct possibility. Tommy told the chairman he believed that a spell in the Third Division would be a lifesaver for the club, enabling him to cut out all the dead wood, blood his youngsters and rebuild towards a genuinely exciting future which could even, in time, bring First Division football back to England's oldest club. In the meantime, he would do everything humanly possible to keep them up, but they had to be realistic. This team was simply not good enough for the Second Division. The chairman seemed not to dissent from all that and Tommy applied himself to the task ahead with renewed vigour.

So keen was Tommy to see this job through that he had agreed to work for six months without wages. County were so cash-strapped that the board had asked him to take a salary drop of £20 a week. "I'm not doing that," he told them. "I'd rather work for nowt until things improve." And 'nowt' suited them very well!

On 6th February 1958 all the problems and politics of Notts County Football Club paled into insignificance when Tommy Lawton listened in deep shock to a news bulletin on the BBC:

Seven Manchester United footballers are among 21 dead after an air crash in Munich. The British European Airways plane caught fire shortly after takeoff this afternoon with 38 passengers and six crew on board.

The footballing world is reeling from the loss of some of its most talented young players, known as the Busby Babes. Their average age was 24 and they included Roger Byrne, the captain, Mark Jones, Eddie Colman, Tommy Taylor, Liam Whelan, David Pegg and Geoff Bent. Eight British sports journalists and several club officials have also been killed.

The Queen has said she is deeply shocked and has sent a message of condolence to the Lord Mayor of Manchester and Minister of Transport and Civil Aviation.

The chartered aircraft was bringing the Manchester United entourage back from a European Cup match against Red Star Belgrade in Yugoslavia and had stopped at Munich's Riem Airport to refuel. On the third attempt to take off the plane overshot the runway, hit a house with its port wing, veered to the right, hit another building and burst into flames. The fuselage did not catch fire and several crew and passengers went back into the wreckage to rescue the injured.

Team manager Matt Busby was described as being the most seriously hurt and is being given blood transfusions in hospital. Star forward Bobby Charlton has been treated for slight head injuries.

According to the Chief Executive of BEA, Mr A H Millward, there was a heavy snowstorm in Munich and the pilot delayed departure because he was dissatisfied with one of the plane's engines.

The whole of Britain was stunned by this disaster. People simply could not believe that so many of Matt Busby's famous 'Babes' had been wiped out; and that another, perhaps the most talented of them all, Duncan Edwards was, like Busby himself, close to death in hospital.

On a cold, snowy morning, a shocked population poured over national newspapers the day after the disaster to read page after page with accounts of the full horror of the crash. Tommy Lawton shook his head in sorrow as he read the list of the dead players and soccer officials and of the appalling injuries to Matt Busby, such a good-natured gentleman when they'd been on the same tour as players. Then he turned to another list – of the journalists who had been killed . . . "Alf Clarke, *Manchester Evening Chronicle;* Don Davies, *The Manchester Guardian;* George Follows, *Daily Herald;* Tom Jackson, *Manchester Evening News;* Archie Ledbrooke, *Daily Mirror;* Henry Rose, *Daily Express;* Eric Thompson, *Daily Mail;* Frank Swift, *News of the World.*"

FRANK SWIFT?

Tommy threw his newspaper to the floor, as if by discarding it he could make it not so. This could not be true. He could not believe it. He would not believe it. Then he picked up the paper and read it again: "Frank Swift Dead. Dead? He *can't* be. Not Frank. Not Big Swifty. Not my mate. No. No. No. Oh for Christ's sake no." But yes, Frank was dead.

Frank Swift, 44, was one of those to be pulled alive from the plane by rescuers. But he died on the way to hospital.

The final death toll of the Munich Air Disaster was 23.

Wing half Duncan Edwards, only 21 but already capped 18 times by England, died 15 days later after an heroic fight for life. After an equally brave battle to stay alive, Matt Busby survived.

England had lost, in Duncan Edwards, a player who would have gone on to become one of the all-time world greats. Manchester United had lost, in eight of those wonderful 'Busby Babes', the core of the most exciting young team ever assembled in Britain. Tommy Lawton had lost, in Frank Swift, a dear, faithful, funny friend he had always thought indestructible.

Frank Swift's cruel death hit Tommy badly. He felt hollow in the pit of his stomach. How he wished, now, that he'd taken more time out in recent years to spend with Big Swifty. He could have done. And Frank would have loved that. He felt as though he'd neglected the best pal a man ever had. Now Frank was dead. It was too late to look him up like he could have done, like he should have done.

For days he kept seeing an image of Big Swifty's beaming face. He could see Frank on those blissfully happy summer days in Blackpool. He could see Frank the day he'd stood in all his glory alongside those naked Roman statues, comparing his assets with theirs while wearing nothing but that silly grin. He could see Frank running out to play in that big match on tour wearing a pair of regulation Army boots. He could see Frank pulling off brilliant, diving saves in front of huge crowds of spectators gasping in disbelief at his athleticism. And he could see Frank carrying that badly injured Scotland player off the pitch, so gently, so carefully, like the lad was a baby in his big, safe arms. He remembered how generous Frank had always been in finding time to give young goalkeepers advice, helping them to correct their faults. He'd even done that for young Bobbie Brown, the Scotland 'keeper before they ran out on opposite sides at Hampden Park. He laughed when he thought of Frank. He cried when he thought of Frank. It was a long time before he stopped thinking about that big, daft, lovely man every day. And he knew that, though the pain and anguish he was feeling would fade eventually, his fond memories of Big Swifty never would.

When football returned to normal after the shock of Munich, Notts County were relegated to the Third Division. Tommy Lawton set about delivering his plan for re-building the team and put in the list of the senior professionals he wanted to retain. This was not a long list. On the longer list of up-and-coming youngsters, he had put a red star against the names of those he believed were most likely to come through quickly, lads like Jeff Astle and Tony Hateley. He couldn't wait to start putting together the team for next season: *his* team; a team he knew would run through brick walls for him; a team he believed could bounce back into the Second Division.

He reckoned that if he could bring back the big gates he had, himself, attracted to Meadow Lane as a player, Notts County could have a great future as one of England's top clubs. He would achieve that by consolidation. He would sign several First Division players, so many of whom he knew as friends: top players just starting to go 'over the hill', so available for affordable transfer fees; clever, skilful, experienced players who would do a great job in Division Three. They would be his foundations, the rock upon which he would build his new team; then he'd perfect his youth policy, grooming youngsters who would learn so much so quickly by playing alongside the older men, just as he'd done as a lad at Burnley and Everton.

The first hurdle would be promotion from the Third. That could be very soon – next season, even – and a year or two later they could be ready to push for the First. He thought it criminal that a big city like Nottingham didn't have a First Division club, while neighbouring Derby, Leicester and Sheffield did. He was the man to put that right. He was excited and highly motivated by what lay ahead. The loyal Jack Wheeler shared his faith, his excitement and his well-founded optimism. This blueprint was, after all, just a more sophisticated variation of the plan they'd both seen succeed so spectacularly at Kettering.

The chairman thought otherwise. Len Machin drove to the Barton in Fabis farm of fellow director, Frank Sherwood and told him, "Get in, Frank. We're going to fire Tommy Lawton." "No, Len," replied Sherwood. "You signed him. You sack him."

Tommy went happily into the boardroom when Machin summoned him, thinking the call was to discuss his retained list and plans for next season. Like most directors he'd encountered in his years in football, he didn't believe Machin knew the slightest thing about the quality of players, about tactics, about the finer points of the game, but he believed he could trust him. After all, Machin had moved heaven and earth to bring him to Meadow Lane.

What followed hit him like a bolt out of the blue: "The board has unanimously decided to dispense with your services," said the chairman.

It took several minutes to sink in. He was fired. Finished. Out on his ear; no job, no salary, no house for his wife and kids. He was dispensed with, like an old pair of boots. Naïvely, he had accepted the job at Notts County without a contract, believing the chairman to be true to his word with his promise of a great future for him at Meadow Lane and his pledge to make Tommy Lawton's Notts County 'the Arsenal of the Midlands'. He'd believed all that. What a fool he'd been. He was devastated, disillusioned, hurt, angry and bitter. *Very* bitter.

Naively, he had shaken hands with Machin on the verbal agreement of a three-year contract but all he got was three months' pay. He had always thought his house in the smart West Bridgford area of Nottingham was his – a gift from the club, he'd believed. Now, he was told the house was required for a new manager and that he had to get out.

"If this is football management," he told himself, "they can stick it." Football, to which he'd dedicated more than 25 years of his life, had repaid him with a vicious kick in the teeth. He hadn't deserved that. This was so unfair. The injustice of it all was so painful. His confidence was shattered. The cocky ebullience which had typified his years as a player had gone. He was beaten and confused. Tommy Lawton walked out of Meadow Lane with his head down, a shadow of the supremely self-assured man who had sauntered in with such a swagger, ordering directors' wives and hangers-on to leave the team coach. Now, in the boardroom, those who had never forgiven him for that sort of "arrogance" were smirking behind his back. In the dressing room some players, not fit to lace his famous boots but sufficiently influential to contribute to his downfall, wore smiles of smug satisfaction.

Writing in the *Nottingham Evening News* on 7th June 1958 Albert Stapleton reported:

The reason for the shock dismissal of Tommy Lawton, £2,500-a-year Notts County manager, is stated to be purely financial. The club, which has already parted with several players and agreed to transfer star forward Ron Wylie, is believed to have felt the urgent need for reducing the overall financial strain.

Lawton, who said he had spent two periods of three months with the club without salary, told me he had made no plans for the future. "This was a real shock to me, especially after the board had gone to so much trouble to get me here," he said.

Mr Machin is keeping silent about the club's financial difficulties and future plans. "No comment" was the reply when I tried to get his views today.

The Notts County supporters were not short of comment about the chairman and the club that had fallen so far since the glory of Tommy Lawton's playing days. They recalled Machin's promise when he unveiled Lawton as the new manager: "The Arsenal of the Midlands?" they moaned. "More like the Arse'ole of the Midlands!"

Tommy Lawton agreed.

Chapter Ten

THE DARK YEARS

T ommy Lawton, dumped on the soccer scrapheap at 39, sat at home with Gay as Carol and Tommy Junior slept upstairs. Gay was as stunned and angry as he was. She came from a background in which 'one's word is one's bond'. How dare they treat her man like this after all he'd done for Notts County? How dare they?! She looked at Tommy, slumped in his chair, eyes distant, mind whirring and she took hold of his hands: "You're a better man than any of them, Tom. You'll bounce back."

But she feared he didn't want to. And he knew he didn't want to. Out of the ashes of the defeat and desperation to which he had descended when Len Machin fired him, that inherent obstinacy was beginning to rise again. No bunch of football club directors would ever get the chance to treat Tommy Lawton like that again. Oh, no.

"I'm finished with football, love," he told her. "I'm going to find a decent job outside the game. With my name and my reputation, that should be easy."

But it wasn't. For nearly 25 of his 39 years, football had been his life, the only thing he knew. Now, he was in a strange, bewildering, alien world which had no role for him. He had no education, no qualifications, no knowledge, no experience, no skills. Football had devoured a talented teenager and now disgorged the bones of a useless, unskilled, unemploy-able man pushing 40. For four months, Tommy Lawton looked for a decent job. There was nothing for him.

He had put some money aside from football but it wasn't much and it was running out. He was a married man with two children to support: he had to do something. All the fair-weather friends who told him he'd never want for work when he was a star were suddenly silent on the subject now that he wasn't. Except for one, who was a manager for the local Kimberley Brewery. "Why don't you and Gay take a pub?" he suggested to Tommy. "Your name would pull in the custom; Gay's got a great personality and she's very attractive. I reckon with a bit of training, you'd both be very good at it."

Tommy knew this was a familiar route for retired footballers but he knew nothing about the pub trade; he'd never been a drinker, save for the occasional pint of beer with the lads and to be sociable and polite at func-tions, so he'd never frequented pubs and running one for a living had never crossed his mind. But there was nothing else on the horizon so it had to be worth looking at.

"Let me know if you're interested and if you are, I'll keep a look out for a suitable place for you," said the man from the brewery. Gay was not keen at first: "Can you see *me* serving people?" she asked her husband. He had to agree that it did not seem a role she had been born to. But finally they agreed. A pub was probably their best option.

In the Nottinghamshire village of Lowdham stood the Magna Charta. Lowdham, its name derived from 'village by the loud stream', was between Nottingham and Southwell, a greenbelt area popular with summer visitors. The Magna Charta, once an old coaching house, was a large pub, one of four in the village and, the man from the brewery told Tommy in a phone call, it had become untenanted. There being no objection from the local licensing magistrates to Thomas Lawton Esq being granted a licence, despite his lack of experience in the trade, he and Gay became tenants of the Magna Charta in October 1958.

It was a decade since he'd shocked the nation by leaving Chelsea for Notts County but the man from the brewery was right. The name of Tommy Lawton still pulled the crowds and now, it was pulling them to the Magna Charta, albeit in somewhat smaller numbers.

Mr and Mrs Lawton, soon discovered that running a pub was hard, demanding work. They were both regularly working 16-hour days.

"It must be lovely to retire to a pub, Tommy," an old friend remarked to the landlord one night. "Retire!" said Tommy, "I've never worked so bloomin' hard in my life!" He reminded his friend that he saw only the few hours a night of bonhomie at the bar – not the cellar work, the cleaning, the washing up, the food preparation and all the paperwork. But they enjoyed it. And they were happy.

That happiness was briefly disturbed at Christmas when Tommy's mother came to stay. Blunt, working-class Lizzie Lawton, the ex-mill girl whose wage had supported a family of eight in the back streets of Bolton, lived in a world apart from Gay Lawton, the ex-wife of a wealthy factory owner with her upper-class ways and fancy language. This was not a relationship made in heaven! In fact, it wasn't a relationship at all. The two women clashed as fiercely as their backgrounds and beliefs were opposed. Neither held their words or hid their feelings. They fought like cat and dog throughout the Christmas holiday. Tommy's mam left in anger and never came near the family again. He would go to Lancashire to see her when he could but that ingrained Lawton stubbornness dictated that she wanted nothing more to do with "that woman".

Landlord Tommy Lawton took a bit too well to the bar and the banter at the Magna Charta. Football fans who wanted to talk to the great Tommy Lawton were prominent among his customers. They liked to boast that they'd been to Tommy's pub and had a chat about football with him and it felt good for him to know that he was still revered. He got rather too accustomed to a seat on the wrong side of the bar, where the punters would hang on his every word and it seemed only natural for the superstar to perpetuate the image by offering one on the house – gratuitous largesse which was repeated far too often and abused just as frequently. He was also too receptive to requests for drinks on the slate which was never completely wiped clean by some of the recipients and he became a soft touch for loans of cash which were often not repaid.

Gay chastised him, often, for this foolish generosity but it was in his nature. He'd been a crowd pleaser since he was a kid and popularity with his public was his oxygen. He couldn't help it. As he sat, too often, drinking with the customers on the wrong side of the bar, there was plenty for Tommy to discuss with them. Football had entered a new decade and the team they were all talking about was Tottenham Hotspur.

In 1960/61, Spurs did the double with a team playing scintillating soccer – a one-touch passing game which was a joy to watch. Every football fan in the country knew that team off by heart: Bill Brown, Peter Baker, Ron Henry, Danny Blanchflower, Maurice Norman, Dave MacKay, Cliff Jones, John White, Bobby Smith, Les Allen, Terry Dyson.

Tommy loved the way they played and would cheer them on as he watched them on TV. Around the bar, the question he was asked most about Spurs was "What do you think of Bobby Smith?" Smith was a stocky, barrel-chested centre forward who'd been in the Reserves at Chelsea in the early 1950s. While all around him in that great Tottenham team were skill, guile, speed and deft touches, Smith was a battering ram. He terrified goalkeepers, particularly Continental ones, as he bore down on them. Bobby was a bruiser: "It's not the way I would play the game," Tommy told his Magna Charta audience, "But, hey, he scores goals and goals win matches. You can't argue with that."

Meanwhile, at Chelsea, another forward out of a different mould from Tommy was scoring goals galore. Little Jimmy Greaves was a sensation. Tommy admired this lad greatly. "Jimmy's got a very rare natural gift," he told the boys in the bar. "He's a predator, a poacher. Totally different from me. He might not touch the ball for 20 minutes, then bang! It's in the back of the net. And that's earned his money."

Money was the biggest football talking point of all around that bar. At long last, the iniquity of the maximum wage for professional footballers, introduced in 1900 and first challenged by a fledgling Players' Union led by Manchester United winger Billy Meredith in 1907, was removed.

Tommy, himself such a prominent campaigner in this ancient battle, had witnessed a paltry rise from £17 a week to £20 a week in 1958, but the players' lot had, proportionately, actually got worse. In 1939, the £8 a week maximum wage Tommy earned was double the average wage paid in industry. By 1960, that gap had narrowed. £20 a week was only £5 more than the average pay packet of a factory worker, even though tens of thousands of spectators were putting massive sums of money over the turnstiles every week to watch those players.

This time the campaign for the abolition of the 'slave wage' was led by the eloquent, bearded boss of the Professional Footballers' Association – Fulham inside forward Jimmy Hill. And this time, the players' leader was more than a match for the powers that be.

Hill was a firebrand who knew how to manipulate the media. He whipped up mass support for the players' case and unlike the ultimatums of previous protests, when Hill's union threatened to strike in January 1961, it was not bluffing. Jimmy Hill had built the union up into a fighting force with a majority membership and there was a very real chance that League football would shut down completely and induce a huge loss in revenue for the clubs.

The Football League had no alternative. The maximum wage was abolished. Jimmy Hill was a national hero. His club, Fulham, under the chairmanship of top comedian Tommy Trinder, created history by making England international inside forward Johnny Haynes the country's first £100-a-week footballer. The floodgates had opened.

But too late for Tommy Lawton who would have been football's highest earner for years if those earlier campaigns hadn't failed. The soccer 'Brains Trust' around Tommy's bar knew that only too well and wasted no time in seeking his views.

Was he angry? Envious? Regretful? No, he told them. Just pleased that this wrong had been put right after so many years: "You want to know what I think?" he added with a laugh, "I think it's a heck of a coincidence that Tommy Trinder is the chairman of Fulham because back in 1945, I complained that the money I earned in a whole year was only a few quid more than Tommy Trinder got in a week for telling jokes. Well, Tommy Trinder is having to pay Johnny Haynes a hundred quid a week – so who's the joke on now?!"

Tommy Trinder and Johnny Haynes aside, money was no laughing matter at the Magna Charta. Tommy and Gay discovered that a trusted barman had done them out of £2,500 by operating a simple but effective scam. His mates would come in, order a round of drinks, pay with a pound note and get change for a fiver. Then they'd share out their ill-gotten gains. With Gay busy on the catering side, which is where the pub's profit was made, and Tommy too engaged in chatting to the hangers-on, the barman had felt safe in his wrongdoing. He was right. It had taken a long time to rack up that £2,500 before he was confronted, admitted to it and was sacked on the spot.

The Lawtons had uncovered the barman's theft when they returned, with the kids, from a caravan holiday at Sutton-on-Sea, a resort on the Lincolnshire coast where their illicit love had blossomed ten years earlier. The caravan was their refuge from the relentless hard work of the pub and the one next door to it was owned and occupied by none other than Gay's ex-husband.

Rex Rose had retired, aged only 42, from his business because of a shadow on his lung. It suited his illness to spend the whole summer in the bracing sea air of Sutton and winters at his home in Mapperley Park. Gay did Rex's washing and ironing and frequently fed him. Tommy liked his wife's ex-husband a great deal and any ill-feeling had long since passed. In fact, the relationship between the three of them was so good that when Tommy, Gay and the kids varied their holiday destination by making an annual trip to the Livermead Hotel in Torquay, Rex went with them – as he did when the family also visited Devon's beautiful Hope Cove, staying at the Anchor, which Tommy and Gay had got to know during their days in London.

Those holidays were of vital importance to the Lawton family. Tommy and Gay had begun to realise that their 16-hour days were not conducive to good parenting. They wanted the very best for their kids but was pub life the best thing for them? Tommy Junior was now leaving the baby stage. The noise from the pub disturbed him at night and they tended to spoil him with toys and other treats to get him to sleep. They knew this was not the right way to do it. Their little lad needed company, not toys and treats. Carol was growing into an attractive young woman and she, too, was left alone a lot. Because of the demands of the pub, she was often out of parental sight, if not out of mind. They started to worry that she might be getting into the wrong company.

One day, they sat down and took stock of all this. They were simply not spending enough time with their kids and it could not carry on like this. There were two courses of action open to them . . . employ good staff so that Gay could spend less time in the pub and more time with Carol and Tommy Junior, or pack in the pub altogether. The former was by far their preferred option, so they looked thoroughly at the figures to see how much they could afford to spend on staff. They were shocked. Not only did their takings rule that out but the exercise brought home something that, because they enjoyed running the pub so much, had never fully occurred to them . . . their 16-hour days were giving them a pretty poor hourly rate of pay for the job. It was not a good wage, certainly not good enough to be jeopardising their children's future for. "There's no choice," they agreed. "We'll have to leave the pub."

This was not the only issue upon which the welfare and future of Carol and Tommy Junior were paramount. Tommy and Gay were determined to ensure that they had the very best education. Gay wanted Carol to grow up smart, intelligent and independent, able to make her own way in the world and to enjoy the wealth and status she had enjoyed as a young woman. Tommy wanted Tommy Junior to grow up a clever young man, academically well equipped to be a success in life without having to rely on something as transient as football. The consequence of their ambition for their kids was that Carol was being taught at the private Wyvil School in Mapperley Park and she was joined there by her brother in 1961. The fees were a considerable expense.

While the Lawtons grappled with the issues around the Magna Charta there was sad news for Tommy. His mother died. The funeral was a simple but dignified occasion, entirely fitting for such a fine, hard-working woman. So many memories came flooding back for Tommy at that funeral: his admiration and gratitude for the way his mam had kept the whole family by working all the hours God sent in that gruelling, unforgiving mill; how she used to sing for them all in that beautiful voice, "Grab your coat and get your hat, leave your worries on the doorstep. Life can be complete, on the sunny side of the street." God knows, there hadn't been much sun on her side of the street in those days. She didn't see much daylight, let alone sunlight. The poor lass laboured away in that mill from morning till night and if she hadn't, they might all have starved.

He recalled his mam's unspoken pride when she appeared in that film with Gracie Fields. That *had* brought sunshine into her life, but she's been much too down to earth to admit it. He remembered how she stood up to the men when they wanted her lad to leave home for Sheffield: "He's not going and that's that," she'd told them. And not one of them dared argue with her. She'd spent a lifetime, Lizzie Lawton, trying always to do her best for others. And though he'd never known him, Tommy cursed his father who had deserted her when he was a baby. Her life could and should have been one of so much less toil and so much more happiness but for that man. Now that life was over.

It was another sad day for Tommy and Gay when they left the Magna Charta but they had no doubt that they were doing the right thing. They rented a bungalow at Stoke Lane in nearby Gedling and Tommy started to look for a new job. Running the pub had at least given him some sort of qualification other than just his name; not much of a *curriculum vitae*, it was true, but better than nothing. He had learned how to serve the public and how (drinks on the house and open-ended loans notwithstanding!) to run a business. He should be more employable now.

But something else had happened. The total disillusionment with football which had so consumed him after his sacking at Meadow Lane had evaporated. Four years on, he was missing football really badly. Like a drug addict tempted after a lengthy clean spell, he felt he could handle it again and he wanted it desperately.

He read every word of the sports pages and he went to football matches whenever he could – particularly internationals at Wembley, where he was treated as a VIP. He discovered that in the wide soccer community outside Nottingham he was still a big name and that that name was still mentioned whenever football was discussed. He'd thought his 20 years in the game counted for nothing when he left Notts County. Now, he knew that was not the case.

Every time he went to a match, he realised how much he missed the atmosphere. The unique sights, sounds and smells of soccer seduced him as they'd always done. What a fool he'd been to give it all up; what a fool not to have taken his sacking at Meadow Lane on the chin and just put it down to experience; what a fool not to have gone for another a job at another club; what a fool not to have bounced back when Gay had told him that he could and should.

The longing to be back in football now tore at his guts but so did his self-doubt: Yes, it was good to know that his name still meant so much in football but it was a name from the past, not one for the future and in those four years, the game had changed so much. There were so many new people at the top now, using new methods. Football didn't just have a new wage structure: it had new systems, new tactics, new techniques. He was only 44, but the extent of the change in the game made him feel old. If only he'd stayed in football, he would have been part of all that change, but he'd shunned the great game, turned his back on it. He cursed himself for walking out on the game, for his headstrong haste and his self-destructive pride. Over and over again, he repeated, "Oh, you bloody fool."

Away from football he was a fish out of water, gasping for the breath to stay alive. Those four years in the pub had only kidded him that he could do without the game. This feeling of regret grew stronger and stronger until it became fierce frustration then deep despair. This was becoming irrational. He hated torturing himself like this. But he couldn't help it. He resented the men who were now in the top jobs; many of them had been little nobodies, not fit to lace his boots. How the hell did they get those jobs when he, Tommy Lawton the legend, was out of the game and out of work at 44? They would surely sneer and look down on him, now, if he asked for their help and that would be unbearable. Others who were old colleagues might feel obliged to help him, but that might be out of pity and he couldn't stand the thought of that, either.

He wanted to swallow his pride and ask them, any of them, for a job, any job, just to get back into the game. But he was scared to ask: scared to face the humiliation of being turned down, scared of the shame of being tolerated where he wasn't really wanted or needed because of the sort of old pals' act against which Tommy Lawton in his prime would have railed and rebelled. No. He'd left it too late to get back. He just had to accept that. But, God, did it have to hurt so much? Best to stay away from football altogether. That way, he might not hurt so badly.

Back home in Gedling, he told himself, "Come on Lawton, pull yourself together, man. Get a grip. You've got a wife and two kids relying on you. Sort yourself out." Then he took a job selling life insurance policies for Imperial Life of Canada. Tommy Lawton, for so much of his life a man people wanted to sell things to, was not a natural salesman. Famous and fêted as he'd been for so long, the rejection which came frequently as just a natural part of this job was hard for him to take. But he took it and tolerated it and got on with the job. He had to.

Four years in the licensed trade had given him lots of contacts and he figured that publicans would be a good target for him. He knew what their immediate problems were and what they would need in later life so he knew what approach to take and what sort of policies to offer. He was right. This was a good market for him. The trouble with publicans, though, is that they live in pubs and if you go into their pubs you are expected to have a drink with them, particularly if you're trying to sell them something:

"What are you having, Bill?"

"I'll have a pint, Tommy – and what will you have yourself?"

"I'll have the same. Now, about this policy."

The conversation was repeated at every pub he visited and so was the round of drinks, often followed by another, then another. After all, you couldn't expect the landlord to buy a policy from you if you refused to drink with him, could you? And there were hundreds of pubs in Nottingham!

Often, while he was talking to a landlord, other customers would recognise the great Tommy Lawton and insist on buying him a drink. How could you refuse to put more profit into the publican's till when you're trying to persuade him to buy a policy from you? Well, you couldn't, could you? And there were hundreds of Tommy Lawton fans in Nottingham pubs!

The drinking started to get out of hand. Every day he stayed longer in the pubs. Every night he was late home.

His relationship with Gay started to suffer. There were rows. And the rows started to get as serious as the drinking. He didn't know it, but Tommy Lawton was on a downward spiral. The longer he stayed in the pubs, the more insurance he was likely to sell and the less likely he was to have another row with Gay. In the pubs, where he was still a famous face, he found the male companionship and camaraderie that he missed so much from his football clubs and a haven from the anxiety and depression now disturbing what had been a happy and tranquil home life.

Tommy Lawton, who for 25 years in football had never been anything but an occasional, casual drinker, was now drinking far too heavily. Gay knew he was drinking too much but had no idea how much.

Both were still intent on giving their kids the best possible start in life. Carol had now moved on to Pitman's Secretarial College and Tommy Junior, clearly a bright little lad, was still getting a private-school education and had passed an entrance examination to the prestigious Nottingham High prep school. The fees were a burden but Tommy was adamant that his lad was going to benefit from the very best education. If there was one thing he had realised since being dumped by Notts County it was the vital importance of having qualifications in later life and if there was one legacy he could leave Tommy Junior it was a life based on the sound foundations of first-class schooling.

At prep school, Tommy Junior, eight years old now, was starting to show some of his father's sporting prowess and his dad was determined that he was also going to inherit some of his famous courage. When Tommy Junior came home crying with badly grazed knees, Tommy senior, extracting grit from the wounds told the lad, "Don't be such a baby. At least this is at the front. Centre halves come at you from behind!"

Tommy Junior was finding out all about such finer points of soccer for himself. Although he was short and tubby, he was surprisingly quick and had his dad's instinctive knack for scoring goals. He was developing into a useful centre forward but his confidence shrank the day he heard an insensitive adult observation from the touchline: "He'll never be as good as his dad." It was true, of course. But it was a thoughtless and callous remark to make within the hearing range of one so young and he was to remember the hurt he felt for the rest of his life.

During the 1964/65 football season, Tommy Lawton was approached out of the blue by Kettering Town FC. They were struggling at the bottom of the Southern League's First Division and asked if he would take over as caretaker manager for the rest of the season with a view to a permanent job if he succeeded. To accept would have meant giving up his job with the insurance company. He was tempted, but this was too much of a risk. Instead, he offered to help Kettering out on a part-time basis. He didn't save them from relegation but he took them on a money-spinning FA Cup run which put both the club and him back in the national headlines for a while. They drew at home with Millwall then beat them 2-1 in the replay before finally getting knocked out by Oxford United. At the end of the season, Kettering repeated their offer. He was still in love with football but he turned it down, settling for what he thought was the security of his insurance company job.

That security was important. Tommy and Gay had moved to Mapperley Park, where they rented a ground floor flat. They were keeping their heads above water financially. Though there was very little left in the bank, they were able to pay all their predictable bills but if any unexpected expense came along, they were hard pressed to meet it. Tommy had, however, discovered a way of solving that problem. He had gathered a wealth of personal soccer memorabilia from his illustrious playing career and he found a ready market for this in the pubs. Ten quid for this, twenty quid for that. This was a useful source of income. With every memento he sold, he was selling a piece of his fantastic football career; losing one of the memories he should have been treasuring for life. He knew that. But needs must.

Thus, Tommy's life after football carried on: selling his insurance policies; when necessary selling another career memento or two; spending too much time in the pubs; taking home just enough money to keep the wolf from the door.

It was 1966 and England was hosting the World Cup but so intent had Tommy been to stay away from football to avoid the pain of not being involved that he was now bordering on disinterest. He wasn't much bothered about the World Cup, or England's performance in it. He didn't have much time for Alf Ramsey, who had succeeded his old *bête noire* 'Summer-arse' as England manager. He'd known Ramsey as a player and he thought he'd got above himself. He told everybody that "Mr lah-de-dah bloody Ramsey" had taken elocution lessons in order to ingratiate himself with the FA establishment!

Nobody knew quite how Tommy was supposed to know that and he never said, so most recipients of this 'inside information' suspected he was just mischievously making it up. But Tommy always imparted the story with straight face and conviction!

With money so tight, the arrival at the Lawton home of two free VIP tickets for the World Cup final between England and Germany at Wembley had Tommy Junior dancing with delight. "Can we go, Dad. Can we go?"

"No, lad, we can't," replied Tommy. He'd promised to open the summer fête at the Saxondale Mental Hospital on World Cup final day: "And no matter what else comes up, you can't let folk down on a promise like that," he said.

Tommy Junior supposed his dad was right not to let those folks down. But it was a very disappointed 10-year-old who sat down at Saxondale to watch the game on TV instead and he regretted not being there even more when England won in extra time and all those fabulous scenes of celebration followed.

What a game it had been: the nip and tuck of the first 90 minutes, ending 2-2; the drama of extra time with the Russian linesman declaring that the shot from Geoff Hurst which rebounded from the bar *had* crossed the goal line; the excitement when Hurst hit a fourth goal seconds before the final whistle, with BBC commentator Kenneth Wolstenholme saying "Some people on the pitch. They think it's all over" then adding, with brilliant spontaneity as Hurst's shot bulged the German net, ". . . It is now!"; toothless Nobby Stiles dancing a celebration jig; little man of the match Alan Ball, socks around his ankles, barely able to walk through sheer exhaustion; Bobby Moore raising the Jules Rimet trophy to the skies. With millions of others all over the country, Tommy Junior had jumped up and down with excitement and glee that afternoon. He and his dad could have been there, watching this game of a lifetime from a VIP seat inside Wembley Stadium. But they were spending the afternoon in a mental hospital because his dad had made a promise.

There was consolation however. Tommy Lawton was a welcome guest at England Test matches at Trent Bridge, particularly when star cricketers who knew Tommy well from his days in London were there and Tommy Junior was always taken along. Colin Cowdrey, Fred Titmus and John Murray were mates of his dad and that made Tommy Junior the envy of his school pals.

A year later, Tommy Lawton was struggling to sell insurance policies. He'd just about exhausted his leads in the licensed trade. It had worked well for a time. In his first year, he had brought in £3,500 worth of business for the company, but it was tough now. He failed to meet his quotas. And they sacked him. He accepted a job with another insurance company but very soon began to feel that there was something not right about it. He felt uneasy about working for them and he resigned. Later, the company went into liquidation, leaving millions of clients without insurance. Tommy's unease had been well founded and his resignation had been principled. But principle wasn't putting money in his pocket.

Just as he was wondering what on earth he could do next, Tommy got a call from a friend named Hunter, a local estate agent who had a shop on Derby Road, Nottingham. Hunter had an exciting proposition for him. He wanted to turn his Derby Road premises into a sports shop and asked if Tommy would become a partner in the venture. The deal was simple. He would provide the premises and the capital. Tommy would provide the big name above the door and run the shop. The business would be called Tommy Lawton Sports Goods.

It took Tommy just a few minutes to accept. At last, a job outside football in which he could take real pride and interest. This was the solution to all his problems, the answer to all his money worries. The potential for selling sports goods in Nottingham was huge, he thought, and with that famous name behind it, this venture surely couldn't fail. He threw himself into this great opportunity.

He embarked on a carefully planned publicity campaign, travelling around Nottingham and district on a soccer lecture tour which took in local football clubs, youth organisations and the sports clubs of the big local factories, Raleigh, John Players and Boots. He reasoned that by offering this service free, the clubs would eventually repay him by using his shop for their sports goods requirements. He worked his contacts at professional football clubs all over the country, aware that they all had bulk suppliers, but hopeful that he might pick up the occasional order by offering personal service and faster delivery. This was a job at which he could excel.

The whole Lawton family was excited and involved. They all helped Tommy clean the shop throughout and prepare the window displays ready for opening. His mates in the local press ensured good coverage of the venture and all was set fair. Come the big opening, Gay was at Tommy's side and she helped him in the shop every day. Often, they were there until 10 pm at night. Carol helped out at lunchtimes and even Tommy Junior joined in on Saturdays and sometimes after school. Tommy's whole heart and soul were in this business. He loved every hardworking minute of it. He'd found his future. And he'd become a stranger in the pubs.

Then, after only two months, his business partner dropped a bombshell. He told Tommy, "We're just not making enough profit. We're going to have to close down." The shop's position, on a busy road out of the city with no car parking, had proved a killer, he said. The business had no future and it was pointless to carry on.

Tommy was devastated. He couldn't understand this at all. His partner owned the shop, so there was no rent to pay. True, he had to buy the stock but he must surely have budgeted for that from day one. Apart from rates and telephone charges, his only other outlay was Tommy's wage and that wasn't enough to break the bank. He took the point about the shop's position but it was not far from where Nottingham's new Victoria Shopping Centre was soon to open and that could bring them a lot of business. In time, they, too, could move into the new centre. "We're throwing in the towel too soon," he pleaded.

There was another problem, Hunter argued. Because they were such a small business some of the big name sports goods manufacturers were refusing to supply them. Larger sports retailers with more potential sales to offer the top manufacturers didn't like small firms muscling in on their territory. Consequently, when customers of Tommy Lawton Sports Goods insisted on top brands, they had to buy in from elsewhere, seriously reducing their profit.

"It's no use fooling ourselves," he told Tommy. "We just have to shut down." Tommy Lawton was no businessman. His partner was. Tommy had a gut feeling that Hunter was making the wrong decision but it was clear that no amount of protest was going to change his mind. "I suppose he must be right," Tommy muttered as he shut up the shop for the last time.

And before he went home to break the bad news to Gay and the kids, he stopped off at the pub . . . Tommy sat at the bar, alone, staring silently into his pint. How could he tell Gay? What the hell were they going to do now? He'd got no money, no job, no future, no hope.

Over the years, dozens of centre halves had tried to knock the stuffing out of Tommy Lawton and failed. He'd always bounced back up with a grin that told them they hadn't hurt him, even though they had. Nobody ever put Tommy Lawton down for long. He'd been confident, cocky and courageous, always the envy of lesser men. But now, he was out for the count. Face down. There was no bouncing back up with a grin from this blow. There were no bruises to show like before; no blood, no broken teeth, no busted nose. He could have coped with that. This was different and he couldn't handle it. All he had left was his pride.

The only source of income now was the dole. And it hurt like hell the day he went to sign on. There was nothing else left for him to do now, nowhere else to turn, but an overwhelming feeling of abject shame engulfed him as he stood in the dole queue. He could see people pointing at him, whispering behind their hands, staring at him, nudging each other: "The great Tommy Lawton, signing on the dole. Who'd have thought it?" Everybody recognised him, not least the Social Security staff. The young man at the counter was a football fan; he called him "Mr Lawton, sir" and couldn't have been nicer but nothing could hide the humiliation; nothing could ease the disgrace that bit deep into his soul. Proud Jim Riley had devoted his life to keeping the grandson he loved safe from such a fate, making sure that his football would look after him and protect him from poverty. "Now look at me," Tommy told himself. "It's all been for nothing." He'd failed. He'd fallen. And he'd dragged his family down with him.

That family really suffered now. They had been living beyond their means for some time, not extravagantly but sufficiently to maintain the lifestyle football had given them. Now, they were deeply in debt. Tommy took to borrowing money from friends to pay his bills. At first, he paid them back diligently but it got to the stage where he was borrowing, knowing that he couldn't pay it back. This he justified to himself with the truism that loads of people had sponged off him in his time and never paid him back. He figured they owed him. They saw it differently and gossip about his borrowing spread throughout the city, adding to his shame.

That shame hit Gay particularly badly. Before she met Tommy, she'd been the spoiled wife of a very wealthy man, wanting for nothing, spending freely, living in a huge house with its own tennis courts. Tommy and Gay had to give up their own smart flat, for which they'd paid a high rent, in Mapperley Park and now rented a much cheaper house on Patterdale

Road, Woodthorpe. That had been hard enough for Gay to take but now she was reduced to hiding behind the curtains or crouching behind the furniture when the doorbell rang because nine times out of ten the caller wanted money she hadn't got. Telephone calls were just as feared and the family invented a code whenever they needed to ring home. You rang three times then rang off then immediately rang again – the signal that it was safe to pick up the phone.

And so life on the dole went on for Tommy and Gay, who had expected something very different from this when she married her soccer star . . . writing cheques they knew would probably bounce in the hope the bank would honour them, borrowing money, paying debts when they could, hiding from creditors when they couldn't.

Tommy was at his wits' end with the worry of it all but one bill he had always managed to pay was the one for Tommy Junior's school fees. Nottingham High School (motto: *Lauda Finem* – 'Praise to the end') was a very fine school. Founded in 1513 by Dame Agnes Mellers it boasted such famous Nottinghamians as D H Lawrence, Jesse Boot and John Player among its old boys. And Tommy Junior was doing very well there.

Tommy and Gay struggled on, trying to make ends meet but failing more often than not, and Tommy marvelled at his wife's strength and patience. How badly he had let her down, he felt and often he told himself he didn't deserve the support he got from her and the kids.

Then some remission from the scourge of unemployment occurred at last for Tommy. At the Liverpool headquarters of Vernon's Pools they heard about Tommy's plight and thought it a crying shame that the man who had so graced the game out of which they made their vast profits was in such dire straits. They offered him a job.

Tommy's role was to appoint coupon collectors in and around Nottingham who would then form their own groups of punters in factories, offices, shops and so on. On Friday nights the group leaders handed in their coupons to the chief collectors who paid their commission and parcelled up all the coupons. On Saturday mornings, Tommy and his boss met all the chief collectors in Nottingham, packaged up all the coupons and rushed them over to Derby to catch the 8:20 am train to Liverpool. There, they had to ensure that the huge packages were placed securely under lock and key in the correct baggage compartment of the train. Failure at any point in this process could lead to lost coupons and potentially a lost fortune of up to £1 million for one of the hopeful punters whose dream of a life of luxury was in that envelope. The pressure, therefore, was considerable and if any of those collectors was late for the crucial Saturday morning rendezvous, the dash to the railway station at Derby through traffic jams, traffic lights and other assorted obstacles made the Keystone Kops look positively pedestrian.

Tommy enjoyed his job with Vernon's and after four months life was beginning to look up a little for the Lawtons. The job wasn't paying Tommy a fortune but it was a regular income and at least it had lifted him out of the doldrums of the dole. Now, they could answer a knock on the door without fear and use the telephone without resorting to the secret family code.

They still had debts, but family life was getting back to something like normal. Tommy was able to watch his son playing football and cricket and Tommy Junior was especially proud the day his dad was there to watch him shine for the school cricket team by taking five wickets in one over! He had inherited his father's jumping ability and there was much family pride when he set a new under-11 school record for the high jump, reaching 3 ft 9 in with scissor kicks.

Then one night there was a surprise phone call for Tommy. It was from the vice-chairman of Notts County Football Club, Bill Hopcroft. The streets of Nottingham, littered with sacked managers from Notts County, were having to make way for yet another one! Notts were faring badly, bottom of the League again and team boss Billy Gray had been booted out. Jack Wheeler, Tommy's mate from Kettering days, had agreed to do the job temporarily on a caretaker basis but, Bill Hopcroft told Tommy, "We wondered if you would like to come back and help us out."

"Whoa! Now just hang on there a minute!" exclaimed Tommy. "Notts County and I have got a bit of history, as you must know." His head was telling him, "Twice bitten, thrice shy. Don't touch this with a ten-foot barge pole!" But his heart was leaping. He was being offered a job in football. He hadn't demeaned himself by pleading for it; it wasn't being offered out of sympathy. He was being asked to come back into the game because he was wanted; because he was needed.

He told Bill Hopcroft, "I've got a steady job with Vernon's and they've been very good to me. We're going to have to have a very long talk before I agree to anything this time." They had that very long talk. Bill Hopcroft, a likeable man, put Tommy at his ease. They levelled with each other. Because Tommy was adamant that he did not want to let down Vernon's, Hopcroft suggested that he took a part-time job with Notts, coaching the youngsters, advising Jack Wheeler and generally helping to get the team back in shape and up the table. This tempted him greatly but he was still hesitant and asked his boss at Vernon's what he thought. The reply was gracious and unselfish: "Look, Tommy," he replied, "We know how desperately you miss football and this can bring you in some extra money, too.

Provided you can fit it in with your duties for us, we have no objection."

So, 1968 saw Tommy Lawton back in football. He was now aged 49. Older certainly. But wiser?

Back where he belonged, back with those sights and sounds and smells, back among footballers, Tommy found fresh vigour. He was loving it. And spending more and more time at the ground. Eventually, even the patience of the considerate folk at Vernon's was stretched to the limit: "Sorry, Tommy. This can't go on. It's going to have to be us or Notts County." Tommy explained the choice he had to make to Bill Hopcroft, who told him the club would employ him full-time as chief scout and coach. He resigned from Vernon's and went back to Meadow Lane.

Months after the headlines had heralded the return of Tommy Lawton they were telling a very different sort of story about another Lawton. His first wife Rosaleen's daughter, Amanda, still bore his surname, though he'd had nothing to do with her since he and Rosaleen divorced.

Amanda was in trouble, appearing at Bow Street Magistrates' Court in London on theft charges; the *Nottingham Guardian Journal* reported the story:

The trouble with Amanda Lawton, 22-year-old daughter of ex-England footballer Tommy Lawton, the Notts County chief scout, was that she had lived a life of fantasy, probation officer Miss Mary Hamilton said at London's Bow Street Court.

Amanda Lawton, appearing on remand, was given a conditional discharge for three years after she had admitted stealing £60 and £100 from American film producer and playwright Mr George Axelrod.

She had also admitted dishonestly obtaining two bottles of brandy worth £8 13s from a wine merchants and asked for 24 other offences involving £2,861 10s, to be considered.

Said Miss Hamilton: "She is a very pleasant girl but is very stupid and has a wrong sense of values. She has squandered money, has lived far beyond her means and has behaved in the most disgraceful manner but she is now very sorry for what she has done and I am sure she will not do anything like this again. Her mother has flown from Jamaica to be in court today and she is prepared to take her back to Jamaica where she will settle down and work."

Miss Hamilton said that Amanda Lawton's stepfather in Jamaica had made arrangements to repay £2,861 10s to Mr Axelrod. The magistrate, Mr Kenneth Barraclough, ordered Amanda Lawton to repay £168 13s.

At an earlier hearing, Detective Sergeant Roger Byrde said that

Mr Axelrod employed Amanda Lawton as a secretary last year. He signed cheques and left her to fill in the amounts when drawing money for his personal expenses and her salary. In 12 weeks she drew more than £2,000 from Mr Axelrod's account by filling in blank signed cheques.

At that hearing, Miss Hamilton had said: "This is beyond me. Miss Lawton is an intelligent young woman but I think she thought this was an easy way of getting money."

Miss Lawton's mother had been married four times and was now married to a Jamaican doctor and living in Jamaica, Miss Hamilton added.

Tommy Lawton never talked about his first marriage, about Rosaleen or Amanda. Gay, Carol and Tommy Junior knew it was a taboo subject. News that the first Mrs Lawton was now in her fourth marriage and living very comfortably with a doctor in Jamaica and that her daughter Amanda had been stealing lots of money from an American film producer was a big talking point and the source of much gossip and speculation in Nottingham . . . but not in the Lawton household.

Tommy read the story in the newspaper, bit his bottom lip and said nothing.

For Tommy Junior there was a very special day on 26th April 1969. Manchester City, managed by his dad's old pal Joe Mercer, were playing Leicester City in the FA Cup final at Wembley and Joe had laid on two tickets and a VIP day out for them. Off went Lawton Senior and Junior for a day the lad would never forget. They took the train to London, walked together up the famous Wembley Way and took their VIP seats to soak up all the preliminaries to the big game. This was the one big football occasion that had eluded Tommy throughout his career and today there was no doubt about which team the Lawtons were supporting . . . Genial Joe's Manchester City. Applauding as he watched Joe lead them out, Tommy wondered how that felt and just for a moment was terribly sad that he would never know.

The Manchester City team that day was very unusual in that every player was from England: Harry Dowd; Tony Book, Glyn Pardoe; Mike Doyle, Tommy Booth, Alan Oakes; Mike Summerbee, Colin Bell, Francis Lee, Neil Young, Tony Coleman. Englishmen, every one of them, including their substitute David Connor and of course, with the flag of St George stamped through him like a stick of rock, their manager! But they looked like a Continental side in their very modern, tight-fitting red-and-black striped shirts and black shorts.

Blue-shirted Leicester City: Peter Shilton; Peter Rodrigues, David Nish;

265

Bobby Roberts, Alan Woollett, Graham Cross; Rodney Fern, Dave Gibson, Andy Lochhead, Allan Clarke, Len Glover. They contained two Scots (Gibson and Lochhead) and a Welshman (Rodrigues), had another Scot (Malcolm Manley) in the number 12 shirt and were managed by an Irishman, Frank O'Farrell.

Tommy Junior sat enthralled and totally absorbed in that unique Wembley FA Cup final atmosphere generated by a crowd of 100,000, leapt to his feet to cheer when Neil Young scored the only goal of the game and watched, spellbound, as City captain Tony Book lifted the world-famous trophy.

Then there was a treat on the journey home – dinner in the British Rail restaurant car with gleaming silver cutlery and crisp white tablecloth. Very posh. The lad loved every minute of his FA Cup final experience. And Tommy Senior was chuffed that, despite everything, he could still give his son a good day out.

Tommy Junior loved soccer, but at his private school he was developing an ever greater sporting love – rugby union. He was starting to look very promising and two men with a keen interest often stood together on the touchline to watch him play. One was Tommy Lawton and the other was an older man. The rugby master, Chalkie White, assumed that this older man, was Tommy Junior's grandfather. It was Rex Rose.

For almost a year, Tommy Lawton was back on top, doing the only job for which he was really suited, the only work he really knew how to do well. He'd been 15 years old when football first employed him: no wonder he wasn't cut out for much else. But he should have known better than to walk back into that black-and-white spider's web. Meadow Lane had not been the happiest of football grounds in the 1960s. Slum clearance had removed the grim housing conditions of the Meadows but with it had gone the traditional breeding ground for Notts County support and County had been usurped as Nottingham's top club by Forest. Nottingham Forest who, in stark contrast to their neighbours, had only one manager, Billy Walker, from 1939 to 1960, won the FA Cup in 1959, beating Luton Town 2-0 in a match in which Forest's Roy Dwight broke a leg, which meant they had to play for an hour with ten men. The days of Tommy Lawton and Jackie Sewell banging in the goals in front of 40,000 crowds were now a distant memory at Meadow Lane and they had become the poor relations.

The Swinging '60s, exciting decade of The Beatles, Carnaby Street fashion, student unrest and enormous social change in Britain, had by-passed the country's oldest Football League club, for whom it had been an era of decline and decay.

Then along came a new chairman. John Jacob 'Jack' Dunnett, London lawyer, businessman and Labour politician, had been chairman of Brentford FC. But after being elected as Member of Parliament for the safe Labour seat of Nottingham Central he switched his football allegiance to Notts County. Jack Dunnett brought his manager at Brentford, Jimmy Sirrell, with him. Sirrell, a tough little Glaswegian who'd played for Celtic, soon set about stamping his own authority on Meadow Lane and his new broom swept away Lawton's role. Tommy was summoned to the new chairman's office and sacked.

Kicked out of football again, he drifted in and out of one or two totally unsuitable jobs but he was unemployed far more often than he was working. The money problems started to build up again and soon they were back to being critical. He started borrowing from friends again, couldn't pay them back and when that supply dried up, he was back hawking his soccer memorabilia around the pubs. After a brief respite from the misery, Tommy Lawton was back down among the dead men of the dole queue.

On the day Tommy Junior arrived to start his third year at Nottingham High School he was sent immediately to the headmaster's office with no explanation as to why. He was made to wait outside the head's office for more than an hour, all that time wondering what on earth he could have done to deserve this. Eventually, the headmaster called him in: "Lawton," he said, "your father hasn't paid the fees. Go home." He went home to Gay and cried his eyes out.

He went instead to a state school, High Pavement Grammar School. There, he was asked early on by a teacher which school he had moved from. "Nottingham High School, sir," he replied – and received a stream of abuse about toffee-nosed kids from posh schools who thought they were better than all the rest. Tommy Junior became withdrawn, mistrust-ing, averse to making friends. But he found great consolation and plenty of self-expression in his rugby. To save money on bus fares he learned to ride an old adult racing bike he found in a shed. It was far too big for him but there was an upside – he grew six inches in a year.

Tommy and Gay had no car now and they walked more than two miles to and from a cheap discount store to do the family shopping, using a calculator to make sure they didn't overspend. This could not have been further removed from the days when they went shopping in London's finest stores while rubbing shoulders with show-business stars but that contrast was nothing compared to the ignominy of Tommy's weekly appearance on the dole queue.

How he hated that dole queue – and how much worse it became after a freelance journalist snatched a picture of him standing in the dreaded queue and sold it to the national newspapers, deepening Tommy's shame when millions of people all over the country saw him, head down, defeated, "queuing for a state handout with the down-and-outs". The picture appeared prominently in all the popular papers, along with lurid headlines wallowing in the "Shame of a Soccer Legend" and the graphic story of how England's 'greatest ever centre forward' was now living in poverty.

But it seemed, for a while at least, that the journalist had unwittingly done him a favour. A furniture company in Colwyn Bay, North Wales offered him a job as a sales rep, a good wage, a company car and an expense account. After attending a training course he was sent back to Nottingham to sell the company's wares but after a short time they told him they were not satisfied with his order book. Again, he was sacked.

The company told him to return his car to Wales and collect his last month's money. He told the company that since they made regular trips to Nottingham they should collect their car from him and bring his outstanding wages with them, arguing that the cost of travelling to and from Colwyn Bay would make a big hole in his last pay packet and he couldn't afford that. The company did not reply and, foolishly, he carried on driving their car.

Unemployed again, Tommy was now visibly depressed. So much so that Rex Rose thoughtfully offered free use of his caravan at Sutton-on-Sea so that he and Gay could get away from all their worries for a time and have a therapeutic seaside holiday. This was not the first kind gesture from Rex, who could have been forgiven for wanting nothing whatsoever to do with the man who had stolen his beautiful wife from him. He was a kind, considerate gentleman. He could not do as much as he would have liked to help the Lawtons because that would look as if he was muscling in on the family, using his money to gain advantage and humiliate Tommy, so he helped in inconspicuous ways – like paying Tommy Junior pocket money for cutting the grass on his huge lawns.

Tommy and Gay accepted Rex's offer of his holiday home gratefully and relaxed by the sea but after a few days Tommy worried that he had been in the wrong not to return his company car and resolved to return to Nottingham before taking it back. The plan was to leave Sutton early in the morning, but the car wouldn't start. With Gay at the wheel, Tommy was pushing the car in an attempt to start it when his head started to spin and he collapsed. A doctor diagnosed a suspected thrombosis and he was rushed to Louth hospital, where he remained for a fortnight, undergoing numerous tests and blood counts and sleeping deeply for day after day. He was, he was told, completely exhausted, physically and mentally.

Absolutely worn out. He was given strict instructions to take it easy from now on: no heavy work, no stress and plenty more rest.

The latter instruction became somewhat difficult to obey when two policemen knocked loudly on the Lawtons' front door at 10 pm. Gay answered, to be told that the officers needed to speak to Mr Lawton forthwith. "He's in bed, resting," Gay protested. "Well, I'm afraid you'll have to get him out of bed, madam," she was told. "We're investigating a report of a stolen car." Tommy told them the car was not stolen, that it was in full view in the drive outside, that it was going to be returned as soon as possible and that the company which had reported him to the police still owed him a month's wages. "Not good enough," said the police and Tommy was hauled off to the police station and held for questioning for several hours. The matter was eventually resolved; the company collected the car and Tommy – while also having to come to terms with the fact that the fit and active life he had led since he was a lad was over at 51 – was left to regret yet another big mistake.

Far from avoiding stressful situations, as the doctors had ordered, Tommy was again lurching from one financial crisis to another: back on the dole; back to a constant struggle to escape penury; back to resorting to transient comfort in pints of beer and whisky chasers in the pubs; back to seeking loans from friends. He could depend on one or two, Jackie Sewell notably and generously among them, to give him money they knew they wouldn't get back when his debts got to the critical stage, but he now began to resent, bitterly and irrationally, those who wouldn't help him. He had been generous to a foolish fault when he had money to spare; he'd been renowned for having an ever-open wallet; a soft touch, he had never been able to stand by and watch people he knew suffer financial distress and they hadn't needed to be close friends – he had only to hear about someone in trouble and he'd been there to bail them out. Now, he was the one who needed help and he cursed the "pathetically small" number who would return the favour.

Too many people, he believed, preferred to look down on him, to gloat over his fall from grace. Though, in his anguish, he tended to exaggerate the extent of this there was more than an element of truth in it and that unpleasant trait which finds satisfaction in observing how the mighty are fallen was manifest among some of the huge number who watched when national television focused on the downfall of Tommy Lawton. On BBC's *Today* programme, Tommy was interviewed by Eamonn Andrews on how it felt to fall so spectacularly from being England's biggest soccer star to the despair of the dole queue. Understandably, Tommy was not at his best on this occasion and for the thousands of people who could remember the bright, handsome, young Jack the lad from his television appearances in the 1950s, Eamonn Andrews's question was answered by the defeated demeanour of the worn-out man of 50-something who now sat so sadly in front of the unforgiving TV cameras.

For every one who gained some sick pleasure from Tommy's plight, however, there were thousands more among those TV viewers who felt desperately sorry for him and these included the owners of a large furnishing company, Catesby's of Tottenham Court Road, London, who approached him with an offer which was beyond his wildest dreams. The offer was to set up a subsidiary furniture company called Tommy Lawton Furniture Ltd, with Tommy himself on the board of directors. He would get a salary of £2,500 a year, plus commission, a company car and an expense account. As an investment in his family's future Tommy Junior would hold a share issue of 38 per cent, the share certificates to be signed by Tommy Senior as his son was a minor.

This represented an incredible turnaround in Tommy Lawton's financial affairs. That salary alone would pay him nearly £50 a week. All he was getting on the dole was £19 a week and, out of that, rent accounted for £8. Then there were all the other benefits, the commission, a smart new car, expenses and young Tommy's share issue. He could not believe it. "Thank God I swallowed my pride and went on that TV show," he told Gay as the Lawton family celebrated some really good fortune at last.

Just as he'd done with the sports shop, Tommy threw himself heart and soul into this new business and one of the first contracts he secured was the furnishing of Derby County FC's new 600-seat social club – an order worth around £5,000.

With the wages, commission and expenses coming through regularly and reliably, he was getting back on his feet financially and spiritually. He was able to pay off some outstanding bills and open a new bank account which, in contrast to recent times, the bank was actually pleased to have. For a time, the Lawton family looked set for some prosperity and normality.

In schools sport, Tommy Junior was continuing to impress on the rugby field. Just like the surgeon who delivered Gay's bouncing baby boy in 1956 had predicted, this Lawton was now a very good player with the oval ball. Tommy took great pride in his lad's progress at rugby but when he was selected for the first XV at 15, he was concerned about him playing against 18-year-olds. Forgetting how, as a much younger child, he'd played pithead football against grown men and overlooking how much fussing fathers embarrass their boys, he went to see the schoolteacher responsible. The teacher had a ready response: "Look, Mr Lawton," he said, "the way your lad tackles, it's the fathers of the 18-year-olds who should be worried!" That was good enough for Tommy. And when, a few weeks later, Tommy Junior was picked to play for the school in the Nottinghamshire under-19s final, Mum and Dad were in the crowd, cheering him on.

Tommy wasn't the least bit put out that his lad was playing rugby and not the game in which his famous name would have opened so many doors. He would much rather Tommy Junior used his education to get a good job so he would not end up like him and the boy's academic progress suggested that he was on the right track.

One way and another, things were definitely beginning to look up for the Lawtons . . . until the misfortune which had dogged Tommy ever since the day he stopped playing football struck again. His bank account started to run down. Even though he was working as hard as he'd done since day one of this venture, his remuneration was not being paid. He made repeated phone calls, wrote several letters and even made personal visits to the firm's headquarters asking for his money to be sent to him. Nothing came. With the naïvety which had typified his life outside football, he didn't worry too much. This was a large, successful, old, established business – a company of honour and integrity. It would all sort itself out and, meanwhile, his bank manager was allowing him to overdraw on his account.

Perhaps he was so badly scarred, mentally, by his previous heartbreaking setbacks that he simply closed his mind in fear of yet another one or maybe that naivety had degenerated into sheer stupidity but, for whatever reason, Tommy continued to ignore warning signs that should have been obvious. When his company car was damaged in an accident, he hired a car to use while it was being repaired, believing that the company's insurance would look after the repairs. But he was told to get rid of the hire car, even though he protested that a potentially big deal meant he had to get to Yorkshire that afternoon.

His petrol and servicing accounts with a local garage were paid by the company and the garage proprietor told him one day that he was worried because his bill had not been paid for two months.

One night Tommy arrived home to find Gay in tears. "What's up, love?" he asked. "What's the matter?" "One of the girls from the head office has just been on the phone," Gay sobbed. "She says Tommy Lawton Ltd has gone into liquidation."

Tommy just did not want to believe this. "No, that can't be right," he told Gay. "There must be some mistake. There's been no official notification." An urgent meeting with his bank manager removed any doubt. "Tommy Lawton Ltd is in liquidation," said the bank manager, who needed to know what Tommy now proposed to do about his large overdraft. Throughout the period during which he'd been ignoring the blatant warning signs, he had carried on regardless, signing cheques when there were no funds with which to honour them.

Back came the floods of worry and despair. And this time, it got even worse. Much worse. A day later, two CID officers went to Patterdale Road, arrested Tommy Lawton, cautioned him and took him away to Arnold police station. As he sat, engulfed in panic, shock and shame, being quizzed in an interview room, the gossip spread around the police station:

"You'll never guess who's just been brought in."

"Who?"

"Only Tommy Lawton!"

"You're joking! What? *The* Tommy Lawton?"

"*The* Tommy Lawton!"

"So what's he in for?"

"Passing dud cheques."

"Bloody hell!"

Detectives examined his bank statements and cheque book stubs and took a list of the cheques that had not been honoured. Then they visited all the people who had accepted those cheques. One or two of these told the police that they wanted the dishonoured cheques to be torn up: "We don't want to see Tommy Lawton in this sort of trouble," they said. "He can pay us back later, when he's got himself straight." Others were ready to assist the prosecution and happy to give statements. Tommy, still in denial, felt cheated by them. On bail and back home, he told Gay, "I don't understand. These are very good friends of mine. I thought they would understand. They've turned against me. And after all I've done for them."

Gay had heard enough. She was distraught, ashamed and furious. Tommy had told her nothing. She had assumed all was well and that all the money Tommy had been spending was accounted for: "Stop, Tom!" she screamed at her husband. "Stop there! You fool! You fool! What have you done to us?"

A few days later Tommy answered the door to two police officers. He assumed that they had come about the case against him, but these two had a different reason to visit him. "Mr Tommy Lawton?" they asked. "Yes. That's me." "We're here about a call we've had from the police at Ipswich. It's about your father. He's in hospital, dying and he's asked to see you. We can . . ."

Tommy cut them off in mid-sentence. "He can f✳✳✳ off," he said. "And so can you." Then he slammed the door. "Tommy!" exclaimed Gay. "What are you doing? You never use language like that!" "The bastard never wanted me before, so why now?" he said. "The subject's closed. Right?"

The family knew you didn't argue with Tommy in this mood. They knew, because he'd told them, that his father had deserted him and his mother when he was just a baby and that he'd never seen him or heard from him since. What they couldn't know was how deep those emotional scars were and that the passage of more than half a century had done nothing to erase the hatred in his heart for that man.

On 6th June 1972, Tommy Lawton, 'England's greatest ever centre forward' stood, head down in disgrace, in the dock at Nottingham's Shire Hall Court. When he was the world's top goalscorer idolised by millions, he'd been flanked by fabulous wingers like Stan Matthews and Tom Finney. Now that role was filled by two sour-faced court officers.

"You are the defendant, Thomas Lawton?" asked the clerk to the court in a loud, clear voice. "Yes, sir," Tommy whispered without lifting his head. "Speak up, please," boomed the clerk. "Yes, I am," said Tommy. "You stand accused of seven charges of obtaining goods and cash by deception. How do you plead? Guilty or not guilty?" "Guilty," said Tommy, eyes to the floor, head still hanging in shame.

Mr David Ritchie was prosecuting. Lawton had chosen to appear without a lawyer. Mr Ritchie laid out the case for the prosecution: Lawton was pleading guilty to obtaining whisky, cigarettes, a car and cash with dud cheques. He was asking for another 20 offences to be taken into consideration.

Apparently believing that Tommy had made a mistake by not being legally represented, there was almost as much mitigation as prosecution in what Mr Ritchie told the court. He said, "A possible reason for the defendant's downfall is that he cannot accept that his days of glamour as an international football star are over."

After detailing Tommy's illustrious playing career, his spell as Notts County manager and his time as landlord of the Magna Charta, Mr Ritchie explained that "the defendant's slide began in 1960".

Outlining the charges, he continued: "When, through no fault of his own, he lost his job, he continued to buy drink and frivolous items, even though his debts were mounting. Again and again he obtained goods, like a colour television set, using dud cheques. Friends were taken in and their loans were repaid with cheques that bounced.

"It was when the cheque passing went beyond mere debt into the realms of criminality that the police investigated the defendant's affairs. The defendant told them that his firm, which had gone bankrupt, owed him £800 and claimed that he believed a further £1,600 would come from another source, which he did not identify. It did not materialise.

"After he lost his job, the defendant has been living on £19 social security and unemployment benefit. He has been unemployed since last September. His debts total about £2,500, made up of £1,200 in county court judgments against him, £638 owing to people he duped with worthless cheques and £597 owing to a bank at Mapperley. The seven charges he admits involve a total of £314.

"A number of the cheques relate to wines and spirits and on one occasion, the defendant told a policeman that he had made some unwise remark 'because of the booze'. It seems very likely that drinking is another problem he is encountering."

When asked if he had anything to say to the court, Tommy replied, "All I can say is that I am very sorry. If I can and when I can, I would like to pay each person back."

Summing up for the prosecution, Mr Ritchie concluded, "These offences were the culmination of a sad chapter in a life which has been one notable for the glamour and excitement that goes with being an international professional footballer. Dishonesty has ruined the defendant's character and added to his misery."

Those last words pierced Tommy's heart like the thrust of a dagger . . . dishonesty, ruin, misery. This lawyer was talking about him. About Tommy Lawton. He wasn't listening as the court adjourned his case until 14th July and granted him bail in the sum of £50. All he could hear were those three words. And all he could feel was the shame they conveyed . . . dishonesty, ruin, misery. Was that the sum total of his 52 years on this earth? He walked out of the court oblivious to the click and clatter of the press photographers and the whirring of the TV cameras, repeating those three words over and over again to himself . . . dishonesty, ruin, misery.

When Tommy's case resumed, he had a lawyer to speak for him, Mr Robert Anderson:

"The defendant had been engaged by Catesby's of London at £2,500 a year, plus expenses, commission and a shareholding in a subsidiary company, Tommy Lawton Ltd. The parent company of the organisation, Donosbru Furnishings, went into liquidation in October last year.

"The defendant should have received £960 when he became unemployed but was paid only £450 and £50 expenses. This man was entitled to expect his wages would be paid but they were not. He was sure some of the money would come and thought the cheques he issued were all right. It was said that the company, with Mr Lawton, would make half a million a year but, the court may feel, it was really Mr Lawton's name they wanted to further their own ends.

"Mr Lawton won 25 full caps for England international matches and 26 wartime caps. He was a sergeant major in the War and had an exemplary character. He was always a gentleman on the field and had always behaved like one off the field. The most he earned as a player was £17 a week – somewhat different from the £10,000 awarded these days."

After listening to Mr Anderson's mitigating speech, the court placed Tommy on probation for three years, and ordered him to pay compensation of £240, prosecution costs of £75 and £25 towards his legal aid. He was told he could pay £1 a week.

Tommy Lawton left the court, branded a criminal, a cruel fate indeed for a man who throughout his life had adhered to the principles of honesty and straight dealing. He could have been sent to prison but he did not think three years' probation was fair and he was very angry that his mug shot, fingerprints and profile were now held in police records with those of crooks, thieves, murderers and rapists. That was so unjust, he believed, when he had been guilty only of naivety, stupidity and placing too much trust in others. The newspapers crucified him: "Tommy Lawton's road to ruin was littered with dud cheques," screamed one front-page headline . . . "Tommy Lawton's dud cheques shame" . . . "Tommy Lawton wrote dud cheques for his friends" . . . and alongside every lurid headline, a picture of the fallen star leaving the court in disgrace.

For weeks, he didn't leave the house: the shame he felt was unbearable and he couldn't face people. When, finally, he did go out he hid within himself, too ashamed to look anybody in the face. At home, the recriminations caused fearsome rows between him and Gay. She knew what a field day the gossips were having: "She left Rex Rose, with all his money, for *him*," they were saying. That hurt. But what hurt much more was the fact that Tommy had kept her completely in the dark about the problems he'd been having and the solutions he'd chosen – stupid solutions that ended in court.

Carol and Tommy Junior were going through the gossip mill, too. Having a famous dad on the dole was bad enough. But a famous dad in the dock? They'd learned how to be tough, though, these two kids. Bravely, Carol faced the wagging tongues at work. Bravely, Tommy Junior faced the cruel taunts at school. But this was hard for both of them.

Soon after, Carol left home and moved to London. For Tommy Junior, who was at a difficult teenage stage without all this, the teasing and the snide remarks made him introverted. He handled the callous treatment from the other lads by ignoring them completely, having nothing whatsoever to do with them. Not the best way, maybe. But it worked for him.

Through all of this, despite everything, Gay stood by her man. She told him that, come what may, she always would and Tommy was intensely moved by this. Gradually, Tommy's shame turned to defiance. He knew he wasn't a crook: "Why shouldn't I look people in the eye?" he told himself. "I've been stupid, yes. But who is faultless? There are many people out there with bigger skeletons than mine in the cupboard. So why shouldn't I hold my head up?"

There were people in the world of football, a world Tommy thought had shunned and deserted him, who knew he wasn't a crook. And a group of his former colleagues got their heads together and decided to help. Tommy, answering a knock on his front door one night, was amazed to find Andy Beattie, with whom he'd played wartime football, on the doorstep.

Andy brought news that, along with Joe Mercer and Sir Matt Busby, he had formed a committee to organise a testimonial match for Tommy. Notts County had offered Meadow Lane as a venue but they had preferred Goodison Park, where Tommy had spent the best years of his career, and Everton had readily agreed. Other old colleagues, Cliff Britton, Harry Catterick, Bill McGarry and Stan Cullis had agreed to join the testimonial committee, Eddie Plumley, the secretary of Coventry City FC had agreed to be the committee's secretary and Bill Shankly, Brian Clough and Don Revie had promised to do all they could to help.

Tommy sank into the nearest chair: "Andy, this is just wonderful. I don't believe this," he said. "All those people prepared to do this for me." Andy told him, "Tom, this is what football's all about, mate. We're very pleased to do it."

Overjoyed at Andy Beattie's good news, Tommy also found himself regretting more than ever having turned his back on football. "Andy's right," he told Tommy Junior that night. "This is what football's all about. The comradeship, the loyalty. And through my big-headedness and stupidity I walked away from all that after just one bad experience as a manager. I should have bided my time, shown some patience, spent more time looking for another manager's job after Notts County sacked me, instead of fretting and saying I wanted no more to do with it. What a difference that could have made."

All those men helping his testimonial had stayed in the game. Joe Mercer was manager of Coventry City, Harry Catterick of Everton, Bill Shankly of Liverpool, Bill McGarry of Wolves, Brian Clough of Derby County, Don Revie of Leeds. Cliff Britton had managed Burnley, Preston and Hull City, Stan Cullis Wolves and Birmingham City. Matt Busby, who had twice been given the Last Rites as he lay horribly injured after the Munich air crash, came back from the dead to lead Manchester United to a European

Cup final triumph in 1968 and was knighted for the achievement. Andy Beattie had managed Barrow, Stockport, Huddersfield, Scotland, Nottingham Forest, Plymouth Argyle, Wolves and Notts County. How was that for staying power?!

All those men had hung on through varying adversities; they'd all taken the blows and come back for more. But Tommy Lawton? 'Five minutes' each at Kettering and Notts County and then off in a huff when, with more patience and tolerance, he could have been as successful as any of them. "Ah, well," Tommy sighed. "As Grandma Riley used to say, 'If *ifs* and *ands* were pots and pans there'd be no work for tinkers!'"

A few days later, Tommy Lawton was back in the national headlines, but this time for all the right reasons. The testimonial for Tommy Lawton captured the imagination of the press. Joe Mercer told them, "Tommy was a wonderful advertisement for football. We played together in the Army, at Everton, for Arsenal and for England. He was a model on the field, a Bobby Charlton if you like, and he brought glamour to the game. He's fallen on rough times now and his old colleagues thought they would rally round and help him." "Football Still Has a Heart" said the *News of the World* headline.

On a Monday night in November 1972 more than £2 million worth of top players turned out for expenses of just £20 between them. Everton were playing a Great Britain XI captained by England skipper Bobby Moore. The teams were:

Great Britain: Gordon West (Everton); Keith Newton (Burnley), Willie Donachie (Manchester City); Bruce Rioch (Aston Villa), Ron Yeats (Tranmere Rovers), Bobby Moore (West Ham); Mike Summerbee (Manchester City), Colin Stein (Coventry City), Francis Lee (Manchester City), Willie Carr (Coventry City), Bobby Charlton (Manchester United).

Everton: David Lawson; Tommy Wright, Henry Newton, Howard Kendall, Roger Kenyon, John Hurst; Alan Whittle, Mike Bernard, Ron Belfitt, Colin Harvey, John Connolly.

About an hour before the match was due to start, the heavens opened and rain thrashed down but that did not deter 12,000 Scouse spectators from turning out to support a man who last played for Everton 27 years ago. They saw a fine game of football ending in a 2-2 draw. Both teams gave much more than an exhibition, providing competitive fare for the fans. Tommy was bowled over by the generosity of those players, giving their time and skills for free, none more so than Bobby Moore, who'd missed his train in London and drove all the way to Liverpool and back to London after the match. All for a man he'd never met, he'd never seen play and knew only from what he'd read and heard.

That, in the words of Andy Beattie, was what football was all about. So was the effort made to be there that night by many of Tommy's teammates from the past, including most of the old 1939 Everton championship-winning side. There was the chance to talk over old times with Joe Mercer, Yanto Jones, Ted Sagar and most enjoyably of all for Tommy, the indestructible Dixie Dean who, at 66, was as fit and sprightly as ever. The clock was turned back more than 30 years as Dixie offered Tommy some private words of wisdom on how he could and should have avoided all his problems, as if he was talking to the fresh-faced teenage kid who replaced him at Everton.

What a night this was for Tommy Lawton. And for Tommy Junior, who accompanied his dad. The emotion that filled Tommy's heart lasted for days after they'd returned home to Nottingham. And there was more to come.

He was invited by the *Daily Express* to attend the Queen's silver wedding anniversary celebration lunch at London's Savoy Hotel. Sporting personalities were there to represent each year of the Queen's married life. Representing 1947, the year of the Queen's wedding to Prince Philip, were Tommy Lawton and Billy Wright, two great England footballers. During the proceedings, the audience watched re-runs of old Pathé Pictorial newsreels on a giant screen and saw Tommy playing for England against Sweden and signing for Notts County for that record £20,000 transfer fee. These old scenes from 1947, such a tumultuous year in Tommy's own life, were greeted with rapturous applause. Tommy could barely see the film through the tears in his eyes.

The plight of Tommy Lawton touched more hearts, too. George Best, who had agreed to play in the match but had to pull out with an injury, sent a cheque for £100 and several fundraising dinners were held around the country.

Tommy told the press:

The people concerned with my testimonial fund have given me the opportunity to make a new life for myself and my family and I am deeply conscious of the fact that very rarely does a man get a second chance. Not only have they helped me get back on my feet, they have filled an emptiness that has been within me for years. I cannot possibly express the gratitude I feel. This could enable me to buy a house for my family, something they richly deserve. It has always been a happy household but in recent years they have shared the brunt of my troubles and misfortunes bravely. All our lives we have lived in rented accommodation. Now I may be able to provide a home of our own.

It was a vain hope. Wisely, given Tommy's track record, Joe Mercer and his committee had made it a binding condition of the testimonial fund that the money was to clear all Tommy's debts completely. Then what was left was to be put into a trust fund for Tommy. But nobody had realised just how bad things were, just how deeply in debt he was, not even Tommy himself. When money became available, creditors crawled out of the woodwork like woodlice from a rotting tree. The testimonial had raised several thousand pounds, but after all the creditors had been paid there was not enough left to open a trust fund. Tommy was no longer hopelessly in debt but he was still unemployed, still drawing his £19 a week dole, still paying £8 a week rent, still left with only £11 a week with which to keep himself and his family. His dream of buying the Lawtons a home of their own in which they'd be beholden to no one and could hold their heads high were shattered.

As 1973 dawned, the perpetual financial crisis in the Lawton home was worse than ever. Bills were going unpaid: the telephone had been cut off; then, in the freezing cold of January, the electricity was cut off. Gay and Tommy sat forlornly in the dark while Tommy Junior studied for his mock A-levels by candlelight. Misery pervaded that house.

Tommy Lawton now plunged to new depths. He told Gay and the family that he'd got a job working for the Berni Brothers of Berni Inns fame. It was a lie. He was leaving home every morning, going into Nottingham, hanging around the shopping centre, the library and the pubs then going home. He was now systematically selling the last and most treasured of his soccer mementoes – his England international caps.

People pointed him out as he sat on benches in Nottingham's Old Market Square or waited in bus queues, or sat for ages with one cardboard cup of tea in a cheap café in the shopping centre: "That's Tommy Lawton," they'd say. "No! Poor man." Drinkers nodded in his direction as he sat on bar stools staring vacantly into the bottom of an empty beer glass, mind far away on some distant proud memory.

People who had once craved his company and basked in his reflected glory now crossed the road to avoid him. There were those among them who had borrowed money from him in the good times and never paid it back. If just half the money he'd been so foolishly generous with was repaid now he'd have no money worries at all and if he'd had just a fraction of the cash he'd put through Notts County's turnstiles he would be a rich man instead of the down-and-out he'd become.

Still, he strove to cling onto his pride. His outer garments had seen much better days, a far cry indeed from those expensive London-tailored suits and coats with which he'd been synonymous in the days when people boasted about seeing him in those same Nottingham streets, but his shirts were always spotless, thanks to Gay, and his shoes always shone, *heels as well.*

Holding onto that pride was so tough, though. He was in deep despair and sometimes he contemplated suicide. 'Trent Bridge would be a perfect place to end it all. Just one leap off the bridge into the muddy brown torrent beneath and it would all be over.' It would be so ironic that the great Tommy Lawton took his own life in full view of Meadow Lane and the City Ground, where tens of thousands of football fans used to watch him leap for those spectacular headers. 'That would make a great headline, wouldn't it? That would make everybody think. They'd all be sorry then.'

But whenever suicide crossed his mind he thought of how he'd felt when Hughie Gallacher killed himself. Tommy had never forgotten how the brilliant little Scottish international once went to so much trouble to advise him on his technique when he was playing against him, nor had he ever forgotten what a sensational player Hughie Gallacher had been. And he remembered how shocked he'd been when he read how the lovely 'wee fella' died.

Hughie Gallacher had also found life after football too hard to handle. Living in Gateshead, he drifted from one meaningless job to another and after his wife died suddenly from a heart condition in 1950, he was lonely and depressed. One evening in 1957, when Hughie came home from the pub, his 14-year-old son was reading a newspaper and when the lad ignored his dad, Hughie picked up an ornament and threw it at the newspaper. The ornament was not meant to hit the boy, just the newspaper, but it caught his head. The boy fled from the house and someone called the police. The police reported an 'assault' to the authorities and the boy went to live with his aunt while a charge was pursued against his father.

Denied access to his son, Hughie Gallacher spent days aimlessly wandering the streets, ignoring anybody who spoke to him. The day before he was due to appear in court, Gallacher posted a brief letter to the Gateshead Coroner expressing his regrets for the trouble he'd caused and saying that if he lived to be a hundred he would never be able to forgive himself for hurting the boy. Later, two young train spotters saw him pacing backwards and forwards on a footbridge over the London to Edinburgh railway line at Low Fell. He was weeping, talking to himself and pounding the bridge railings with his fists. Then he stepped down from the bridge and walked in front on an oncoming express train.

At the time, Tommy had been stunned and moved by Hughie Gallacher's death. He'd thought it such a tragic, pointless waste of the life of a fine man and it had made him think that suicide could never be the answer to anybody's problems because of the anguish it left behind. Hughie Gallacher was 54 when he died, the same age as Tommy was now. No. Suicide was not the answer and he recalled another of Grandma Riley's old sayings: 'What cannot be cured must be endured.'

Bad as things were, there was yet more to be endured by Tommy Lawton. Among his unpaid bills were those for his rates and when the arrears reached £74.66 he was ordered to appear before Nottingham's Shire Hall magistrates where Mr John Smith, treasurer of Arnold Urban District Council asked for his committal to prison for three months.

Tommy Lawton told the magistrates that the arrears had arisen "through a complete misunderstanding" and they adjourned the case for three weeks so that he could sort this 'misunderstanding' out. Mr Smith told the court that if the arrears and costs, totalling £79.66, were paid the case would be withdrawn.

There was no misunderstanding. He was just playing for time, clutching at straws, hoping like Mr Micawber that 'something would turn up' to save him from three months in prison. It didn't and the ultimate disgrace was about to fall on the famous head of Tommy Lawton as he faced the magistrates again.

But as he stood in the dock awaiting his fate, Mr Smith got to his feet with a message for the bench: "Your worships, I've just had a telephone call from the Shire Hall saying that a letter has been received in relation to this case. I have not myself yet seen this letter but I am told that it is from Arsenal Football Supporters' Club who say they would like the privilege of paying these arrears." Tommy had escaped gaol – thanks to the supporters of one of the clubs he graced as a player. He told reporters outside the court: "I'm very grateful for the gesture. This is typical of Arsenal."

But there was another court case for Tommy Lawton to face. He had 'borrowed' £10 from a friend, publican Roland De'Ath, telling him he needed the money to get to Coventry to collect money from his testimonial match. When, six months later, Tommy had not paid him back, Mr De'Ath told a couple of police officers who frequented his pub. The police decided to prosecute and on 14th August 1974 Tommy was back in the dock, pleading not guilty to obtaining money by deception.

Mr David Ritchie, prosecuting, told the court that Lawton needed the £10 for household expenses but borrowed it on the pretext of wanting to get to Coventry to see Joe Mercer, who was manager of Coventry City FC. Joe Mercer was summoned as a witness and Tommy shrank in shame as he looked out from the dock and across the courtroom, watching his old mate Joe taking the oath and telling the court: "We knew he had come on hard times and was heavily in debt. A team of all-stars played an Everton team and raised about £6,000. A trust was formed, trustees being myself, Sir Matt Busby and Andy Beattie. We found by the time we had paid his creditors that it was not worth setting up a trust."

Roland De'Ath, licensee of the Horse and Jockey, Bulwell, told the court, "Lawton came into the pub in June 1973 and told me he needed £10 for petrol and expenses to get to Coventry. He said he would repay the £10 later that week but he didn't. I complained to the police six months later."

Detective Sergeant Brian Davy said he saw Lawton in February and told him that by telling a false story to borrow money he had committed an offence, to which Lawton had replied, "I did tell Ron a lie but I had to have money. We had no food in the house. I was desperate." Giving evidence, Lawton denied having said that and denied that he had obtained the money dishonestly: "After getting the £10 from Mr De'Ath, I set off for Coventry but the car broke down before I reached the M1 and I decided to abandon the journey because by the time I got there it would have been too late to see Joe."

Defence lawyer Mr Michael O'Connell submitted that the police interview with Lawton was on the basis that he could not possibly have obtained money from his testimonial fund because there was no money left in it, but this was wrong. The fund was not wound up until later. Lawton was not dishonest: he really did intend going to Coventry.

That wasn't enough to convince the magistrates. They found Lawton guilty and remanded him on bail until 4th September. At the resumed hearing, he was sentenced to 200 hours' community service. Magistrates' chairman Dr Hugh Rice said the bench had considered 27 similar offences. Lawton was sentenced to another 200 hours' community service for breach of his probation order, the sentences to run concurrently. He was ordered to pay £40 costs, of which he offered to pay £10 within seven days and the remainder at £2 a week.

Doing community service, menial tasks like sweeping up leaves, was humiliating but Tommy turned it to some advantage. He went to a call box and rang *The People* to ask if they would like to buy an exclusive picture of the great Tommy Lawton doing his community service. The £25 *The People* gave him for that picture paid for a new suit for Tommy Junior so that he looked suitably smart when he started his first job at Barclays Bank.

Before that community service sentence was passed, Tommy's defence lawyer told the court, "The defendant and his family have already suffered embarrassment and distress because of the extensive publicity given to this case." That was an understatement. But still, the courts hadn't finished with Tommy Lawton.

On 11th December 1975 Lawton was again summoned for non-payment of rates. Again he faced Mr John Smith from the council across the Shire Hall courtroom. Tommy was admitting non-payment of £84.46 in rates due from 1st April 1974. Mr Smith told the court that a distress warrant was issued on 20th March and with costs the amount owed was £92.56.

Mr Smith said, "The defendant has made various offers to pay, none of which have materialised and I now ask for his committal to prison." Lawton told the court he had not been in a position to pay because he had been sick and was on social security. He offered to pay the arrears in full in seven days, adding, "It would save my family a lot of suffering." But it was pointed out to him that he had been arrested on the warrant of 15th November and Mr Smith told the bench, "We have done everything we can to help, but rates for another year, totalling £110.50 are now due."

Tommy pleaded with the court: "I expect to receive some money in a few days then I can pay." But Mr Smith replied, "Your worships, the defendant gave us the same assurance in September." The court had heard enough excuses from Tommy Lawton. The chairman of the bench asked him, "Do you have anything to say before I pass sentence?"

Tommy shuddered, then began to shake all over. Sentence? He was going to be sent to prison. His eyes darted all around the courtroom and those eyes were pleading in vain to the police officers, the lawyers, the reporters, the court clerks, the magistrates. What was he going to do? He hadn't said anything at home about this latest debt. Gay and the kids didn't even know he was here. And now he was going to prison.

He stuttered his reply to the magistrates: "With the press being here and everything it is very humiliating to find myself in this position. I am thinking of my wife and family. I would rather they heard about this from me than hear it on the radio or see it in the papers just because I used to be in the public eye."

His plea counted for nothing. The chairman told him, "We sentence you to three months' imprisonment. You will be taken from here to Lincoln Prison."

Two burly police officers grabbed an arm each and Tommy Lawton was marched down the steps, out of the court and into the police cells. His belt and his tie were taken from him, his pockets were emptied and he was put into a cell. The cell door slammed shut and suddenly all was silent. He was alone. Completely alone. And for the first time in his life, he felt real fear. His whole body now shook from head to toe. He couldn't stop shaking. He sat down on the bench that passed for a bed in that dark, dingy, smelly cell. He held his head in his hands. And he wept.

Tommy had to stay in that police cell until the court had finished its business. There would probably be more than one prison sentence today and all the prisoners would be taken to Lincoln in one big van. So, he had to sit in his cell, waiting and worrying. His head was in turmoil. What about Gay and the kids? Gay would be frantic with worry when he didn't come home – and then she'd find out he'd been sent to jail. Oh, God, what was he doing to her? And the kids? The shame they would feel. Their dad in prison. And the newspapers: "The great Tommy Lawton, the best centre forward England ever had – a jailbird!" God, what a field day they were going to have with that. And what about Tommy Junior's future? What use is a good education now that his dad's a convict? He hadn't just wrecked his own life. His whole family was ruined. And what would become of him? The loneliness and humiliation of being locked in a cell was already unbearable and he had to face three months of this. How the hell was he going to be able to cope? And when he wasn't locked up and lonely he'd be with real villains: "Oh, my God. How has it all come to this?"

Back upstairs in the courtroom, there was a break in cases and the clerk whispered to the chairman of the bench, "There's a development in the case of Lawton, sir. Someone has turned up offering to pay his rates arrears." "Really?" asked the magistrate. "Is it genuine?" "It appears so, sir. I'm told it's a Mr Oliver Tame." "Well, we'd better call him."

Oliver Tame worked with Tommy at Imperial Life ten years earlier when he was selling insurance. They'd been good pals. News of what had happened to Tommy had reached Tommy Junior who, completely unaware that his father was in court, had been playing rugby and had just walked off the pitch. Tommy Junior rang Oliver Tame, who now took the witness stand and made his offer formally to the court: "I just have to help a man like Tommy Lawton, your worships. He has been left high and dry by an unkind world. People have such short memories. It breaks your heart to see the people who once clung to his coat tails now forsaking him."

The magistrates nodded in agreement and thanked Mr Tame for his kindness. "Just one thing, your worships," he replied. "Could you please ensure that my name does not get out? I would hate people to think I've done this for some sort of reflected glory. Tommy is a good man and that's the only reason I want to help him. So I must do it anonymously, please." The magistrates agreed. The press would be told only that Mr Lawton's rates had been paid by a friend who wished to remain anonymous: "Thank you Mr Tame and good day."

Tommy heard a key turn in the lock of his cell. That must be it, then. Court must have finished. Now he was going to be taken to prison. He lifted his head from his hands and pulled back his shoulders. No one was going to see him like this. He would grin and bear it.

A police officer opened the cell door: "You're free to go, Tommy," he said with a smile. "Somebody's coughed up for you."

"What! Who?"

"Can't say. Don't know. But you're out of here, pal. Off you go!"

"Thank you. Thank you so much."

"Just one thing, Tommy . . ."

"Yes?"

"Can I have your autograph, please?"

Tommy Lawton was a free man and the next day's newspapers all splashed the latest news about Lawton. That was hardly surprising. It was a cracking story. But Tommy was beginning to wonder what all the headline writers would do without him. And Gay hadn't finished with him yet!

Tommy agreed, after a prolonged ear-bashing, that he would never, ever keep anything like that from her again. He knew that he wasn't going to hear the last of this for a very long time to come. But, hey, he could have been in prison!

The shock of that awful experience had a salutary effect on Tommy Lawton. He and Gay were no better off and they weren't going to be, although Tom Junior had paid Oliver Tame back the money that had saved his father from prison, thus restoring at least a modicum of pride and peace had descended on the Lawton household. Money was probably going to be tight for the rest of his life. He just had to come to terms with that, stop feeling cheated by a cruel world, stop thinking that football owed him a living, stop living on past glories and stop drinking so much. In his mid-50s, Tommy Lawton was telling himself, "It's time you grew up!"

For more than ten years he had been dwelling on his glorious past, living subconsciously off his famous name, still believing that football would provide for him and when it didn't, blaming everybody but himself for his troubles. Sullen and self-pitying, he'd been living in a daze of drink and debt for far too long. Sitting, shaking and alone with his thoughts in that cold, lonely police cell had brought him to his senses and from now on, he would be a different man.

So what of football now? Tommy still loved the game. And he always would. Football was, however, doing its best to ensure that professional purists like him didn't love it back!

They were a strange looking lot, these 1970s footballers. Glam rock had introduced odd chaps like David Bowie, Gary Glitter and Sweet to the music scene: blokes who dressed like women, wore make-up and lipstick and had shoulder-length hair. Now the footballers looked the same: 'big girl's blouses' with perms (perms, for God's sake!) and they wore skimpy, tight, thigh-hugging shorts, so short they barely covered their backsides.

Worse, they played the beautiful game so cynically now, cheating in ways that only ex-professionals like Tommy could see was cheating: trying to kid the refs; falling over to get penalties; rolling the ball away along the ground when opponents got throw-ins; time-wasting and arguing; using aggression craftily, nastily, sometimes going way beyond tough-tackling into the realms of what non-soccer folk would call criminal assault. This was not the game he knew.

Then there was the crowd behaviour. This had started to degenerate in the 1960s but now it was truly horrific. Obscene chanting and singing; baiting black players with disgusting displays of racism; bloody street battles between armies of thugs masquerading as supporters; mass brawls inside the grounds; destruction of stand seats; pitch invasions. These weren't soccer stadia any more: they were warzones.

But still, Tommy watched football, mostly on television because who wanted to stray into a warzone on a Saturday afternoon? He was so proud of his number 9 protégés from Nottingham. Jeff Astle and Tony Hateley were coming to the end of their top-flight careers but they'd done so well: Astle for West Brom and England; Hateley for Aston Villa, Chelsea, Liverpool, Coventry City and Birmingham City. Tommy knew they'd be good 'uns and how right he'd been.

He could still spot a player and he even had a couple of ideas which football might like to accept from him. For example, his own experiences had led him to think, often, that if he'd had someone to look out for him after Jim Riley died, things might have been different. Why shouldn't *every* professional footballer have a representative, an agent, who negotiated contracts, pay, transfers? With his own vast experience, nobody would be able to do that job better than him? He bounced the idea off several of his contacts in the game, including the Professional Footballers' Association. "No," they all told him, "it would never work. The clubs are too powerful."

He thought he knew how this dreadful soccer hooliganism could be tackled, too: "All-seater stadia," he said. "Can't happen," they told him. "Too expensive."

Watching Tom Junior play rugby had given him an idea on how to curb bad conduct on the soccer field. "Look at the ten-metre rule in rugby," he told them. "If you don't go back straight away or argue with the ref, you're sent back another ten metres. This would be an excellent way of calming down footballers and getting respect for referees back," he argued. "Nah, that's rugby," they said, "a different sort of game."

Tom Junior's rugby was coming along very well now and so was his job in Barclays Bank. With his dad still on the dole, Tom's wage was vital to the family and Tom was proud to be doing his bit, even though he thought Gay's demand for £10 a week out of the £25 he earned was a bit much.

Tom injured his right knee ligaments playing rugby for Barclays in North Yorkshire and the next day he was in such pain that a doctor was called to treat him at home. But the doctor was much more concerned about Tom's dad. Tommy had suffered with stomach problems for a long time and now he was in agony. The doctor had him rushed immediately to Nottingham City Hospital, where an operation was performed on a duodenal ulcer.

In 1977, Tom Junior married Elizabeth Cockayne, a farmer's daughter from Bingham, who he'd met at a disco. He was just 21. It was a grand wedding at Bingham Parish Church and his mum and dad were very proud, especially Gay because this was her sort of occasion, but she fretted over how much they were going to miss the money young Tom brought home. Carol, too, had got married – to her boss, Bob Butchers, for whom she'd been PA. She and her husband were now living in an old windmill they'd restored in Skelmersdale, Lancashire.

In 1978, young Tom was player of the season at Mellish Rugby Club but because it seemed that every time Tommy went along his team would lose, he'd banned his father from watching him play. "Stay away, Dad. You're a jinx," he told him. Tommy smiled. "OK, son," he said. But it was a jinx of a different kind, injury, that forced Tom to pack in his beloved rugby. Playing in the Three Counties sevens semi-final he snapped the cruciate ligament and tore the medial and lateral cartilages in his left knee.

A year later, Tom had moved to Leicester and as he watched the East Midlands playing Lancashire one Wednesday evening he was spotted by his old rugby master at Nottingham High School, Chalkie White. As well as being Head of Physical Education at Nottingham High for decades, Chalkie had coached Leicester Tigers since the early 1970s. Chalkie was a superb analyst of people and a great motivator.

"How's your rugby, Tom?" inquired Chalkie. "I had to quit," Tom told him, "My knee's knackered." Chalkie's reply was unequivocal: "Monday evening; seven o'clock; training. We'll sort you *and* your knee out." Tom said, "Yes, sir!"

And that was how Tom Lawton Junior came to sign for Leicester Tigers, the best senior rugby union team in the country. He made one stipulation before signing. There was to be no publicity about whose son he was. He'd inherited his dad's stubborn streak and if he was going to make it in rugby union it was going to be down to him, not his famous father.

The Leicester squad was very strong, full of international players and it was two seasons before Tom got the chance to play in the first team. His debut was against Cambridge University and he told his dad, "Don't you dare come and watch me. You'll put a jinx on us." Tommy smiled: "OK, son."

Tom was playing blindside and the Cambridge fly half, a certain Rob Andrew, broke down the blindside in the Tigers' 22 and thought he was clear through for a try, but Tom launched himself at the flying fly half and they both finished up in the front row of the stand . . . "Great tackle, Lawton!" shouted Chalkie White. "Get in there!" shouted somebody else. Was it? Yes, it was. After the game, Tommy Lawton confessed to his son. He had been ignoring his ban all along!

Meanwhile, on the Nottingham soccer scene, Forest's reign as the city's top club was continuing – and how! Brian Clough became the manager of a struggling Second Division side in 1975 and won promotion in the 1976/77 season. In their first season in the top flight, Forest won the League Cup, beating Liverpool 1-0 in a replay at Old Trafford and the League championship, beating Liverpool into second place. From 27th November 1977 until 9th December 1978 Forest went unbeaten for 42 games, the equivalent of a whole season.

Then in 1979, Forest won the European Cup, beating Malmö of Sweden 1-0 in the final with a goal by Trevor Francis. Brian Clough had transformed Nottingham Forest from unfashionable Second Division also-rans into champions of Europe. It was a truly fantastic achievement by the man whose brilliant career as a centre forward had been cruelly cut short by an horrific knee injury in 1962.

Clough had been a goalscorer of Lawton-like magnificence. He'd hit 197 in 213 games for his home town club Middlesbrough and 54 in 61 games for Sunderland until that fateful day when he collided with Bury goalkeeper Chris Harker in one of those sickening crunches that immediately silence a soccer crowd.

Tommy Lawton was delighted at Clough's sensational feats with Forest. He felt a lot of affinity with Brian:

Like him, Clough came from a poor, working-class, Northern background.

Like him, Clough had been a precocious talent and a prolific goalscorer.

Like him, Clough was confident, blunt and outspoken.

Like him, Clough had open contempt for those 'lah-de-dah buggers'.

But above all, Brian Clough's Nottingham Forest played the game the way it was meant to be played, the way Tommy Lawton wanted to see it played: fast, fluent, to feet; in the air only for as long as it took to find the centre forward's head. "If God had meant football to be played in the sky, he'd have put bloody grass up there!" Clough famously once said. And how Tommy Lawton agreed.

While snarling indiscipline, cheating and arguing the toss over referees' decisions had become endemic in British football, woe betide any Forest player who stepped out of line with the boss's strict disciplinary code. "It wasn't a penalty because the referee didn't give a bloody penalty," Clough would say. And how Tommy Lawton agreed.

Brian Clough made soccer history by paying Birmingham City £1 million for Trevor Francis, then immediately played Britain's first million-pound player in the Reserves. Just like Dixie Dean had done with Tommy, Clough was keeping the lad's feet on the ground. And how Tommy Lawton agreed.

And so, the 1970s drew to a close. It had been a dark decade for Tommy. He was 61 years old now. Older and wiser? "You bet," he said. "And not before time!"

1980 dawned on a much quieter Lawton home in Patterdale Road. With Carol and Tom Junior now gone their separate busy ways, Gay and Tommy were alone. By living within their means they had got their finances under control. There were no debts but money was tight and the rigours of the last decade had taken its toll on both of them, mentally and physically. Both looked older than their years. They were worn out. The old house, too, looked tired and unloved. It was hard to love it. It had been a home of such unhappy times. The furniture was shabby, the paintwork cracked and worn. A single bar of an electric fire kept the worst of the cold at bay but offered little comfort. The walls and shelves were devoid of any clue to the great man's illustrious football career. He'd sold all his mementoes during the dark days. There was just one tiny old medal on the mantelpiece and if you looked very closely at this you could just make out the inscription:

T Lawton, Bolton Town Schools Football, 1930.

It was the first recognition he'd ever had. How proudly he'd carried it home to show to Jim Riley, his mam and his uncles. And what a life had been waiting for the lad who'd won it. But that life had long gone now.

Tommy and Gay spent their days in that drab house reflecting: Tommy on all that had happened to him; Gay on the life of luxury she gave up for him. They rarely went out together; even if they could afford to, there was nowhere they wanted to go, but most days Tommy walked to the Co-op and called in at the pub. There was no hard drinking now, just a couple of pints then off home. When he went out, he did his best to look smart in case someone recognised him. Gay made sure he always had a nice clean shirt and he polished his shoes religiously, *heels as well*, but he needn't have bothered because nobody linked the old fella in a worn-out raincoat to Tommy Lawton, 'England's greatest centre forward'.

The boredom was lifted now and again when Carol took them to stay in the hotel in Chester which she ran with her husband or when Tom, who had moved to Leicester, called to see them, but mostly it was an unremitting routine of doing nothing in particular.

It was just the same in 1981 and in 1982 and in 1983 and in 1984 . . . Going nowhere, doing nothing, drifting listlessly into old age on a flat sea of endless monotony.

Back on top of the world

Chapter Eleven

RESURGAM!

T he schoolboys' match had long since finished. The playing fields were empty now. A hush had descended, along with a thin autumn mist. And it had turned cold. Tommy Lawton shuddered: "Blimey, this is Goose Fair weather – and a month early, too. How long have I been sitting here?"

He'd been obliviously absorbed in his memories ever since he slumped down on that bench, bristling from the rudeness of that young school-teacher who'd asked him who the bloody hell he was. Two or three hours must have passed and he hadn't realised. "Silly old sod," he chastised himself. "Getting lost down Memory Lane. Gay's going to think I've been in the pub."

He opened the front door, put his Co-op carrier bag down and took off his coat.

"That you, Tom?"

"Yes."

"You've been ages. Have you been in the pub?"

"No. Well, yes. I did call in for a couple but that's not where I've been. I stopped off to watch a kids' match and . . . well, never mind, I'm here now."

"Did you remember the ham?"

"Yes."

"Not cut too thick?"

"No. Just as you said."

As they sat down to their boiled ham, potatoes and peas, Gay suddenly remembered: "Oh, there was a telephone call. A chap called John Holmes from BBC Radio Nottingham. They want you to go on their sports programme on Saturday afternoon."

"Crikey," said Tommy. "Nobody's wanted to talk to me for years. Radio Nottingham? Did they say why?"

"Some anniversary or other. Will you go?"

"No. I shan't bother. Who wants to listen to me these days?"

Then he remembered what that rude young man on the playing fields had said, "Who the bloody hell are you?" He was still angry about that. "On second thoughts, I will go. Yes, I will."

Barrie Williams, the editor of the *Nottingham Evening Post* was driving his Daimler to the City Ground to watch Nottingham Forest. He was football mad and having moved to Nottingham from Kent to become the best paid editor in the regional newspaper industry in 1982, he was able to watch both Forest and County, a feast of football upon which he gorged happily. Both clubs had welcomed the new editor of the prestigious *Evening Post* with open arms. He'd been a surprise appointment, a young man in his 30s when newspaper editors, especially of big, traditional newspapers like this one in Nottingham, had always been older, wiser men. It was a pleasant change for the clubs to have an editor who was so enthusiastic about the game and he'd become a firm friend of the football folk at both the City Ground and Meadow Lane.

Williams always listened to BBC Radio Nottingham on his way to the matches. He liked to hear the team news and listen to the build-up chat. As he drove past Nottingham University from his home on the Nottinghamshire-Derbyshire border, he switched on his car radio. A man with a Lancashire accent was talking about football in the old days and the presenter was asking him about a goal he had scored for Notts County against Nottingham Forest at the City Ground in 1949. It was Tommy Lawton.

"Tommy Lawton," Williams thought. "My dad should be listening to this." He had grown up in Oswestry, where Shropshire borders Wales, and his dad talked often about Tommy Lawton. His mum's family were from Liverpool, Evertonians every one and Tommy was a legend to them. Williams's best pal for a time in his schooldays was Alan Ball, the Alan Ball. Like Tommy, Alan came from Bolton. Like Tommy, he played for Everton and Arsenal and England. Alan's father, Alan Senior, was a jour-neyman footballer and the Balls were in Shropshire because he was player-manager of non-League Oswestry Town. That didn't pay a fortune, so he also kept a local pub, the King's Head. In their last year in primary school and first year in grammar school in the late 1950s, young Alan Ball and Barrie Williams used to have impromptu football training sessions with Alan's dad among the empty beer barrels in the pub's yard and on the wall of the shed behind Williams's council house home, they painted a circular heading target in pale blue paint they pinched from the shed. Williams's dad, Stan, another football fanatic, would watch them as one threw a tennis ball for the other to head at the target. When they hit the target, Stan would cheer and shout "Tommy Lawton!"

This all came flooding back to Barrie Williams as he listened to the legendary Lawton on the radio. Then he remembered stories about Lawton's troubles in the 1970s. How the great man had fallen. He made a mental note: "We must get this man's life story. It'll be a great read."

When Tommy came home from his walk the following Monday, Gay had another message for him: "I've had a reporter from the *Evening Post* on. They want to know if they can come and pick you up to talk to their editor."

"What?" said Tommy. "First, Radio Nottingham. Now the *Evening Post*. They've all ignored me for years."

"Will you go?"

"No. I don't want to speak to the editor. He'll be some lah-de-dah bugger."

At that night's editorial conference, Williams asked his sports editor, Trevor Frecknall, "How did we get on with Tommy Lawton?"

"No joy, I'm afraid, boss. Don't think he wants to know. Can't say I blame him. He had a hell of a time in the '70s, you know".

"Of course I know! That's the whole point. That man's life is a great story. Get back to him, Trev – and make sure he knows I'll pay a bloody good fee for it."

Trevor Frecknall was a good journalist. He knew his boss was not going to take 'no' for an answer on this one. So he went around to Patterdale Road himself. It took one more visit from Trevor and a great deal more persuasion but eventually, a reluctant Tommy Lawton got into the sports editor's car to be driven to the huge city-centre offices of the *Nottingham Evening Post*.

As he walked along the highly polished floors through wood-panelled corridors with the faces of wing-collared Dickensian newspaper barons peering from gold-framed oil paintings on the walls, Tommy's preconceptions about this editor chap seemed to be confirmed. He expected him to look just like one of those blokes in those paintings.

The editor's secretary, Mavis Brand was a fan of Notts County who'd once had a crush on one Leon Leuty, a County player from Tommy's era. Mavis was thrilled to meet Tommy. "What a nice lady," he thought as Mavis poured him a cup of tea and made him welcome in her office, next door to the editor's. "What's he like, your boss?" Tommy asked her. "A 'lah-de-dah bugger' I suppose." "I think you'll be surprised," said Mavis with a smile.

Barrie Williams jumped up from the big desk behind which he sat and bounded across to Tommy as he walked through the door with Mavis: "Tommy, you old bugger. We've got you at last!" he beamed.

Tommy was taken aback. This wasn't one of those blokes off the wall. This was just a lad, young enough to be his son. His hair was quite long, he wore a white suit and a trendy pink shirt with a flamboyant broad tie and when he offered him a cigarette, he noticed that he wore a silver bracelet. "Blimey," thought Tommy. "When policemen and newspaper editors look like kids, you must be getting old!" But there was something else he hadn't expected about this newspaper editor. He was no 'lah-de-dah bugger', but a council-house kid who talked his language.

Williams was similarly surprised. He'd never seen Lawton play, of course, but he'd seen pictures of him in his old soccer albums: the big muscular frame, the wide strong shoulders, the slick, healthy hair; the supreme athlete, more often than not pictured in one of those incredible leaps to head the ball. Could this frail, faded fellow with his stooped shoulders, grubby raincoat and Co-op carrier bag possibly be the great Tommy Lawton?

First impressions soon became irrelevant and these two hit it off immediately. There was an instant natural rapport between them as they talked about the newspaper's proposition: "Tell you what, Tommy," said the editor after a while. "Let's go across to the Blue Bell. We can finish talking this through over a pint." "Now, that's a good idea, mate," said Tommy. And that's exactly what both of them knew they were going to be from that moment on: mates.

The fee that the *Nottingham Evening Post* was paying Tommy Lawton for his life story was more money than he and Gay had seen for years. Barrie Williams paid in advance and raised a cheque from his finance director immediately so that he could take it home with him.

Back at Patterdale Road, Tommy teased Gay: "Guess what I've got in this envelope!"

"Oh, I don't know. You've been in the pub, haven't you?"

"I have, yes, with the editor of the *Evening Post*. And you and I have got something to celebrate, my dear."

"Oh, go on, then. Show me what's in your envelope."

"Only this!" said Tommy – and handed the cheque to his wife with a flourish.

"Gosh!" exclaimed Gay. "Fifteen hundred pounds!"

"That's what the editor thinks I'm worth to his paper," said Tommy. "And do you know what? He and I really got on well. I'm going to enjoy doing it."

The task of writing Tommy's life story was given to sports reporter David Stapleton, who had followed his dad Albert into the newspaper business. Tommy had a great deal of time for Albert when he used to report on Notts County. "Your old fella were a good 'un," he told David. And they sat down and got cracking.

Knowing that his editor was always impatient when he was on to a good story, David Stapleton devoted several full days and nights to the task of writing the early instalments before knocking nervously on his door to tell him: "The Tommy Lawton stuff's ready for you to see, boss." Later, the editor summoned the writer to his office: "This, David old son, is bloody good stuff," he enthused, " ... and it will get even better."

Williams rang the *Nottingham Evening Post's* promotions manager, Bob Britten: "Bob, I've got something a bit special here. Can we talk about how we launch it, because I think that has to be special, too?" There could have been nobody better equipped for this task than Bob Britten. He'd been a professional footballer, a half-decent winger on Nottingham Forest's books, before a dodgy knee forced him to try something else. This was the sort of promotional assignment he loved getting stuck into.

After a lengthy meeting, editor and promotions manager were agreed. The serialised *Life Story of Tommy Lawton* would be launched via a *This Is Your Life*-type presentation on Tommy. That would capture the imagination and provide some belting good copy and pictures to kick off the series. Then they'd plaster the city with picture posters of Tommy in one of those brilliant heading shots.

A great compère for the *This Is Your Life* show, they agreed, would be top comedian Charlie Williams. Charlie, too, was an ex-professional footballer. A black man, a rare sight indeed on football pitches in those days, he'd been a tough centre half with Doncaster Rovers in the 1950s. When he quit football he became a performer on the equally tough Northern nightclub circuit and when TV producers were looking for stand-up comedians for a show they called *The Comedians*, Charlie was chosen. The show, with its non-stop, quickfire gags, was a massive hit. It became a long-running success and Yorkshireman Charlie, along with the likes of

Bernard Manning, George Roper, Frank Carson and Mike Reid, was one of its biggest stars.

Viewers loved his self-effacing routine, drawing the fire of any racists by telling jokes about his own colour. It was a unique brand of humour and Charlie, with his broad accent and cheeky chuckle, went on to become one of the biggest show-business names of the 1960s and 1970s. Still much loved and still doing his comedy routine, Charlie's link with football would make him a brilliant compère. Williams and Britten went to Sheffield to make him an offer: "Ee, Tommy Lawton," Charlie chuckled. "Now, 'e were a great player, owd love. I'll be reet chuffed to do it for 'im."

With the compère signed up, the editor then drew up a list of significant personalities from Tommy's proud past to be the *This Is Your Life* guests. His was the easy bit. Bob Britten had to track them down, persuade them to appear, organise transport and hotel accommodation, and get them there on the night: a daunting challenge and very little time in which to do it, but Bob loved every minute of it.

Next task for the editor and the promotions manager was to sit down for several hours with Charlie Williams and thrash out the contents of the 'Big Red Book' – the script. Then Bob Britten had to locate backdrop material for the stage: pictures to be blown up to life size, of Tommy's birthplace, his old schools; photographs of memorable moments in his career; old Pathé Pictorial newsreels.

This was hard work, but if ever there was a labour of love, this was it. One of the toughest parts of this whole assignment was to keep Tommy totally in the dark. This had to be a complete surprise for him. They didn't think that Gay, bless her, would be able to keep it to herself, so they kept it all from her, too. The secret would be safe, though, with Tom Junior and Carol and they could help.

Williams and Britten were delighted to learn from Tom Junior that, by coincidence, the date they had chosen for the event was Tommy's 65th birthday and a splendid cake was swiftly added to Bob's surprises for the night.

The venue was to be the spanking new social club at Meadow Lane and an audience of around 150 people were invited. In the interests of secrecy, the invitations had to go out ridiculously late, the day before the event and even then they were all asked not to say a word to anybody. It was still a bit of a risk, but it would be no good without an audience. Barrie Wiliams rang Tommy Lawton a couple of days before the big night:

"Tommy, I thought it would be good if you and Gay could join me for a drink to celebrate the start of the series in the paper. I'll bring my wife, Pauline and the four of us can have a nice evening together."

"Oh, yes. We'd like that. Where?"

"The new Meadow Club at Notts County's nice. Just opened; very smart."

"Well, Meadow Lane's not exactly my favourite place. But for you guv'nor, we'll be there."

"Great. I'll send a car for you. About seven."

Come the night, Bob Britten had worked his socks off and prepared a masterpiece of organisation. The smart new club looked a treat; the stage setting was absolutely first class; the members of the audience were in their seats, primed to be quiet. Charlie Williams was ready for the off, Big Red Book under his arm, famous toothy grin from ear to ear. Bob, proving that among his many talents he was a more than adequate warm-up man, told the audience, "When the lights go out, which will be any minute now, I want you to be absolutely silent. Right?"

Bob had arranged a system of signals to plot the course of Tommy and Gay right up to the minute they got to the big double doors of the club-room. "Sshh-Sshh," he whispered into the microphone as the lights were switched off, plunging the room into total darkness and silence. It was so quiet that they could hear Tommy and Gay pushing at the doors and Tommy saying, "Flippin' door's shut, what sort of a bar is this?!"

Then the doors flew open, the lights went up and more than 100 people rose to their feet, cheering, clapping and whistling. Tommy looked stunned. Gay laughed. Charlie Williams walked over to the couple and took Tommy gently by the arm: "Come with me, Tommy, owd love. We've got a few surprises for you." As Charlie led Tommy past the table where Barrie Williams and his wife sat with their guests, Tommy said, "You bugger!" But the smile on his face and the glint in his eye told the editor that he was really thrilled to bits.

The applause did not die down until Tommy and Gay sat down on stage with Tom Junior and Carol beside them. Charlie Williams opened the proceedings by introducing himself, as if that were needed, and raised the first of many laughs that were to come by telling the audience, "I were a centre 'aff, me. I couldn't play. But I could stop the buggers 'oo thought they could!"

The compère proceeded to conduct *Tommy Lawton – This Is Your Life* with the laid-back charm of a true professional, putting everybody involved at ease with his spontaneous gags and infectious laugh.

One by one he brought on the stars from the great Lawton era to rapturous applause, each one shaking Tommy by the hand and hugging him: Tom Finney, Raich Carter, Peter Doherty, Neil Franklin, Stan Cullis, Johnny Carey, Jackie Sewell. An especially large cheer greeted one of the combatants from epic battles with the Auld Enemy giant Scottish centre half George Young. The years had done nothing to diminish the stature of this affable man mountain and he and Tommy engaged in some spontaneous mock jostling, with Charlie Williams encouraging Tommy to "whack the big bugger from be'ind!"

When Charlie Williams finally closed the Big Red Book and handed it to Tommy with a warm handshake, the audience stood in an ovation that lasted several minutes while the star of the show, flanked by all those old mates, stood under the spotlight smiling broadly through the tears that flowed from his eyes.

The next day, Tommy took the bus down to the city to watch the first instalment of *The Tommy Lawton Story* coming hot off the press. A splendid, happy picture of him with Charlie Williams and the Big Red Book had pride of place on the front page of that day's *Post*. The whole of page 3 of the paper was dedicated to more pictures and the full story of the triumphant *This Is Your Life* production. The first instalment of Tommy's life story occupied another full page to itself. Tommy was the centre of attraction again when he joined the editor and the lads from the sports department for a pub lunch at the Blue Bell, where they all replayed the events of that fabulous evening, guest by guest.

On the bus ride home, Tommy sat with a warm glow of satisfaction, the like of which he hadn't felt for years. As the bus chugged along, a young man wearing a black-and-white scarf approached him diffidently: "Excuse me, Mr Lawton. Could I have your autograph, please?" "Of course you can, son," said Tommy. "Of course you can."

Week by week, *The Tommy Lawton Story* was told in the *Post*. And the editor knew he'd done a shrewd bit of business when the sales of his paper went up.

The series was being avidly consumed by readers, for many of whom it was rekindling memories of the great man and (this being Nottingham!) reigniting old arguments as well. Many of those readers were putting pen to paper with their feelings and the bonus of *Tommy Lawton Letters Specials* was further proof that the fee the editor had paid Tommy was worth every single penny.

As it drew to its close the series was producing something else . . . lots of interest from the national press. All the popular papers picked up the jaw-dropping human-interest story of the decline and fall of this soccer legend.

Now, that famous face was splashed over all the national sports sections and questions were being asked about how England's greatest goal scorer could possibly have suffered such a sensational fall from stardom to a police cell. It was as if the stories of his dark years had never been told before. They had, of course – that had been part of the shame – but they'd been published sporadically, one by one, so that the impact of the whole sad, sorry story had never been fully felt on Fleet Street. Now, a decade later, the national press interest was not cruel and prurient like before. This time it was sympathetic and considerate. Television and radio also picked up the story, locally, at first, then on the national networks.

Barrie Williams had known all along that *The Tommy Lawton Story* was a good 'un. But this? The reaction was incredible. After two or three months of continuing national interest, he and Tommy sat in his office, wading through a pile of national newspaper cuttings his librarians had put together: "Bloody hell, Tommy!" "Bloody hell, guv'nor!"

Later, Williams took a call from Brentford Football Club. It was from Eric White, the chairman of the Supporters' Club. They'd read the story in *The People* and wanted to put on a testimonial match for Tommy. "We can't believe that such a great player has suffered so much," said Eric, "and we want to do something for him." Brentford Football Club and Eric White got cracking.

Frank McLintock, the former Arsenal, Leicester City and Queens Park Rangers star was managing Brentford and he threw his full support into the plan. Yes, of course his team would turn out. And, yes, he would help Eric put together a team of All Stars from the London area for the testimonial match for which the date of May 20th 1985 had been chosen.

The first of those All Stars to agree was Gerry Francis, of Tottenham and QPR, former captain of England and an iconic midfield player in the 1970s. He agreed to captain the side. When news of the game reached Thames Television they produced a brilliant half-hour documentary contrasting Lawton's football fate with the fortunes of Francis and comparing, particularly, the difference in earnings between the two.

Gerry played a big part in putting the team together for the testimonial: Pat Jennings (Arsenal), Kevin Bond (Southampton), Micky Droy (Chelsea), Tommy Caton (Arsenal), Frank Lampard Senior (West Ham), Vince Hilaire (Crystal Palace), Gerry Francis, David Armstrong (Southampton), Ian Allinson (Arsenal), Alan Curtis (Swansea), Jimmy Case (Brighton).

Brentford were to line up: Gary Phillips, Denis Salman, Jamie Murray, Keith Millen, Steve Wignall, Terry Hurlock, Chris Kamara, Robbie Cooke, Bob Booker, Keth Cassells, Gary Roberts.

There was also to be a warm-up game of veteran ex-players from Brentford and Chelsea, including Franck McLintock, Andy McCulloch, Jim McNichol and the brilliant Stan Bowles. At centre forward for the

Chelsea side was one Tom Lawton of Leicester Tigers, who had promised that he'd try his best not to pick up the ball and run with it!

The London newspapers did a great job promoting the match, with a big spread about Tommy in the *Evening Standard*. And he was invited to appear live on *TVam* on the morning of the match, for a breakfast time interview with Jimmy Greaves. Barrie Williams had booked Tommy and Gay into a plush London hotel for two nights. His newspaper was picking up the bill and they were to spare no expense, he told them. It was a hotel with extra special memories for Mr and Mrs Lawton – thirty three years earlier they had spent their honeymoon night there. On *TVam,* Tommy was brilliant: relaxed, confident, articulate and funny.

The match programme featured a great front page picture of Tommy leading out Brentford in 1952 and inside, Eric White wrote:

This evening we honour one of the greatest players ever to wear an England shirt, Tommy Lawton. His stay here was brief, yet dramatic. Who can ever forget, for example, his brilliant back header against Aston Villa. In recent years, fate has not smiled in Tommy's direction but we hope to have a bumper turnout this evening so that Londoners can pay tribute to this great star from the past.

There was also a special tribute from Liverpool manager Bob Paisley:

Modern defenders look at old films of Tommy Lawton and think they would have stopped him scoring. No way. Tommy had a gift that comes along once in a century. He could head a ball at any angle or speed he wanted to. Unstoppable in the air and just as good on his feet. He would still be scoring thirty or more goals a season if he played today.

And so the scene was set. It was a balmy May night. There was a decent turnout by Londoners and they gave Tommy a standing ovation as he led out the two teams. Tommy looked immaculate in a smart new light grey suit, spotless white shirt, bright red tie and shoes polished to gleaming, *heels as well.* He had shed 20 years as he walked onto that pitch, his shoulders back, his chest out, his head high, raising both arms in the air to acknowledge the cheering crowd.

Barrie Williams watched this wonderful scene from the stand. And it was his turn to shed a tear.

As Tommy left the pitch, a long queue of people waited patiently for his autograph and among the avid signature hunters that night was the match referee Colin Downey, who had been at Griffin Park as a 10-year-old to witness Tommy's debut for Brentford.

Another fan had made a 200-mile round trip from Chepstow to see

Tommy, who had a special word of thanks for yet another, who had travelled from Langley in Buckinghamshire for a glimpse of 'the great man' despite having a broken foot in a heavy plaster cast.

Fans brought gifts galore for Tommy, including a splendid oil painting of him in his Chelsea kit and blown- up pictures of him as a teenage star at Everton. An elderly lady fan gave him a copper kettle and there was a lovely bouquet of flowers for Gay – courtesy of *The Guardian* newspaper.

Tommy had plenty of fans in the dressing rooms, too – where not one of the players even charged expenses to come and play for him. Their feelings were summed up by Northern Ireland goalkeeper Pat Jennings who said: "I volunteered for this match because there was nobody better than Tommy." And Frank McLintock added: "If Tommy had been playing today, he'd have been a millionaire. Nobody deserves more respect than him."

An overwhelmed Tommy told the gathering of press men: "Brentford was the club I did the least for in my career, yet look at how they've repaid me. I shall always remember this night. Londoners are the salt of the earth."

The wonderful Brentford tribute raised around £4,000 for Tommy – but what it did for his spirit was incalculable.

There was now a strong bond between the legendary soccer star and the newspaper editor. And when the series on the life and times of Tommy Lawton had run its successful course in his newspaper, Barrie Williams did not want it to end there. He offered Tommy a job as a soccer columnist on the *Post*. Tommy was delighted to accept and he wondered what Big Swifty would have thought because, many years earlier, his old pal had suggested that this was something at which he could be very good. Here was a lifeline: something at last with which to occupy those long, lonely days; something to give him pride and purpose and pleasure – not to mention a weekly fee of £120.

And it wasn't just the readers of the *Post* and the people of Nottingham who had rediscovered Tommy Lawton. Following all the national publicity his resurgence had generated, he was getting frequent invitations to attend top sporting events. Once again, he was treading the streets of London, a place so dear to his heart. Tommy Lawton, 65, was back on top.

The fortunes of football, however, had declined in direct proportion to those of Tommy. Gates were down; fans were disillusioned; the game had become stale and stereotyped and hooliganism was a desperately serious problem. The police, charged with the almost impossible task of keeping the hooligans under control, were employing riot techniques. Appalling armies of sadistic, snarling, spitting so-called 'supporters' were being herded, chanting obscenely, through towns and cities between ranks of mounted police. Hundreds of rival thugs, masquerading under the colours of the clubs whose names they sullied, were baiting each other outside railway stations, in city centres and on the perimeters of the football grounds, hurling missiles and disgusting abuse at each other over the thin blue lines of overstretched police officers trying to keep them apart. Often that line was breached and pitched bloody battles ensued. Terrifying violence was commonplace. All in the name of the 'beautiful game'.

High fences to cage the crowds, a sight which had so shocked Tommy and his teammates when they first saw them in Italy before the War, were now keeping thugs off the pitches in all the country's Football League grounds. Too many of those grounds were antiquated relics of the past with substandard conditions and the old-fashioned standing terraces, into which hooligans and decent spectators alike were packed, provided both the perfect terrain for the violence and the protection of anonymity for the perpetrators.

Ten days before Tommy's big day at Brentford, 56 supporters had died and 265 were injured when a ferocious fire destroyed the ancient stand at Bradford City's Valley Parade. A carelessly discarded cigarette end ignited accumulated rubbish under the old wooden stand and the consequences of the fierce blaze which followed were truly horrific. Most of the dead were children or elderly people who were crushed in the rush to flee the inferno. It was a terribly tragic afternoon which had started in happy celebration as Bradford City captain Peter Jackson was presented with the Third Division championship trophy.

Hooliganism played no part in the Bradford City fire disaster but, just nine days after Tommy's Brentford testimonial, there was another soccer disaster in which it did. The 1985 European Cup final between Liverpool and Juventus of Italy was being staged in the ageing Heysel Stadium in Brussels. An hour before kick-off, rival fans were taunting each other and that atmosphere of imminent violence which had become so familiar to football prevailed. A section of Liverpool supporters stormed an area containing Juventus fans and as the Italians tried to escape a wall collapsed. Thirty-nine spectators were killed and hundreds more were injured. In a decision which shocked the world, the game went on despite the tragedy because it was feared that abandonment would cause even more trouble. Juventus recorded a sickeningly hollow 1-0 victory. In the inevitably acrimonious aftermath, UEFA immediately banned all English clubs from European football.

Tommy Lawton, soccer columnist, was not short of subject matter. And Big Swifty was being proved right. Tommy's weekly column, titled

Lawton's Law, was an immediate success with readers. It was, like the man himself had been in his prime, fearless, forthright and feisty. He immediately championed the cause of the working-class spectators who were football's lifeblood, campaigning vehemently for some of the many millions of pounds that were still coming into football, despite its many ills, to be reinvested in improving conditions for them.

He had been calling for all-seater stadia when nobody wanted to listen to him. Now he had a powerful platform from which to state his case. And he did so with great passion. He was appalled by the moral injustice of directors and hangers-on sitting comfortably in heated seats in their boxes and enjoying the posh corporate executive facilities while the real fans were kept in squalor. If you treat people like wild animals, they will behave like wild animals, he argued. Take down the fences, have them all sitting down and the thugs among them would lose the protection of anonymity which thrived in those packed terraces; the police would then have easier access to the hooligans and the decent spectators, who just wanted to enjoy the match, would help the police to sort them out until they became a manageable minority.

It was, like all Tommy Lawton's opinions on the game he loved, a solution that was way ahead of its time. In stark contrast, one of his columns suggested a 'back to the future' approach that provoked a flood of readers' letters, many against but a clear majority in favour. He wrote:

The 'old-fashioned' way is the only cure for our ailing modern football. To lure back the missing millions, to master the defensive systems that have spoilt the game as a spectacle, we have got to revert to the 2-3-5 line-ups of my day. Two fullbacks, three halfbacks, five forwards.

It would take ten years for the seed to flower into full blossom again and the young lads at school would have to learn the basics, but it would prevent football from withering away.

Every match is the same today. Stereotyped. Lacking in unorthodoxy and personalities.

I accept that the big money handed out to players is a factor but cash was a dangling carrot in my day, too. Your £2 win bonus would buy the groceries for a week, so it was an immensely attractive incentive!

At just after three o'clock on a Saturday afternoon, I see the ball pushed back, squared here and squared there. Seldom a through pass, seldom a switched ball with a player running towards the right touchline and cutting it back to the outside left. That was what I call an 'Alex James pass'. The Arsenal and Scotland master craftsman specialised in the cross-field ball that split the opposing defence wide open, with a really fast winger, like the Gunners' Joe Hulme, running onto it.

I have this lovely vision of watching an England team lining up old-style against Continental or South American opponents. Before they got over the shock, we'd be two goals in front.

I don't care what today's so-called geniuses believe. The only way to beat the rest of the world is from your own half of the field, through moves like the 'Alex James pass'.

No wonder the once soccer-crazed public have become disenchanted by the lack of wingers. You can't go through defences, you can't dig underneath them with a spade and come up on the other side. The only way is to have wingers going round the back of defences.

Sir Alf Ramsey, manager of England's 1966 World Cup-winning side, has rightly taken a lot of stick for his scant regard for wingers. He won the World Cup on his own 'midden', Wembley, at the expense of British soccer. His predecessor as England manager, Walter Winterbottom, was the initiator of negative attitudes with his coaching methods, but Ramsey carried it on to an extreme.

The old-timers who could make a football 'talk' must be turning in their graves at the sight of the game today; at the lack of personality players, of characters. Even at school – and there's one a goal kick away from my home – an individual isn't allowed to express himself without getting a blast from his schoolteacher. How relieved I am that no such inhibitions existed in my own early years.

For me, one of the most damning indictments of the modern game is watching a centre forward clearing the ball off his own goal line. Had I done that my defenders, after they'd got over the shock, would have delivered a well deserved kick at my backside and told me that my business was not in my own penalty area. They would have told me to get upfield and do my own job – scoring goals.

Football suffers acutely because people can now watch the game on television. Almost invariably, the football coverage consists of highlights. If your face fits, they show the best of you. Certainly the face of England and Manchester United captain Bryan Robson fits. British journalists and TV pundits go overboard about him. They enthuse over his 'world-class' status. Bryan is a very good player, yes. Great? Never. The widespread view that he is merely mirrors the poor standard of our game and in my day, the public wouldn't have been so easily kidded because they could only form their opinions of players by seeing them in the flesh, for a full 90 minutes.

The other Robson, manager Bobby, doesn't impress me, either. He seems to lack the ability to make up his own mind. I could have cried when he declared, after the unconvincing 1-0 win over Northern Ireland, that he had decided to open up a school "to find two wingers". Robson should have been thinking that way before he took up his Lancaster Gate appointment in September 1982 and if he really wanted a lead he could have taken it from Watford manager Graham Taylor in 1982/83. We have as much chance of winning the World Cup with Robson's ideas in general as I have of playing in the next FA Cup final at Wembley – and I'll be in my 66th year by then!

Today's hierarchy will point to that age as a sign that I don't know what the modern game's all about, that it's different. I'll tell you how it's different. It's different because you've got more managers, more coaches, more blackboards; too many people telling players how to play.

Don't run away with the idea, though, that I am resolutely against coaching. Up to a point, it is a very good thing. Improve your weaknesses, strengthen your strengths. That's my coaching maxim. What I am against is coaching that says 'You will do as I say' and 'This is the way you've got to do it at 3:15, then like this at 3:30 and like this at 3:40.'

No doubt jealousy will be an accusation levelled against me. But from the bottom of my heart, I want this tiny island of ours to win everything in sight. Nobody would be more proud and pleased if we did.

Lawton's Law didn't pull its punches. And Tommy now lived for the two or three days a week that he'd hop on the bus and head for the *Nottingham Evening Post* offices to prepare his columns with the lads on the sports desk. When the pressure of deadlines was off, he loved to sit and talk to those lads, Trevor Frecknall, John Lucy, Nick Lucy, Mick Holland, Duncan Hamilton, David McVay (who shared with Tommy the experience of having been a Notts County player: David was a talented fullback in the mid 1970s side).

Those lads were all real pals now, just like his old teammates in his playing days. There was comradeship and togetherness. Those lads all loved Tommy – as did every female in the office. The old charmer had lost none of his knack with the ladies. Then there were the days he got to chew the fat with the genial Harry Adamson, one of his Notts County teammates from 1949, who worked in the newspaper's maintenance department. Then, the many functions and special occasions to which he was being invited as a star guest, often with Gay at his side.

Tommy Lawton was happier now than he had been for as long as he could remember. He told the editor one day, "Guv'nor, you've no idea how much you've done for me." "Bollocks, Tommy," said the editor. "It's not even half as much as you've done for my newspaper."

So, the good life continued for the reborn Tommy and Gay, and Tommy never ceased to express his gratitude to the editor. Sometimes, when he'd been presented with mementoes at functions, he would sneak into Barrie Williams's office when he was out and leave them on his desk – a gift, "with thanks from Tommy".

Gifts like a beautiful cut glass goblet with the inscription: "Presented by the Variety Club of Great Britain to a Living Legend – 15.12.1986" which he'd received at a posh black tie dinner in Manchester. Gifts like a set of exquisite porcelain figures of an 'All Time Greats XI' from the 'Golden Years', perfect replicas of each player in his club colours: Frank Swift; Johnny Carey, Eddie Hapgood; Danny Blanchflower, Neil Franklin, Joe Mercer; Stan Matthews, Wilf Mannion, Tommy Lawton, Raich Carter, Tom Finney. This superb limited edition collection, mounted on a solid, polished wood stand, was crafted after a star-studded collection of soccer stars, all born before the Second World War, were gathered together at Old Trafford to select their 'All Time Greats XI' from the years between 1920 and 1970. Those making the choice included Tommy Lawton, Gordon Banks, Neil Franklin, Raich Carter, Stan Mortensen, Danny Blanchflower, John Charles, Stanley Matthews, Tom Finney, Johnny Carey, Cliff Jones, Ray Wilson, Billy Liddell and Joe Mercer. They were not, of course, allowed to vote for themselves. When the results were pooled, Lawton was the majority choice at centre forward over players including Dixie Dean, Jackie Milburn and Nat Lofthouse. Bobby Charlton only made substitute, along with John Charles!

Whenever one of these gifts appeared on his desk, Barrie Williams sought out the persistent benefactor and implored him to take them back but that famous Lawton stubborn streak kicked in and he resolutely refused to do so: "Tommy, for heaven's sake. This is yours. I can't take it." "It's for you, guv'nor. It's the only way I can thank you."

For his part, the editor was delighted to see Tommy, of whom he had now grown so fond, back on his feet, enjoying life to the full. When, frequently, he put tables of guests together for sporting functions in Nottingham, Tommy's was always the first name on his list. On one such occasion, a black-tie do at Nottingham Forest's Jubilee Club, the star speaker was Brian Clough. When he got to his feet to speak, Clough asked his packed audience a rhetorical question: "Gentlemen, I was a pretty good centre forward, yes?"

When the audience shouted its agreement with this typically immodest assertion, Clough went on: "But there's a man here tonight who was better than me. Much, much better than me. I've just spotted him, over there on Barrie Williams's table. It's Tommy Lawton." As the audience applauded, Clough beckoned over to Tommy: "Come on, Tommy lad. Come up here with me." Tommy walked, chest out, shoulders back, to the top table and stood alongside Brian Clough who grabbed his arm and raised it, like a boxing referee saluting the winner, shouting: "Gentlemen, Tommy Lawton." When the audience stood to give an ovation to Tommy, Clough planted a kiss on his cheek and told him, "You were the best, man."

Tommy rated Brian Clough so highly that this was the greatest tribute he could possibly have been paid. He walked back to his table, stopping to shake eagerly outstretched hands, feeling ten feet tall.

There were tributes paid to him over the river at Meadow Lane, too, where he was invited to officially open the new Lawton Bar. As Tommy stood behind the bar, pulling the first pint, Notts County director John Mounteney, a warm, kindly man who had watched Lawton play for Notts as a lad, sang the ditty from the Kids' Pen of those days:

Put another ninepence in,
In Notts County's turnstile tin,
All we want is Notts to win,
And Lawton, Lawton, Lawton.

The opening of a bar named in his honour was a very cordial occasion, in contrast to an earlier episode when John had invited his boyhood hero as his guest into the old Notts boardroom. Frank Sherwood, the local farmer who was on the board that sacked Lawton and was now a life president, was also there and had not been best pleased when Tommy, having enjoyed a snifter or three, banged repeatedly on the wood panels and shouted, "Come on Mr Sherwood. Where's all the cash I earned for this club hidden?!"

Tommy Lawton's resurgence was described beautifully by top sports writer Patrick Collins who, in an article in *The Mail on Sunday* on 20th December 1987, wrote:

The old gentleman sat in his living room, reached for his spectacles and stared at the letter in his hand. And although he was smiling, the tears were uncomfortably close.

"Look at that," said Tommy Lawton. Complete stranger, lives

in New York, he's just sent me a cheque for a hundred dollars. He says I was very kind when I signed an autograph for him at Ipswich. In 1943."

The past has a habit of creeping back to the sturdy little house on the edge of Nottingham, especially at this time of year. It was in this month, more than half a century ago, that young Lawton signed a form which made him the most expensive 17-year-old footballer in the game's history.

Burnley, the club which discovered him, saved themselves from bankruptcy with their staggering fee of £6,500. And for their money, Everton acquired the finest centre forward that British football has ever been able to offer.

Even now, at the age of 68, he seems to have stepped from one of the cigarette cards of youth: hair Brylcreemed black as jet with its parting dug in a deep channel through the middle of his scalp, the way centre forwards ought to look. And as he settles by the fire, he recalls the day of that famous transfer with entrancing clarity.

After describing Lawton's early days at Burnley and Everton and the 'sadistic' training routines of Ray Bennion, Patrick Collins's article continued:

The enduring impression of Lawton is of a 13-stone striker leaping high above defenders to thump terrifying headers. He faintly resents the image. "I could play on the deck as well," he insists. "I got twice as many goals with my feet. Stands to reason, doesn't it? I've got one head and two feet."

By head or by feet, the goals came in droves. At 19, he was a full international and scoring the winner against Scotland: "There were 154,000 people at Hampden and me mam and me granddad were the only people cheering," he says.

He scored four against the Scots in a wartime international, four more against the Dutch in 1946 and a further four against Portugal in Lisbon when England won 10-0 and fielded the mouth-watering forward line of Matthews, Mortensen, Lawton, Mannion and Finney.

"I loved every second of it," he says. "Fit as a flea, scoring goals, playing with the best. I were a bit mean, too. Anything around the box was mine and I didn't care who was in the way. I'd have been sent off today, the way I clattered goalkeepers. But in those days, the likes of big Frank Swift and Sam Bartram would clatter you right back.

"I travelled the world for nowt, elite class: planes, boats, trains, the lot. And I never gave money a thought. It never seemed important."

That attitude did not survive his retirement in the mid-1950s. As a player, he had lived at the summit and revelled in his gifts. As a civilian, he was ill-prepared to negotiate the financial and business minefields which more mundane men take in their stride.

He touched rock bottom. The rent and rates were a constant struggle, the fuel bills were an embarrassment and social security was his lifeline. His chief consolation lay in the devoted support of his wife Gay, in whose eyes he had never been less than a hero.

After describing the circumstances of Tommy's revival, Patrick Collins went on:

The Post then offered him a job, commenting on the modern game and he took it with the grateful glee of a child on Christmas morning. "Three days a week I take the bus into Nottingham and write me bits and pieces then on Saturdays I go and watch Forest or County," he says.

"I don't push myself forward. I give an opinion only when I'm asked and sometimes I see a few of the old lads and we have a few laughs. I'm back in the game I love. Gay says it's like I've been reborn and she's dead right.

"I don't envy the lads who play today, mind. Sure, the money's gone daft but that's not their fault. If somebody offers them £2,000 a week, they'd be mad to turn it down. I don't know if they really appreciate it all, though. They don't look as if they're enjoying themselves the way we used to.

"Still, I could be wrong. I mean, who wouldn't enjoy himself playing football? There's nothing better in all the world, is there? Never has been."

It promises to be the happiest Christmas for the Lawtons. Gay is making a fine recovery from an operation, the work is going well and Forest are providing splendid entertainment in their little patch of Nottingham. For all his 68 years, there's a bounce in Tommy's step as he guides his visitor to the front gate.

The taxi driver winds down his window and does a theatrical double-take. "That's Tommy Lawton," he says. "Bloody hell. Tommy Lawton! I saw him when I was a kid. D'you know, he could head the ball harder than some of these modern fellers can kick it."

Lawton was waving farewell as the cab turned the corner of the road. The driver glanced in his mirror. "Tommy Lawton," he said almost to himself. "Wait till I tell my lad who I've seen today."

On March 26th, 1988 Tommy was interviewed by John Motson on BBC TV's *Football Focus*. He spoke eloquently about how much he had enjoyed all of his playing career but said that his experience as a manager with Notts County had been "a disaster."

He told Motson: " I could have stayed in the game, but I thought: 'If that's what football thinks of me, I don't want any part of it.' The offer of a job as a *Nottingham Evening Post* columnist rescued me from the hard times and put my faith back in the game. It's only just lately, these last few years, and thanks to the *Nottingham Evening Post* who've given me a new lease of life, that I've become involved in football again."

Soon after that, Barrie Williams was asked by his brother Les if he could provide a soccer star for a special occasion. Les Williams, a very good local footballer who had been on Shrewsbury Town's books, was a member of a committee which ran the Graham Edwards Memorial Fund. This was a fund set up in aid of leukaemia research to honour another fine young local footballer who had died from the disease. Every year, teams from villages around the Shropshire-Wales border competed for the Graham Edwards Trophy and every year, the fund committee made the final a bumper affair to raise as much cash as possible. Barrie Williams suggested to his brother that they might like Tommy Lawton to do the honour of presenting the trophy and medals. Les and the committee were thrilled. Tommy was delighted to help.

Early on the Sunday morning of the match, Barrie and Pauline Williams picked up Tommy and Gay at Patterdale Road to drive to Shropshire. Gay had been suffering from stomach problems but she was recovered, she thought. The following week, she was to go for tests to confirm that, or otherwise. Gay was in a happy mood. Barrie and Pauline had thought her, from previous acquaintance, to be quite difficult: very defensive, abrasive and a bit too inclined to remind people of her wealthy past, but they had never spent that much time in her company. Today, they were to spend many hours with her.

As the four of them journeyed to Shropshire, the editor and his wife began to get a very different impression of Gay. Relaxed, she was enjoyable and amusing company. Tommy, too, was intent on enjoying the day to the full. A good time was going to be had by all. They stopped, *en route*, for a traditional Sunday lunch at a posh hotel just outside Shrewsbury and the party was greatly amused when Pauline found a dead wasp in her gravy. An extremely apologetic head waiter offered a free bottle of wine as compensation for the deceased wasp and this was graciously accepted.

A few minutes later, Tommy, straight-faced, summoned the head waiter, who was hovering anxiously, clearly upset that his hotel's extremely high standards had slipped sufficiently to allow a wasp, dead or otherwise, to inhabit the gravy: "Yes, sir, what can I do for you?" he asked Tommy. "There are *12* wasps in *my* gravy. Do I get a dozen bottles?" His gravy was, of course, entirely insect-free but even the head waiter appreciated the practical joke and immediately ceased his anxious hovering.

Next stop was at Oswestry, the home of Barrie Williams's parents, so that his mum and dad could meet their Everton legend. They were thrilled to bits.

When they got to the football ground at Gobowen, venue for the Graham Edwards Trophy final, Tommy's appearance had boosted the gate and when he got out of the car he was immediately surrounded by autograph hunters.

The four VIPs from Nottingham sat on the touchline, watching a good, competitive game of village football and Tommy was enjoying every minute. Then after half an hour, the heavens opened and the rain fell like it can in and around Wales – in torrents. They retired to the club house to watch the rest of the match and the frequency with which Tommy cleared the condensation from the big double windows proved that his apparent absorption in the game was not affected. As the game headed for the final whistle, a youth of agricultural appearance and low alcohol tolerance, bellowed across the club house, "'Ave some of this!" dropped his trousers in front of the VIPs and displayed his credentials. Gay, as quick as the flash itself, told the lad, "Oh, you poor boy. Is that the best you can do?!" When the offender had been removed by acutely embarrassed committee members, they apologised profusely but the laughter with which the four visitors from Nottingham were still rocking showed that no apology was necessary. Tommy did the presentation honours with aplomb, preceded by a nice little speech and Gay was presented with an enormous bouquet of beautiful blooms, with a 'lovely card thanking 'Mrs Lawton for her generous support of the event'. Gay received the bouquet and the sentiments graciously, with obviously genuine pleasure and gratitude.

On the drive home, interrupted for an extremely pleasant light dinner, Tommy, Gay, Barrie and Pauline chatted and joked constantly. There was not so much as one break in the conversation and they laughed and laughed, with nobody contributing more to the mirth than Gay. The Gay they dropped back home with Tommy was an entirely different woman to the one they had expected to spend the day with and it had been a most pleasant surprise. Williams concluded that the hard face Gay always wore in public, leading many people to think her not very likeable, was just a veneer built up layer upon layer, as she battled the ravages of those dark years with Tommy and fought to protect her husband from a world which had turned so cruelly against him. That weekend, the real Gay had emerged, the one Tommy knew and loved to bits. And for the first time they understood why he did.

Gay's medical tests brought the worst news imaginable. She had cancer of the pancreas. Surgeons operated and carried out a bypass. Tom Junior asked the specialist, "What will this do for her?" The specialist told him, "It should give her an extra six to eight months."

Gay went home to spend those months in the care of her husband. Tommy nursed her like a baby. He had to. That beautiful, strong, dominant lady had wasted to a tiny skeletal shadow weighing only four stones when she died, two days after her 67th birthday. Tommy was absolutely grief-stricken.

The funeral, in a Roman Catholic church, was a very quiet affair. Williams was annoyed at the brief and superficial soliloquy from the priest, the main point of which appeared to be that Gay was a lapsed Catholic. He thought she deserved so much more than that. At the back of the sparsely populated church a well-dressed man sat entirely alone, speaking to no one. He disappeared immediately at the end of the service. Tom Junior identified him as Gay's brother – a member of the family which had ostracised her completely for the rest of her life when she divorced Rex Rose. How sadly ironic that they could never forgive her while Rex could.

There were no flowers, by request, at the funeral but on Gay's coffin lay one solitary red rose. It was from Tommy. And it said it all.

Gay's death hit Tommy really badly. For a while he became reclusive, locked away in that tired old house, alone with his thoughts. Gradually, with gentle encouragement, he emerged. He got back in touch with the lads on the sports desk at the *Post* and resumed those punchy columns. But he never got over the loss of the love of his life, the wife who'd been such a rock for him through the dark years when it would have been so much easier for her to walk out on him: "And, God knows, I couldn't have complained if she had."

Back, thundering out his outspoken *Lawton's Law,* Tommy constantly drew attention to the way ordinary supporters, or real supporters, as he called them, were being treated at football grounds. No one denied the need for strict, heavy policing to beat the hooligans but, Tommy argued, the baby had been thrown out with the bathwater and decent people were being treated worse than cattle. This had to stop, he said. He was ashamed that football, his game, was treating its supporters like this. It was a view that was proved to be tragically correct by the events of 15th April 1989 with a disaster which, for the people of Nottingham, was very close to home.

Brian Clough's brilliant young Nottingham Forest team were playing Liverpool in the semi-final of the FA Cup at Sheffield Wednesday's Hillsborough Stadium. At ten minutes to three, it was a wonderful scene: a beautiful spring afternoon, with bright sunshine beaming down from clear blue skies onto the lush green turf. This was the quintessential English Saturday afternoon, the sort that football was made for. The packed stadium, alive with the tingling anticipation that only football can engender, echoed to the singing, cheering and chanting of thousands of excited fans. But half an hour after kick-off that scene had turned to one of sheer horror. The stadium no longer echoed to singing, cheering and chanting but to the chilling wails of sirens, to screams of pain and cries of anguish. The pitch, so perfect for a great game of football, had become a killing field, littered with dead bodies; many more lay injured, limbs broken, heads bleeding, throats choking.

Thousands of Liverpool fans, still outside the ground after the match had kicked off, had surged into Hillsborough's Leppings Lane Stand after police had opened a set of gates to ease a dangerous crush. The human stampede of supporters into the stand caused a much more severe crush and the consequences were horrendous. Unable to escape because of the hooligan-proof cages which contained them, men, women and children were crushed to death where they stood. Ninety-six people were killed and nearly 800 injured, many of them very badly. The emotional scars on hundreds more who survived the crush and thousands who witnessed the carnage were incalculable. Recriminations were rife, with most people blaming mismanagement by the police but some making allegations about the conduct of Liverpool fans.

A full public inquiry would look into all that later but on the night of that tragedy, one stark and horrifying truth was already incontrovertible: it would not have happened if the ordinary supporters, Tommy Lawton's real supporters – the vast majority of whom were just decent, well-behaved fans – had not been caged like dangerous animals in a zoo. And Tommy Lawton, respected football columnist, was saying so in no uncertain terms.

Tommy's job at the *Nottingham Evening Post* continued to be his lifeline: his trips to those huge offices in Nottingham city centre were his reason for being; his friends at the *Post* were like family to him, but being home alone without his beloved Gay was desperately hard for him. Neighbours at Patterdale Road were very kind, helping with his laundry and meals on wheels were arranged, but by mid-1989 it was becoming obvious that he wasn't coping at all well. He began to lose weight, to look a bit frail.

Late one evening in September, Barrie Williams rang Tom Junior, who now lived in London, to share his concerns about his dad. They agreed to think things through. But what to do? Tommy didn't want to leave Patterdale Road because that old house was his last link with Gay. Moving to London was not an option; Tom Junior had embarked on a new career, establishing a training company for banking that involved travelling the world and his marriage was in difficulties (like his father, he had married young and, time was telling, he and his wife had little in common).

Then, just as the two men were discussing the problem, fate took over and the matter was taken out of their hands. Tommy tripped over the carpet, fell and broke his hip. He was found by neighbours and taken to Nottingham's Queens Medical Centre. When Barrie and Pauline Williams went to visit him in that vast hospital, they were taken aback to find he was not on the ward they'd been told he was on and the staff didn't know where he was. "What did you say his name was?" Williams was asked. "Lawton, was it? Tommy Lawton?"

"Bloody hell," exclaimed Williams, "I know this is a big place but how can you lose England's greatest centre forward?!" Eventually, they located Tommy on another ward and when they told him of the difficulty they'd had in so doing, he laughed: "There's quite a few people who'd have liked me to get lost over the years. But this lot actually did it!"

Tom Junior and Carol convened a meeting at the Queens Medical Centre to discuss where Tommy was going to live when he came out of hospital. Tommy had been befriended by a social worker, who was also called Tommy. (His dad was a lifelong Notts County fan and he named his son after a certain centre forward!) He attended the meeting and suggested they contact the Abbeyfield Society.

Abbeyfield, a not-for-profit organisation dedicated to making the lives of older people easier and more fulfilling, had more than 500 houses and care homes across the UK, including one at Bakersfield, Nottingham. Tom and Carol liked what they heard about Abbeyfield, with its resolve to help its residents live independently. Their dad had made it perfectly clear to them that he "wasn't ready for the knackers' yard" and they knew that the independence Abbeyfield offered would be just right for him.

But would he be just right for them?

On a Saturday morning early in December, Tom Junior drove his father to a meeting with the local Abbeyfield committee. That famous Tommy Lawton charm worked again and a place in the Bakersfield home was made available for him. Here, Tommy had his own self-contained flat but constant care. Abbeyfield was run by a lovely lady called Irene who treated Tommy like one of her own family. He was very happy at Abbeyfield and while he never recovered the robust good health he enjoyed before Gay's death, he was looking much better: back on his feet, albeit with the aid of two walking sticks. That incapacity didn't stop him from getting a bus and making his three trips a week to the *Post,* where *Lawton's Law* still graced the sports pages and all his friends still greeted him so affectionately.

When editor Williams ran a campaign he called 'Old and Cold', which exposed the scandal of many old folk dying from hypothermia because they couldn't afford to keep warm, the *Post* came up with a great idea to raise money for the paper's resultant Old and Cold Fund. A *Nottingham Evening Post* roadshow would be taken around the vibrant working men's club circuit featuring good bands and comedians. A highlight of the shows would be a quiz based on the contents of the previous week's newspapers and the *Post's* top names would be there to meet and greet the readers. All the proceeds from ticket sales would go to the Old and Cold Fund. Like all Bob Britten's ideas it was a belter. The readers loved the twice-weekly shows, they were raising lots of money for the fund and the most popular personality on the *Post* team was Tommy Lawton. Tommy, who never missed a show, signed hundreds of autographs and chatted happily with them all. The number of football fans who not only claimed to have seen him score *that goal* against Forest but described it in every detail was truly amazing and Tommy loved reliving it for them . . . "Get in there!"

On the evening of one of these shows, the weather turned brutal. It was freezing cold, there was a biting east wind and snow was falling heavily. Fortunately, it would take more than that to stop the big-hearted folk of the working men's clubs from supporting a good cause, but Williams was hoping Tommy Lawton would stay indoors and when he hadn't arrived for the start of the show, he was relieved. He should have known better. The charity evening had been going for half an hour when a bedraggled figure on sticks hobbled through the club doors, thick white snowflakes on his jet black hair, face almost blue with cold.

"Tommy! What the hell are you doing coming out on a night like this?"

"Guv'nor, I'm old, I'm cold and I'm 'ere so just get me a pint and stop fussing."

Tommy sat down with his pint and was immediately besieged by autograph hunters. "Bad night?" he told them. "We used to play in worse than this!"

Every week for the next five years, Tommy Lawton carried on writing *Lawton's Law*: three days a week he caught the bus to the *Post* office.

Rain, hail, snow – nothing could keep him away from that sports desk and his columns were as good as ever. Back at Abbeyfield, Irene and her staff continued to treat 'Our Tommy' like a king. Tom Junior had been so determined to find the right care home for his intensely proud old man and what a great choice he'd made.

But, well though he looked, Tommy was obviously getting older by the year and there was one last piece of the jigsaw of his resurgence with which editor Williams wanted to complete the picture of this exceptional man. He had thought, ever since the *Post* serialised Tommy's life story that this would make a brilliant piece of cinema, TV film or theatre drama. "You couldn't make a story like Tommy's up," he would say to Pauline and he wondered about trying to contact David Puttnam, whose *Chariots of Fire,* his brilliant film based on the story of two young British sprinters competing in the 1924 Olympic Games, had been a massive worldwide success. One night, as they watched television together, Pauline exclaimed, "Robert Lindsay! Now, he'd make a fantastic Tommy." 'How right she was,' thought Williams.

Robert Lindsay, such a fine actor. He'd appeared in BBC TV Shakespeare productions such as *Much Ado About Nothing,* in which he played Benedick and *King Lear,* in which he played Edmund opposite Lord Olivier. But he was best known and much loved for his role as Wolfie Smith, the hilariously incompetent revolutionary leader of the Tooting People's Front in the BBC's smash hit TV sitcom *Citizen Smith*. He could play Tommy Lawton brilliantly and better still, Robert Lindsay was a local lad, born and brought up just down the road from them at Ilkeston, where his mum and dad still lived.

The next day, Williams wrote a letter to Robert Lindsay, setting out his idea, enclosing cuttings of the story and asking the star actor if he might be interested in it. He mentioned, in passing, that he lived at Trowell, just a few minutes from Robert's parents. Several weeks later there had been no response from Lindsay and Williams had figured there never would be. Then, early one Saturday morning, as he and Pauline sipped coffee at home, a panting man in overalls appeared at their breakfast table. It was Reg, a local plumber, who was working at their house: "It's him. It's him!" gasped Reg. "That Wolfie Smith off the telly. He's at the front door, asking for you!"

Williams went to the door to find Robert Lindsay, smartly dressed in a suit and expensive overcoat: "Hi, you must be Barrie," he said. "I'm Robert Lindsay. D'you know, I've often wondered what your house looks like from the inside. I used to come scrumping in your orchard when I was a lad. How are you?" "Much the better for seeing you," Williams told him and Robert replied, "Obviously what I've really come for is to talk to you about Tommy Lawton. I think your idea is very interesting. My dad was *always* talking about Tommy Lawton when I was a boy. He was a huge star, wasn't he? Tell me more."

Half an hour later, Robert Lindsay was in the front seat of Barrie Williams's Jaguar being driven to Bakersfield to meet Tommy Lawton. Tommy opened the door of his little flat with a beaming smile: "Robert, I think you're absolutely brilliant," he said, shaking Lindsay's hand. "Hey. You weren't so bad yourself, Tommy," said Robert, "and it's a real honour for me to meet you."

Inside, Tommy had laid out all his newspaper cuttings and old photographs. There were no mementoes left to show Robert (he preferred to forget how he'd sold all those during the dark years), but there were some wonderful pictures, so evocative of the periods of his prime. Robert loved those old pictures, particularly one of Tommy with Lupino Lane, the original star of *Me and My Girl*. Robert himself had starred in a tremendously successful West End and Broadway revival of that wonderful old musical and his fabulous *Lambeth Walk* stopped every show. Lindsay, the star of current stage and screen and Lawton, the star of football's bygone age, were getting on so well that three hours later, they were still deep in conversation. Robert, himself a football fan, was clearly captivated by Tommy, his dad's big hero, and for Tommy that warm, positive feeling of respect and admiration was obviously mutual.

As they drove back, Robert Lindsay enthused to Williams about the possibility of a Tommy Lawton project and kept reciting Tommy's unique little phrases in an uncannily accurate impression. He said, "I see it as a one-man show with music and old newsreels. I think it can be very good indeed. I'll talk to Alan Bleasdale about writing it. He's football mad. He'll like it, I'm sure." After insisting on calling back at the house to thank Pauline for the coffee she'd given him earlier, Robert took his leave: "I'll definitely be in touch," he said.

"What a lovely man," said Pauline. And that was a view shared by Tommy when Williams rang to tell him of Lindsay's enthusiasm. "That was one of the nicest blokes I've ever met," he said. Much later, the editor had heard nothing from Robert Lindsay but he came out of a board meeting one day to find a message had been left with his secretary: "Please tell Barrie I'm still interested in the Tommy Lawton idea and I'm sorry I haven't been in touch, but if he watches Channel 4 on Friday night, he'll see why."

On Channel 4 that Friday night was the first episode of *GBH*, a groundbreaking new drama series written by Alan Bleasdale about corruption in local government. It became hugely successful and highly controversial.

Robert Lindsay was sensational in *GBH* in the leading role of a corrupt politician who eventually got his comeuppance. He won a BAFTA for his performance and was now more in demand than ever.

Despite being incredibly busy, Robert Lindsay still found time to leave another message for Barrie Williams: "Please tell him, I haven't forgotten about the Tommy Lawton proposal but I'm now committed to a London run of *Henry IV*."

And so it continued for Robert Lindsay. He'd been a big star when he'd first met Tommy Lawton. Now he was huge, with one massive TV or theatre role following another. Tommy and the editor were disappointed but understood fully and both were so pleased for such a genuinely nice man they felt privileged to have met. But this was not getting the Tommy Lawton story onto stage and screen and Williams wanted so much to complete that jigsaw and get one last big payday for his mate Tommy, so he wrote to Bill Kenwright, late of *Coronation Street* (in which he played Betty Turpin's son), now a massively successful theatre impresario and better still, the chairman of Everton Football Club. Bill Kenwright rang within a couple of days: "This is interesting. Have you got a writer?" "No," said Williams. "Well, get one then come and see me."

As it happened, Williams knew a very fine young writer. Billy Ivory (the son of a Nottingham journalist, Bill Ivory, who had worked with Williams as news editor and assistant editor of the *Post*) was very highly rated. Young as he was, Billy already had a hit TV comedy drama series, about the exploits of a crew of bin men, to his credit. Despite its unconventional subject matter, *Common As Muck,* starring Edward Woodward, Roy Hudd and Tim Healy, was critically acclaimed for the quality of its writing. Better still, Billy was an avid Notts County fan. Was he interested? "Tommy Lawton? You bet I am!"

Williams and young Ivory went to see Bill Kenwright in his palatial London office. When told that Robert Lindsay had seen the Tommy Lawton story as a one man show with music, Kenwright turned to Billy Ivory and asked him rhetorically, "That's not the way you see it, is it son?" This was a stage play, Bill Kenwright decreed, and he told Billy Ivory to go and write it.

"Great. Job done at last," thought Williams as he went to tell Tommy all about the latest idea. Weeks later, the editor had a visit from Billy Ivory. He was concerned that Tommy didn't seem enthusiastic "I can't get him to talk freely. He just doesn't seem to relax with me," said Billy. "I'll have a word," said Williams, but when he raised the subject with Tommy, he simply smiled. No answer came. Then it dawned on Williams: "I know what it is, you stubborn bugger! You feel that you've promised it to Robert

Lindsay, don't you? But Robert has got far too much on and we've got to get on with it."

Tommy accepted this assessment from the 'guv'nor', sat down with Billy Ivory and carried on with the project but, just as had happened with Robert Lindsay, the exceptionally talented young writer then achieved success after success and became incredibly busy himself, so the *Tommy Lawton Story* hadn't quite made it on to stage or screen after all.

"But," the editor told Tommy over a pint one night, "I'm sure that one day it will, mate."

On Grand National Day in April 1990, Tom Junior was assembling new wardrobes for his dad in Tommy's flat when he broke the news that history had repeated itself . . . he, too, had fallen for a fantastic pair of legs, belonging to a lovely girl called Gillian and he was getting a divorce. Tommy warned his son to be sure that this time, he was choosing the right girl, as he had done with Gay and he told young Tom: "I'm very happy for you." To celebrate, the pair put £20 each way on a horse called Mr Fisk in the Grand National. Their day was complete when Mr Fisk won at 20-1!

That summer saw Tommy Lawton, along with millions of others, cheering on England in the World Cup being played in Italy. Under manager Bobby Robson, England had a very good, settled side and there was a strong belief that this could be the year they finally matched the great achievement of 1966. That optimism looked justified when England made it through to a semi-final against . . . Germany!

Tommy settled in front of his TV to watch what turned out to be one of the best World Cup semi-finals of all time. This England team – Peter Shilton, Paul Parker, Stuart Pearce, Des Walker, Terry Butcher, Mark Wright, David Platt, Chris Waddle, Paul Gascoigne, Peter Beardsley, Gary Lineker – was in fine form with Lineker and the massively talented, if temperamental, Gascoigne particularly impressive.

After an hour of a pulsating match, Germany won a free kick in a central position just outside the England box. The ball was knocked short to Andreas Brehme whose shot took a wicked deflection off Paul Parker, then looped up and over Peter Shilton into the net. The serenity of the sedate Abbeyfield Home for the elderly was shattered by the howl of protest from the flat of one of its residents: "Fluke! Fluke! Jammy German buggers!"

Twenty minutes later, Gary Lineker equalised for England. The serenity of the sedate Abbeyfield Home for the elderly was again shattered, this time by the crashing of two walking sticks against the ceiling of the flat of one its residents and a bellowing shout: "Get in there!"

At full-time, the score remained 1-1. Millions of people all over the country sat on the edge of their seats, Tommy Lawton among them, as the game went into extra time. Both sides went flat out for the winner; Paul Gascoigne was booked and shed the tears that made that moment ironic. But the sides could not be separated and it all came down to the drama of penalties. With the scores at 4-3, after Stuart Pearce's effort had been saved, Chris Waddle was left with the task of keeping English hopes alive.

Waddle had to score. But he looked too tense for the comfort of the watching millions back home; Tommy Lawton said, "He's going to miss this." Waddle ran up – and blazed the ball way over the bar! The serenity of the sedate Abbeyfield Home for the elderly was shattered again, this time by a loud, wailing cry from the flat of one of its residents: "Bloody Germans! Bloody Adolf Hitler!" For two days after that, Tommy Lawton refused to eat.

On 24th August 1991, Tommy was in London, looking his dapper best in a smart new dark blue suit, spotless white shirt and bright red tie. His shoes were polished to gleaming, *heels as well*. The occasion was the wedding of his son, international banking consultant Thomas James Hugh Lawton to Gillian Alison Linda Blackburn, daughter of a retired business-man. The proud father of the groom was besieged by autograph-hunting wedding guests, many of whom were Arsenal supporters. Long after the bride and groom had left for their honeymoon, Tommy was enthralling the throng which had gathered around him in the bar with story after story of football the way *he* played it. This audience with the great Tommy Lawton was still going on late into the night. None of them wanted to go to bed. Least of all, the storyteller.

That bewitching Lawton way with words was still captivating the readers of the *Nottingham Evening Post*, too. Age might have been weakening his body now, but that punchy column was as strong as ever. However, the wonderful working relationship between 'England's best ever centre forward' and the newspaper editor who'd become such a friend was about to be broken.

The *Post*, which had been owned by the same local family for well over 100 years, had been sold to the Daily Mail and General Trust for a staggering £93.4 million. Barrie Williams's newspaper was now going to be one of a big stable under the control of Northcliffe Newspapers, the provincial wing of the *Daily Mail*. Williams had nothing whatsoever against the new owners but his job, widely recognised as the best in the business under the family owners, was now going to be on a par with all the rest, just one of many.

Like his pal Tommy, he had a stubborn streak of his own and he told the chief executive of Northcliffe, Ian Park, that he felt in need of a complete change. What he meant was that after many years in newspapers he wanted to try something completely different but Park came back to offer him the editorship of the group's flagship regional morning newspaper, the *Western Morning News*, serving Cornwall, Devon and Somerset. A very different sort of newspaper. An exciting new challenge. In the beautiful West Country. After 13 years in Nottingham this was an offer he simply couldn't refuse.

Things move very quickly in the newspaper business and Tommy Lawton suddenly found himself at a farewell dinner for his mate. It was a private affair; just 20 of the editor's closest colleagues. Halfway through the dinner, Williams looked across at his pal and saw Tommy shaking his head slowly and sadly from side to side, as if to say "Don't go, mate." But he had to. Everybody at the dinner had written a farewell inscription for the departing editor. Tommy's said simply "If it wasn't for Barrie Williams, I probably wouldn't be here."

But he was there, thank God. And still hitting home with opinions on football which were as accurate and incisive as his world-famous shots and headers.

One of his lasting laments remained the lot of the real supporter. The Taylor Report into the Hillsborough disaster had recorded failure of police control as the cause of the tragedy but its strident recommendations also resulted in all-seater stadia, the removal of those grotesque fences, and a vast improvement in spectator conditions and facilities in general. Tommy had been campaigning for that 20 years earlier but there was a by-product to this long overdue development which most certainly didn't please him. Ticket prices to all these swanky new grounds were rising so high that he feared the game was losing touch with its working-class supporters, in danger of becoming too much a domain of those dreaded 'lah-de-dah buggers'. God forbid! There was one thing for sure and certain. He was one of the biggest names in football's history, but Tommy Lawton had never lost touch with his working-class roots.

In May 1995, Tom Junior was away working in Sri Lanka when his wife Gill rang with some marvellous news. She was pregnant. With twins!

Immediately, Tom rang his dad. Tommy was so overjoyed that he leapt into a mock Red Indian war dance, like the one he'd performed with such inspirational success in the Notts County dressing room at the City Ground all those years ago. This time, though, he kept his clothes on. And this time, the effect was not so beneficial. As he whooped and hollered in his dance of delight around his flat, he twisted his knee badly, making walking on his sticks even more difficult than it already was for weeks afterwards!

But his joy was boundless and even more so when, on 21st November 1995, Gill gave birth to the Lawton twins, a boy and a girl, Anthony Philip Thomas and Zoe Alicia May. Tom Junior sent a car to collect his dad in Nottingham and take him to Hampshire, where he and Gill now lived, to meet his new grandchildren. As Anthony and Zoe's happy granddad held the babies in his arms and kissed their little heads his pride shone as brightly as his shoes. He had just one regret. His beloved Gay was not there to share the moment. Then, he took Tom Junior to one side and told him, "Now, you have three depending upon you. Don't let them down."

Back home in Nottingham, Tommy's authoritative opinions on football, locally and nationally, were still valid and valued, more than 60 years after his professional career began. In September 1996, in an interview with Jimmy Armfield on Radio Five Live, he predicted, generously, that Alan Shearer, who moved from Blackburn Rovers to Newcastle United for a world record £15 million, would become "the greatest centre forward of all time".

But, alas, Tommy's health was failing fast now: the body, once so strong and muscular, was bent and brittle; the voice, once so powerful as it barked instructions on the field of play, was weak.

In October 1996, with Tom Junior away working in Malawi, Gill got a call to say that Tommy was seriously ill. He had pneumonia and the punishment his body had taken over the years, including the heavy drinking of his dark years, had finally caught up with him. The battered, stressed and strained body of Tommy Lawton had cried 'enough.'

Immediately, Tom Junior flew home and dashed to his father's bedside. Tommy knew he didn't have much time left. He had a heart to heart with Tom Junior in one of those intensely private and personal exchanges that only a father and son can have.

Then he asked if he could have a pint of lager! Why not? It couldn't do any harm, they said. They helped Tommy as he slowly sipped his pint. "Thank you, that was lovely," said Tommy. Then he closed his eyes and drifted into unconsciousness. For the next week, Tommy drifted in and out of consciousness and who knows what thoughts and memories he had in those waking moments.

As his health was deteriorating, Tommy had told the lads on the *Post*'s sports desk, "I'm not afraid of dying. Gay will be up there waiting for me. She'll probably bollock me for being late but it'll sound so sweet. Big Swifty will be there, too. He'll get the cards out and start dealing and he'll say, 'Hey, Tommy, lad. What kept you?'" Maybe that's what he was thinking just before he died.

But what we do know, for sure, is that Tommy Lawton, 77, died a man at peace: at peace with himself; at peace with the world.

A week later, Nottingham witnessed a big funeral. The body of Tommy Lawton was driven slowly in procession from the funeral parlour in Sneinton, towards the River Trent and Meadow Lane. Outside the huge iron gates of England's oldest football club, the cortège stopped. A crowd of Notts County supporters, some old, some middle aged, some young, had gathered to pay homage to the man who had once put an extra 30,000 spectators through those gates, just to see him. As they'd waited in the late autumn sunshine for the cortège to arrive there had been much talk about *that goal* he'd scored against Nottingham Forest. And there were red-and-white scarves amidst the black-and-white, for admiration of this man knew no tribal boundaries.

The old men there to pay their tributes reflected on what a different environment now surrounded the old football ground; the new red brick and concrete of lifeless, faceless modern businesses where once there'd been terraces of back-to-back houses, full of character, full of people, full of life. Slums, they'd called those houses when they'd pulled them all down. Well, maybe they were. But was this better? Not bloody likely, it weren't.

They all bowed their heads in front of Tommy Lawton's coffin from which, contrary to some speculation, there was not a shout of "Where's all the money hidden, you buggers?!" But for all any of them knew, there might have been.

On the cortège went, to Bramcote Crematorium on the fringes of the city. Here, such a big congregation had gathered that many had to stand outside, where arrangements had been made to broadcast the funeral service to them. Television cameras were much in evidence, as were radio crews, press photographers and reporters. BBC Radio Five Live was broadcasting the funeral ceremony live to hundreds of thousands of listeners. In death, as in life, Tommy Lawton was headline news.

Inside, the scene was a *Who's Who* of famous faces from football's past and present, Sir Stanley Matthews and Sir Tom Finney among them. Should it have been Sir Tommy Lawton too? On achievements and contribution to the game he had graced for so long, yes it should, but with his turbulent middle years and his lifelong penchant for upsetting the establishment, that was never going to happen. Fresh-faced young Nottingham Forest and Notts County players, with much to look forward to, were there, immaculately turned out in club blazers, conducting themselves with a quiet maturity which was beyond their years, showing all present that age was no barrier to respect of greatness. Many true friends, with so much to look back on, were there, like Jackie Sewell and Jack Wheeler, heads bowed as they sat with their memories of times recalled as vividly as if they were yesterday.

Tom Junior had been determined to ensure that that his dad would have a send-off worthy of the great man and he hadn't let the old fella down, but it hadn't been easy. The 'lah-de-dah buggers', it seemed, were not prepared to put themselves out too much for Tommy Lawton, even now. Desperate to locate some memorabilia for the funeral, Tom had contacted the Football Association to ask if they could lend him an England international cap to place on the coffin. The reply? "Can't help." Tom then asked if he could have an FA flag, with the Three Lions, to drape over the coffin. The reply? "Suppose so, but only on loan."

Tom had asked Barrie Williams to deliver the soliloquy. It was tough to do as, along with everybody else in that packed crematorium, he mourned Tommy. But he was immensely proud to have been asked. Williams, choked with emotion, told how he'd found Tommy back in 1984 and chronicled the events that had made them such close friends. He told of those mysterious gifts that would appear on his desk and how Tommy steadfastly refused to take them back. And he concluded:

I am glad, now, that he wouldn't take those souvenirs back because they are mine to remind me of a real pal. I shall cherish them, as I will my many personal memories of Tommy and his stories of the big times, the bad times, the sad times and above all, the funny times which, with his wicked sense of humour, he liked telling best of all. Tommy Lawton, the great sporting legend, was a fine man, too. A loyal man, a man of principle, a man of integrity and I consider it an honour to have been granted his friendship.

As Barrie Williams stepped down from the lectern, he glanced across at Tommy's coffin and saw that sitting poignantly, proudly on top was one of his England international caps. This brought him to tears. He knew that Tom Junior had scoured the country in an exhaustive quest to find one of his dad's caps for the funeral but thought he had failed – as indeed had Tom. But at the eleventh hour BBC sports presenter John Inverdale had come to the rescue. John had invited Tom to go on Radio 5 Live to be interviewed, with the outside chance that there might, even at that late stage, be someone out there who would hear and help. Tom told John's huge radio audience how Tommy had, sadly, sold all his England caps around the pubs during his dark years and pleaded for anybody who might know where he could locate one to get in touch immediately.

John Inverdale's thoughtful assistance had paid off. A collector contacted Tom to tell him that he had a cap which Tommy had earned representing

England against Holland and, yes, he was welcome to borrow it for the funeral. Tom had got hold of it at the very last minute and placed it, alongside the FA flag, on his Dad's coffin.

After the funeral, an FA representative introduced himself to Tom Junior and told him, "We'll need the flag back. Get the undertaker to deliver it to the City Ground." Then, promptly, he left.

Tom Junior and Barrie Williams, discussing the abrupt departure of the man from the FA, concluded, "He was probably scared that Tommy would reach out of the coffin and drag him in!" And as they laughed, they were sure that somebody up there would be laughing with them!

Chapter Twelve

REFLECTIONS

I t is truly amazing that 75 years after his magnificent playing career began, 55 years after it ended, 15 years after his death, you can still mention the name of Tommy Lawton and get instant recognition, even from youngsters.

Tommy Lawton . . . Say the name with pride, for it is a name of which this country can be forever proud; a name which is indelibly engraved into the history of the great game in which he made it; a name synonymous with football brilliance and scoring goals, which he did better than anyone else in the world.

And if anybody was in any doubt as to why we should say that name with pride, we hope that reading this book will have provided the answer. That's why we wrote it, his son and his friend, because we wanted to honour his memory with our own personal and heartfelt version of his extraordinary life story.

The game Tommy Lawton loved so dearly has changed dramatically in many ways since he first made his impact in 1935. But in some ways, it's hardly changed at all. Take his old clubs, for example:

Burnley – still unfashionable and small fry financially but always punching above their weight, always playing good football, always assured of solid support from fans with an inherent knowledge of the game.

Everton – still a big club with family values, loyal to players, loyal to managers; despite so many years in the shadow of Liverpool FC, still a standard-bearer for the way football should be played and, above all, enjoyed.

Chelsea – still the Jack the lads of London football; exciting, flash, showbiz; dressing room full of sexy stars who are never out of the headlines and not always for football reasons; unpredictable, mercurial but always entertaining.

Notts County – still underachieving and prone to pie-crust promises of brave new dawns which always seem to end in penury, yet still faithfully supported by a fan base which takes blow after blow but always comes up smiling and singing its unique song *I Had a Wheelbarrow; the Wheel Fell Off.*

Brentford – still the warm and welcoming small club of London football; the poor relation with a big heart, never more worn on its sleeve than on the night it staged that wonderful testimonial for Tommy, such a generous gesture even though he'd only spent a short time with them; still deservedly going strong in spite of the massive competition from the capital's big boys.

Arsenal – still the hereditary aristocrats of British football, rich in history and understated class; even though they've moved out of Highbury, with its palatial marble and polished-wood elegance, still exuding top-drawer, double-barrelled, old-school-tie elitism.

Among the many things that have changed since Tommy's day is, of course, the massive wealth of modern players. Football's 'feudal' maximum-wage structure meant that his earnings ranged from £7 a week when his career began to £17 a week when it ended. That final figure, the most he ever earned, would today have been worth about £300 a week. In the whole of his glittering playing career Tommy earned the equivalent of about £210,000 in today's money for 20 years as a top-class player, as an international star reckoned at one time to be the best centre forward in the world.

Compare what Tommy was paid to the salaries of well over £100,000 a week paid to the Premiership star strikers of today, such as Wayne Rooney or Didier Drogba. They earn in just two weeks what Tommy earned in the whole of his 20-year playing career. Yet Drogba and Rooney are of no greater stature in the world game, indeed arguably considerably less, than when Tommy was at his peak.

Compare what Tommy was paid to the salaries of other English soccer multi-millionaires, such as John Terry (£170,000 a week); Frank Lampard (£150,000 a week); Steven Gerrard (£140,000 a week) and Ashley Cole

(£120,000 a week). And that's not to mention the hundreds of thousands of extra income these men get from today's lavish sponsorship and advertising deals.

Can anyone even begin to imagine, in today's game, a situation in which one player adds an extra 30,000 paying spectators to a club's gate but receives not so much as one penny of all that increased revenue for himself? That's precisely what happened when Tommy made that dramatic drop from Chelsea in the First Division to Notts County in the Third and throughout the four and a half years that followed, the presence of Tommy Lawton secured huge attendances at Meadow Lane: gates that had never been seen before and have never been seen since. That's not to mention the thousands more he put through the turnstiles of every club Notts County played away from home. And what did the man himself, the man solely responsible for generating all that revenue, get out of it? Nothing!

Twice, Tommy was sold for record transfer fees: in 1936, when Everton bought him as a teenager for £6,500 (today's equivalent: £240,370) and in 1947 when Chelsea sold him to Notts County for £20,000 (today's equivalent: £519,000) and out of what were, in those days, astonishing sums of money he got a total of less than £600 for himself. Nor was there any financial recognition of his enormous personal contribution to the development of Jackie Sewell, for whom Notts County received another record fee of £35,000 (today's equivalent: £797,300) when they sold him to Sheffield Wednesday in 1951.

The brilliant Tommy Lawton made vast fortunes for football while football paid him comparative peanuts in return, then quibbled about twopence on his expenses. Such was the lot of top footballers in the 1930s, 1940s and 1950s when the indefensible maximum wage allowed the scandal of outrageous exploitation of players to go unchecked for so long. It would, today, be utterly inconceivable that a man considered to have been the best player in the world at his peak could end up hiding behind the curtains because he couldn't afford to pay the electricity bill.

Now, of course, many people would argue that the pay pendulum has swung crazily to the other extreme, with even average players in the Championship being paid thousands of pounds a week. If he'd earned a fraction of today's riches, Tommy would never have had to live through those desperate days of debt which ended in the deep despair of being locked in a police cell. That said, in his halcyon days, he was better off than many people and there's no doubt that he wasted a lot of money that could have been saved for the rainy day on which, in his case, it positively poured.

But how many young men, plucked from poor working-class obscurity and catapulted to head-spinning stardom, would have been any more careful with their cash? With his impoverished background, who could blame him for enjoying the trappings of fame? He thought it would never end. And when it did, it was too late.

Tommy Lawton was no saint. He would have been the first to scoff at any suggestion that he was and there were some parts of his life of which he was anything but proud. There are a couple of elements of Tommy's story – his disastrous first marriage to Rosaleen and his disowning of Amanda – about which more could not be written because he would never discuss them in other than cursory terms. However, he was not reticent to talk about the many problems which soured and shamed his middle years and he never tried to deny that some of them were self-inflicted.

There's no denying, either, that in the dark years before the *Nottingham Evening Post* restored and revived him, Tommy drank far too much. We don't believe he was ever an alcoholic, but drink was his escape when life outside the cocoon of football became too hard to handle. Like George Best and Paul Gascoigne years later, football ate him up when he was little more than a child and spat him out woefully ill-equipped to face the harsh realities of the world outside.

He was empty. That's tragic for someone whose life has been so very full and if it had not been for the strength and support of Gay, the woman he loved so much, he could have died a relatively young man, possibly by killing himself. Thank God that didn't happen and that his final years brought back the pride and dignity to which he was entitled following his fantastic feats as one of the world's best footballers.

Don't let anyone tell you, by the way, that it was easier to perform those feats in Tommy's time. With that heavy leather ball, with defenders kicking lumps out of you and employing strong-arm tactics that would have them frequently suspended, if not banned for life, these days, it was arguably harder to score goals back then.

Similarly, let no one dismiss wartime football. It was every bit as professional, well-organised and officiated; just as hard and skilful, particularly in the frequent home internationals and representative matches, as it was before and after Mr Hitler's untimely intervention.

What would Tommy, the football columnist, have been writing about today's game? We're sure he would not have been complaining about the enormous sums of money the players earn. Good luck to them, he'd say, better it goes into their pockets than into the fat wallets of the 'lah-de-dah buggers' in the boardroom!

But we're equally sure he'd be very unhappy about the way football has continued its inexorable drift away from its working-class supporters.

It now costs more than twice as much to watch a top game as Tommy earned in a week. He'd have had a very great deal to say about that and would no doubt have been complaining in his column that football clubs ignored Lord Justice Taylor who, in his report on the Hillsborough Disaster, said that the provision of all-seater stadia should not be used as an excuse to put up prices. That's just what they did: ticket prices have continued to soar ever since and Tommy would deeply deplore the fact that watching football is now out of the financial reach of so many people – his people.

He'd have hated the toffee-nosed trappings, despised all the extracurricular activity at the 'posh' end of the game, reviled the prawn-sandwich brigade so rightly ridiculed by Roy Keane. As for those corporate clowns who stay stuffing their faces in the hospitality suites at Wembley after the second half's started? He'd have had the buggers shot! "You don't go to a football match for your dinner!" he would say and he'd tell you that all spectators got in his day was an enamel mug of scalding hot weak tea served from a giant urn in a shack with a corrugated iron roof.

He'd tell you, too, about the primitive toilet 'facilities'. These were merely concrete walls. Behind the walls were funnelled floors through which would surge raging torrents of foaming recycled beer. On cold days, clouds of steam would hang over the latrines, for most of them had no roof and if, as often happened, the crowd was too dense to allow sufficient freedom of movement to get to one of these bogs, a rolled-up newspaper provided the conduit through which you relieved yourself where you stood, with no sympathy whatsoever from your companions, who'd tell you, "You should have gone before you came in!" It's difficult to imagine today's corporate 'toffs' putting up with that.

Of course, nobody, least of all Tommy Lawton, would advocate tolerance of conditions like those in this day and age but far too many football fans have been lost because they've fallen through the vast gap between the extremes and Tommy would have been desperately disappointed to know that so many lower earners now have to pick and choose their games because they can't afford to go to as many as they would wish and that so many fathers can't afford to take their sons, so they don't go either. That's not the game that Tommy Lawton graced for 20 years.

Talking football with Tommy in his last decade was a joy: the bitterness had gone, the anger had dissipated and he so enjoyed sharing his memories, telling his stories and offering his opinions on the modern game.

His favourite centre forward? A close call between Alan Shearer and Les Ferdinand. Both strong, quick and clever leaders of the attack; both powerful strikers of the ball with feet and head. Unlike some of those who look back to the 'good old days', Tommy had a lot of time for contemporary strikers like Alan and Les. And today? How he would have loved Wayne Rooney at his best and what a shame he didn't live to see Wayne play.

Tommy Lawton graced the shirt of Everton at the same tender teenage stage as Rooney did and, like Wayne, he's been eminently newsworthy ever since. When, in the autumn of 2009, the story broke about a row over moving Tommy's ashes from the football museum (to which Tom Junior donated them) at Preston, to a new venue at Manchester, it appeared in all the national newspapers, on TV and radio and in the *Nottingham Evening Post* it made the front-page splash.

Tommy Lawton, still making headlines 90 years after the lusty lungs of that big baby boy heralded his arrival into the world on 6th October 1919.

THE END?
(D'you know, we don't think it will be!)

Barrie Williams   Tom Lawton Junior

LAWTON FAMILY UPDATE

G ay's first husband, Rex Rose, continued to be a friend of the family up to 1989, when he died at the age of 75. Rex had moved from Mapperley Hall Drive in Nottingham to Seacroft, Skegness in 1978. In 1988, when he was on holiday in Cornwall, Rex suffered a thrombosis as a result of which he lost his left leg and he was wheelchair-bound until his death.

Rex left a substantial inheritance for his daughter, Carol, who sadly died from Crohn's disease in March 1998 at the age of 51.

Tom Junior set up his own global business, training bankers, in 1989. Since then, he has travelled the world, running programmes in 53 countries. His second wife, Gillian, who had worked for Standard Chartered Bank, joined him in his business after they married in 1991. In 2004, they moved to Majorca, where the twins were educated at King Richard III College. The family moved back to Hampshire early in 2010 so that the twins could complete their education in the UK.

The Sporting Family Lawton maintains a record of goalscoring debuts:

Tommy scored on his debuts for Burnley, Everton, Chelsea, Notts County and England.

Tom Junior scored on his debut for Nottingham High School.

Anthony scored on his debut for Calvia, in Majorca.

And Zoë, playing in her grandfather's number 9 position, scored on her debut for Robert Mays School in Odiham, Hampshire in March 2010.

It seems that the name of Lawton will always be associated with scoring and achieving goals!

THINGS THEY'VE SAID ABOUT TOMMY

"He came out looking like a film star, jet black hair parted down the middle, slicked back. It was his heading that amazed me, not just the power of it, but his ability to get up there before everyone else and then just hang there. He was classic, absolutely classic. Two wonderful feet and so mobile, so quick. The mark of a great player is that he makes other players play well. Tommy could do that, too."
– *Arthur Milton, Arsenal and England footballer and England cricketer*

"We have seen many incomplete centre forwards who were first-class players and some of them played for England. Some could run and shoot, like Milburn, who liked the ball on the ground; some could plan like Revie, from behind the line; some, like Drake, were powerful and could shake off punishment; some were bold and dangerous, like Trevor Ford; some were cool, accomplished dribblers like Finney; delicate and accurate, like Allen; some were big and strong and found the open spaces, like Kevan. Some could beat a man on the ground, some in the air; some could shoot on the turn, some could snap onto a through-pass; some could marshal the line, some inspire it. Tommy Lawton could do it all."
– *Maurice Edelston and Terence Delaney*, Masters of Soccer, *1962*

"Tommy Lawton would lead my ideal forward line. He'd be under considerable pressure from Stan Mortensen, Nat Lofthouse, Tommy Taylor, Jackie Milburn and Gary Lineker, but he was the best of the bunch. He was the greatest header of a ball – his headers had the power of shots – and there has never been a better all-round number 9. Tommy was a Lancashire lad, like myself, with a lovely sense of humour."
– *Sir Tom Finney, Preston and England forward*

"GET IN THERE!"

"Tommy Lawton's climbing and sense of time and distance are as near perfect as possible. Leaving the ground at exactly the right moment he appears to hover in the air at the height of his climb. Any cross from the wing is directed goal wards as though jet-propelled."
– *Maurice Edelston, Reading and England wartime international*

"There were a few great centre forwards – Lofthouse, Milburn, Mortensen, Trevor Ford, John Charles – but Tommy Lawton was the best of the lot. There was something different about Tommy, an aura. The height he jumped to was just amazing and then he'd hang in the air for so long and you wondered how on earth he did that. Did he have wings? Nobody, before or since, could head a ball as hard as Tommy. You'd watch Nat Lofthouse, John Charles, John Toshack and think they were brilliant headers of a ball – but not if you'd seen Tommy Lawton!"
– *Derek Tapscott, Arsenal and Wales forward*

"Believe it or not, Tommy could actually *steer* a ball with his head. When you sent over a cross that you felt was worthy of a goal it was more likely than not that Lawton would nod it in the back of the net. I had all the time in the world for Tommy, both as a player and as a person. He was the best centre forward I have ever seen."
– *Denis Compton, Arsenal and England winger and England cricketer*

"The ball came in the air down the inside-left channel to Lawton. His outside left, Les Smith, moved into position but as Tommy went up he saw Ron Suart coming across to intercept and with the ball still coming, Tommy seemed to hang, adjust, let the ball go just a little bit further then nod it inside Suart for Les Smith to run onto. Tommy made his decision and his adjustment *after* he'd jumped!"
– *Ron Greenwood, Brentford centre half and manager of West Ham and England*

"Tommy is fast-moving, beautifully balanced and, for a big fellow, a brilliant ball player."
– *Frank Swift, Manchester City and England goalkeeper and journalist*

"Tommy was big, strong, quick and accurate and he was a great header of the ball. Some of the goals he scored simply amazed me. You just

couldn't afford to allow Tommy a kick. He only needed half a chance and the ball was in the back of the net."
– *T G 'Yanto' Jones, Everton and Wales centre half*

"When Tommy moved from Chelsea to Notts County he brought glamour to the city of Nottingham. As he walked around the streets, immaculate in his camel coat, he was the centre of attraction, just as David Beckham would be today. I was only 12 but, to this day, I can see Tommy standing on the centre circle, rubbing his hands together, ready to kick off. Tall, handsome and athletic, a magnificent specimen of fitness and strength. He was without doubt the best header of a ball the game has ever known. I can visualise him now as he appeared to hover in the air and so perfect was his timing that the ball always went like a rocket even though it was very heavy in those days, particularly when it was wet."
– *John Mounteney, former Notts County director*

"I've always counted it a privilege to have played with so many great centre forwards. Ted Drake was the first one, on my England debut. Then there were Nat Lofthouse and Stanley Mortensen. With Tommy Lawton, I could guarantee he would make contact with nine out of ten crosses. He was simply a brilliant header of the ball."
– *Sir Stanley Matthews, Blackpool and England winger*

"The one thing Tommy earned was respect and that's a commodity money can't buy in these days of multimillion-pound transfer fees and wages. He never ducked an issue or flinched from a controversial challenge. He was prepared to call a spade a spade and say what he thought, whether about the high, the mighty or the humble. Tommy remains a giant in the beautiful game."
– *David McVay, Notts County footballer, journalist and author*

"Tommy was truly a great player, one of the best centre forwards there has been anywhere in the world, yet as a bloke he fitted into the set-up like anyone else. There was always a good camaraderie and atmosphere when Tommy was around. We played for the love of the game."
– *Wilf Mannion, Middlesbrough and England forward*

"Tommy was the lightest mover of any big man who ever played football."
– *Alex James, Arsenal and Scotland forward*

"Tommy Lawton knew how good he was, he was aware of his brilliance, but it never came through in any way arrogantly or offensively. He remained a nice man, a very kind man. It was always a privilege to meet him and I'm proud to say that I knew Tommy Lawton."
– *George Edwards, Swansea, Cardiff and Wales winger*

"I recall one goal above all others, scored by Tommy for England against Italy in 1948: a first-time shot that barely rose four inches from the ground. No hesitation, no nerves, just the work of a truly great player – a natural goalscorer."
– *Billy Wright, Wolverhampton Wanderers and captain of England*

"Tom was the best centre forward I ever saw; not only was he the best in the air, he had two exceptionally good feet. The man had incredible presence and brought a tremendous amount of pleasure to spectators. I could never speak highly enough about him, both as a player and as a man."
– *Jackie Sewell, Notts County, Sheffield Wednesday and England forward*

"Whenever I went back to Nottingham, I would call and see him. Thin and fragile in later years, he walked slowly, occasionally using his stick, but his back was straight and his head was held high with that famous Lawton nose jutting proudly at the world. One Saturday in October 1996 I knocked at his door. He seemed smaller than usual, frailer. "I've got something for you," I said and handed him a copy of Cliff Morgan's autobiography. Tommy peered at the message which Cliff had carefully inscribed on the title page, "To my great friend and hero, in appreciation of your class and style." Tommy's eyes immediately filled with tears. Recognition from one sporting legend to another."
– *Andy Smith, Radio and TV sports reporter and presenter*

"I played against Tommy Lawton as a young centre half for Northampton Town in 1950. Notts County had won promotion and there was a crowd of more than 31,000 at Meadow Lane. Notts beat us 2-0 and Tommy scored both goals. I can see one of them now – we were just outside the penalty area when a cross came in from the left. I went up for it with him but was amazed that my head was only level with his waist! He did no more than flick his head and that was it. Our goalie had no chance. Tommy was chatting to me all the time; he called me by my Christian name and even though I was his opponent, I felt he was looking after me. He had

done everything in the game and I was just a 22-year-old novice but he was so kind to me – a friendly man, a lovely chap, a gentleman."
– *Ben Collins, Northampton Town defender*

"Tommy Lawton? Simply and surely the greatest number 9 of all time."
– *Joe Mercer, Everton and Arsenal wing half and manager of Manchester City, Coventry City and England*

TOMMY LAWTON